Mutative Metaphors in Psychotherapy

of related interest

Shakespeare as Prompter
The Amending Imagination and the Therapeutic Process
Murray Cox and Alice Theilgaard
Foreword by Adrian Noble and Ismond Rosen
ISBN 978 1 85302 159 6

Shakespeare Comes to Broadmoor
'The Actors are Come Hither' – The Performance of Tragedy
in a Secure Psychiatric Hospital
Edited by Murray Cox
Foreword by Sir Ian McKellen
ISBN 978 1 85302 135 0

Structuring the Therapeutic Process
Compromise with Chaos: The Therapist's Response
to the Individual and the Group
Murray Cox
ISBN 978 1 85302 028 5

Coding the Therapeutic Process
Emblems of Encounter: A Manual for Counsellors and Therapists
Murray Cox
ISBN 978 1 85302 029 2

The Group as Poetic Play-Ground
From Metaphor to Metamorphosis:
The 1990 S H Foulkes Annual Lecture
Murray Cox
ISBN 978 1 85302 203 6

Mutative Metahpors in Psychotherapy

The Aeolian Mode

Murray Cox
and Alice Theilgaard

Foreword by Philip Brockbank
Introduction by Malcolm Pines

Jessica Kingsley Publishers
London and Philadelphia

First published in the United Kingdom in 1987 by Tavistock Publications Ltd

Published in the United Kingdom in 1997
by Jessica Kingsley Publishers
116 Pentonville Road
London N1 9JB, UK
and
400 Market Street, Suite 400
Philadelphia, PA 19106, USA

www.jkp.com

Copyright © Murray Cox and Alice Theilgaard 1987 and 1997
Foreword copyright © Philip Brockbank 1987
Introduction copyright © Malcolm Pines 1987
Printed digitally since 2007

Library of Congress Cataloging in Publication Data
A CIP catalog record for this book is available from the Library of Congress

British Library Cataloguing in Publication Data
A CIP catalogue record for this book is available from the British Library

ISBN 978 1 85302 459 7

for
Pooh and Piglet
and
The child in us all

Authors' Foreword

This book was first published ten years ago. During the interim metaphor has become a topic which has attracted steadily increasing therapeutic interest. Books, articles and conferences – at local, national and international level – all testify to metaphor's hermeneutic potency. For example, a network of Danish interdisciplinary researcher on metaphor in culture and cognition, of which Alice Theilgaard is a member, has been inaugurated by the Institute of Philosophy, Pedagogy and Rhetoric at The University of Copenhagen. It is funded by The Humanistic State Research Council and holds regular meetings.

The relevance of mutative metaphors in psychotherapy – the particular focus of this book – is explored in Murray Cox's supervision groups in London, Copenhagen and Oslo. It now forms a component of the training curriculum of The Institute of Group Analysis (London) and is furnishing material for academic dissertations.

Metaphor has not only come to stay, it has been here all the time and carries thought across many hitherto unbridgeable chasms.

Murray Cox and Alice Theilgaard
Spring, 1997

Contents

When it comes, the Landscape listens –
Shadows – hold their breath –
When it goes, 'tis like the Distance
On the look of Death –
(Emily Dickinson, 'There's a certain Slant
of light')

In a dark time, the eye begins to see,
I meet my shadow in the deepening shade;
I hear my echo in the echoing wood –
(Theodore Roethke, 'In a Dark Time')

'It may well come to be recognized that the contemplative prelogical mode of knowing exhibited so forcibly in art, the knowing that terminates in recognitions and not in "conclusions", is the source from which all valuable action flows. For my own part, I am convinced that prelogical knowing is not only more reliable and comprehensive than the intellectual knowing of analysis, abstraction, generalization, and verification, but that it is in fact – in its directness and vividness – the prototype to which all human knowledge is referred in action, in actual events of reality.'

(George Whalley, *Poetic Process*)

'To deny associations is most painfully to risk alienation, unreality and a thinning of the personal life.'

(Barbara Hardy, *Tellers and Listeners: The Narrative Imagination*)

'Only connect the prose and the passion . . . and both will be exalted, and human love will be seen at its height. Live in fragments no longer. Only connect, and the beast and the monk, robbed of the isolation that is life to either, will die.'

(E. M. Forster, *Howard's End*)

Acknowledgements

'We have . . . great cause to give great thanks.'
(*Coriolanus* V. 4, 60)

– so great, indeed, that it is impossible to do justice to it. Family, friends, and colleagues from several disciplines, and of many persuasions, have gradually nudged our thinking in an Aeolian direction. The Group Analytic Society (London), the Danish Psychiatric Society, and the Danish Society for Psychoanalytic Psychotherapy provided the soil in which our ideas germinated. Though we cannot name all who should be thanked, they know who they are. But we hope they will allow Professor Philip Brockbank and Dr Malcolm Pines to be named on their behalf, and to receive our gratitude for their cumulative influence. Philip Brockbank and Malcolm Pines have encouraged our collaboration since it began in Copenhagen in 1980. We are also grateful to them for their contributions which place this book in its literary and therapeutic contexts.

Professor Sir Desmond Pond and Professor Edgar Rubin were deeply influential in their reminders that two worlds are really one, that figure and ground can be reversed, and that the whole is more than a sum of the parts. Dr Patrick McGrath, a close colleague for many years, is a continuing influence. And we are indebted to Dr Peter Walker, the Bishop of Ely, for discussions about things poetic which point beyond themselves.

But our patients must take the greatest thanks. In every sense, the Aeolian Mode could not have developed without them.

Diana Cookson typed numerous drafts and the final version. Ashi Brant and Jeanne Møller typed material for various lectures and seminars which, over the years, evolved into the theme here presented. We are jointly in their debt too.

Without the expertise of three librarians, the text and the bibliography would be impoverished. We wish to set on record our thanks to Susan

Brock, Jill Duncan, and Alison Farrar of The Shakespeare Institute, The Institute of Psycho-Analysis, and Broadmoor Hospital, respectively.

On page 9 the reader will see the reference 'Hobson 1985'. And although Bob Hobson had told us of his interest in metaphor, it was our misfortune that we had not read *Forms of Feeling: the Heart of Psychotherapy* (R. Hobson, Tavistock 1985) until we had virtually finished our writing, because there are several points at which our thinking converges. He kindly read our entire typescript and made valuable suggestions which should ease the reader's task.

Finally, we wish to thank Gill Davies, Editorial Director, Tavistock Publications Limited, whose creative response to our points of urgency was a constant encouragement. She exerted an aesthetic imperative upon us in the kindest possible way.

Murray Cox, London
Alice Theilgaard, Copenhagen
November 1986

The authors and publishers are grateful to the following for their kind permission to reproduce copyright material:

Anna Akhmatova: Weidenfeld & Nicolson for an extract quoted in *Nightingale Fever* edited by Ronald Hingley (1982).

Emily Dickinson: Extracts from 'There's a certain Slant of Light', 'After Great Pain, a Formal Feeling comes', 'Tell all the Truth but tell it Slant', 'We grow accustomed to the Dark', 'Ample make this Bed', and 'I felt a Cleaving in my Mind', taken from *The Complete Poems of Emily Dickinson*, edited by Thomas H. Johnson. Copyright 1914, 1929, 1935, 1942 by Martha Dickinson Bianchi. Copyright © renewed 1957, 1963 by Mary L. Hampson. By permission of Little, Brown and Company.

T. S. Eliot: Faber & Faber Ltd for extracts from *Murder in the Cathedral*, and from 'Choruses from "The Rock"', 'Burnt Norton', and 'East Coker' (from 'Four Quartets'), all taken from *Collected Poems 1909–1962*. In *The Complete Poems and Plays* (1969). From *Murder in the Cathedral* by T. S. Eliot, copyright 1935, 1952 by Harcourt Brace Jovanovich, Inc.; renewed 1980 by Esme Valerie Eliot. Reprinted by permission of the publisher. From 'East Coker' in *Four Quartets* by T. S. Eliot, copyright 1943 by T. S. Eliot; renewed 1971 by Esme Valerie Eliot. Reprinted by permission of Harcourt Brace Jovanovich, Inc. From 'Choruses from "The Rock"' in *Collected Poems 1909–1962* by T. S. Eliot, copyright 1936 by Harcourt Brace Jovanovich, Inc.; copyright © 1963, 1964 by T. S. Eliot. Reprinted by permission of the publisher. From 'Burnt Norton' in *Four Quartets* by

T. S. Eliot, copyright 1943 by T. S. Eliot; renewed 1971 by Esme Valerie Eliot. Reprinted by permission of Harcourt Brace Jovanovich, Inc.

Paul Éluard: © Editions Gallimard for an extract from I, 394 taken from *Oeuvres Complètes* (1968).

U. A. Fanthorpe: Peterloo Poets for extracts from 'Rising Damp', taken from *Standing To* (1982) (Peterloo Poets, 2 Kelly Gardens, Calstock, Cornwall PL18 9SA).

Robert Frost: the estate of Robert Frost, Edward Connery Latham, and Jonathan Cape Ltd for extracts from 'Neither Out Far Nor in Deep' and 'A Leaf Treader' taken from *Selected Poems* (1955).

Edwin Muir: Faber & Faber Ltd and Oxford University Press, New York, for extracts from 'The Poet', 'The Prize', and 'The Combat' taken from *Collected Poems* (1960).

Kathleen Raine: George Allen & Unwin for an extract from 'On a Deserted Shore', taken from *Collected Poems 1935–1980* (1981).

Theodore Roethke: Faber & Faber Ltd for extracts from 'In a Dark Time' and 'The Waking' taken from *The Collected Poems* (1968). Excerpt from 'The Waking' copyright © 1960 by Beatrice Roethke as Administratrix of the Estate of Theodore Roethke from the book The Collected Poems of Theodore Roethke. Reprinted by permission of Doubleday Publishing Group.

Wallace Stevens: Alfred A. Knopf, Inc. and the author for extracts from 'The Man With the Blue Guitar' and 'Prologues to What is Possible' taken from *The Collected Poems of Wallace Stevens* (1954).

Norman Thelwell: Methuen London for a cartoon from *Up the Garden Path* by Norman Thelwell.

Dylan Thomas: J. M. Dent and David Higham Associates for an extract from 'Do not go gentle into that good night' taken from *Collected Poems 1934–1952* (1952).

W. B. Yeats: A. P. Watt Ltd on behalf of Michael B. Yeats and Macmillan London Ltd for extracts from *The Winding Stair and Other Poems* (1933), 'The Circus Animals' Desertion', and 'The Curse of Cromwell' taken from *The Collected Poems of W. B. Yeats* (1950).

Fons et origo

All the references arising in the course of the ensuing pages will be found in the bibliography which, apart from the indexes, comes at the very end of the book. All, that is, except one. This stands on its own, because of its significance for the Aeolian Mode.

We found that our provisional formulations had been crystallized in a sentence written by Gaston Bachelard (1884–1962), the French scientist–philosopher–poet. It is paradoxical and at variance with the traditional psychoanalytic approach of 'starting superficially and working deep'. We shall return to these words many times, and from many angles, in our exploration of the coherence between creativity, aesthetic imperatives, and dynamic psychotherapy. The key passage comes from the introduction to *The Poetics of Space* (English translation 1969):

'But the image has touched the depths before it stirs the surface.'

Bachelard encapsulated that which we had slowly come to learn from our psychotherapeutic attempts with the psychotic, the borderline, and the psychopathic patient. Nevertheless, it should not be forgotten that the significance of associative sensitivity is not confined to the clinical field. Indeed, it enhances all deep human encounters. We found that an image could safely hold experience which was too painful, too brittle, or too broken to be firm enough to tolerate analysis. Such patients enabled us to see that the image, activated by metaphor, could be the location of exploration or the fabric of support.

It is for this reason that the simple reference '(Bachelard op. cit.)', which occurs intermittently throughout these pages, carries our gratitude.

Notation

1. In order to simplify the presentation of dialogue between patient and therapist we have adopted the following notation. The therapist's words are always inset to the right of those of the patient. For example, the following exchange –

> PATIENT: 'I can't talk to them. . . . They know all about me.'
> THERAPIST: 'But if they knew *all* about you?'
> PATIENT: 'If they knew *all* about me, then they'd understand.'

is presented (as on p. 120) in this way:

> 'I can't talk to them. . . . They know all about me.'
>> 'But if they knew *all* about you?'
> 'If they knew *all* about me, then they'd understand.'

If the patient's words evoke a thought which the therapist does not speak (as on p. 74) this will be shown by means of italics.

2. We have sometimes referred to 'the therapist', sometimes said 'we (M.C.)' or 'we (A.T.)', and sometimes used the first person singular. This was spontaneous and arbitrary. We cannot justify the decision, except to say that it felt right. Each chapter has been our mutual concern, and the writing was a joint endeavour – although, for obvious reasons, our relative contributions varied.

3. Names, histories, settings, and other identifying features have been changed, so that confidentiality is assured.

It should be presumed that a patient is 'speaking', whenever the 'spoken' word is printed and is not followed by a specific reference.

4. We have usually used 'he' when referring to 'the patient'. This is simply to avoid the rather clumsy use of 's/he, him/her' and should be taken as meaning a patient of either sex.

5. In a book so densely populated with literary quotations, we have had to exercise discretion in the depth of bibliographic detail. For example, Augustine and Luther are quoted without precise 'location'; Ibsen is given a date, e.g. '*Ghosts* 1881'; whereas Eliot is quoted as '*East Coker* I 1940', though the full bibliographic reference is also given: '*Complete Poems and Plays* 1969'.

PSYCHOANALYTIC LITERARY CRITICISM

The specialized field of analytically-orientated literary criticism is a large one and has an extensive bibliography of its own. Though related to Aeolian issues, and of great intrinsic interest, it is not of direct clinical relevance. For this reason, and in the interests of space, we have therefore kept the topic at arm's length except, perhaps, on p. 33. We do, however, refer to Elizabeth Wright (1984) who is a stimulating guide to the complexities of the relationship between the literary-aesthetic process and the psychoanalytic one.

Foreword

Shakespeare's Aeolian Mode

When Murray Cox first visited the Shakespeare Institute he remarked
'Whereas for you Macbeth and Lady Macbeth are fiction, for us they sometimes make their presence felt in everyday clinical encounters.' He seemed
to measure the space between the therapist's immediate exposure to
'infected minds' that 'To their deaf pillows will discharge their secrets' and
the academic Shakespearean's safe contemplative distance from them.
From that distance there is reason to admire those who minister to diseased
psyches, without the formal solace of aesthetic order and delight. Yet
Shakespeare was aware of the proximity of his own art to the therapist's
and of his own state to the patient's. When Hamlet is made to act as bone-
setter to the times that are 'out of joint', he uses the play itself as a
therapeutic device; and in the sleep-walking scene of *Macbeth*, a delinquent
makes her own play, unconsciously re-enacting her part before a Doctor of
Physic who is auditor and spectator. Shakespeareans, including the
professional kind, are spectators without being therapists, but they
resemble therapists because they are required constantly to re-compose
their own understanding in response to the experience of others, and often
have reason to recognize that 'The lunatic, the lover and the poet Are of
imagination all compact.' For the Shakespearean *Macbeth* can be seen at
once as a case-history, a political history, and a festive tragedy. If Murray
Cox and Alice Theilgaard are right, however, it may also be seen as a
complex of metaphors indirectly at the disposal of the practising therapist.
The play is a major episode in the history of civilization, and in 'the
common cultural heritage' (see p. 154) of most therapists and many
patients; but there is also, in the play and outside it, a more obscure
common inheritance of metaphoric and metamorphic fields of language
and experience to which therapist and patient have occasional access.

The title of the present study has itself undergone several metamorphoses, the mode of analysis being variously described as 'Aeolian', 'mutative', and 'metaphoric'; but all are consistent with Shakespeare's exploitation of the metaphoric properties of the language to create and transform his 'characters'. Shakespeare's characters are at once personal and impersonal, born into the present from 'the hatch and brood of time'. So, it might be said, are we all: 'not I', cried D. H. Lawrence, 'but the wind that blows through me. A fine wind is blowing through me in the direction of time'. The story of the Aeolian Harp looks back to the myth of Orpheus, upon whose harp (or lute) the wind continued to play after he had been lynched by the maids of Lesbos. The instrument itself, designed specifically for the wind to play upon, was perfected in the eighteenth century, an elegant item of garden or conservatory furnishing. Its history as metaphor is more complex. Edmund Spenser used it to commemorate Sir Philip Sidney in *The Ruins of Time*, and before it reached Coleridge it had served the purposes of a transcendental and a mechanical understanding of spiritual and psychological processes, and his Aeolian preoccupations have a history both in the poetry and the philosophy of the later eighteenth century.

The Bedlam poet, Christopher Smart, recovered an old tradition (from Jacob Boehme) which found in the created world the 'automatal harp' of the Supreme Being; poets (Orpheus, David, Smart himself) re-sounded their Maker's praise. In the pre-Romantic decades the figure of the Bard (Gray, Collins, Thompson, Akenside) swelled that incantatory concert of harps and offered as 'inspiration' what Swift at the start of the century would have been content to call 'wind' (see his reflections on the Aeolists in *A Tale of a Tub*). While Thompson's readers were listening to the 'soul-dissolving strains' of the 'harp of Aeolus' in *The Castle of Indolence*, David Hartley was at work on his associationist psychology, refined from ideas adumbrated by Locke and Hume. Coleridge named his son after him and entertained himself with the thought that the infant Hartley was 'inspired by the God Eolus, & like Isaiah, his "bowells sound like an Harp" '. Disengaging from the confident rationalism (as he supposed) of earlier generations, Coleridge initially welcomed the notion that consciousness was ordered by associative processes that remained active when the self-conscious reasoning faculties were suspended. The 'Bardic trance', variously cultivated by pre-Romantic and Romantic poets, yielded some high accomplishments ('Khubla Khan', 'Ode to a Nightingale') and much inconsequential absurdity (particularly from the febrile brains of the so-called Spasmodics). In his finest poetry and most searching criticism, however, Coleridge disengaged from Hartley and claimed a creative and re-creative role both for 'reason' and for the complex faculty he called the 'secondary imagination'. It was this range of interests and insights that prompted him to a rediscovery of qualities of Shakespeare's language that had been neglected or undervalued in the age of Johnson and which could, in some senses of the term, be described as 'associative'.

Characters are often shaped and re-shaped in Shakespeare's plays through the sounding and re-sounding of metaphoric harmonics. It is said of the Koch harp that the dissonances of the 11th and 13th overtones are heard in shrill discords as the wind grows stronger, only to give place to beautiful harmonies as it dies down. The instrument thus offered the eighteenth-century optimist the expression of a divine aesthetic order beyond the turbulence of ordinary life. Such solace in Shakespeare's plays is harder to win and may be offered not to the character but to the spectator. In the pages that follow Dr Cox and Dr Theilgaard make use of 'vignettes' that afford glimpses of metaphor at work in afflicted and destructive minds. For the therapist the mind of the patient is projected and organized, however imperfectly, by the patient himself; but for the play-goer the experience of 'the other' is projected both by the character and by the play-wright and poet.

Making a vignette from the play *Macbeth*, a therapist might ask the killer an apparently straightforward question, 'Were you in your cups?', and get the oblique answer, 'I had to do it quickly'. A straight answer could be made available from the action ('I'd had quite a few'), since the feast was occasion for hard drinking and drunken hopes, but Macbeth in the play is not merely an individual (*ideote* as the Greeks would say) but an inheritor and representative of a tradition of values which includes the sanctities of hospitality and the communal table. His words 'If it were done when 'tis done, then 'twere well It were done quickly' spoken as servants cross the stage to serve Duncan his last supper, recollect Jesus speaking to Judas, 'what thou doest, do quickly', and anticipate an image of the communion chalice, now 'poisoned' and a symbol of betrayal. Macbeth, moreover, is a warrior hero and usurper in a monarchy committed to dynastic inherit-ance. His virtue ('I dare do all that may become a man'), his inhumanity ('who dares do more is none'), and his obsession with children ('a barren sceptre in my grip') have therefore an impersonal as well as a personal genesis. But the relationship between the impersonal inheritance and the personal experience is only intermittently and imperfectly clear to the characters in a Shakespearean play; connections are lost in what Prospero, trying to stir Miranda's ancestral memory of sovereignty and usurpation, calls the 'dark backward and abysm of time'; hence, both in intimate and public awareness of language, the fading of 'metaphor' and the genesis of what is here called 'cryptophor' (see p. 106). In a play much concerned with the equivocal values of a tradition and society in which sanctities are sustained by an ability to 'unseam' a man 'from the nave to the chops', the cryptophor is a leading dynamic of the language, including that of Macbeth's soliloquies. The 'bank and schole' of time is not a stable metaphor fit for social or narrative discourse, but a volatile and cryptic pun; a 'bank' is a bench when we think of a 'school', but a sand-bank when we think of a 'shoal of time' and its treacheries and insecurities. 'Jump the life to come' means 'risk the hereafter', but pre-echoes 'vaulting ambition' and the soldier's fear of crashing down on the other side as he leaps superbly into the saddle. The cryptophors are mediating between Macbeth's personal drives and those inherited from the larger society of 'bloody instruction', warrior virtue, and temporal insecurity. That larger society is a part of the play's structured experience, and the significance of the cryptophors are therefore apt to be clearer to the play-goer than to the characters. While the experience and language of 'everyday Macbeths' and their larger world have not been organized by a poet and playwright working in a tradition thousands of years old, there is enough continuity between ordinary life and language and highly ordered versions of them to give the cryptophor an analogous significance in the relationship between patient and therapist. The everyday Macbeth who wants to 'get on', 'get on top', 'get to the top', and 'make a killing' (or 'a bomb'), will take from the common stock whatever myths and metaphors give meaning to his experience and try to make his own story and image of himself; but again, the onlooker may see more of the game.

From another point of view Macbeth's ordeal is a state of division expressed by the primordial metaphor, 'Now o'er the one half-world Nature seems dead, and wicked dreams abuse the curtain'd sleep'. Shakespeare's theatre often recalls us to the divided self in a divided world. That world may be pagan – the natural and unnatural one where 'Light thickens and the crow Makes wing to the rooky wood; Good things of day begin to droop and drowse'. It may be urban – London with its blue coats and tawny coats, patrician and plebeian Rome. Or it may be national or even imperial. In a Shakespearean play the 'time and space beyond story' (see p. 2) are sometimes evoked as the history of the community (Lear's Britain, for example) and sometimes as a condition of the society (trade and usury in Venice, the marriage market in Padua).

The love of Antony and Cleopatra is at once intimate and political, expressing a critical moment in the history of Roman empire; in conquering Egypt the Romans are exposed to a transfiguring and destructive engagement with Egyptian values. Murray Cox and Alice Theilgaard are not concerned here with the impersonal sources of story and metaphor in the history and dispositions of the larger society. They do, however, offer an impersonal neuropsychological perspective which, while not of course offered in the play, is (cryptophorically at least) consistent with it. The movement from the west to the east Mediterranean is like that from the left to the right hemisphere of the brain described in chapter 7. Terms applied to the left hemisphere, 'verbal, analytical, abstract, rational, temporal . . . univocal, linear, conceptual, and abstract . . . bleak and rigid' might plausibly be diverted to Caesar's Rome; and Cleopatra's Egypt does not resist labels attached to the 'colourful imagination' of the right hemisphere, 'synthetic, analogical, ikonic and intuitive' (see pp. 203–4). Romans and Egyptians alike must live in both spheres, but differing potentials respond to differing cultural histories. Antony's Roman self dissolves in dissolute Egypt, finding its metaphor in the clouds of the evening sky ('The rack dislimns, and makes it indistinct As water is in water . . . Here I am Antony, Yet cannot hold this visible shape'). He is re-formed, as Imperial Roman ikon, in Cleopatra's (and Shakespeare's) Egyptian imagination ('His legs bestrid the ocean, his rear'd arm Crested the world'). When Cleopatra challenges Dolabella, 'Think you there was, or is, such a man as this I dreamt on?', she gets the Roman answer, 'Gentle madam, no' (which Ben Jonson would have endorsed), and offers an Egyptian retort, 'Nature wants stuff to vie strange forms with fancy'. 'Fancy' then (as now) looked one way towards 'fantasy' or 'imagination' and another towards sexual love. Since 'the lover and the poet are of imagination all compact', Shakespeare's characteristic language realizes itself most fully in Cleopatra's vision. What Coleridge called a 'happy valiancy of style' gives maximum significance to Antony's life. But effects of transcendence have a human history; the lover's fantasy is made from Rome's Mediterranean presence as Shakespeare interpreted it from the pages of Plutarch.

Sometimes, it seems, the therapist is in search of a story, to be told and retold by the patient until its significance is clear. Macbeth's apathy (compare the blank condition of mind described in vignette 3.1, p. 66) finds life, in a celebrated story-metaphor, to be 'a tale, told by an idiot, full of sound and fury, signifying nothing'. The story needed to confer significance upon his experience cannot be told by the 'idiot' who is totally cut off from the community and its values. It is a feature of the mode of analysis described by Dr Cox and Dr Theilgaard that metaphors seemingly distant from the narrative can clarify and intensify its meaning. Shakespeare's language offers many instances. Othello wins the love of Desdemona, and of her father, by telling her the story of his life. Thereafter his story can be told either outwardly, by relating Iago's designs against him, or inwardly, by tracing through the play's metaphors the history of his imaginative experience. At the centre of that experience we find this passage of visionary geography (III. 3, 453):

Never Iago. Like to the Pontic sea,
Whose icy current and compulsive course
Ne'er feels retiring ebb, but keeps due on
To the Propontic and the Hellespont,
Even so my bloody thoughts, with violent pace,
Shall ne'er look back, ne'er ebb to humble love,
Till that a capable and wide revenge
Swallow them up.

The metaphor seems to create the destructive momentum of Othello's passion and epitomizes the plot of the play. Sea-words and thought-words are interrelated until they reach not a wide *ocean* (as ordinary language would require) but a capacious and wide *revenge* that swallows up bloody, icy, compulsive, and violent thoughts. Everyday Othellos are in this perspective hard to come by, but oscillations between ice and fire, violence and stillness, often find metaphoric expression in the present study (and see vignette 2.1, for another celebrated Othello metaphor).

The movements of the Mediterranean sea and the warrior's experience of them (like the storm encountered on the way to Cyprus) are built into the poetic and dramatic structure of *Othello*. Shakespeare's plays, written at a time when 'every day some sailor's wife, The master's of some merchant, and the merchant' had 'themes of woe', often make metaphoric use of the voyage, with its quests and hazards. Egeus in *The Comedy of Errors*, telling the story of the shipwreck that overtook his family, speaks of 'the always-wind-obeying-deep'. But while the wind and the sea seem often to contend with human determinations and designs ('The seaman's whistle Is as a whisper in the ear of death'), they can also fulfil them, as in Viola's Illyria, in the Pauline voyages of Pericles, and at the sea's edge where Timon dies.

It is in *The Tempest*, however, that the metaphor of wind and sea finds its fullest expression, and the sea's movements, the sea-sounds and sea-airs can seem in the theatre to restore what they take away. It is as if the 'wind-obeying-deep' is a profound state of awareness, acted upon by invisible but formidable pressures and influences from outside the 'proper self'. 'Destiny, That hath to instrument this lower world' (Ariel's phrase in *The Tempest* III. 3, 53) is at once retributive, morally restorative, and musical, resolving discords to harmony. The 'deep and dreadful organ-pipe', says the usurper Alonso, 'pronounc'd the name of Prosper; it did bass my trespass'. Prospero himself we may see both as playwright, sorting out the plot, circumscribing the characters; and as therapist, using versions of shock-treatment, hypnosis, induced hallucination, story-telling and retelling, and work. There is nothing in such an account of the play that would have startled the Paracelsan physician Oswald Croll (who used all these techniques in Shakespeare's time) and much that the offender-therapist might still find congenial. It would seem that in Prospero's therapy there is much that in the current jargon we would call 'judge-mental', but the judgements in Shakespeare's Aeolian mode are meta-phorically charged and designed to satisfy the aesthetic as well as the ethical imagination (V. 1, 79):

> Their understanding
> Begins to swell, and the approaching tide
> Will shortly fill the reasonable shore
> That now lies foul and muddy.

There is the prospect in which Shakespeareans and therapists might choose to meet.

Philip Brockbank
Director of the Shakespeare Institute
University of Birmingham

Introduction

Late twentieth-century psychology has assembled many maps of the mind. Psychotherapists need and make use of them as they embark with their patients on journeys of meetings, of exploration, believing that to journey together in search of hidden meanings may result in the healing of hurt minds.

Many claim the psychoanalytical map to be the most modern and reliable, yet there are noticeable differences between maps as issued in the various countries. The North American map is technically brilliant, printed in bold type and clear colours for each area of the mind – id, ego, super-ego, making the origins and depth of strata evident. Areas are marked oedipal, pre-oedipal, triadic, diadic. The navigator is warned of the defence systems used by the different tribes that he will meet. Some are fairly civilized and open to rational discussion, even prepared to give up their magical beliefs and to adopt the ways of Western man – which he himself believes to be adaptive to their circumstances. Other tribes are much more primitive and dangerous, will defend themselves cannibalistic-ally and have devised effective, explosive devices to use against their enemies.

Maps issued in London give much more of the area of mind over to the primitive world. They warn that, under the superficial veneer of civilization, most world inhabitants harbour primitive fears and fantasies which constantly threaten to erupt from their depths; unless they have been tamed by the lengthy process called psychoanalysis, which allows for the benign meeting of a calm, informed explorer with these untamed primitives, ignorant infants who lie at the heart of the modern psyche.

Continental maps are almost unusable by Anglo-Saxon navigators. The French maps require months of argument and explanation before it becomes clear how they are to be used, for the meaning of each word is controversial and has to be defined. Other continental maps show a

German influence, one that seems non-psychoanalytic and that portrays areas of spirit and soul that do not appear on the other maps. Though intriguing and evocative, they are difficult for actual use in the task of clinical navigation.

Contemporary psychologists seem to have forgotten the older mind maps that man used to picture his psyche before the rise of Western schools of psychotherapy. They were put aside because they had not been constructed by scientists, as defined by nineteenth- and twentieth-century standards. They were the work of philosophers, dramatists, poets, visionaries, men of religious faiths. Being neither reliable nor valid, they were discounted. Yet now there is movement for rediscovery taking place.

Psychotherapists are rediscovering that psychotherapy is not primarily a precise technology of accurately used words, as tools of effective interpretations. The depths of the mind are reached and touched by simpler words that speak in images and metaphors, speak in a universal, timeless language, pre-dating contemporary ideas. A language that touches the heart, the ancient seat of the emotions, that speaks to the soul, that aspect of the human being that nineteenth-century science thought to have eliminated, as bespeaks the suppression of that word in Strachey's translation of Freud, whereas in his native German Freud used the word frequently.

Not only do we rediscover the need for such language to help us in our exploration, but modern science, such as neuropsychology, helps us to understand the nature and effect of these words. They are ways in which man can re-experience wholeness, a sense of being a person, a self, whose head, heart, and soul are not divided by cognitive categories.

We need new maps, and in this book the authors, English and Danish, united by a common love and deep understanding of language, have given us maps that would have been recognized by the ancient Greeks who bequeathed us fundamental ideas about the psyche that we were in danger of forgetting.

In *The Mirror and the Lamp* (1953), Abrams tells how the classical metaphor for the mind was that it was a mirror reflecting nature. Later, men began dimly to recognize the mind's vast inner dimensions and then the poet was portrayed as an explorer of the deep, his journey dimly illuminated by the poetic imagination. Another less well known metaphor for the poet's mind then became the Aeolian Harp.

The Aeolian Harp was hung from the branch of a tree, its music created by the stirring of the wind playing through its strings. This was the music of nature. One day the authors of this book and I were journeying at sea on a Danish ferry and discussing what might be an appropriate title for the work. Knowing that the desire of the authors is to show how the therapist's mind can be stirred by the communication of the patient, and how, unselfconsciously, the therapist finds himself responding at depth to the patient's hidden meanings, I suggested to them, 'The Aeolian Mode' as a suitable title. By using this image from ancient Greece, we ourselves in the twentieth century re-make contact with the ancestors of the Western world mentality, whose insight we are still exploring.

All psychotherapists will be stimulated to review and ponder their own experiences while reading this book and all will, in some ways, be wiser and changed by the experience.

Malcolm Pines
Consultant Psychotherapist
The Tavistock Clinic

Prologue

The Aeolian Mode of psychotherapy takes its name from the Aeolian Harp. It depends upon the therapist's capacity to pick up the 'music in the wind', and 'The Aeolian' was originally an early musical mode. It is, in itself, a metaphor which conveys customary clinical concerns. But it does more than this. The Aeolian Mode also facilitates response to the numerous nuances, and the hints of 'other things' which so often people therapeutic space.

Psychotherapy is concerned with a story which is so disturbing that, however painful the telling may be, it must be attempted. The 'teller' seeks an opportunity to explore, appreciate, and appropriate his story, so that it loses its hold. The Aeolian Mode is therefore a way of responding to, and furthering the telling of, that story of which it is also an unfolding part.

The Aeolian Mode is endowed with 'double trust'. First, it augments stringent clinical precision. And it does so by helping the therapist to become increasingly attentive to the patient's presence, and to what he does – or does not – say. Secondly, it both mobilizes and utilizes the therapist's associative activity. And the blending of both functions – the discriminative and the associative – leads to the creative use of imagery and metaphor. The latter, when it induces change, it justly named 'mutative'.

It can either facilitate endopsychic change or reduce endopsychic instability; the option depending upon conventional clinical 'indications'. It does not imply new criteria for therapeutic interventions. But it offers the capaciousness of metaphor, and the impact of fresh images, as resources for texturing and sharpening such dynamic initiatives. Transference interpretation is one specific form of metaphoric mutation, through which presence, affect, and naming are vicariously relocated, whereas in supportive psychotherapy such mutation brings about the consolidation of existing defences.

THE BRIDGING EFFECT

There are parallel patternings between the processes implicit in the fields of experiential, interactional, and neuropsychology. And they underlie various kinds of dynamic 'bridging'. The linking of two spheres of experience takes place in psychotherapy – the here-and-now and the there-and-then. This is brought about through transference – and its resolution. Indeed, 'bridging activity' lies in the very word itself. 'Transference' means 'to carry across' in Latin. As does 'metaphor' in Greek.

The linking of the two cerebral hemispheres takes place through the Corpus Callosum. And metaphor, seen from a neuropsychological perspective, integrates the ikonic mode of the right hemisphere and the linguistic mode of the left.

THEORETICAL FOUNDATIONS

Theoretically, the Aeolian Mode rests upon a tripartite foundation.

Developmental psychology, which offers both structural and functional perspectives:

1. Mainstream psychoanalytic psychology, which stresses the significance of the 'developmental line', personality structure, and the effecting of dynamic change through transference interpretation and resolution. The flexibility of the Aeolian Mode ensures that it can be active and efficacious in both interpretative and supportive psychotherapy.
2. Organismic psychology, which maintains that developmental progression proceeds from a state of relative globality and lack of differentiation, to a state of increased differentiation, articulation, and hierarchical integration. The Aeolian Mode facilitates this progression, but it does not diminish the intrinsic importance of antecedent levels of functioning. On the contrary, it attaches special significance to physiognomic perception, concrete thinking, and primordial affects. Such phenomena are not automatically regarded as unwanted, regressive symptoms to be 'treated'. Indeed, they often afford access to essential, early and authentic experience which cannot be attained in any other way.

Neuropsychology, which is congruous with the Aeolian Mode as a whole. In particular, it contributes to the understanding of this Mode in terms of the significance of hemispheric lateralization, the relationship between novelty and the mutative process, and the means whereby an appropriate cognitive–affective stimulus can 'bypass' the repression barrier.

Phenomenological existential psychology, which is attentive to the immediacy of experience. It maintains a constant pull towards the particular, the present, and the pleroma of experience. It defies all attempts at reductionism, underlines the impact of the larger story which encompasses the story of our life, and places greater weight upon understanding than upon explanation.

Chapter 7 explores the interrelationship of these theoretical foundations.

JUNG'S INFLUENCE

It is difficult to know where to state the impact which Jung's thought has had upon our writing. The number of 'Jungian' entries in the bibliography bears no relation to the pervasive influence of his thinking. But our concentration upon the significance of archaic language is closely linked to those symbolic and archetypal aspects of experience which Jung stressed (see p. 143).

A CAUTIONARY NOTE

We have written this cautionary note to serve as a reminder that a patient 'hearing voices' or 'seeing things' may initially need anti-psychotic medication or even surgical intervention for an intra-cranial tumour. And the fact that much of this book is about aesthetic imperatives and mutative metaphors does not imply that we ignore conventional clinical concerns. On the contrary, we have cause to underline the importance of assessing each patient from every relevant clinical angle.

But, having said this, wherever and whenever therapist and patient ultimately meet, and whatever the clinical presentation, Aeolian initiatives always stand the chance of offering the therapist more finely tuned responsive precision.

AN OPTIMISTIC NOTE

'As we learn steadily that the depths are not only the wellsprings of neurosis, but also of *health*, of *joy*, of *creativeness*, we begin to speak of the healthy unconscious, of healthy regression, of healthy instincts, of healthy non-rationality, of healthy intuition. And we begin to desire to salvage these capacities for ourselves.'

(Maslow 1965)

NEGLECTED COHERENCES

'Surprise and wonder always fly beside him [Pegasus]. There is no poetry where they are not.'

(*The Poet*, Emerson 1841)

An attempt to restore neglected coherences lies at the heart of this book. We refer to links between analytic, linear thinking and the associative thought of imagination and metaphor; between determinism and creativity;

between the power of *poiesis* to sustain novelty and, paradoxically, its simultaneous capacity to reinforce the archaic and the primordial. These neglected coherences fired our curiosity, because they converged upon the therapeutic process.

Nevertheless, in spite of providing clinical examples to flesh out the three theoretical foundations, we remain acutely aware that we have only stirred the surface of things. And, although Bachelard comes to our aid should we touch the depths, we are left with two lines from Edwin Muir hovering about us:

> 'What I shall never know
> I must make known.'
> (*The Poet*, Muir 1960)

Paradox is one of the features of the Aeolian Mode and, as we write as co-authors, Edwin Muir, slightly adapted, gives us the necessary 'once-upon-a-timeness' to begin the story:

> 'What we shall never know
> We must make known.'

THE ESSENTIAL PROCESS

We are sometimes asked for a 'thumbnail sketch', the essence of the Aeolian Mode in a nutshell.

This can be given in three brief, condensed lines – although it takes nearly 300 pages to explore its implications.

Attend. Witness. Wait.
Discern, formulate, potentiate, and reflect mutative metaphoric material.
Attend. Witness. Wait.

1
The story

'But the moment I asked him to tell me a story, he was instantly on his guard, pretending he had no idea what I was talking about. It was only after many days, when he had come to trust us more, that he confessed to having stories and told us some of them; but even so I always had a feeling that there was deep in his heart a story of stories which needed far more time and sharing of experience to communicate than I could afford just then.'
(Homesick for a Story, Van der Post 1961)

The disturbing story

This book begins and ends with statements about the significance of story, the human story as it is experienced and as it is told. But it is not concerned with the telling of just *any* part of the story. And it certainly has no intention of telling *every* part of the story. On the contrary, it centres upon those aspects of his story with which a person needs to come to terms because they 'disturb' him and because they sometimes lead to 'disturbed' behaviour which may be 'disturbing' to those around him. We speak of being 'thrown' by the unexpected, which recalls us to the Latin root of the word. *Disturbare* means 'to throw into disorder', *turbe* itself meaning 'a tumult, turmoil, or crowd'. And man's condition of 'thrownness' is a crucial existential attribute. It is not surprising that 'parable' – a fictitious narrative containing deep truth – comes from the Greek for 'thrown alongside' (*paraballein*). It encapsulates the triple themes of the story, the larger story, and 'thrownness' (see also pp. 241–2).

The story of the patient's unfolding experience always matters. And, as it is told, it usually has the double quality of being both vigilantly descriptive, yet also rich in metaphoric potential. The therapist is offered detail of

1

experience and circumstance so that, as Cecil (1949) says of Turgenev, we are 'aware of time and space beyond the story'.

Much of this book is concerned with the therapist's task of enabling the patient to engage with his own evolving story and, as such, it is 'down to earth', practical, and clinical. However, in the last chapter we venture to look at the way in which each individual story is related to the story of Everyman and to 'the greater story that encompasses the story of his life' (Dunne 1973). Nevertheless, even in these opening pages it seemed relevant to draw attention to the numerous similarities between the patient's story, and his telling of it in clinical disclosure – no matter whether this occurs in the setting afforded by individual or group psychotherapy – and those other tellings which come from the wider landscape of general literature.

Indeed, a momentary diversion from the clinical to the literary world finds us in the company of *The Story-Shaped World* (Wicker 1975), *Tellers and Listeners: the Narrative Imagination* (Hardy 1975), *The Genesis of Secrecy: On the Interpretation of Narrative* (Kermode 1979), and *The Story-teller Retrieves the Past* (Lascelles 1980). Each of these books explores different, though cognate, aspects of the relationship between the intrinsic fascination of 'story-telling', the interpretation of narrative, and that degree of 'fiction' which is necessary to carry the 'fact' of human experience.

Spence (1982) raises the crucial question of whether the therapist 'hears' the same story that the patient is 'telling' in *Narrative Truth and Historical Truth: Meaning and Interpretation in Psychoanalysis*.

But it is to Romanyshyn (1982) that we are indebted for the exploration of the psychological significance and etymology of the word 'story'. He tells us that 'psychological understanding proceeds by way of story . . . [which is] primarily a way of seeing, a guide, something which shows the way'. And the idea that 'story' refers not only to the way of disturbance that has been taken but also to the 'showing of the way' means that the *via dolorosa* and the *via illuminata* are linked in the matrix of meaning.

A fragment of dialogue from *Othello* takes us on the way, both mimetically and metaphorically, by reminding us that encounters at depth between one person and another, even in dynamic psychotherapy, are inevitably partial and provisional.

> 'I pray you bring me on the way a little . . .
> 'Tis but a little way that I can bring you.'
> (*Othello* III. 4, 196)

The patient is involved in gradual re-engagement with repressed experience and re-cognition of painful aspects of his story. But 'clinical' though the task may be, the Aeolian Mode through which this is achieved is essentially 'aesthetic' in Bateson's sense (1979). That is, it involves a search for 'the pattern which connects'.

It is a search in which both the patient and the therapist participate, although they each approach the scene of the search from different starting points. And there is an inescapable aspect of 'liminality', or threshold-crossing, in which they are each engaged. For the patient, this involves the threshold between the unconscious and the conscious, which may be crossed by words or images. And the importance of the latter can never be exaggerated. The patient's story may be so disturbing that it is repressed and thus banished beyond the possibility of verbal access. Indeed, it is often the impact of repressed experience which leads to that story which is so disturbing that the patient seeks the opportunity to tell it; so that he can learn his own life-story at first hand.

The therapist's threshold is a different one. And it is a double threshold. It is, in part, that of discerning 'the pattern which connects'. And it is, in part, through empathy and transference, being present with his patient as the threshold of insight is crossed. A patient who was reflecting upon his need to tell 'the disturbing story' and who felt that the therapist had drawn back from the threshold which he knew he had to cross, said:

> 'I took it further.
> He did not take it further enough.
> *I can take it further still.*'

And he did. Slowly. And often in silence (see also p. 215). 'Further still' carries an echo from Bernard of Clairvaux (1090–1153): 'My curiosity has led me to explore my lowest depths as well, only to find that He went deeper yet. If I looked out from myself, I saw Him stretching farther than the farthest I could see; and if I looked within, He was more inward still.' And this, in turn, recalls a question which everyone asks himself, at some point along the way: 'Travel you far on, or are you at the farthest?' (*The Taming of the Shrew* IV. 2, 73). A book which brings together many aspects of threshold–crossing is Hendry's (1983) *The Sacred Threshold*.

Silence

But therapy is also concerned with the significance of the changing eloquence of silence. And Isak Dinesen (1957) reminds us that 'where the story-teller is loyal, eternally and unswervingly loyal to the story . . . silence will speak'. Silence is not always evidence of resistance. McGuire (1985) has studied Shakespeare's 'Open Silences' in his book *Speechless Dialect* – a title taken from *Measure for Measure*. The open silence is a recurrent feature in the unfolding of the human story within therapeutic space.

Its 'precise meaning . . . emerges only in "performance"'. And Leslie Kane (1984) has surveyed *The Language of Silence:*

> 'The dumb silence of apathy, the sober silence of solemnity, the fertile silence of awareness, the active silence of perception, the baffled silence of confusion, the uneasy silence of impasse, the muzzled silence of outrage, the expectant silence of waiting, the reproachful silence of censure, the tacit silence of approval, the vituperative silence of accusation, the eloquent silence of awe, the unnerving silence of menace, the peaceful silence of communion, and the irrevocable silence of death illustrate by their unspoken response to speech that experiences exist for which we lack the word.'

She refers to the 'unspoken response to speech' in her discussion *On the Unspoken and the Unspeakable in Modern Drama.* But silence within therapeutic space is often the silent response to silence, at the still point of the unspoken response to speech. In this unfathomable stillness, the Aeolian Mode may serve as a reference point. And so it may in the quiet of volcanic turbulence before an eruption. Silence of this significance is a characteristic of offender-therapy, as the following 'memory' described by a schizophrenic offender-patient indicates.

'She said nothing . . . So I killed her . . . Then nothing was said.'

Havens' book *Making Contact* (1986) is of relevance here. He describes three forms of absence and ways of 'speaking to absence'. Olinick (1982) considers the psychoanalytic significance of silence in 'Meanings Beyond Words', and Homan (1980) explores *Shakespeare's 'More than Words can Witness': Essays on Visual and Nonverbal Enactment in the Plays.*

The other story

Silence speaks of many things. Indeed, when a patient tells part of his story too easily, this usually signifies that this is not the part of his story which needs to be told. This argument has a special relevance when the therapist is working with extremely narcissistic patients, clinically described as psychopathic. The novice therapist may be surprised that such a patient gives the story of a killing with detail – often horrifying detail – of the victim's last struggle. But casual 'telling' always implies that there is another story, often a much earlier story – which the patient can only blurt out fitfully and partially – if he can tell it at all.

'True, . . . he's telling *a* story. . . . But it's not *the* story for him.' It is difficult to imagine a group of listeners who would be more difficult to 'lead up the garden path' than seven other psychopaths who are fellow

4

members of a therapeutic group. They, above all, would be best equipped to detect whether they were hearing 'a story', '*the*' story which one of them needed to tell, or whether the necessary story was still being kept at bay by the 'merciful function' of repression – to use Bettleheim's helpful phrase. Often the re-telling of the story is no mere repetition. Paradoxical though it sounds, re-telling often carries older, more deeply buried cognitive–affective overtones. Thus the repeatedly searched memory of the killing of a parental surrogate leads to the following reflection:

> 'It weighs on my mind. In bringing it out I think of fresh things each time. I don't dwell on it in the same way. There are no barriers anymore . . . not now.' [The dots might represent five silent, but very long, active minutes.]

For example, when some dahlias, sent as a gift to one of the group members, are described as 'looking like dried blood', and another patient remarks, 'I *am* what I've done', there are deeper echoes of personal pain which previous tellings had not reached. And when the associative phrase 'like a breech in nature / For ruin's wasteful entrance' (*Macbeth* II. 3, 111) appears in his mind unbidden, it startles the therapist. He is aware that the group matrix is vigorously alive with reverberations of fact and fiction, past and present, conscious and unconscious aspects of experience.

It was as the members of a therapeutic group were comparing their individual stories that the following arresting reflection emerged: 'It's the process of unfolding that's the same . . . the telling of the story is the same.' Although the developmental stages through which each individual passes must, of necessity, be the same, the individual elements of each story will differ. Content will vary, but the 'process of unfolding' will be the same. This observation recalls the words of Malan (1979): 'the aim of every moment of every session is to put the patient in touch with as much of his true feelings as he can bear'. In other words, one of the tasks of dynamic psychotherapy is to enable the patient to tell his story so that such disclosure can lead to a change in the way in which he sees himself and his world. This, in turn, leads to changes in personality organization. Whatever the individual psychopathology may have been, there is a generic quality about dynamic psychotherapy which is concerned with 'the process of unfolding' and 'the telling of the story'. This points us in the direction of Robert Graves (1961) who wrote: 'There is one story and one story only / That will prove worth your telling' ('To Juan at the Winter Solstice').

Hoffman (1967) described 'Graves' special virtues, his incantatory rhythm, his primordial imagery, his embodiment of contemporary experience in a mold archaic, mysterious, and compelling'. In Chapter 5 we shall be considering the depth of dynamic disclosure within therapeutic space in which archaic language, imagery, metaphor, and myth reverberate. But here we note that Graves raises the issue as to whether the 'one story' refers to the irreducibly personal, or to the generic human story of birth, struggle, joy, pain, and death.

Perspectival world and personal story

A cognate concern is the relationship between 'The story of my life' and 'The life of my story'. We shall see how they converge as archaic language is invoked, because it alone can carry the affective weight. 'The life of my story' is less time-bound and is closer to the fable.

'LOOKING FROM WHERE I AM'

A patient once prefaced the description of escalating domestic disruption with the words 'Looking from where I am'. Yet, apart from defensive distancing through dissociative or psychotic dislocation, it is impossible for a patient to look from anywhere else. One of the perennial tasks of psychotherapy is to help a patient look at his life in a new way, so that he can appropriate his experience and get into his story. It was with a sense of considerable achievement that John said:

'I said "My name is John" and then I got into my story.'

In many respects this simple sentence sums up the purpose of the Aeolian Mode. It offers the therapist a way of helping a man to say 'My name is John' and then to get into his story, looking from where he is. It is never easy and it requires courage to enter one's own story. The Aeolian Mode facilitates this difficult task because it intensifies empathic precision. Indeed, empathy (see p. 170) can be regarded as the *sine qua non* for entering the perspectival world[1] of another, because the therapist comes alongside John and joins him in looking at his life from where, for the time being, they both are. This shared perspectival point is always at the therapist's discretion. It is partial and reversible, because effective psychotherapy demands that the therapist also continues to attend to the patient's story from other perspectives.

But when the patient has a multiple personality, a different dimension of empathy is called for. The affirmation then becomes

'My name is Legion; for we are many.'

(*Mark* V, 9)

The daunting prospect of 'getting into several stories' simultaneously seems almost insuperable, though it cannot be avoided. The associative freedom encouraged by the Aeolian Mode, when grounded in basic psycho-analytic theory, can augment therapeutic possibilities in such an unpromising predicament.

Getting into his story and looking from where he is imply that the patient is prepared for the painful self-scrutiny of turning to himself. This is far removed from narcissistic withdrawal. On the contrary, the turning indicates a capacity to endure the vulnerability of diminished defensiveness. This turning point is of wider significance when a therapeutic group begins to look at itself from where it is. 'My name is Legion; for we are many' can stand for the name of the group-as-a-whole.

Homan (1981) describes the way in which 'the theatre turns to itself'. And he considers this theme in relation to the aesthetic metaphor in Shakespeare. In our view, there is a direct link between the various components involved in a 'live' dramatic production and another kind of 'live' dynamic event, namely a therapeutic group. Homan refers to 'the presence and function of the audience'. But in the unfolding life of a therapeutic group the 'audience' may, at any moment, change places with those who 'deliver' the story. Those who receive, and those who 'get into their own story', are unpredictably interchangeable. And although each member of the 'audience' forming the group-as-a-whole has his own story to tell, there is also the growth and differentiation of the corporate experience, the story which they are all 'in'. It is for this reason that the aesthetic metaphor described by Homan is so close to the aesthetic imperative (see p. 26) which is active at a pivotal place in the Aeolian Mode.

The theatre turning to itself, as audience and actors intermingle, reminds us that 'theatre' means 'that which we gaze at'. And the aesthetic imperative makes for clarity in our understanding of the inner and outer stages upon which the action occurs. Joyce McDougall's *Theaters of the Mind: Illusion and Truth on the Psychoanalytic Stage* (1985) is a rich elaboration on this theme.

In the following pages we draw attention to the tapestry of exchange between the part played by the aesthetic metaphor in poetry and drama, and its enabling function in dynamic psychotherapy. It seems to us that each world can be an energized beneficiary of the other.

In our attempt to understand the meaning of the patient's personal story, by linking it to the larger story, we need a frame of reference which embraces the pattern which connects. Yet to look for this pattern is not to make a straight-line, cause and effect connection. As Bateson (1979) points out: 'Logic and quantity turn out to be inappropriate devices for describing organisms and their interactions and internal organisation.' The *story* always needs to be viewed from different perspectives, not least when it is a question of integrating the theoretical frames of reference upon which its

7

understanding rests. One theory does not make another redundant. This syncretic approach does not necessarily lead to a cacophony of ideas drawn from different sources. On the contrary, it is often a coherent picture which emerges rather than one which is capricious, controversial, and incomplete.

To say that the objective of psychotherapy is to understand and experience the relationship between thoughts, feelings, and actions is to link the reflection cited from Malan (see above, p. 5) and these theoretical considerations. Meaning and context are linked to each other. And, without context, words and actions have no meaning at all. Without attempting to integrate the seemingly disparate theoretical ideas, the framework will be fragmented. Therefore our aim has been to call upon ideas from developmental psychology, neuropsychology, phenomenology, and existentialism. And we have done so in the hope of showing that the Aeolian Mode can be viewed from a variety of perspectives which still make sense, whether they are considered individually or as part of a coherent whole.

This introduction serves to emphasize the importance of thinking in terms of the story. And here, the 'story' refers not only to the patient's experiential story. It refers also to his manner of telling the story, its integration with the greater story which encompasses the story of our life, and its relationship to the theoretical background upon which the therapist structures and responds to the story he is told. Dunne (1973) implies that the therapist's life-story also comes within the ambit of 'the greater story'. The life-stories of both patient and therapist are inevitably linked in a more profound way than technical terms may suggest. Thus, phrases like 'countertransference phenomenon' and 'transient projective identification', technically necessary though they may be, may shield a therapist from discerning a dimension of mutual predicament it is unwise to ignore.

In the following example the therapist can only know about love and hate, fire and ice because of their impact upon his life. He may have academic knowledge of positive or negative affects, but the experience of fire and ice he recognizes in the patient is of another order. Before most of the members of a weekly therapeutic group had even sat down, one member said:

> 'I want to talk about something . . . but I want you to start it off because I don't know how. I can't start. I could use psychological jargon, like ''positive'' or ''negative'' feeling, but that is impersonal and uninvolved.'
>
> 'How about loving or hating?'
> 'That's nearer.'
> 'Or fire and ice?'
> *'That's it. That's me all over. There is no inbetween.'* [Energetically, immediately, and with a flash of relief and recognition on his face.]

This is a fragmentary glimpse into therapeutic space. It emphasizes the universal pull of the primordial. It is an intrinsic part of the psychotherapeutic process in which a patient comes as close to his true feelings as he dares. Furthermore, it exemplifies a recurring phenomenon which is evident throughout the ensuing pages, because it is irrespective of education and social class; although its exact epiphany is not independent of the patient's personality structure. The psychotic is often much closer to omnipotence, destructive rage, and insatiable love than his neurotic counterpart. If he is an arsonist, he may even experience a consuming fire of passion or anger in concrete rather than metaphorical terms. Nevertheless the metaphor affords the possibility of engagement with those primordial themes to which all our experience gravitates.

Hobson (1985) has described the importance of metaphors about the human body as conveying the deepest levels of experience. A patient who tells the therapist that he is afraid there is something wrong with his heart receives the reply: 'Yes. It's broken.' We agree with Hobson that images and metaphors about the body are of major significance. They help our understanding, not only of psychosomatic illness, but of every kind of emotional disturbance. And, as in many dramatic works, 'body metaphors' abound in *Coriolanus*: 'I am known to be . . . one that converses more with the buttock of the night than with the forehead of the morning' (II. 1, 53). Sue Jennings (in press) refers to the epic metaphor, a 'larger than life metaphor which can often communicate our most profound state of being'. Nevertheless, powerful though these body and epic metaphors are, we feel that the primordial metaphors, which are linked to primal chaos and our deepest fundament, have even greater potential for housing anguish or ecstasy. This is evident in the dialogue just cited. Positive and negative feelings are detached academic assessments of human experience. Love and hate are, as the patient said 'nearer'. Whereas the primordial metaphor of fire and ice takes us immediately into the preserve of the dawn of things. Masterson (1976) shares this view, and has invoked the aid of the Horsemen of the Apocalypse – famine, war, flood, and pestilence – because '*Technical words are too abstract to convey the intensity and immediacy of these feelings* (depression, anger, fear, guilt, passivity, helplessness, and emptiness and void) and therefore the primacy they hold over the patient's entire life' [our italics].

It is easy to see why loving and hating, and fire and ice, are the raw material of so much *poiesis* that leads to formal poetry. But poetry, in an orthodox sense, is not our concern here. Whereas the process of *poiesis*, in which 'something is called into existence which was not there before' (see below, p. 23), is central and ubiquitous. Two associations induced by the discussion of this theme refuse to remain silent:

> 'But from my grave across my brow
> Plays no wind of healing now,
> And *fire and ice* within me fight
> Beneath the suffocating night.'
> [our italics]
> (*Collected Poems*, A. E. Housman 1939)

> 'This is the Hour of Lead –
> Remembered, if outlived,
> As Freezing persons, recollect the Snow –
> First-Chill-then-Stupor – then the letting-go –'
> (*Complete Poems*, Emily Dickinson *c.* 1862)

We can now discern why a patient who was afraid of 'slipping off the world', and who knew of 'the letting go', almost hurled the reply 'YES' across the room when he was asked if he felt very cold. The pull of the primordial again. In a letter to his friend Myers (1904), John Ruskin wrote: 'But it is partly a help to know that one does not work in the shadow alone.' These words are peculiarly apt as a description of that depth of experience which the patient and the therapist recognize in each other as they gravitate towards the primordial. After he had said that fire and ice were 'me all over' and 'there is no inbetween', the patient went on to express extreme ambivalence towards his parents. This had never been glimpsed during previous formal 'interviews'. The mutative power of the metaphor had enabled him to feel and say that which had been 'safely' banished. This 'uncovering' brought him to the brink of a psychogenic psychosis, but there was no short cut to integration which could bypass this encounter with self. To discover that the 'voices' which he had previously 'pretended to hear' had eventually become real must have been a frightening experience. His fear was such that, even from the grave, there was no wind of healing across his brow; but this disclosure within therapeutic space induced that vital mutation whereby the intolerable becomes tolerable. And the unsafe safe. Or at least safer.

'I always prepare myself for the sight of myself.' In this thought-provoking phrase Virginia Woolf has touched upon an essential aspect of psychotherapy, namely, that it takes time to 'prepare myself for the sight of myself'. And a premature 'therapeutic' intervention is always counterproductive because the patient is not 'prepared'. Should this happen, the patient, like Virginia Woolf in *The Waves*, will 'quail'. The full passage is as follows: 'It was only for a moment, catching sight of myself before I had

time to prepare myself as I always prepare myself for the sight of myself, that I quailed' (1931).

'ON THE WAY A LITTLE': TOWARDS THE INACCESSIBLE

Our mood of caution in introducing the Aeolian Mode is caught by the phrase 'on the way a little' (*Othello* III. 4, 196). This therapeutic emphasis grew out of our attempts to work dynamically with patients traditionally regarded as 'unsuitable' for psychotherapy – even after extensive 'preparation'. Nevertheless, Aeolian initiatives can encourage such preparation on account of their non-invasive quality. They reach the depths precisely because they adopt a non-invasive approach. Although, to be more accurate, they do NOT REACH the depths, because they START there (Bachelard op. cit.). This heterodox momentum is looked at more closely under the heading of poetic induction (see p. 48). It means that therapeutic initiatives do not primarily attempt to overcome resistance, or try to gain access through an inadequate defensive protection to a fragile and precarious core. On the contrary, the Aeolian Mode engenders movement which originates in the depths of experience. In other words, the patient himself mobilizes resources for self-scrutiny which, *ab initio*, are already safely behind his distancing defences. Paradoxical though it initially appears, such an approach has proved to have pragmatic efficacy. To start in the depths is 'a new reality and not a logical riddle' – as Tillich (1957) said of paradox. What we hope to offer is not solely academic and detached from the clinical 'coal-face'. Far from it. It is at the point of encounter when a patient becomes 'inaccessible', so that further movement seems blocked, that the mutative metaphor comes into its own.

THE AUGMENTATION OF CLINICAL STRINGENCY

The Aeolian Mode is not a soft option. Because *poiesis* features prominently, it should not be presumed that it encourages casual clinical thinking. Or that diagnostic categories cease to count. Or that 'DSM III' is irrelevant. On the contrary, it can sharpen the discernment of 'first rank symptoms', or help to differentiate the pseudo-psychotic from the schizophrenic. And we constantly underline the fact that the Aeolian Mode does not bypass conventional clinical assessment criteria. It enables the therapist to employ a wider range of 'tuning devices', so that he has a greater chance of access to, and empathic reception of, the perspectival world of his patient. When it comes to the clinical challenge of distinguishing suicidal or homicidal *fantasy* from the sombre, crisis-creating phenomenon of suicidal or homicidal *intent*, the Aeolian Mode is not relinquished for more 'forensic tools'. Indeed, even when medication is indicated or physical intervention is urgently called for, the associative

11

delineation of inner-world object-relationships can be regarded as a *sine qua non*, not an optional extra.

The Aeolian Mode supplements established assessment and therapeutic strategies. And the fact that poetic thinking and inferential investment is involved does not mean that it lacks clinical rigour. For example, when assessing a homicidal assault from the point of view of the inner-world phenomena of the assailant, it may be significant that blood spilt – and subsequently produced as forensic evidence – was that of the assailant, not the victim (see vignette 3.2, p. 72). And a phrase from *Coriolanus* may have 'forced its way' into the therapist's observing attentional 'perceptual set'.

> ''tis not my blood
> Wherein thou seest me mask'd; for thy revenge.'

But the 'deictic stress' (see p. 116) may render the following mutation of implication:

> ''tis NOT MY blood
> Wherein thou seest me mask'd; for THY REVENGE.'
> *(Coriolanus* I. 8, 9)

Thus a 'displaced victim' may result from psychopathology in which 'self' and 'other' are confused. Coming to this interface from the side of poetry, we find Julia Kristeva (1984) writing on 'poetry that is not a form of murder'. And just where and how the clinical and the aesthetic are interwoven, so that enhanced clinical precision – rather than contaminated clinical distortion – follows, we hope the ensuing pages will illustrate.

The Aeolian Mode in action: a vignette

The Aeolian Mode may take us 'on the way a little'. This is modest movement. Yet it is in the right direction and better than no movement at all. At this stage an illustrative vignette may serve as a hook on which to hang subsequent discussion. Our first example is easy to describe. Even if it succeeds in taking us on our way a little, its dynamic implications are far from pedestrian.

VIGNETTE 1.1
'But how will I be tonight?'

Mary, a frightened, intermittently paranoid young woman, cuts into a reflective silence with a gratuitous statement of her predicament. Her gaze-pattern is that of a jerky searchlight probing every corner and possible hiding-place in the room:

> 'I'm all right today.
> And I'm all right now.
> But how will I be tonight?'

12

She was scarcely asking the therapist a question and seemed to be absorbed in wondering how she would be when darkness fell. Interpretation was out of the question. But an empathically supportive echo was urgently indicated. 'Feeling like a river . . . almost overflowing its banks?' was the therapist's way of indicating that he understood her fear of not being contained or containable. Mary responded to the metaphor[2] as though she had actually chosen it herself. And, with the more relaxed tone of someone whose inner world has been recognized – and who is somehow no longer a stranger to her own experience – she replied:

> 'That's a good way of putting it. Yes . . . It's an overflowing feeling . . . like a bubble in me is going to burst.'

DYNAMIC IMPLICATIONS OF VIGNETTE 1.1

It is true that the therapist might have discerned that Mary was dreading nightfall as much as she was dreading death. Yet this would be a retrospective justification of events. In this instance, it was not only the archaic cadence which led the therapist towards an associative linking with the following passage:

> 'If thou hast run with the footmen, and they have wearied thee, then how canst thou contend with horses? and if in the land of peace, wherein thou trustedst, they wearied thee, then *how wilt thou do in the swelling of Jordan?*' [our italics]
>
> (Jeremiah 12, 5)

The 'Jordan' quotation remained latent, but yielded the manifest image of flooding.

We will now try to explain why the therapist allowed the association from *Jeremiah* to activate his specific response to a frightened psychotic. It is difficult to explain exactly why the echo from *Macbeth*, which was prompted by 'a bubble in me', was *not* acted upon: 'The earth hath bubbles, as the water has, / And these are of them.' (*Macbeth* I. 3, 79). It presents another daunting theoretical challenge. What is beyond doubt is the fact that we are dealing with an overdetermined countertransference phenomenon.

There is the fear of approaching night; the sense of swelling, of an incipient overflowing of experience and the bursting of an internal bubble. There are unstable introjects, ill-defined ego boundaries, volcanic id-derivatives, and an overall confusion of inner and outer world phenomena. But such considerations cannot take us sufficiently close to the composite insight whereby an archaic cadence: 'But how will I be tonight?', found such an exact echo in an English translation from a Hebrew prophet: 'How wilt thou do in the swelling of Jordan?'

This, in turn, led to the dynamic metaphor of hitherto unverbalized experience being described in terms of a river overflowing. Furthermore, there was the superimposed catastrophic implication that the river of death was about to burst its banks. So that death, itself, was out of control. It is not surprising that in narrow, strictly clinical terms, the patient was intermittently paranoid.

In order to counteract the impression that the Aeolian Mode rests upon an echo, and that alone, we will now attempt to grapple with the numerous questions which inevitably arise. Although the echo forms an integral part of the dynamic exchange, it is no simple 'clang-association'. Other and deeper resonances are present and active. We look at these with 'contra-clang' as a hazard warning light.

'CONTRA-CLANG'

Why did the therapist choose this particular metaphor? Was it merely the similarity of the archaic cadence: 'How will I be tonight?' – 'How wilt thou do . . .'? Could it be a 'clang-association' linking the statement of the patient and the passage from *Jeremiah*? Was the connection determined by the accident of their rhythmic contiguity? An unwitting selection of associations occurring automatically? Or is the reaction of the therapist goal-directed? Is there a determining tendency toward selection from the many possible 'appropriate' associations?

The ultimate goal is to help the patient, and the proximate goal is to formulate the thought about to be captured within a specific theme. This means that the therapist's primary and secondary processes have to work in concert. Such goal-directedness determines the association, even though it is not conscious at a given moment (Ach 1905; Lewin 1926).

Within metaphor, paradox, allusion, and image facilitate the emergence of repressed ideas. But the Aeolian Mode can only capture preverbal thoughts and their hidden relationships if the therapist's associations are 'goal-adequate' ideas. They must stand as representatives for the strivings, wishes, drives, and feelings of the patient.

Creative, innovative thoughts, which always have a random component (Bateson 1979) can be described as divergent – as opposed to convergent – thinking. This mode of thinking is essentially related to the right hemisphere – whereas digital thinking is related to the left hemisphere.

It can be claimed that creative thought is fundamentally stochastic, which implies that *two* components are at play. In this instance there is both a random component and a process of selection. The latter is as important as the former. Random material *per se* can be manifest as thought disorder. And whether it is meaningful or not depends upon its context. This is akin to Jung's concept of synchronicity. He describes this as 'an acausal connecting principle' which throws light upon meaningful coincidences. He writes (1972): 'Synchronicity is a phenomenon that seems to be primarily connected with psychic conditions, that is to say with processes in the unconscious . . . they are subjectively convincing but are extremely difficult to verify objectively.'

Although the Aeolian Mode has an affinity with the concept of synchronicity, its therapeutic effect lies in its capacity to provoke reorganization. This depends upon the integration of both primary and secondary process phenomena, as well as the two components of creative thought, namely, that which is random and that which results from the process of selection. The language of the primary process – kept in check by repression – is linked to that of the secondary process. This is a dialectical activity in which two opposite modes move towards integration. As Ogden (1985) points out, 'the integration is never complete; each integration creates a new dialectical opposition and a new dynamic tension'.

Empathy also occurs within the context of a dialectical exchange between patient and therapist. It is a question of balance between being and not-being 'the other' (see pp. 170–80). It is the empathy, the goal-directedness, and the capacity for integrated dual modes of thinking, which are prerequisites in the application of the Aeolian Mode. It is not a question of an arbitrary connection of associations coming to consciousness because of too little selective suppression. Nor is it a train of associations based merely on habit, subordination, and linear thinking.

Consensual validation – the patient's 'Eureka' experience – is an indication of accuracy in the therapist's response within the Aeolian Mode. Its capacities can be described as follows: It encourages the patient to experience the richness of symbolic equivalence and affective value; it allows 'reasoning' to proceed by a non-linear mode of association which is not restricted to syllogistic logic; it uses images which reflect a pre-conceptual level of psychic functioning. Appelbaum (1966) points out that the most effective interpretations are likely to be multilayered. The patient responds at different levels of mental organization originating from different developmental stages.

In vignette 1.1 Mary is not surprised by the novelty of an interposed image. When affective matching is as accurate as therapeutic empathy allows, the patient sometimes accepts apparent novelty as though it is familiar. Empathic congruence is the key concept. 'The swelling of Jordan' was congruous, because of its implicit aura of barely controlled catastrophe. And this is exactly how Mary felt.

In this example the patient needed dynamic support rather than interpretive or exploratory intervention. Subsequent vignettes will illustrate the dual quality of metaphor. It can be honed to razor-sharp precision. Or it can act as scaffolding for supportive consolidation. Yet it can also be as invitational and 'open-ended' as a projective test.

Precise though it is, there is nothing 'absolute' about the Jordan image. It was efficacious because it emerged from the therapist's aesthetic reservoir as offering 'the best fit' for the perceived awareness that Mary had of her own predicament. In other words, it 'fitted best' as an echo of how the patient herself felt about her inner and outer world. There are, of course, numerous other possibilities which the therapist might have chosen. But these are the words which actually clothed his affective response. Affective precision and psychodynamic discernment are what matter. Their degree of reciprocal 'fit' and their reception by the patient are what matter most.

The therapist will already have known Mary's story and her current defensive organization. During the session she brings him up to date about her present predicament. The therapist's 'goal-directedness' determined his choice of an image. This was compatible with the frightening 'fluidity' of Mary's turbulence.

Theoretically, this vignette illustrates certain characteristics of the Aeolian Mode which can be *summarized* as follows (see also p. 56):

1. Its effect depended upon accurate empathy. This in turn was linked to partial, temporary, and reversible projective identification. The therapist was aware of intensified homospatial (see p. 194) experience which the patient also sensed, with a feeling of recognition and relief: 'That's a good way of putting it.' This belongs to intuition. It is global and sudden. And it is predominantly a right hemispheric function (see pp. 200ff.).

2. Repressed memory is often stored in non-verbal images. And in this example there is both an aesthetic and a kinaesthetic empathic (see p. 173) imperative, which tend to bypass the repression barrier. There is an unavoidable awareness of coherence and of the response of the body as a whole: 'How wilt thou *do* in the *swelling* of Jordan?' Swelling, and the risk of inundation and flooding, convey the potential hazard of uncontrolled drive derivatives. But these are rendered safe by the therapist's temporary fusion and the implicit diminution of boundaries.

3. The therapist endorses the validity of Mary's statement. He links it to the archaic cadence of poetry, uttered in a time of potential peril. Yet this linking does not depend solely upon the language of archetypal echoes. Its specificity depends upon the globality of Mary's 'presentation': her posture, her gesture, her facial expression, and her intonation all contribute to the therapist's 'chosen' association. It should be noted that the therapist does *not* quote the exact passage, or cite its

origin. In our view, a central dynamic issue is that his empathic presence implies that Mary's is not an alien experience. Others have been this way before.

4. Mary's experience is accepted as particular and primordial. It is not *exclusively* categorized, or dismissed as a diagnostic pointer in the direction of paranoid anxiety; although the therapist's 'left hemispheric', 'scientific', and 'clinical' faculty is coding what he observes (see p. 203). Siirala (1969; 1985) has described this reductive tendency of regarding everything as 'nothing but an object' as primary objectification. Technical terms like 'projective identification' describe parts of the mutual experience. But they do not confine or control it. A sense of mystery, astonishment, and uniqueness persists which transcends any descriptive technicalities.

The call into being

We have tried to offer suggestions, but we cannot explain exactly why the unspoken linking of Jordan, swelling possibly to the point of bursting, exerted such a calming influence upon a frightened woman.

We have already referred to the process of *poiesis* and it is one to which we repeatedly return. This is because of the centrality of its position when therapy is undertaken in the Aeolian Mode. In the following chapter we shall distinguish between the processes of poetic appropriation and poetic induction. They both involve the process of *poiesis*, because 'something is called into existence which was not there before'. Within the Aeolian Mode they each bring this about in a slightly different way.

It seems fitting to comment upon the paradoxical nature of the Aeolian Mode. A subsequent section is devoted entirely to the importance of paradox. At this juncture we wish to stress that the Aeolian Mode only seems to be paradoxical when it is viewed from the perspective of orthodox psychoanalytic psychology. For example, it initially appears to be diametrically opposed to Greenson's discussion of 'the old rule: begin every interpretation from the surface' (1967). It is for this, and related, reasons that we have devoted the whole of chapter 7 to the three theoretical foundations on which the Aeolian Mode rests.

Nevertheless, taken on its own terms according to which creative imagery and the mutative metaphor start from within and 'work superficially', the Aeolian Mode is not paradoxical. It is in fact congruous with a substantial bibliography on poetic imagery and poetic thinking. This can only receive passing mention here, but we have in mind *Poetic Process* (Whalley 1953), *Poetic Thinking: an Approach to Heidegger*

(Halliburton 1981), *The Poetic Image* (C. Day Lewis 1947), and *The Chequer'd Shade: Reflections on Obscurity in Poetry* (Press 1958).

One of the early books which links the two disciplines under discussion is *Archetypal Patterns in Poetry: Psychological Studies of Imagination* (Bodkin 1934). Its preface contains the following sentence:

> 'An attempt is here made to bring psychological analysis and reflec-
> tion to bear upon the imaginative experience communicated by great
> poetry, and to examine those forms or patterns in which the universal
> forces of our nature there find objectification.'

It seems pertinent to point out that our work as clinicians leads us to reverse Bodkin's trajectory. By this we mean that the flow of his sentence could change direction, so that it reads:

> 'An attempt is here (in the Aeolian Mode) made to bring the imagin-
> ative experience communicated by great poetry to bear upon psycho-
> logical analysis and reflection.'

In other words the Aeolian Mode is about the impact that 'great poetry' – and other aspects of the creative imagination – makes upon clinical phenomena, in particular the phenomenon of dynamic psychotherapy.

Clinical experience leads us to the conclusion that conventional interpretive and supportive psychotherapy can be facilitated by the use of image and metaphor. We suggest that deep affective material in the patient's inner world can be contained, changed, or consolidated by the appropriate use of *poiesis* in which new resources are called into being. And these resources fulfil the criteria of *poiesis* because, as far as the patient is concerned, something has been called into existence, in the shape of new capacities and enhanced resilience, which was not there before.

This paradox and apparent dichotomy between the direction of psycho-analysis which starts superficially and works deep, and that of the creative image which touches the depths before it stirs the surface is more apparent than real.

Our strong suggestion is that a mutually enhancing, synergistic con-vergence is possible here. This is because one of the prime objectives of analytically orientated psychotherapy is to render the unconscious con-scious. And it is this particular transition which the mutative metaphor so often expedites and facilitates.

It is now self-evident that an adequate theory of linkage is called for. Some of the questions already implicit in this introduction must be faced if the Aeolian Mode is to have clinical and aesthetic credibility. The dis-cussion about a frightened schizophrenic and 'the swelling of Jordan' may have been a partial answer. But there is still a pressing question in relation to the clinical relevance of the implicit subject-matter of the books whose titles have been listed and the day-to-day task of conducting dynamic psychotherapy. Do we run the risk of a capricious translocation of knowledge from one frame of reference to another? Or of being eclectic to the point of confusion? These are some of the questions which we endeavour to face in the pages which follow.

The retreat from being

The patient is frequently frightened by a feeling of impending catastrophe which is about to engulf her. Mary's experience in vignette 1.1 was just such an instance. Wilshire (1982) cites a passage in which it is suggested 'that something behind the text was almost too hot to handle!'. *Role-playing and Identity: the Limits of Theatre as Metaphor* tackles the themes of theatre as metaphor and playing as disclosure. Much of our work explores the limits of metaphor as theatre – not forgetting the etymology; the Greek meaning 'that which we gaze at'. Therapy undertaken with the psychotic, for whom concrete meanings often replace the metaphor, bring us sharply to the limits of metaphor. For example, 'a killing look', 'the final touch', 'dead quiet', or 'burning anger', *when taken literally evoke active clinical intervention, not poetic reverie*. But the Aeolian Mode sometimes enables us to reach such patients who are otherwise dynamically inaccessible and impervious to every attempt at empathy.

Working within the Aeolian Mode there is a sense of risk-taking.[3] That is in the nature of things. Without it the inaccessible is not rendered accessible, and we are not even taken upon our way a little.

This introduction ends where it started, with a reminder of the uniqueness of all that underlies the telling of each patient's 'one story and one story only'. In 1963 Jaspers wrote 'The power of the story is rooted itself in the animation of present sight: "The same story as it happened cannot be told twice".' But it is not only the telling of the one story that implies risk-taking; there are also hazards for those whose task it is to listen. And training can never obviate this. If it could do so, the vital spark of the exigent would be lost. Therapy is conducted in the unfolding moment to which the past looked forward:

> 'That when the exigent should come, which now
> Is come indeed.'
>
> > (*Antony and Cleopatra* IV. 14, 63)

> 'Sail forth – steer for the deep waters only,
> Reckless O soul, exploring, I with thee, and thou with me,

For we are bound where mariner has not yet dared to go,
And we will risk the ship, ourselves and all.'
(Passage to India IX, Walt Whitman)

Searchings and certainties

'Thou art the thing itself'
(King Lear III. 4, 104)

'She must try to get hold of something that evaded her. . . . Phrases came. Visions came. Beautiful phrases. But what she wished to get hold of was that very jar on the nerves, the *thing itself before it has been made anything*.' [our italics]
(To the Lighthouse, Virginia Woolf)

'For years after it occurred, I dreamed of it often. I have started up so vividly impressed by it, that its fury has yet seemed raging in my quiet room, in the still night. . . . I do not recall it, but see it done; for *it happens again before me*.' [our italics]
(David Copperfield, Charles Dickens)

'All the past rose on the instant and confronted me.'
(First Love, Ivan Turgenev)

'Memory seems to have insisted that the whole story got told somehow, however obliquely.'
(Tellers and Listeners, Barbara Hardy)

'He thought it must all be a dream and tried to wake up, but there was no other, waking world. It was real snow which lashed his face and settled on him and numbed his right hand.'
(Master and Man, Leo Tolstoy)

'And they said then, "But play, you must,
A tune beyond us, yet ourselves,
A tune upon the blue guitar
Of things exactly as they are."

Throw away the lights, the definitions,
And say of what you see in the dark
That it is this or that it is that,
But do not use the rotted names.
              Nothing must stand

Between you and the shapes you take
When the crust of shape has been destroyed.'
('The Man with the Blue Guitar',
Wallace Stevens)

'The metaphor stirred his fear. The object with which he was
   compared
Was beyond his recognizing. By this he knew that likeness of him
   extended
Only a little way, and not beyond, unless between himself
And things beyond resemblance there was this and that intended to
   be recognized,
The this and that in the enclosures of hypotheses
On which men speculated in summer when they were half asleep.'
                    ('Prologues to What is Possible', Wallace Stevens)

'I was not subject to influence from any quarter; there was nothing to
hustle me. I learnt to restrain speculative tendencies and to follow the
unforgotten advice of my master, Charcot: to look at the same things
again and again until they themselves begin to speak.'
                                              (Freud 1914a, p. 22)

   'The land may vary more;
   But wherever the truth may be –
   The water comes ashore,
   And the people look at the sea.'
              (Neither Out Far Nor In Deep', Robert Frost)

   'Birds greater than the wind
   Do not know where to rest their wings.'
                                        (Paul Éluard)

   'For if the trumpet give an uncertain sound,
   Who shall prepare himself to the battle?'
                    (*Corinthians* I. 14, 8)

      'What kind of a story are we in?'
                    (*Time and Myth*, John Dunne)

2

The Aeolian Mode

'If you want to give your unconscious a chance you must keep your
eye on something else.'

(Louis MacNeice 1935)

THE STORY GATHERS

The Aeolian Mode is a mode of dynamic psychotherapy in which an
aesthetic imperative augments the patient's access to his inner world. The
therapist catalyses this process by means of *poiesis*. Discussion of a phenomenon as complex as the Aeolian Mode inevitably involves a degree of
repetition. But the introduction and elaboration of a concept such as *poiesis*
could never lead to 'repetition', in the sense of passive reproduction. On
the contrary, it is an intrinsic part of the vitality and buoyancy of the
process of *poiesis* that it always presents itself in a new light, casting a fresh
constellation of shadows.

Two interrelated, though distinct, processes need to be explored before
the Aeolian Mode itself can be clearly defined. These have been called the
dynamic components and the therapeutic initiatives respectively. And it is
debatable which should take precedence. On balance, we have decided to
consider the dynamic components first, because they form an integral part
of any possible therapeutic initiatives.

Dynamic components

There are three dynamic components which are always present and always
active, although their significance varies from session to session and from
phase to phase within any particular session. They are *poiesis*, aesthetic
imperatives, and points of urgency.

POIESIS

Plato's *Symposium* provides us with the primary source for the term *poiesis*. It is the process of 'calling something into existence that was not there before'. Heidegger refers to it as a 'bringing-forth', using this term in its widest sense. He thought of 'poetry' which required the poet; but we hear from Halliburton (1981) that he also thought of: 'a poetry without poets – the blooming of a blossom, the coming-out of a butterfly from a cocoon, the plummeting of a waterfall when the snow begins to melt. The last two analogies underline the fact that Heidegger's example is a threshold occasion, a moment of ecstasis when something moves away from its standing as one thing to become another.'

A cursory glance through these pages reveals poetic quotations, ranging from a truncated phrase to an extended passage. And it must be made crystal clear that our concern has a direct connection with the etymological link between *poiesis* and poetry. This sentence calls for elucidation.

The intrinsic part that *poiesis* plays within the Aeolian Mode is that, when the therapist is attentive to the total presence of the patient, he is standing on perceptive 'tip-toe', trying to detect what is on the brink of being called into existence for the first time. The numerous citations which people these pages do so because they carry a particular affective loading. This resonates with that within the patient which is called into existence.

Poiesis holds the centre of the stage in the Aeolian Mode. And it has no direct connection with the particular therapeutic modality known as 'poetry therapy' (Leedy 1969; Lerner 1978). Important though poetry therapy is in its own right, it is not our focus here. The copious quotations from previously published poetry are in themselves examples of an earlier *poiesis* which resulted in a poem. By this we mean that when the original poem was being composed, then, and only then, was *poiesis* taking place in the mind of the poet. At one level such *poiesis* cannot be repeated, although every time a poem is read or quoted there is a fresh encounter between the original poem and that within the reader or listener which is called into being. It is only in this second existential sense that it could be claimed that there exists a link between the completed poem and *poiesis* as it is used within the Aeolian Mode.

For our purposes, it is poetic thinking, with its strongly hybrid cognitive–affective connotation, which is a characteristic of *poiesis* as a dynamic component of the Aeolian Mode. Halliburton (1981) refers to poetic thinking in these terms: 'Rigorous in its own way, it is at once playful and sober, innovative and traditional, carefully argued and arbitrarily avowed.'

The process of *poiesis* is the pivot upon which the Aeolian Mode balances. Its essence is novelty; because, by definition, it is impossible to

become habituated to that which is new. That which is called into existence cannot, by definition, have been there before. Arieti (1976) devotes a
chapter to 'Poetry and the Aesthetic Process', although the whole book
Creativity: the Magic Synthesis is expressly relevant.

The calling into existence always implies the crossing of a threshold, and
the threshold to be crossed may initially be that of the patient's capacity to
trust the therapist and, subsequently, the patient's capacity to trust himself. From another perspective, it declares itself as the movement towards
insight gathers momentum. *Poiesis* may thus be the process whereby inner
emptiness, initially experienced as insecurity, fragility, and hollowness, is
gradually transmuted into affirmative depth; a phrase coined by Halliburton (1981) when he said 'we do not, after all, fall into a void but into a
kind of affirmative depth' – a cadence in which every connotation counts.
Poiesis is inherent in creativity.

Winnicott has important things to say about creativity, play, and
psychotherapy; but it must not be forgotten that such 'play' may be that
sombre search for self wherein a psychopath, who has previously been
homicidal, learns to 'face his own music'.

> 'Psychotherapy takes place in the overlap of two areas of playing, that
> of the patient and that of the therapist. Psychotherapy has to do with
> two people playing together. The corollary of this is that where play-
> ing is not possible then the work done by the therapist is directed
> towards bringing the patient from a state of not being able to play
> into a state of being able to play.'
>
> (Winnicott 1971)

> 'The place where cultural experience is located is in the *potential space*
> between the individual and the environment (originally the object).
> The same can be said of playing. Cultural experience begins with
> creative living first manifested in play.'
>
> (Winnicott 1967)

Ogden (1985) took up Winnicott's theme in a paper entitled 'On Potential
Space'. He develops the idea that 'projective identification is the negative
of playing'. And it is our suggestion that the Aeolian Mode can generate a
state of mind necessary for playing.

Serious and playful

Apter (1975) underlines the importance of the therapist's capacity to
'respond playfully'. And the Aeolian Mode often gives the opportunity for
an intensification of serious playfulness and/or playful seriousness. In
Apter's words, 'the therapist should be ready not only to regard some of
the schizophrenic person's activities as playful, but to respond playfully'.

Bohr sees a complementary relationship as the essence of play (in Blædel 1985). And Garland (1981) has usefully extended the therapeutic play space to the larger arena of the group in *The State of Play*.

In a provocative passage which links *poiesis* in literature and psychotherapy, Kaufmann (1965) writes:

> '*Troilus and Cressida* is a brilliant dramatic mutation. In its analytical brilliance we follow it *as if we were writing the play with Shakespeare*. It provides a spectrum of life-visions, or value systems within the action itself. The play provides the dramatic equivalent of a colossal Rorschach inkblot test, each reader confronted by separate alternatives, identifies *where he must*, and thereby pragmatically indicates his own sympathetic stance within the heteronomy of its suspended judgements.' [our italics]

The phrase 'as if *we* were writing the play' has exactly captured that invitational edge of unfolding experience as it is disclosed within therapeutic space. We feel as if we are perennially in the 'crest of the wave' about to break. The momentum of the moment, *poiesis*, is there. This illustrates a recurrent theme. We are concerned NOT with the quotation of a 'known' poem. On the contrary, our concern is with the echoes evoked by the 'swarming shadows' of literary associations. This may energize the process of *poiesis*, as we attune our response to the patient. Once again, it is the activity of *poiesis* which characterizes therapeutic space; such *poiesis* activates the growing awareness of creative possibilities in new options and the endorsement of a more coherent sense of self. However, mere awareness of earlier creative work, even if it is that of Shakespeare, may have a restricting and obsessionally binding effect if it does not liberate the patient's own creativity. An extreme example would be that of a patient whose perseveration precluded him from saying anything other than 'Tomorrow and tomorrow and tomorrow'.

It is the use to which literary associations are put which will determine whether they are contaminants to be avoided or catalysts to be welcomed by the therapist. In *The Edge of the Image*, a title central in this discussion, Weatherhead (1967) refers to Coleridge's comment on Shakespeare: 'You feel him to be a poet inasmuch as *for a time he has made you one* – an active creative being' (our italics). Putting Kaufmann's statement alongside that of Coleridge provides a dual affirmation of the enhanced creativity available to those within therapeutic space. The therapist's need of creativity is just as great as that of the patient. They need it for a common task, although they inevitably approach it from different angles. 'We feel as if we were writing the play . . . [we have been made] active creative beings.'

25

Freud (1937) described psychoanalysis as 'an impossible profession'. Oates (1976) brings out aspects of other impossibilities in her lucid study, *The Edge of Impossibility: Tragic Forms in Literature*. She describes *The Brothers Karamazov* as 'almost a novel in the making, a novel as it is being written, *in the very process of being imagined*', adding that Dostoevsky gives us 'the vision of the unfathomable raw process of creation as it leaps from the unconscious'.

It is not difficult to see how such catalytic associative material could facilitate the 'double impossibility' where work in 'an impossible profession' is furthered by resources from 'the edge of impossibility'. The patient's own 'unfathomable raw process of creation . . . leaps from the unconscious'. But, although it may sometimes 'leap', it only does so at the 'point of urgency'. We suggest that the swarming shadows of associative literary material can enhance the therapist's restructuring capacity. If the point of urgency is clinically discerned so that *poiesis* in the form of a mutative interpretation can be made, then endopsychic change will occur. *Poiesis*, in the creativity of an apt intervention, will have resulted in a slight but stable change in personality structure.

AESTHETIC IMPERATIVES

This, perhaps of all the sections in the book, is the most difficult to write. Not because we are uncertain what we mean by an 'aesthetic imperative', but because it is such a delicate and elusive concept that attempted definitions may kill it and attempted illustrations prove inert (see Altieri 1971).

Although Sartre (1950) was the first to use the phrase, our understanding of an aesthetic imperative comes from linking Bateson's definition of aesthetic as the 'pattern which connects' (1979), to an imperative, an irresistible summons to action. This perspective needs clarification. An aesthetic imperative might imply the active passivity of preserving something because it is 'right' – a harmony, a colour, or a shape. It can legitimately refer to the recognition of form which is appropriate because it is coherent within a larger gestalt. Thus illustrating the law of closure. But, for our purposes, it is a mandatory initiative.

In particular, it is the precise action of making a therapeutic intervention. It is that which makes the therapist act when and how he does. In the clinical task of conducting psychotherapy in the Aeolian Mode, the 'pattern which connects' refers to the integration of a conventional psychodynamic appraisal of the patient's prevailing needs, and his overall existential predicament. This is linked to the therapist's reverberative echoes, activated in response to the particular *timbre* of his patient's 'presence'. An aesthetic imperative is equally 'insistent', whether the patient's personality structure is that of the neurotic, the borderline, or the psychotic. The prime significance of the imperative nature of 'the pattern which connects' is the fact that it cannot be readily ignored. The power of an evoked association seems to connect many patterns. At the same time, it releases creative energy within the patient so that he is taken further 'on the way a little'. According to Green (1979) 'aesthetic pleasure resides in the simultaneous arousal and control of the drives'. Whalley (1953) has so aptly described the attitude of mind which is called for by aesthetics: 'For aesthetics there is required . . . a restless centre of emphasis guided by a sensitive flair for relevance; a subtle tact in discovering and gently unfolding the self-revealing processes.' They are in fact adjectival of the *aesthetic imperative*. It may be a counsel of perfection, but when therapy is undertaken within the Aeolian Mode, the therapist, as far as is humanly possible, needs 'a sensitive flair for relevance; a subtle tact in discovering and gently unfolding the self-revealing processes'.

Poets frequently describe their chosen language by saying that what needed to be said could not be expressed in any other way. Similarly, patients often imply, or state explicitly, that what needed to be said could only be said as it was said (Cox 1978).

Few would disagree that many of the lines of great literature carry an autonomous authority which would be trivialized and ruined if words were changed. And even with the words of a relatively unknown poet, such as Anne, Countess of Winchilsea, it would be blasphemous to do so:

> 'Trail all your pikes, dispirit every drum,
> March in a slow procession from afar,
> Ye silent, ye dejected men of war!'
> (Pool 1945)

Similarly, when Gerard Manley Hopkins (1844–89) writes 'There lives the dearest freshness *deep down things*' (Hopkins 1967) [our italics], we recognize the authenticity of completed *poiesis* (the poetic line) and its current poetic engagement with our experience when something fresh is called into existence. Nevertheless, when we change frames of reference from that of poetic appreciation to the clinical context of a therapeutic group conducted with offender-patients in a secure hospital, we hear the following words as a reply to the question, what kind of things do you talk about in the group?: 'The *deep down things* that keep on coming up.'

This reply is powerful, not because it echoes a phrase from Gerard Manley Hopkins, but because of the sense of coherence. It exists between past and present, between feeling and thinking, and between the particular life trajectory of an individual patient, the lives of the seven other group members, and the corporate life of the group-as-a-whole. In short, the therapist was aware of an aesthetic imperative. *This means that the words spoken by the patient, and the surrounding affective penumbra in which they were embedded, exerted an imperative effect upon the therapist.* At this juncture it would be imprudent to explore in greater detail the exact nature of the therapist's response. This is because considerable detail is necessary if sense is to be made of a concept as far-reaching as the aesthetic imperative. It is for this reason that we have already cited an example (vignette 1.1) in which an affect-laden disclosure of inner world turbulence 'but how will I be tonight?' acted as an aesthetic imperative and influenced the quality of the therapist's response. The following chapter contains other vignettes which illustrate the aesthetic imperative in action. Many involve kinaesthetic empathy (see p. 173) in one way or another.

The aesthetic imperative is that irresistible call to activity which is experienced by the therapist as he responds to the spoken and unspoken disclosure of the patient's experience. And this response may take the form of a conventional intervention, but it may be a changed orchestration of an existing silence. It is important to bear in mind that non-verbal communication, such an axiomatic feature in all psychotherapy, may activate the aesthetic imperative.

> There's language in her eye, her cheek, her lip;
> Nay, her foot speaks.
> (*Troilus and Cressida* IV. 5, 55)

Sometimes the patient's language is lucidly and unambiguously trenchant: 'I want to kill you (him, her, it, them).' Sometimes it is opaque, invasive, and encircling: 'There's a death in the house, but nobody's died . . . there's a sort of bereavement . . . but it's me.' And sometimes, as Brockbank (1982) has said of many passages in Shakespeare, 'the language does not quite surface'. In such instances there is massive implicatory significance, affective loading and existential weight, but precise contours and content cannot yet be discerned. They are solitary islands of utterance in a sea of silence. And potential meaning is distorted if the language is pushed too far. Brockbank's phrase reflects Wells' classification (1924) of 'sunken' and 'expansive' images. The former is 'one which powerfully affects the imagination without conveying a definite picture', whereas the latter 'is one in which each term is strongly modified by the others'.

Cardinal (1981), embarking on a chapter entitled 'Engaging with the Poetic', writes: 'Occasions which seem to proclaim the desire of the world to reveal itself to human consciousness are moving experiences which demand to be recorded.' These words are equally applicable when 'the desire of the *inner* world to reveal itself' takes place within a therapeutic setting. Indeed, this 'desire' is another facet of the aesthetic imperative.

28

It is the impact of the inner world of the patient on that of the therapist, and vice versa, which promotes movement. It also makes demands. And the linking of this 'demand' to the 'pattern which connects' constitutes the clinical phenomenon of the aesthetic imperative.

Like every art form, visual art may also exert an aesthetic imperative. Non-naturalistic pictures sustain our attentiveness through the use of daring distortion and abrupt modification in the intensity of colour and contrast. Naturalistic, representational art may also hold the observer's attention, lodge in his memory, and thus form part of an associative reservoir. As far as the therapist is concerned, a landscape painting has all the potentiality of a 'listening landscape'. But it is non-naturalistic visual art which has an elective affinity with 'sunken images'.

In such art it is the very strangeness that suggests its inferential and evocative significance. And the aesthetic imperative is linked to its ability to disturb the spectator. He may accept it as dream-like, so that it has the quality of an ill-defined but provocative 'sunken image.' It is strange yet familiar. The artist himself, with every brush-stroke, influences the impact his work makes. He, too, has to rely on his unconscious sensitivity in scanning the construction concealed in his painting. This is because subliminal vision is at work. And in the same way that Kaufmann (1965) writes of *Troilus and Cressida*, 'as if we were writing the play* with Shakespeare', so the spectator may have the creative sensation 'as if he were painting the picture'. This, in turn, leads to the application of the aesthetic imperative in psychotherapy. The Aeolian Mode has the capacity to intensify an empathic awareness – not 'as if we were writing the play' or 'as if we were painting the picture' – but as if we were living the life. Because of this, the patient can gain an enhanced sense of re-living his life. In fact, the patient often feels that he is living (*really* living) his life for the first time.

Ehrenzweig (see Hogg 1969) pointed out that 'The aesthetic effect of the Golden Section suggests an unconscious vision free from normal spatial differentiation.' That such vision exists has long been known by creative artists. Bergson sees creative intuition as a form of vision in which incompatible things blend with each other and co-exist in time and space. This is closely linked to Rothenberg's concept (1979) of homospatial thinking (see pp. 194–5).

The aesthetic imperative induced by poetry, visual art, and other art forms suggests the contours and *timbre* of the therapist's response, although this is 'indicated' on conventional clinical grounds. It emanates from an undifferentiated matrix in which the law of contradiction does not apply.

A good example of the aesthetic imperative 'at work' is vignette 3.2 (pp. 72ff.) in which it energized a disclosive association to the memory of the shoplifting of perfume. A poet, in this instance Edith Sitwell (1948), has this to say about the blood-theme in *Macbeth* (later echoed by Lady Macbeth's: 'Here's the smell of the blood still'): 'For it seems as if all the blood had fled from the heart of Macbeth, to join the blood that had been shed. Blood will haunt his spirit for ever, but will leave the veins like that "most ghastly thing in Nature", the bed of the ocean from which the ocean has fled.' Little wonder that *Macbeth* yields such a rich harvest of imperatives in that arena of offender-therapy in which 'blood is their argument' (*King Henry V* IV. 1, 145).

We have quoted this passage by Edith Sitwell because it exemplifies the way in which an aura can amplify a particular affect – and make it even more finely focused. 'The bed of the ocean from which the ocean has fled' is a remarkably provocative association to stabbings and veins drained of blood. Within the exigency of the moment a therapist, wondering exactly how he might phrase a transference interpretation (involving the linking of the verifiable, forensic fact of previously killing a victim and the fantasy of killing the therapist, killing his father, and killing himself), may find that an oblique construction of violence flowing from the metaphor of an ocean fleeing – a sea running away – is something the patient can just affectively contemplate. Should this metaphor prove to be *en route* to a full classical interpretation of the wish to kill his father, it could truly be described as mutative. In this event the aesthetic imperative would have enabled a dynamic initiative to develop in an area which was otherwise too heavily defended.

Writing of the therapist's style of responding to the patient's dream-life, Meltzer (1984) links 'the presence of an aesthetic object' and 'circling about in the material'. This has Aeolian affinities and implies an aesthetic imperative.

> 'As the excitement of comprehension and a sense of being in the presence of an aesthetic object grows, the tendency to talk for the purpose of holding the situation suspended gives way to a different type of talking in which the patient is less inclined to join until he is an experienced dream-interpreter himself. This type of talking has a spiral feel to it, circling about in the material, uttering interpretive notions, waiting a moment for some response, going on to another aspect and notion, and so on, until a fabric of interpretation begins to weave itself together.'

Paffard (1976) asks 'What is it that makes these "unfading recollections" come rushing back into the mind? Sometimes they come "In vacant or in pensive mood" flooding in, as it were, to fill a vacuum. But they may equally well come elbowing their way into a mind already preoccupied with present business.'

'Elbowing their way' has exactly caught the sense of resisted intrusion which the aesthetic imperative exerts upon the therapist, who is 'pre-occupied with [the] present [psychotherapeutic] business'.

We recall the description of nostalgic memories: 'Others I summon; this comes of itself' (White 1964). Or again, 'But moments like this could not be forced, they came of themselves or not at all' (Hillyer 1966).

The therapist does *not* 'summon' associations. Neither can he 'force' them. But, once they have elbowed their way across his horizon of awareness, he wonders whether they facilitate his prime task of taking the patient as close to his feelings as he has the capacity to endure. At the same time, he asks himself whether they are countertransference contaminants which are antitherapeutic.

The therapist is aware of the aesthetic imperative as he listens to what the patient says, and feels its affective thrust. Many of the ensuing pages will be taken up with a detailed discussion of why a particular reverberatory circuit is activated in the therapist's responding, yet non-invasive, presence. Friedman (1953) writes: 'Poetry which manages to tap these (mythical) roots of the human psyche is liable to appeal deeply and permanently to all men. The reason for this profound vitality which all sense in the words of men like Dante, Goethe, or Shakespeare is simply that they traffic continually in archetypal symbols and emotions.'

Working within the Aeolian Mode the therapist finds that long-buried, repressed experience is unearthed, no matter whether it is that of a homicidal psychopath or a frightened psychotic. These words of Friedman's ring true. His chosen words, 'deeply', 'permanently', 'all men', 'profound vitality', 'traffic continually in archetypal symbols and emotions', echo and re-echo as the story unfolds.

POINTS OF URGENCY

'But who, I ask Thee, who art Thou?
Tell me Thy name, and *tell me now*.' [our italics]
(Charles Wesley, 1707–88)

The length of this section is inversely proportional to its significance. It is short because the three dynamic components are so closely interlinked that, by inference, much that relates to 'points of urgency' has already been said. Nevertheless, its clinical significance justifies a separate section.

The term was originally employed by Strachey (1934) in his seminal introduction of the concept of the mutative interpretation. It implies a moment of incipient dynamic instability, in which endopsychic patterning is such that the patient is optimally receptive to the therapist's initiative. It is then that a mutative interpretation may activate the capacity for insight,

31

and change the structural organization of the patient's inner world. This is in contrast to the purely informative 'dictionary' type of interpretation which, according to Strachey, will be non-mutative. Although he originally introduced the term in connection with analytic work, we suggest that there are similar points of urgency in supportive work. In this case, however, it refers to a degree of incipient endopsychic fragmentation, when a stabilizing reinforcement of precarious defences is urgently indicated.

The 'point' of urgency is a point in time. It may be evident as the moment of urgency when breakdown seems inevitable. This may be the breakdown of hitherto effective defensive organization. It may also refer to the brink of decompensation when the patient may have 'a breakdown' if appropriate therapeutic initiatives are not forthcoming. In either case 'points of urgency' refer to an optimal point in time, a genuine point of *kairos*, when the patient is receptive for either a mutative interpretation or a stabilizing initiative.

All the vignettes to come, and many of the minor passages of dialogue, illustrate various aspects of therapeutic initiatives at the patient's point of urgency. However, as we are considering them in relation to the aesthetic imperative, a distinction needs to be made. Whereas the aesthetic imperative is connected with form and the gestalt theory of closure, the points of urgency are always points in time.

Dunne (1973) reminds us that: 'We are alone, it seems, because we can know more than we can tell. . . . Still, we can listen to one another, not only to the things we can tell but also to each other's awareness of things we may not be able to tell.' Clinically, we might add that we can listen to each other's awareness of things we may not YET be able to tell. One of the central concerns of dynamic psychotherapy is that the patient is progressively enabled to tell that which was hitherto withheld. It may be deliberately withheld as the result of conscious choice. But by far the greatest pathological momentum, which results in a wide variety of clinical presentations of inherent psychopathology, is due to that which the patient is unable to tell because it is unconscious. He himself is unaware of it. We recall Foreman's comment (1979; see Wilshire 1982) that certain plays 'sort of "break down" formally in a way that suggests that *something behind the text was almost too hot to handle*' [our italics] (see pp. 19, 150). 'Too hot to handle' is an effective jargon version of experience at the brink of the 'point of urgency'.

It is a common clinical experience, endorsed by non-verbal communication, that behind the patient's spoken words is feeling which is 'almost too hot to handle'. This is one of the reasons why we are often aware of that experience of patients about which they are unable to speak. Many patients are so heavily defended that analytic approaches cannot reach them. But the aesthetic imperative can help the therapist in reaching the depths while the surface remains intact. This is because the aesthetic imperative and the patient's point of urgency are inextricably related both to each other and to the dynamic of *poiesis*.

A tightrope of contingency

Lady Macbeth is alone in 'A room in Macbeth's castle', as the stage directions tell us. A messenger tells her that Duncan 'comes here to-night'. When the messenger has left, the following words are in her mind:

> 'the raven himself is hoarse,
> That croaks the fatal entrance of Duncan
> Under my battlements.'
>
> *(Macbeth* I. 5, 38)

Although this passage is dense with manifest meaning, it also conveys a sense of ominous incipience. It is Macbeth's castle and she refers not to 'the', 'his', or 'our' battlements, but to *my* battlements. There are fatal implications in the raven-heralded entrance of Duncan under her battlements. Battlements not only in terms of the obvious fortification of Macbeth's castle, but also in terms of those other battlements which are soon to be 'unsexed' and 'top-full of direst cruelty'.

It would not be surprising to find that this passage came to mind when a female patient with sadistic fantasies speaks simultaneously of the outer-world setting (the battlements of my castle) and the inner world of castrating fantasies. These are somatically symbolized in the thought of the risk-taking and potentially fatal entrance of a present-day Duncan under the anatomical battlements of a heavily defended pubic arch.[4]

Neither would it be surprising if, at the earliest hint of such complex psychopathology, the therapist was aware of an unheard call for cosmic protection in which Heaven might 'peep through the blanket of the dark, / To cry, "Hold, hold!"' *(Macbeth* I. 5, 53). In this instance 'Hold, hold' might be congruent with a need for a supportive 'holding' approach rather than an exploratory uncovering initiative. Although each *might* follow an isomorphic aesthetic imperative, conventional clinical indications would determine which was called for in a particular instance.

The Aeolian Mode may appear to depend too much upon a tightrope of contingency so that it is difficult to be taken seriously as a valid clinical activity. At first sight it seems to be so closely linked to what the therapist may have read, a selection so obviously dependent upon predilection, chance contacts, and other uncertain contingencies that its application in the professional setting is suspect. Yet it must never be overlooked that the therapist's intervention in the Aeolian Mode is closely linked to his appraisal of the patient's endopsychic structure, the patterning of his object relationships, and his defence organization about which, within broad limits, Freud, Klein, and their professional progency would agree.

These reflections about the aesthetic imperative emerged in therapeutic space:

'It's urgent. It has vitality and momentum.'
'It's the only continuity.'
'It provokes a sensation of voyage – without the distortion of the
    commonplace.'
'It propels us into something larger.'

'That broad general sympathy with life and people'

Having spoken of the 'actual living' which the trainee therapist knows at first hand, Ella Freeman Sharpe (1930) turns to discuss avenues through which human nature may be vicariously encountered. 'He will also have ranged to some extent through some pathway of literature; biography, history, fiction, poetry or drama. In some field of literature he will have met, in addition to his actual contacts with people, phases of life and conduct that will have given him *that broad general sympathy with life and people* which no textbook of scientific principles can ever inculcate' [our italics].

She then describes a fragment of a therapeutic session in which a patient suddenly refers to Portia and adds, 'I won't think of her, I don't like her.' The author comments: 'The patient has unconsciously, with unerring instinct, selected a representation of her own unconscious psychology. If I do not know the role of this Portia in the play, I shall be slower in getting on to the track of the unconscious motivation.'

There is no doubt that the therapist's horizon of awareness can never be too wide. Nevertheless, although we agree with Sharpe's affirmation of the importance of 'that broad general sympathy with life and people' which is nurtured and extended by literature, this is only obliquely connected with the part that literature plays in the Aeolian Mode. Put more precisely, it can be unequivocally stated that *poiesis*, poetic appropriation, and poetic induction do not depend upon whether the therapist and the patient each have first-hand knowledge of the same literature. The Aeolian Mode does not depend upon a prior knowledge of the patient's reference to 'Portia, not that Portia, but Brutus' Portia'.

We do, however, strongly endorse Sharpe's enthusiastic encouragement of wide reading. And it is for this reason that we are quoting the following paragraph:

'In any reading for analytical qualification I would make compulsory the following books: Nursery Rhymes, the Alice books, Hunting of the Snark, Grimm, Andersen, the Brer Rabbit books, Water Babies, Struwelpeter, Undine, Rumpelstiltskin, Peter Ibbetson, Greek Myths and Tragedies, Shakespeare's Plays.'

There is a second avenue leading to 'that broad general sympathy with life and people' which comes from such books as *The Abnormal Personality Through Literature* (Stone and Stone 1966). Here the reader will encounter many of the classical introductions to inner world turbulence given us by Dostoevsky and Chekhov, to name but two. Nevertheless, the prime introduction to a broad general sympathy with life and people must come through the therapist's 'actual living'. And it is good that Sharpe gives us her persuasive encouragement towards wider reading after 'actual living'. And not before.

Elizabeth Irvine (1974) has also made a strong case for using literature as a way of enhancing psychodynamic understanding and clinical expertise. 'It seemed to me that the exercise enriched what had been learned in other ways, and did much to ensure that what was cognitively mastered was also experienced in feeling, and related to personal experience.' And at the end of her Lydia Rapoport lectures she used a phrase which could apply to the Aeolian Mode. Having made the point that no teacher should be coerced into using this particular mode, she wrote: 'I only wanted to *set free* those who would enjoy teaching like this.' We suggest that this is also one of the Aeolian characteristics. It 'sets free' those who would enjoy working in this way.

Working in the Aeolian Mode the therapist draws upon every kind of nourishment which enriches his capacity to acquire 'that broad general sympathy with life and people'. Davis (1981), writing on 'Exchanges with the Humanities', makes the following comment which links with our theme: 'Of special interest to psychotherapists are those plays in which reconciliation is mediated by an outsider, and in which as a result there is remission or recovery in an illness.'

Summary

The Aeolian Mode[5] is a complex phenomenon. Its efficacy depends upon optimal synergism between three dynamic components:

Poiesis: a process in which something is called into existence which was not there before. The patient cannot become habituated to that which is

35

new. The freshly minted image and metaphor ensure the necessary novelty.

Aesthetic imperatives: the therapist's experience of a sense of 'fit' and coherence, linked to an imperative urge to respond to a patient in a particular way. The perceived coherence is one between evoked associative echoes in the therapist, the patient's clinical predicament, and the organization of the latter's inner world. In other words, conventional therapeutic initiatives of an interpretive or supportive nature are 'contoured' and textured to a degree of 'fine tuning' by the therapist's associative resonance.

Points of urgency: a moment of incipient dynamic instability, in which endopsychic patterning is such that the patient is optimally receptive to the therapist's initiative. In analytic work the point of urgency indicates that a mutative interpretation is called for (Strachey 1934). In supportive work the point of urgency refers to a degree of incipient endopsychic fragmentation, when a stabilizing reinforcement of precarious defences is urgently indicated.

The mutative metaphor as the equivalent of a 'trial interpretation'

At first sight this section seems premature. It is included because it so clearly demonstrates the therapist's action at the patient's point of *potential* urgency. It should be linked to the main study of mutative metaphor (see p. 98), and it is also an example of paronomasia (see p. 113).

A trial interpretation is one in which the therapist seeks to determine how much the patient is able to reflect upon his inner world. It also gives an indication of his capacity to endure those of his 'true feelings' which are alien to his sense of self.

The instance which follows comes from the opening of a group session for offender-patients. Anne arrives late for the session because she was having her hair restyled. She has been in therapy for several years and has often spoken of her 'crime'. She had been involved in a fatal assault. As she entered the room she was asked why her hair was parted as it was. And she told us that it was connected with the position of her 'natural parting'. Each time she has described the scene of the offence, she has gone into more intimate details of her feelings as the 'events' unfolded. The therapist was uncertain whether she had reached the point where she could fully explore the psychosexual aspects of the killing. Had her capacity to endure her own experience, without the protection of repression, increased since she last lingered at the place where she confronted herself?

'It all depends on the place of my natural parting.'

'What about the place of your un-natural parting, Anne?'

The ensuing corporate reflection about 'un-natural partings' left the therapist in no doubt of the depth to which the patients were prepared to go. The mutative metaphor employed was only *potentially* mutative. Un-natural partings might have been taken to refer to the site of a 'comb-track', whereas they were taken to imply not merely dying, but the 'parting' which killing had made inevitable. This is a simple example. In many ways it is similar to the risk of 'skating on thin ice' (see p. 78). Nevertheless it illustrates how the metaphor can be as challenging as the patient is prepared to let it be. It cannot force its way into the depths. On the contrary, it engages with the patient 'before it stirs the surface'. The flexibility of the therapeutic potential of the metaphor is shown by setting the titles of three papers side by side: 'The Analysis of Metaphor' (Voth 1970); 'Interpretation Within the Metaphor' (Cain and Maupin 1961); and 'The Noninterpretation of the Metaphors' (Katz 1983).

All group members are 'on trial' in every session. And so, existentially, is the therapist. As Oscar Wilde (1949) sharply points out: 'All trials are trials for one's life' (and see p. 165). And the life of the group-as-a-whole is always on trial. We suggest that the mutative metaphor can be mobilized by the aesthetic imperative, so that the group is not tried beyond its breaking point.

On following an associative clue

'However certain our expectation
The moment foreseen may be unexpected
When it arrives. It comes when we are
Engrossed with matters of *other urgency*.' [our italics]
(*Murder in the Cathedral*, T. S. Eliot 1935)

It may be an advantage to follow an associative clue, or it may be a disadvantage. It may be 'safe', with no adverse sequelae. It may be risky and confront the patient with more than he can take. The essence is to try to discern which way the balance lies. The ensuing story is a case in point.

Bill, referred for a dynamic assessment, has a history of admissions to numerous psychiatric hospitals and has been given several custodial sentences. He is adept at confusing clinicians, having had twenty years' experience of inventing 'original' constellations of pseudo-psychotic phenomena. Although there is an aura of genuine anxiety, he still conveys a tantalizing and provocative ethos which is initially baffling. He gives the impression of being able to play games and run rings round conventional clinical attitudes, so that the interviewer can almost hear him thinking 'If you'd like a little bit of word salad, you can have it. Yes, I've had pseudo-hallucinations . . . and if you would like to hear about my hallucinations,

well, I've seen reptiles, spiders, bugs, rabbits . . . I've heard voices for
twenty years. They whisper and add words like "if", "when", "who",
"then", "now", "go". These words are mumbled and it's my subcon-
scious talking to my ego. And I have no control.'

Having casually referred to the range of animals which gave variety to
his visual hallucinations – a comprehensive range scarcely equalled by
Noah's Ark – he said:

'I've seen rabbits . . . in fact I've seen a snake eat a rabbit in my cell.'

'Head or tail first?'

'By the tail.'

This unorthodox question was followed by a change in Bill's complexion,
posture, and entire demeanour. Whereas he had previously given the
impression of utter confidence, twisting the therapist round his little
finger, he now appeared pale, sweated profusely and his originally fixed
gaze became flickering, furtive, and evasive.

'How are you feeling *now*, Bill?'

'When you asked that I sort of went cold. Like cold flushes running
down my back. I wasn't prepared for it . . . I had to think very
rapidly . . . *It got next to me. It was frightening and relieving.*'

'I wonder why that should be?'

'There was a greater feeling of being trapped . . . The rabbit didn't
stand a chance, it might have done if the snake had started at the other
end . . . it might have got away . . . it's like me, I feel trapped. I was
always in the wrong space at the wrong time . . . I was born at the
wrong time.'

Why had the therapist asked the unorthodox question about the details of
a snake's swallowing habits? He had done so because he had just read
Arieti's account (1976) of Kekulé's dream: 'Kekulé identified himself in a
dream with a snake swallowing its tail, and saw an analogy to the benzine
molecule as a ring rather than a chain of carbon atoms.' As the therapist
walked from his office, where *Creativity* lay on his desk, Kekulé's dream
was on his mind. Within fifteen minutes Bill described his visual hallucinations and reached the point at which he referred to a snake swallowing a
rabbit. Initially, the therapist tried to banish what might be an intrusive
association about Kekulé's dream and Kekulé's snake. Yet, with all the
adhesive persuasion of an aesthetic imperative, coupled with the patient's
clinical point of urgency, this association refused to relinquish its hold on
his attention. He quickly 'stood back' from the immediate dilemma and, as
far as he could, assessed the risks of making this unconventional response.

At the time, he could see no contra-indications. Indeed, it appeared that this might exert the impact of *poiesis*, because it was probable that Bill would be confronted by that which he had not known before. As it transpired, numerous physiological concomitants of anxiety, and a wide range of other pointers to changed inner feelings, rendered it indubitable that Bill was made to pause in his easy flow of pseudo-disclosure. He was confronted and 'stopped in his tracks'.

This vignette clearly demonstrates the double effect of the mutative metaphor; linking the described current experience (snake eating rabbit), the affective transference identification (Bill 'caught' unexpectedly 'from behind'), and the 'trapped feeling' with his mother – his repressed early experience.[6] The risks of such an intervention can be exaggerated. The worst that could happen would be that the therapist was regarded as being 'clever' because he was 'playing little therapeutic games'. But little serious harm is likely to be done; because, if the patient's defences were not by-passed, they would remain intact, thus fulfilling their original purpose of defending the patient from himself and from others. Nevertheless, if the patient's defences are breached, this happens within therapeutic space and the therapist is there, alongside the patient, to be with him as fresh realization about himself dawns.

Gordon (1961) has described the process of *synectics* as the 'joining together of different and apparently irrelevant elements'. And, as Arieti (1976) observes, 'a state of readiness for catching similarities' is one of the conditions for promoting creativity. And the Aeolian Mode is, above all else, concerned with the use of creativity, by both the therapist and the patient with whom he shares therapeutic space (see also *The Dynamics of Creation*, Storr 1972).

'The force of poetry'

We have frequently drawn attention to the fact that the Aeolian Mode rests upon *poiesis*, and not upon poetry. But the 'force of poetry' (Johnson 1751) is such that the balance needs to be restored. Johnson wrote: 'In this passage is exerted all the force of poetry, that force which calls new powers into being, which embodies sentiment, and animates matter.' And Fell (1979) speaks of the evocative power of words in these terms: 'The writing of poetry by poets is most profoundly disclosive when it remembers and evokes anew this original founding, when it does not simply treat words as basically signs or tools but "hears" what words evoke.'

As we spend time with people who are frightened, depressed, hopeless and chaotic, we cannot fail to recognize the 'poetic style' of expression. It is adopted by even the most prosaic-minded patient when he tries to express the 'inexpressible'. And it does not rest on a single, fortuitous observation. On the contrary, it suggests a disclosive flow, irrespective of the patient's 'diagnostic category', which has the force of poetry. In these circumstances the patient attempts to convey his awareness of mystery. It baffles him because it seems to disclose and yet conceal itself. As Tracy (1981) comments: 'The reality of mystery is, after all, experienced and understood as mystery only on the other side of the breakdown of the clarity of the everyday.' We have already written (Cox 1978) of a poetic disclosure which can act as surrogate for many others: 'I'm blind because I see too much, so I study by a dark lamp.' It is inherently powerful. The more so because the words are those of a schizophrenic patient. Kierkegaard was aware of the discerning capacity of 'an insane observer':

> 'Frater Taciturnus establishes the following order: A curiously interested observer sees much; a scientifically interested observer is praiseworthy; a concerned, interested observer sees what others do not see, but an insane observer sees perhaps most, his observations are more sharp and more enduring.'
>
> (*Collected Works*, Kierkegaard)

In writing about the Aeolian Mode we are trying to present the theoretical foundations upon which a poetic style of verbal expression, or the awareness flash-point of *poiesis*, rests. If we succeed, it is because the bridging between hemispheric functions, though neglected until recently, is nothing new (see pp. 200ff).

Poetry spreads a four-fold significance before us as we write about the Aeolian Mode.

First, poetry does something which nothing else can do (see pp. 64, 138). In T. S. Eliot's phrase (*East Coker V* 1940) it is 'a raid on the inarticulate'. It enables the poet and the reader to gain a purchase on awareness which is too elusive or overwhelming for other language to contain. It can take us to the limit of what is expressible. It can 'evoke new energies of apprehension' in 'Things Hard for Thought' (Knights 1980).

Secondly, those whom we have met in the intimacy of therapeutic space have become poets (see pp. 25–6) when they describe and reflect upon their darkest realities and their brightest joys. Forrest (1965) has studied *poiesis* and the language of schizophrenia. And Rosenbaum and Sonne (1986) have scrutinized psychotic speech and explored idiosyncratic significance embedded in metaphor. Egan (1972) tells us that '*King Lear* must establish an image of existence that will remain valid in the face of the darkest realities of experience.' And when a psychotic girl says that 'the night would come in properly if we spoke the more human way', she has touched primordial experience – the infancy of language – 'when it is all poetry' (Barfield 1928).

'If you could really talk the more human way, the night would come in properly.'

'It's time to get our belongings together and go home.'

> *not our 'things'*
> *not our 'bits and pieces'*
> *but our belonging – yours and mine – our 'belonging' to each*
> *other – our belongingness.*
> *Together. Home.*

Such language as this is part of a cataract of human testimony which is so easy to ignore because of legitimate professional distractions. For example, preoccupation with categorization can distort perception, so that cadences of expression such as 'the night would come in properly' are missed.

Thirdly, both poetry and psychotherapeutic endeavours ultimately fall silent in the face of the deepest feelings. Yet, before language fails, poetic language, almost an 'otherness of language' because it 'stands for the infinite possibilities of language' (Kristeva 1980; 1984), bridges the gap between that which is 'inexpressible' and feelings which make their presence known through massive non-verbal evidence. The rest *is* silence. Though both poetry and therapy can change the cadences in the language of silence which may be sub-audible. But not sub-empathic.

Fourthly, our central concern is the force of *poiesis* in enabling a man to tell his story. Hammer (1978) points out that poetry and therapy share the same goal, when they link the universal with the particular. Ricks (1984) writes: 'Some of Empson's most valuable vigilance has been in defence of story, seeing in real terms the situation out of which a person speaks.' It is no coincidence that this sentence occurs in *The Force of Poetry*. It has a direct link with the Aeolian Mode, which depends upon the force of *poiesis* and the aesthetic imperative through which a man defends, proclaims and becomes his story. It *is* possible to go blind (literally and metaphorically) if one sees too much; and the force of poetry can furnish both therapist and patient with a 'dark lamp', a reminder that 'Poets and psychotherapists are blood brothers' (Rothenberg 1972).

Therapeutic initiatives

The three dynamic components just considered energize those initiatives through which the therapist hopes to reach the patient at his point of urgency. There is almost no limit to the number of possible initiatives which the therapist may make. For the sake of discussion, however, they can be grouped under two headings. Inevitably there will be particular instances where the dynamic of the Aeolian Mode does not fall neatly into either group. These initiatives depend upon the process of *poiesis*. Each may be used to bring about endopsychic change in interpretive psychotherapy, or to reduce endopsychic instability in supportive psychotherapy. They are known as poetic appropriation and poetic induction respectively. We shall consider poetic appropriation first. It is easier to describe, and involves a less elaborate mechanism of *poiesis* than poetic induction.

POETIC APPROPRIATION

This refers to the use of an image which is immediately apparent to the individual patient or the group-as-a-whole. It may involve sight or sound, smell or touch. Thus there may be a visual image, such as a butterfly flying into the room, or a light bulb suddenly 'dying'. There may be an auditory image, such as the sound of shooting from a distant rifle range, the first cuckoo, or a passing train. There may be an olfactory image, such as autumnal woodsmoke, leaking gas, or the strong provocation of garlic as a reminder of a recent meal. Other senses and synaesthetic experience may all provide images which carry psychodynamic, phenomenological, and existential weight.

A simple example of poetic appropriation is furnished by a group therapy session in which all the members crowded round the window to watch a bee-keeper endeavour to take a swarm which had settled on an adjacent wall. One patient, denying any fear, blandly dismissed the anxiety of his fellow members by saying: 'Bees are OK, they don't sting if you understand them.' To which the therapist replied: 'I wonder if people are like that?'

This illustrates the way in which the three dynamic components are integrated by an apposite use of poetic appropriation. Furthermore, the therapist's use of the stored energy released in a mobilizing metaphor in the simple phrase 'I wonder if people are like that?' linked the point of urgency of one group member to that of the group-as-a-whole. At this juncture the reader may wish to turn to page 164 to consider this example in greater detail.

The apparently limitless availability of suitable imagery remains a source of perennial surprise. We have an almost daily appreciation of the fact that there are so many potential images and metaphors which we have not used. This initiative has been given its name because the therapist appropriates an easily available image for the purpose of facilitating *poiesis*.

Poetic appropriation involves the incorporation of a polyvalent image into the therapeutic matrix. It is equally applicable whether the matrix is that of the therapeutic group, or that of therapeutic space in which one patient and one therapist meet – although both individual and corporate space are always 'peopled' by constantly changing fantasies. There is sometimes an irresistible sense of thrusting incipience from images waiting to be carriers of cognitive–affective communication, linking the past with the present and the future. Poetic appropriation is best learned in the free exchange of a supervision workshop. The one-way response traffic of a book inevitably blocks spontaneous associative response. Nevertheless, we are encouraged by Kenner's comment (1948) on Chesterton's way of seeing the world when he writes 'he is not inventing illustrations, he is perceiving them'. Similarly, although creativity is involved, during the actual unfolding of a therapeutic session the therapist is not aware of 'inventing' images. On the contrary, he perceives them. The usual difficulty for the novice is not that he sees too few potential images, but that he sees too many and is unable to decide which to engage. It has become established practice to look not only for the metaphor which links the three dynamic components for the individual patient, but also for the one which is appropriate for the other members of a group. And, if possible, for the one which serves as a vehicle for the corporate life of the group-as-a-whole. The example on page 48 about bedroom walls and walls between people highlights these features.

Experience related by one member of a group can be transfigured, so that it conveys not only the experience of all the individual group members, but also the corporate experience of the group as-a-whole. This is illustrated in the following vignette. It demonstrates the way in which the poetic appropriation of an image can be potentiated by reflection, so that the mutative metaphor exerts its effect of 'touching the depths before it stirs the surface'. The opening words spoken by Lise, a relative newcomer to the group, as she sat on the edge of her chair, were in answer to a question on the nature of genital herpes, from which she had stated she was suffering.

'It is something which starts deep down inside, and then makes its painful way to the surface.'

(At this point Finn enters, apologizing for being late.)

'Finn, we've just been talking about something which starts deep down inside, and then makes its painful way to the surface. What might this be?'

'Well, I don't know exactly, but it must have something to do with the unconscious.'

Because of the nature of the mutative metaphor, the therapist had the assurance that by reflecting Lise's phrase about the source of her discomfort, he was mobilizing the metaphor. This must, in some way or other, evoke reflection about experience which 'makes its painful way to the

43

surface' for every member of the group. Furthermore, in the developmental life of the group-as-a-whole there would also be the pain – which was gradually surfacing – and was felt by all.

We have given this example relatively early in the book, long before we have discussed the theme of metaphor with the detailed attention it demands, because it serves as a hook on which to hang many clinical and theoretical considerations; as well as issues of technique.

Another example stems from David, a nurse, whose staccato remark about the 'cuts' in medical supplies to a relief organization had an ominously personal reference as well.

'Something has been stopped.'

'And the group is a place of unstopping?'

The therapist, who had been silently attentive for thirty minutes, was certain that the reflected question would impinge upon David and the group-as-a-whole. This is because both the phrase and the feeling were appropriate for the current immediacy of concern about the stopping of supplies. And for this reason he stayed in the idiom, although he expanded its potential connotations. But it also ensured universal relevance because of its primordiality. There is ubiquitous apprehension – which may be unleashed as primitive terror – if vital supplies (oxygen, warmth, food, holding, love) may possibly constitute the 'something' which has been stopped. It is not surprising that, although David's manifest statement referred to health service resources, his affect gravitated towards the uncomfortable disclosure:

'I want someone to put his arms around me and say, "It's OK".'
'Something has been stopped.'

This has the quality of a nuclear disclosure (Cox 1978). This is such an essential aspect of inner world phenomena, that it evokes and captures the essence – the thing itself. It is for this reason that poetic appropriation is most effective, when it centres upon a key component of an intrapsychic struggle, or an active nodal point in a group matrix. Thus, Mary's response to the need for 'unstopping' was:

'I blame him because he stopped me from doing anything with any other man.
I blame him most of all because I can't love myself.
I blame him because love has been stopped . . . *strangled*. Spontaneity and trust has been stopped.'

The concurrent archaic howling, which made 'love has been stopped' almost indecipherable, proved, beyond doubt, that this was a nuclear disclosure. By contrast, other dynamic events were peripheral. In this instance poetic appropriation was so rudimentary as to be almost super-fluous, were it not for the slight shift in dynamic emphasis. 'Stopped' implied ending and failing resources. 'Unstopping' implies not only the restoration of supplies, but also the release of 'stopped' ('dammed up') affect which clamoured for release. But the release of affect, vital though it might be, unaccompanied by fresh insight, would only be cathartic, and therefore afford only transient relief. And effective dynamic therapy depends upon the integration of release and augmented insight. One with-out the other is incomplete. Such integration is facilitated by the Aeolian Mode.

Ibsen (1884) wrote of the life-lie (*The Wild Duck*): 'Deprive the average man of his life-lie and you've robbed him of happiness as well.' *Per contra*, a nuclear disclosure could also be regarded as a *Life-sentence*. This has a dual connotation. It is a sentence which captures the essence. For example, 'I'm always next door' can be an emblematic metaphor of always being else-where, never being present, constantly distracted – as well as literally talking with the neighbours 'over the garden fence'. But the 'Life-sentence' also carries implications of judgements made, restrictions imposed, and confirming boundaries stipulated 'for the rest of natural life'. Therapy attempts to bring new freedoms where intrapsychic movement previously seemed impossible.

The *Life-sentence*, once detected, often has the quality of a descriptive life-theme, a psychological ground-base which lies so deeply within the personality that it is equivalent to a musical key in which an individual's life-theme is orchestrated. If a therapist can discern this he has found not a reductive category, but a mobilizing motif. The usual meaning of a Life-sentence is loss of freedom and incarceration. And many patients embark upon therapy because of a sense of being imprisoned within themselves for life, and fear they may never know release. When the story changes, so does the story-teller. *Poiesis* enables change to occur within the patient, but its effects are most in evidence when the thematic Life-sentence changes. Thus, the man who is 'always next door' ceases to be 'miles away' and becomes affirmatively present where he is. Such changes in the capacity to relate to other people are usually heralded by intrapsychic change.

The Aeolian Mode can help to locate and throw light upon a patient's Life-sentence. This in turn becomes part of the metaphorical confrontation with self which is an integral part of dynamic psychotherapy. Sometimes the Life-sentence seems to invest the patient as though it is an emotional legacy from a previous generation. Unexpressed affective loadings may be handed on to their successors by those who were unable to tolerate experience which was rightly theirs. This is no new phenomenon.

'The fathers have eaten sour grapes
And the children's teeth have been set on edge.'
(*Jeremiah* 31, 29)

In *Ghosts* (1881) Ibsen actually quotes this text in his elaborate, inferential disclosure of illicit sexual relationships and dubious parenthood. He describes the way in which people are not free to live their own lives, because of the secret lives of their parents. The latter seem to hover over an existence which is denied its longed-for authenticity. In the words of Mrs Alving:

'It isn't just what we have inherited from our father and mother that walks in us. It is all kinds of dead ideas and all sorts of old and obsolete beliefs . . . Inside me it's the dead who live. Ghosts . . . I'm struggling with ghosts – inside and out.'

'I am fighting my father's battles.'

Indeed much family therapy revolves around transgenerational pathology. Boszormenyi-Nagy and Spark (1973) discuss the 'invisible fabric of loyalty' and the impact of transgenerational existential obligations, an impact conveyed through poetry in *The Inherited Boundaries* (Barry 1986).

Poetic appropriation is one of the ways in which a Life-sentence can be activated as a mutative metaphor. The patient may be confronted to the point at which his capacity to endure ceases. Beyond this crucial stage the Aeolian Mode fails to be invitational and the depth will not be touched before the surface is stirred.

Poetic appropriation exerts its effect by activating images which are brought into sharp relief in the associative matrix of the group. Having explored the scope of poetic appropriation with different populations of patients, calling for a wide range of psychotherapeutic strategies, we have come to the conclusion that certain groups of images are likely to prove more efficacious than others. Our experience points to the fact that the more archaic and primordial the image, the more likely it is to have universal relevance. This means that image and metaphor rooted in natural phenomena best lend themselves to the Aeolian Mode. It is for this reason that darkness, thunder, fire, ice, daybreak, dusk, and the four seasons not only speak of physiognomic perception but carry messages of growth and decay, living and dying.

Nevertheless, poetic appropriation can flourish if there is some obvious agent which 'speaks for itself' to the individual or the group. For example, a Christmas tree whose roots had been 'killed' so that it could never be replanted, spoke to the group of that which appeared to be living and yet stood no chance of further life. It had acted as a focal point for festivities.

Yet the celebration was tarnished by an aura of wistfulness. When the decorations were removed, the tree would be relegated to the scrap heap. In this instance the group was not slow in exploring the way in which each member had to maintain the vitality of his own roots if future life was to be productive. This incident recalls Hans Andersen's fairytale about the *Fir Tree*. Fairytales and myths are rich in associative potential (see *The Uses of Enchantment*, Bettelheim 1976).

On another occasion an unfinished jigsaw puzzle had been left in the group room:

'In some ways, the group seems like a jigsaw.'

'We are all one big puzzle . . . we are each an unfinished puzzle . . . life is one big jigsaw, there is always a piece missing . . . you only find the missing piece when you die . . . that's when the puzzle is complete.'

As the group therapist learns to trust the group – an attitude repeatedly encouraged by Foulkes (1964) – so he learns to trust the images in, of, and from the group. A butterfly trapped in the room was eventually helped to liberation by opening the window, but as it flew out, a wasp flew in . . . 'so often when you safely let something out, your defences go and something worse comes in.'

These few random examples illustrate the way in which a material, concrete 'happening' in the group can mobilize and loosen endopsychic structures. It can be seen that poetic appropriation is the appropriation of an image, transmuted through metaphor into that which speaks from the patient to the patient and from the group to the group. That which was called into being in, say, the butterfly–wasp substitution, was the patient's confrontation with repressed experience and toxic introjects. As he became open to good feelings, so he became aware of bad feelings. This followed a period of denial when he had distanced himself from the painful parts of his history-laden present. Poetic appropriation allowed him to speak of either being so 'blind' that he saw nothing; or of finding that as his eyes gradually opened, so that he could see a butterfly, he also ran the risk of seeing a wasp.

Three further examples must suffice before we explore the more complicated process of poetic induction. One group member looked distracted and said that his attention was held by the 'sound of the shovels'. (The foundations of a new greenhouse were being dug by a team of 'diggers' outside the open window.) The combined effect of intensified group associative activity was profound in its precision, poignancy, and power. It was a beautiful, sunny, warm autumnal day.

47

But, in an instant, 'the sound of the shovels' had taken us to think and feel about:

'Grave-digging'
'Death'
'Funerals'
'Concentration camps'

This, in turn, evoked the painful recall of those deaths for which the group members were not only witnesses, but also agents.

In another group, one member described the loneliness of being an only child:

'But we lived in a terraced house. I used to knock on the bedroom wall and the girl next door used to knock back. We couldn't talk, but it was a kind of message.'

> 'Isn't this something like the group? Though there may be walls between us, we can hear the knocking and get a kind of message.'

'Like prisoners tapping on pipes . . . you know you're not alone.'

'But why not speak?'

> 'Language sometimes fails to carry our feelings?'

'Yes . . . and anyway there may not be any words for what we feel.'

The final example of poetic appropriation should be enclosed in a brief but intensely reflective silence. The solitary place and the place of sharing are linked in the imagery of playing and there are reverberations between there-and-then and here-and-now.

'When we'd played in the street, I went in alone.'

> 'When we'd played in the group, I went out alone?'

Silence.
Silence.
Silence.

'Mmm . . . that's interesting.'

POETIC INDUCTION

'He is not inventing illustrations, he is perceiving them.'

(see p. 43)

'You don't begin at the surface.
Not because you begin at the depth.

48

But because *you* don't begin.
You induce beginning in me.'

'You induce the beginning in me of a story . . . a small story.'

'It is most dramatic when it connects with something larger . . . a larger story.'

'The closer we get to something that is out of *both* of our depths, the more at home I feel and the more I actually feel *I know more than you about everything, including me.'*

'It could be that I put it in your mind because I know the springboard I need.'

'I know which door I want you to open on my behalf.'

This is how a patient chose to describe her experience of psychotherapy when the therapist used the initiative we have described as poetic induction. It is inherently more complex than poetic appropriation. It is also far harder to describe. It involves the paradoxical reversal of initiatives. The therapeutic process is facilitated because the therapist responds to a hidden initiative in the patient. It is this by which the patient enables the therapist to 'open the door' which needs to be opened on his behalf. It is therefore not a question of the therapist forcing the opening of an inappropriate door. It is rather a matter of 'deep calling unto deep', as the therapist responds to 'a primitive communication not decodable in the usual way' (McDougall 1974).

The effect of poetic induction can be stated with brevity and clarity. It holds the patient in his experience. But more than this, it allows the patient to reach areas of his experience which were hitherto inaccessible to introspection. In this sense, poetic induction can facilitate that degree of precision of interpretation which the patient unconsciously needs.

We cannot reach a satisfactory definition of poetic induction by amalgamating the separate definitions of 'poetic' and 'induction', although the fact that induction can be regarded as the production of energy through proximity takes us in the right direction. Poetic induction is inextricably linked to empathy, transference, and countertransference. And each one of this triad is of equal logistic and theoretical importance.

The paradox is complete when we recall that poetic induction both facilitates the patient's capacity for reflective free association, and at the same time augments the therapist's resources for more finely tuned attentiveness. The therapist is able to sharpen the precision of an exploratory intervention because of an enhanced degree of affective 'fit'. Before we continue this study of the nature of poetic induction by looking at an illustrative vignette, a few markers are called for. States (1978) points out that 'pockets of emptiness are never reliably insignificant'. And the process of poetic induction pushes this enigmatic statement still further. By this we mean that the therapist often enables the patient to reach pockets of presumed affective emptiness which prove to be reliably significant. In more conventional terms, it can be said that the defences of denial and repression, often clinically presenting as amnesia, yield an affective loading whose buried significance for the patient's subsequent emotional life could scarcely have been guessed.

The dynamic of poetic induction

Poetic induction has the quality of an analytic interpretation, or a defence-strengthening supportive initiative, and, like every other aspect of the Aeolian Mode, it is effective at the patient's 'point of urgency'. Nanette Auerhahn's comments (1979) about the plurality of interpretations are relevant here.

> 'Reality is an overabundant fullness that perpetually outstrips our attempts to express it. . . . To attempt to arrive at a single interpretation for a patient's statement in an analytic session is to misconstrue the nature of meaning. There is no single interpretation to any statement . . . Language by its very nature is polysemantic. . . [but this] does not constitute arbitrariness.'

Her discussion about intuition is congruous with the theme of poetic induction and the 'aesthetic imperative'. It is this which helps the therapist to determine the patient's point of greatest urgency.

By way of summary: Instead of regarding uninvited, 'spontaneous' associations as contaminants to the conduct of psychotherapy, such experiences are valued and encouraged. But this heterodox response to apparent distractions only applies when they are perceived as being over and above all that conventional psychodynamic appraisal necessitates. In other words, the extra dimension of harmony and sonority which the Aeolian Mode offers is only relevant as an adjunct, or catalyst, to the psychodynamic melodic line. *It is an addition and must never be a substitute.* 'Wild quotation' is as much out of place as is 'wild analysis'. As Hammer (1978) says: 'The empathy, the daring, the sensitivity, and the creativity of the artist-side must be balanced by the objectivity, the rigour, and the discipline of the scientist-side.' Further exegesis follows consideration of a detailed, but generic, example.

Poetic induction in action: vignette 2.1
'I was killing part of me'

Jane, a 24-year-old unmarried mother, describes her escalating anger and frustration at her baby's incessant screaming:

> 'I suddenly found that I had put a pillow over his face. And was keeping it there. I kept it there till it stopped . . . the screaming

stopped, I mean. When I took it off, he was blue and still. But alive
. . . I felt I had really meant to put a pillow over my own face because
I couldn't stand any more of his screaming . . . it was my screaming,
the screaming of years that I wanted to stop for ever . . . I was killing
part of me.'

In addition to his developing dynamic assessment of events, the therapist's
hovering attentiveness is set 'oscillating with something else' when he
hears of the smothering. The 'something else' is a complex association
involving smothering-Othello-flickering candles; and the following words
jump into his mind: 'Put out the light and then put out the light' (*Othello*
V. 2, 7). He waits, holding together the image of the candle, the patient's
description of the ambient circumstances of the incident, and his current
understanding of her inner world. The latter is coloured by the prevailing
transference–countertransference phenomena. *There are no technical words
(fortunately) which can exactly describe what takes place within the therapist as he
waits*. It has something to do with an increasing sense of inevitability about
the irresistible oscillation between his response to the patient, and the
mutative metaphor's capacity of 'quenching a flaming minister' to carry
the weight of the composite dynamic structure. It is then, and only then,
that the therapist acts. *What does he do? What is his intention?* He does *not*
'quote' *Othello* to Jane.

He wants to offer her the possibility of exploring, as far as she is able, her
murderousness towards her baby and towards herself. But he senses that
the issue is far too explosive for an unambiguous, conventional 'interpretation'. Nevertheless, he is aware that the patient is almost telling him that
projective identification is the predominant defensive operation: 'It was
my screaming . . . I was killing part of me.' He is aware of Jane's clamant
need for supportive, non-judgemental listening. He decides that by offering the candle image he gives the patient the option. The flickering candle
is invitational. It could either lead to deep analytic material; or to a supportive image in which she could safely rest, and yet continue to express
feeling at a tolerable depth. The image offers the patient a Heideggerian
'clearing', in which her presence can be manifest in all its individuality, its
disturbance, and its creative potential.

Let us now imaginatively reconstruct the dialogue from the point of our
digression, when the therapist could not possibly have known how Jane
would continue. We have called the sequences A and B:

'. . . I was killing part of me.'

'And the candle almost flickered out?'

A. 'It *just* didn't, thank God. She's three now – and do you know, she
has "flaming" red hair! Funny, when you come to think about it.'

or

B. 'Death was the only thing living when I was a kid. Everyone died. And the pillow was handy so I used it – screaming, any screaming, I still can't stand. My Dad died screaming – he fell under a bus. I've never heard you scream but I think you might – Dad was silent before he screamed. And you're often silent . . . terribly silent . . . and it frightens me.'

The therapist was unable to predict whether the patient would continue with the first option or the second, and it can be seen that two entirely different disclosure sequences ensued. A and B are different in wording, direction, affect, and implication.

But there is one dynamic constant about an aptly timed mutative metaphor, no matter whether the mode is that of poetic appropriation or poetic induction. It is uniformly the case that the patient *never* regards the image as intrusive or inappropriate. Neither does she accuse the therapist of 'changing the subject'. To an uninvolved observer, there is such a patent violation of sequence that it evokes discordant jarring. But the patient regards it as entirely reasonable. We have noted this phenomenon many times.

Reverting again to the choice-point where the mutative metaphor 'entered', we encounter *poiesis*. An image is 'doing' something:

'. . . I was killing part of me.'

'And the candle almost flickered out?'

The following aspects of the process of inducing mutative *poiesis* through a metaphor should be noted:

1. It was certainly not a quotation from *Othello*, although the words were in the therapist's mind. And it is of no consequence whether the patient 'knows' *Othello*, *pace* Ella Freeman Sharpe (see p. 34).
2. It was not even an accurate paraphrase, although an affective equivalent was present.
3. A conglomerate associative image of smothering, and putting out the light, had formed part of the therapist's total response to the patient as a whole person. This encompassing, global response was also coloured by the countertransferential implications. This will have both conscious and unconscious aspects. There was a linking of an unconscious response to the 'left hemispheric', deliberately cognitive appraisal of the patient's endopsychic patterning.

It must be emphasized that if the therapist had been asked by an external 'examiner' about his appraisal of current dynamic events, he should have been able to describe the patient's predominant defence organization, libidinal orientation, ego-strength and other related issues. Working within the Aeolian Mode does not bypass these technical necessities of professional training. The therapist does not formulate dynamics solely in terms of *Othello*! To the best of his ability, he assesses and monitors the patient in conventional psychodynamic terms. But we suggest that *Othello* helps him to frame a 'weight-bearing' image. This is always tailor-made. Yet it is tolerable and acceptable to the patient as she comes to terms with hitherto unacceptable parts of her experience.

The flickering candle used as a creative image in this instance illustrates Coleridge's statement (see Abrams 1953): 'I hold that association depends in a much greater degree on the recurrence of resembling states of feeling than on trains of ideas. . . . I almost think that ideas *never* recall ideas, as far as they are ideas.' Poetic induction offers an integrated cognitive–affective association with an inherent capacity for catalysing dynamic activity in the patient's inner world. But, as in all psychotherapy, the optimal structuring of time, depth, and mutuality is vital if poetic induction is to prove efficacious.

Jane showed a degree of surprise as the flickering candle illuminated part of her previously 'unknown' experience. Reik (1936) wrote on *Surprise and the Psycho-Analyst* and drew attention to the surprise quality of unconscious content as it appears during a session (see p. 207 for the neuropsychological significance of surprise). At a purely affective level, other 'flickering candle' images might have declared themselves. *But they did not do so.* We have in mind the end of *Anna Karenina*, where Tolstoy describes how the candle 'flared up . . . flickered . . . grew dim and went out for ever' as Anna threw herself under the wheels of the train. We also think of Elton John's haunting lines: 'And it seems to me you lived your life / Like a candle in the wind.'

Yet Jane's candle did not 'go out for ever'. And the image from *Anna Karenina*, well known and powerful though it is, would have been a diverting contaminant. Whereas *Othello* facilitated the therapeutic work. Neither was Jane's life extinguished 'like a candle in the wind'. With another patient, *Othello* or Elton John might have been contaminating and *Anna Karenina* facilitating. Yet again, the 'candle in the wind' might have carried an aesthetic imperative. Clinical discernment is what matters.

Returning to a phrase from the example just given we wish to draw attention to the implications of one sentence: 'There are no technical words (fortunately) which can exactly describe what takes place within the therapist as he waits.' And this is the dilemma we have to live with, because 'what takes place within the therapist' is the arena where poetic induction operates. If there are no technical words then we either have to invent them or do without them. Our reason for returning to this sentence is to underline the attempted integration of psychodynamic understanding, the appreciation of the patient's ambient circumstances, and the fragile-yet-tenacious presence of the image of the candle. We have noted that the therapist waits and holds together these three facets of experience (see also pp. 180–1).

THE STORY GATHERS MEANING

Having explored the interaction between the dynamic components (*poiesis*, aesthetic imperatives, and points of urgency) and the therapeutic initiatives (poetic appropriation and poetic induction) in the context of various clinical examples, we are now in a position to give a fuller answer to the question 'What is the Aeolian Mode?'

The Aeolian Mode was originally called the associative mode (Cox 1982a; 1983). But the problem confronting us in the early days was that the title 'associative mode' was not new. Whereas there were numerous connotations of the significance of association in the field of psychological study, in the world of literary studies there was indeed specific reference by name to the associative mode (*Swifter than Reason*, Day 1963). Similarly, the two processes of poetic appropriation and poetic induction are not new to the poet in his discussion of the activity of the poetic image, although, as far as we can tell, the particular names we have chosen for these processes are original. Thus Day Lewis, in *The Poetic Image* (1947), when comparing patterns of images used by Browning and George Herbert, writes:

> '[Browning] did not ask himself what image would best represent "the pain of finite hearts that yearn", and, after long deliberation, decide that five beetles in a fennel cup would do the trick nicely. I imagine him, rather, brooding upon the theme of human love, its aspirations and dissatisfactions; and *suddenly, thrown up by memory, or present observation perhaps, the beetles appear, tugging at his sleeve*, so to speak, and whispering "We are important, you need us." And similarly "the champaign with its endless fleece" was not deliberately chosen as a symbol of "infinite passion", but rather *drawn into the magnetic field of a theme* which was just so much the *more clearly realized when it appeared*.' [our italics]

Here, it seems, is an example parallel to the therapeutic process of poetic induction, when an image, linked with a psychoanalytic understanding of events, 'tugs at the therapist's sleeve'. Day Lewis continues: 'This is not to say that poems have never been composed on lines of *imagery laid down in advance* [our italics]. George Herbert surely did it time and again; and his great poem, *The Collar*, shows how successful this method may be. It is an example of the strictly functional use of images; their use, that is, to point to a theme already defined.'

This, in a non-clinical setting, is the process of poetic *appropriation*. The imagery is 'laid down in advance' and it points to a 'theme already defined'.

It is not difficult to see the isomorphic balancing of matching processes from the fields of literature and dynamic psychotherapy. This mode of psychotherapy was given its new name, the Aeolian Mode, in 1985 at the suggestion of Malcolm Pines (see p. xxv). The image of a harp, which was so loosely tuned that its strings could detect the slightest breeze and turn it into music, was a compelling metaphor for our purposes. An aesthetic imperative, in fact.

It is strange to recall that in the early days of exploration of the possibility of 'Aeolian initiatives' in psychotherapy, one of the first instances was when a few lines from *Macbeth* hovered among a group of institutionalized psychopaths: 'Though you untie the winds, and let them fight / Against the Churches' (IV. 1, 52). This was immediately seized upon by one active protagonist, who firmly defended his peers by saying 'But *we* do *not* cause disorder.'

There is something primordial, speculative, and invitational about the archaic phrase referring to the 'untying of the winds'.' There is a feeling that cosmic disorganization might ensue, and with it the impossibility of sanctuary in either the outer or the inner world. It was only later that we came to learn that Aeolus was the 'keeper of the winds'. Being a god, Aeolus could release the winds as gentle breezes or overwhelming hurricanes as he chose. And the metaphor of the 'wind of healing', or the psychic tornado against which apathy is defenceless, does not need to be elaborated.

Our first reference to the Aeolian Mode (Theilgaard 1987) was brief, and limited to the Rorschach technique. This is therefore our first extended attempt to discuss the nature of this therapeutic process. The complexity of the material under discussion inevitably implies repetition and a degree of overlapping because we approach the centre from many different points on the periphery. And there is always the danger that a description and definition may be so circumscribed that an impression of reductive aridity is unavoidable. If, on the other hand, the discussion is over-discursive, there is the risk of not seeing the wood for the trees. But, bearing these strictures in mind, the Aeolian Mode can be described as dynamic psychotherapy in which the therapist's augmented access to the patient's inner world is catalysed by poetic association and poetic induction. It depends upon the three dynamic components which we have already discussed. The therapeutic initiatives have the effect of bringing about endopsychic change or enhancing endopsychic stability, depending upon the clinical constellation.

Some characteristics of the Aeolian Mode can be listed as follows (see also pp. 16–17):

1. Its emphasis is invitational and not adversarial.
2. Though invitational, it can still be interpretive. Though confrontational, it can still be supportive.
3. Paradoxically, it can be both supportive and confrontational simultaneously.
4. It is equally appropriate for individual or group psychotherapy.
5. It is not only the patient who discovers enhanced self-awareness. The therapist can do so too.
6. If often evokes precise perception of current events, and, by lifting the repression barrier, it sharpens the details of memory hitherto shrouded by amnesia. It also has the capacity to enlarge reflective potential, so that both the therapist and the patient are increasingly aware of 'the larger story'.
7. It is catalytic, spontaneous, and enabling, rather than predetermined and reductive.
8. Although it is congruous with analytic developmental psychology, it carries a heavy existential loading and thus strengthens the patient's sense of living his own life. In Havens' expressive phrase (1976), the patient develops an intensified sense of his 'history-laden present'. The Aeolian Mode therefore enhances the perception of the irreducible particularity of things, including the individual's unique style of living his own life. The capacity to strengthen individuality, and defy reductive labelling, is of significance for the patient with low self-esteem. This is as necessary outside the institution as it is within, and it is exemplified as follows: 'If I don't get out of here soon, I won't have a life to lead anywhere.'

The pivot upon which the Aeolian Mode rests is that there is no possibility of a patient becoming habituated to that which is novel. In chapter 7 when we look at neuropsychology as one of the theoretical foundations upon which the Aeolian Mode rests, we shall see that the novelty of the stimulus maintains the state of arousal. This has the clinical corollary that, for example, the aggressive psychopath has no means of detecting what a 'correct' answer would be to an original and 'once off' question raised by the therapist. He cannot prepare a response to the already discussed (Cox 1983) tangential and unexpected remark: 'I wonder why death's flag is so pale?'

Similarly, the psychotic who needs support so readily detects if the therapist is bored and is 'just trotting out the usual cliché', or saying the 'usual thing' he says to 'all the other patients'. But, working within the Aeolian Mode, the therapist concentrates upon the breaking edge of the wave of fresh imagery. And this can never become jaded; either for the patient or for the therapist. There will be times when the therapist finds himself sinking back into pale, worn clichés ('the bad breast' or 'the Oedipal situation', Holmes 1985), but this is laid at the therapist's door and not at that of the Aeolian Mode. He may be tired. He may be ill. He may need a holiday. The Aeolian Mode, however, depends upon *poiesis* which is always calling into existence that which was not there before. And this gives a unique stamp to the transference–countertransference atmosphere which the patient and the therapist breathe together.

Davie (see Donoghue 1964) described W. B. Yeats as 'trusting the image just as fearlessly outside the world of poetry as inside that world'. Yeats had 'this way of standing by the image through thick and thin'. Here, in a nutshell, is a description of fidelity to the image which is one of the distinguishing features of the Aeolian Mode. But it is not a question of 'standing by' *any* image which *might* be useful. On the contrary, there is a quality of inductive assurance which rests upon the neglected coherence between an appraisal of endopsychic structure, transference–countertransference phenomena and a sense of the aesthetic imperative. Although the images which have a pivotal place in the Aeolian Mode *apparently* arise *de novo*, and engender the feeling of surprise, they often rest upon unconscious determinants which are initially inaccessible to introspection. This deeper coherence seems to be integrated with archetypal rather than regressive experience. In this way the image serves a dual purpose of being a vehicle for interpretation or support, dependent upon the patient's endopsychic patterning and his affective needs.

It must be dogmatically stated that working within the Aeolian Mode is no short cut, no expedient, 'alternative' therapy. The therapist needs the fullest possible understanding of the patient's personality structure and defensive organization if he is to appreciate the significance of current transference phenomena. *And it is only when he comes to that crucial choice-point of how to frame, with cognitive–affective precision, his 'interpretation', his 'intervention', his 'clarification', or his supportive 'consolidation' that the Aeolian Mode can offer the therapist a 'fine-tuning' instrument.*

The ensuing vignettes will illustrate the way in which the therapist uses metaphors, images, and other associative linkings as he responds to the patient's free association. The Aeolian Mode is a capacious therapeutic resource. It may be of value in analytic therapy during the early stages of establishing a therapeutic alliance, during the middle phases of transference interpretation when both therapist and patient are in 'mid-Atlantic', or as therapeutic closure and termination call for the tranquillity of safe disengagement. On the other hand, it affords the possibility of that paradoxical quality of supportive psychotherapy in which the patient gradually becomes aware of an active endorsement of hitherto unknown resilience and energizing stability.

It will have become clear that we attach as much weight and space to supportive psychotherapy as we do to analytically orientated psychotherapy. In our view, supportive psychotherapy is not the poor cousin of psychoanalysis. With the severely disturbed psychopath, the psychotic, the borderline, and the explosive offender-patient, the skills of supportive therapeutic work are no less demanding, in terms of either theoretical understanding or logistic engagement, than is analytic work. But neither are they more demanding. We hope to illustrate that the Aeolian Mode allows poised concentration within both therapeutic approaches, so that the patient may be offered that which he needs, at the time he needs it, and in the form in which he can assimilate it. Sometimes the mutative metaphor is 'uncovering' and leads to greater insight. And sometimes it can heal by covering that which is too readily seen to be tolerable; in such instances it can 'Make the visible / A little hard to see' (Wallace Stevens (1879–1955) 1954).

What the Aeolian Mode tries to do

This book is essentially clinically orientated (see particularly chapter 8). This means that the sole criterion by which it is to be judged is the degree to which it enlarges a therapist's armamentarium. It stands or falls by its efficacy, whether or not it offers something new.

Although the Aeolian Mode is congruous with analytic orthodoxy, it is heterodox in that it places central emphasis upon the induced image which emerges 'spontaneously' during the therapeutic session. But it is the way in which the image is used which gives the Aeolian Mode its distinctive hallmark.

It is over seventy years since Freud (1917b) wrote

'Observation shows that sufferers from narcissistic neuroses have no capacity for transference or only insufficient residues of it. They reject the doctor, not with hostility, but with indifference. . . . They remain as they are. . . . They manifest no transference and for that reason are inaccessible to our efforts and cannot be cured by us.'   (p. 447)

However, since those early analytic days there has been increasing professional interest in the possibility of working analytically with narcissistic personality disturbances and borderline patients. We think of Chessick (1977), Kernberg (1975), and Masterson (1976), although many other authors have written on this topic (see also p. 228), and we link this theme with the work of Frosch (1983) on *The Psychotic Process*.

The Aeolian Mode can support the profoundly decompensated, disturbed, and disturbing patient because it does not threaten to invade penetrate, or overpower him by forced entry from without. On the contrary, the poetic image is induced deep within the patient who welcomes it as a growing inner reinforcement. This has the logically baffling effect of strengthening the surface against alien onslaughts from the outer world. And it is here that Bachelard's paradox becomes most acute.

1986 has seen the publication of *Essential Papers on Borderline Disorders: One Hundred Years at the Border* (M. H. Stone (ed.)). In this wide-ranging selection of papers, Stern writes on 'negative therapeutic reactions'. And his comments illustrate the need for the kind of Aeolian initiative we described in the last paragraph.

'The margin of security of these patients is extremely narrow, and an enlightening interpretation throws them, at least for the moment, into despondency, so that only rarely does one notice a favorable reaction to discoveries. Furthermore, in estimating the significance of the negative therapeutic reaction one must bear in mind that the marked immaturity of these patients, and their insecure, depleted narcissism impel them to react to interpretations as evidence of lack of appreciation or love on the part of the analyst. With these patients analytic therapy is like a surgical operation.'

It was just such a patient who made the decision 'to take it further still'. He followed the gathering of meaning: 'from dream and being, from laughter and from tears a meaning gathers' (Rilke (1875–1926) 1964: For Count Karl Lanckoronski).

That the story gathers meaning is true in a double sense. First, it accumulates meaning and significance as it unfolds. Experience is incorporated, associations develop and the inner and the outer world significantly influence the progressive growth of the story which is to be told. Secondly, the story also gathers meaning in the sense that retrospective significance begins to be discernible at the centre and the horizons of life which, hitherto, were partially hidden by proximity and preoccupation.

Psychotherapy is concerned with a story which is so disturbing that, however painful the telling may be, it must be attempted. The 'teller' seeks an opportunity to explore, appreciate, and appropriate his story, so that it loses its hold. This sentence will be recognized from part of the prologue, but it is here set in a wider context. It is at this point that one of the inevitable and creative tensions of analytically orientated psychotherapy makes its presence felt: because, no matter whether we are concerned with that particular story which is not merely a 'history' but also a 'case history', or whether we are concerned with fragmentary glimpses of the human story which the poet and the lover know, we are brought up against the fact that, ultimately, the deepest feelings cannot be put into words. Language fails. Silence reigns. Marcus (1984) in *Freud and the Culture of Psychoanalysis* studies Freud's attitude to the patient's story. Freud himself (1905) said that treatment started 'by asking the patient to give . . . the whole story of his life and illness', and Marcus reviews Freud's comments on the shortcomings of narrative: 'these narratives are disorganised, and the patients are unable to tell a coherent story of their lives'. Psychoanalytic treatment is, in part, the fashioning of a coherent life story. Marcus continues:

> 'A complete story – "intelligible, consistent, and unbroken" – is the theoretical, created end story. It is a story, or a fiction, not only because it has a narrative structure but also because the narrative account has been rendered in language, in conscious speech, and no longer exists in the deformed language of symptoms, the untranslated speech of the body. At the end – at the successful end – *one has come into possession of one's own story*.' [our italics]

It is an indisputable fact that language fails to be a sufficiently capacious vehicle to describe ultimate experience. This is true whether it is that of religious ecstasy: 'silence heightens heaven'; or that of abject terror: 'I *was* tongue-tied and terrified.' It is logically and experientially impossible to say 'I *am* tongue-tied!' As T. S. Eliot (1957) reminds us: 'the poet is occupied with frontiers of consciousness beyond which words fail, though meanings still exist'.

Furthermore, there may be other dimensions of the 'depth' of experience in which meaning is so fragile, and yet profoundly significant, that it might be destroyed by trying to encapsulate it in language. When discussing 'absolute poetry', Hamburger (1969) adopts the simile of 'using a lasso to catch a humming-bird'. The very instrument employed in the catching might damage and destroy the thing caught. Much of the fragility of experience which comes to life within therapeutic space is of this quality. Further, it is not only true for the psychotic that language may be unable to contain experience, even with neologistic support. Everyone, as he comes into possession of his own story, is aware that it is so ultimately personal that 'the rest is silence' (*Hamlet* V. 2, 352). Burckhardt wrote 'the poet's purpose is to tell truths – truths which escape the confines of discursive speech' (quoted in Hamburger 1969). And Rilke's silence recalls Hamlet's, 'Oh, how often one longs to speak a few degrees more deeply! . . . one is left with a mere intimation of the kind of speech that may be possible there, where silence reigns' (see also Leishman and Spender 1939).

Steiner (1978) refers to Heidegger as being 'the master of astonishment . . . [who] put a radiant obstacle in the path of the obvious', and Leishman (1964) comments that 'we are perpetually surprised' when reading Rilke. Both these comments are also adjectival to the attitude of the therapist as he waits with his patient whose story gradually gathers meaning. And we are back to Reik (1936), with a modified title *Surprise and the Psychotherapist*.

If the therapist is too predatory he may damage the humming-bird with his lasso. Yet, if he is insufficiently associatively attentive he may have failed to notice that light had thickened, and have either ignored or failed to detect the ominous significance of the fact that the crow was making 'wing to the rooky wood' (*Macbeth* III. 2, 51).

The Aeolian Mode and the primacy of the poetic

Writing in *The Development of Shakespeare's Imagery*, Clemen (1951) states

'The images are formed in the very act of composition; one word engenders another. . . . The fact that we so often only gradually become conscious of what image is meant, indicates that Shakespeare no longer inserts the image 'from outside', but that while writing, *he begins to see something in a particular light and then creates an image out of it*. At first this image is only suggested in metaphors; its realization follows later.' [our italics]

This passage describes many aspects of the therapist's experience when he is working in the Aeolian Mode. He does not 'insert images from outside'. And as the creative process of psychotherapy unfolds, so 'he begins to see something in a particular light and then creates the image out of it'. Clemen closes the chapter with words which could so easily be part of a clinical assessment of a disturbed patient's 'mental state': 'Summing up, we observe as characteristic features . . . the following: mingling of the concrete and the abstract, concentration of content, ambiguity, connection of the parts by association and suggestiveness.'

Continuity through apparent discontinuity

We are aware that writing a book of this kind implies that many short cuts and risks must be taken. Whenever a vignette is offered there is an inherent danger that insufficient explanation may give the impression that a response within the Aeolian Mode is either naive or 'clever'. For example, the following fragment from a therapeutic session cannot possibly convey what underlay the therapist's global appraisal of dynamic material which led him to make a 'specific' intervention. But it furnishes yet further evidence of the fact that the patient himself perceives the intervention as part of an entirely natural 'sequence'; whereas a third party might feel that the therapist was changing the subject.

Vignette 2.2
'trap . . . cage . . . duet'

Jessica, a research chemist, is casually sketching with a soft pencil on a sheet of paper produced from her briefcase:

> 'I'm drawing a trap . . . it's not a trap . . . it's a cage.'
>> 'What kind of a duet did you have with your father?'

> 'Certainly not in singing . . . the more I think about it, I didn't have a relationship with my father. He was older. We weren't friends. We didn't do things together. He didn't play with us. I reminded him of his own father. He was changing and sociable. I don't think my parents . . . liked me very much. Daddy would have liked me to be a boy.'

To try to explain why the therapist introduced the image of a duet at this point in the long trajectory of individual interpretive psychotherapy runs the risk of killing its relevance. Oedipal issues were in the air and Jessica's ambivalence towards her father is unmistakable. She had started 'doodling' during a phase of free-floating reverie about life at home when she was a young girl. There were also transference-intensified feelings of being trapped and yet attaining a greater sense of freedom as she faced these issues within therapeutic space.

This example has been given, not because it has anything new to say about such traditional analytic concerns as the Oedipal triangle, but because of the *poiesis* implicit in the creative outlet of singing. It is interesting to note that the therapist did not, in fact, mention singing. And it was Jessica, herself, who responded by saying 'certainly *not* in singing'.

Maybe the therapist was subliminally aware of an association between 'It's not a trap . . . it's a cage' and 'We two will sing like birds i' the cage', but at the moment of inducing this metaphoric substitution he would have been hard pressed to call up this earlier reverberation.

All in all, the affective exchange with Jessica enabled the deep affection–hostility, which constituted her ambivalence towards her father, to be thought through and felt through. Moreover, poetic induction had ensured that there was a fresh image in which to engage with such vital material; rather than a jaded, cliché-ridden restriction to exploration which can hang like a suffocating fog over 'yet another Oedipal problem'.

Although the therapist's response certainly has the superficial appearance of a disjunctive deflection, the patient did *not* experience the 'duet' association as either intrusive or diverting. Indeed, at a deeper level it was received as being integrative. It had the effect of pulling preconscious material within the patient's horizon of awareness.

Reflecting on this duet theme during a subsequent session, Jessica said:

'It wasn't changing the subject . . . it was the same subject but more friendly. It was bending it so that it comes nearer than it really is, like a stick in a swimming pool. It makes the relationship with my parents less remote . . . I felt quite envious of other people's relationships with their parents . . . of being friendly with them. *The theme was in the air.* But it had not been discussed before in terms of singing a duet with one's father . . . it implies that you have something to do with him . . . a cage is a trap after it's been sprung.'

In fact the associative linkage was through that paradoxical statement of freedom-within-restriction which occurs towards the end of *King Lear* (V. 3, 8). Lear and Cordelia are surrounded, trapped, and *en route* to prison. Yet Lear is able to transmute the experience of being captured into one of invitation:

'Come, let's away to prison . . .
We two will sing like birds i' the cage.'

We suggest that the use of imagery and metaphor, which is a central feature of therapy undertaken within the Aeolian Mode, allows an exact sense of fit and detailed engagement because of its capacious openness and potential for particularity. This is linked to one of Heidegger's favourite themes of 'releasement' and 'letting-be'. This, in turn, is close to the capacity of negative capability described by Keats in his famous letter of 1817:

'several things dove-tailed in my mind, and at once it struck me what quality went to form a Man of Achievement especially in Literature and which Shakespeare possessed so enormously – I mean *Negative Capability*, that is, when a man is capable of being in uncertainties, mysteries, doubts, without any irritable reaching after fact and reason.'

In our experience, when the therapist is in the presence of the aggressive psychopath, the psychotic offender, or the borderline patient, he is without doubt in the presence of 'uncertainties, mysteries, and doubts'. Yet, his analytic training with its stress upon the centrality of psychic determinism will give the corrective balance to the hovering, evocative, 'letting be-ness' of *poiesis*. One without the other is defective. Together they are synergistic and often enable the story which the patient needs to tell to gather meaning. Ultimately, one may need to follow Moltmann's example (1980) and 'stand aside from . . . all the telling'. And this brings us back to the words of Isak Dinesen (1957): 'When a story teller is true to the story . . . silence will speak.'

We have repeatedly drawn attention to the distinction between *poiesis* and the rich network of associations which centre upon 'poetry'. And we have explained why it is important for the therapist to remain aware of the different emphasis between the process of *poiesis* and the phenomenon of poetry. Having said this, the lecture by A. E. Housman in 1933 on 'The Name and Nature of Poetry' is so in tune with psychotherapy undertaken within the Aeolian Mode, that we intend to link passages from the lecture with various relevant psychodynamic concepts.

Graves (1979) writes: 'Housman declared that the peculiar function of poetry was not to transmit thought, but to transfuse emotion: To set up in the reader's sense a vibration corresponding to what was felt by the writer.' Although Housman did not use the specific words, many of the central dynamic issues of the Aeolian Mode were evident. Such as

Kinaesthesia (see p. 173)
Empathy (see p. 170)
Poiesis (see p. 23)
Archaic language (see p. 138)
Primordiality (see p. 147)

These are exemplified in the following brief extracts from his lecture:

'Poetry is not the thing said but a way of saying it.'

'I can only say, because they are poetry, and find their way to something in man which is obscure and latent, something older than the present organisation of his nature, like the patches of fen which still linger here and there in the drained lands of Cambridgeshire.' [see also p. 140]

'Experience has taught me, that when I am shaving of a morning, to keep a watch over my thoughts, because, if a line of poetry strays into my memory, my skin bristles so that the razor ceases to act.'

'elements of their [Collins, Cowper, and Blake] natures were more or less insurgent against the centralised tyranny of the intellect.'

3

Vignettes: the story
in the telling

'he receives the word from the voice of another, and the word arrives
in his context from another context which is saturated with other
people's interpretations. *His own thought finds the word already inhabited.*' [our italics]

(Bakhtin 1973)

Although we have already given examples of the Aeolian Mode 'in action',
they have been interspersed among discussions of related themes. This
chapter consists of nothing other than illustrative clinical vignettes and their
scrutiny from various perspectives.[8] In the interest of brevity, we have only
looked in detail at the first vignette from each of the three theoretical foundations. And we hope that the subsequent associative episodes should, through
the reader's critical appraisal, speak for themselves. Of necessity, they can
only be fragmentary glimpses taken from therapeutic sessions. They have
been chosen because they highlight various styles of response evoked in a
wide range of therapeutic settings. They each illuminate the possibility of
non-invasive encounter at depth for which the Aeolian Mode is particularly
appropriate. They come from individual and group psychotherapy sessions
in which either interpretive or supportive initiatives were indicated. Furthermore, they do not come from one field of therapeutic work. They represent
psychotherapy undertaken with patients as different as the conflict-ridden
neurotic and the psychotic offender-patient. We hope that the central
emphasis on dynamic material is maintained in spite of the brief descriptive
sketches.

VIGNETTE 3.1 INDIVIDUAL THERAPY
'I've gone blank'

Martha, an elderly, single, retired social worker, is explaining how she has
always been regarded as the reliable member of the family. 'By not feeling,

I got on with what I had to do. I was an activist.' Whenever there is sudden illness, or any other crisis, the numerous members of the family always call upon her. She is expected to relinquish whatever she is doing, travel to the eye of the storm and bestow calm, purpose, and presence to those in need. No attention has ever been paid to the possibility that she might have needs of her own. The dynamic events of this vignette took place while Martha was enjoying an easy and uninterrupted flow of reminiscent, nostalgic disclosure about good experiences in her early years. Without any hint of what was to come, the benign effusion of speech was interrupted by a sudden silence:

'I've gone blank.'

[Quietly, in an evocative tone of reflective reverie]
'a dead blank feeling came upon me, as if I were approaching to some frozen region yet unseen, that numbed my life.'

[Continuing *as though she had introduced the theme* of a numbed life]
'Of course I've always known I've been frozen . . . I've been keeping it at bay all my life . . . It's safe and acceptable . . . and it's just safe. There's the risk of melting . . . of coming alive . . . a block of ice . . . others not wanting to get under the ice . . . if I came alive I should be unacceptable. I was always the same . . . always a block of ice . . . IF I UNFROZE . . . I SHOULD WANT TO GOUGE HIS EYES OUT . . . HE WOULD BE OUT OF THE WAY . . . I want to bring it out here . . . I wanted to get him out of my sight . . . he diverted Nanny's attention from me.'

Perspectival reflections on vignette 3.1

It will be recalled that the three interlocking theoretical foundations upon which the Aeolian Mode rests are developmental psychology, neuropsychology, and phenomenological existential psychology. It is important to remember that, although each of these foundations plays a part in understanding the dynamics of the chosen vignettes, the significance of each perspective varies from example to example. However, it seems appropriate to make a few general observations about the therapist's intervention in vignette 3.1, before looking at the theoretical aspects of the dynamics in detail.

First, it is to be noted that if the therapist's words are deleted from the dialogue, Martha's words have the following sequence: 'I've gone blank . . . Of course I've always known I've been frozen.' Poetic induction is well exemplified here. An image has been used which offers the patient a metaphor as a safe vehicle for making the transition from one area of experience to another. The patient continues as though she herself had introduced the theme of a frozen region which numbed her life.

Secondly, it could be argued that the therapist had diverted Martha's flow in such a controlling manner that the river of disclosure could not but follow a predetermined, re-routed course. It is therefore important to state in unambiguous terms that the therapist did not try to 'conjure up' the most appropriate association which he could muster. Indeed, he would only make such an intervention if it was felt to be 'irresistible': this comment appears in different forms in connection with each vignette described, but it cannot be emphasized too often.

The therapist perceived a high degree of coherence between the patient's endopsychic patterning, her prevailing psychotherapeutic needs, and the transference–countertransference *ensemble*. In other words, it was as he heard the words 'I've gone blank' that he found himself encountered in reverie by words from *David Copperfield*. And these words 'held' him. He did *not* question himself as to whether there was a literary passage, possibly by Dickens, which *might* be relevant. On the contrary, he tries to offer the freely hovering attentiveness of conventional psychotherapeutic response. At the same time as he is concentrating upon Martha's personality structure and her defensive patterning, he tries to remain accessible to the perception of what is about to be called into existence. This sense of *poiesis* sustains creativity within therapeutic space. And this is work undertaken at the 'coal-face' of psychotherapy.

During a subsequent session, when Martha was recalling this 'frozen region' episode, she was asked whether she felt that the therapist had changed the subject when he introduced the theme of a 'numbed life'. She replied: 'You didn't change the subject . . . because it was the same. It kept me on course.' Though defensive, the cold and the ice were also containing, firm, and predictable – and by melting there was the risk of dangerous spontaneity.

It was possibly less than a minute from the time when she said 'I've gone blank' until she was saying, with reference to her younger brother, 'I should want to gouge his eyes out . . . he would be out of the way.' If the therapist had remained silent, or had merely reflected the patient's words with a conventional Rogerian reflection:

'I've gone blank'.
      '. . . gone blank?'

it is unlikely that the deeper significance of buried aggression and sibling rivalry would have been reached. As it was, she moved almost effortlessly from the statement 'I've gone blank' to 'I should want to gouge his eyes out.' And she did so with a depth of affect and an intensification of presence which is still vivid. Ambiguity is present in: 'I want to bring *it* out here.' This was therefore an unconscious feeling which had been clinically evident as ill-defined and generalized anxiety. But, as soon as it was located, it was recognized as familiar buried affect which she had needed to explore within the safety of therapeutic space. *And when the focal anger had been released, integrated, and understood, she lost her generalized anxiety.*

This book would become too lengthy and cumbersome if each vignette was to be studied in this depth. It is therefore our intention to restrict systematic perspectival reflections to this single vignette.

Caveat:

1. In many places we have stressed that the therapist does not quote or make any direct reference to the associative linking which the patient's experience has evoked within him. Vignette 3.1 is therefore an exception and can be taken to illustrate the flexibility of the Aeolian Mode. It is indeed virtually unknown for the therapist to make any direct citation in response to those aspects of experience which his patient discloses. But in this vignette it should be noted that after Martha had said 'I've gone blank' the therapist, as it were, extended her sentence, 'in an evocative tone of reflective reverie'. This is important. The ethos was that of gently floating a theme upon the surface of corporate reverie. There was no hint of directive control. Martha's tone of voice indicated that she continued speaking as though *she* had introduced the theme of a numbed life.

2. In the ensuing perspectival appraisal of the 'numbed life' vignette, we shall show how each vignette draws upon the three theoretical foundations to a different degree. The fact that the following sections are widely discrepant in length and significance is deliberate. For reasons which are self-evident, perspectival reflections on other vignettes would find these proportions reversed.

DEVELOPMENTAL PSYCHOLOGY

Psychoanalytic psychology

Martha's disclosure illustrates Malan's statement (1979) that 'the aim of every moment of every session is to put the patient in touch with as much of his true feelings as he can bear'. Repression had successfully defended her from the pain of recalling her fierce murderousness towards her brother, whose eyes she had wanted 'to gouge out'. He had been a rival for Nanny's attention. And Nanny, a mother surrogate, was a human transitional object. Martha did not exhibit the denial which the hysteric shows, with its undue preoccupation on 'the good things of life'. On the contrary, the good things were described because they were safely remembered, whereas the deeper feelings of resentment were beyond awareness because of 'the merciful function of repression'.

In this instance, the process of poetic induction allowed the patient safe access to hitherto buried experience. In classical terms, the unconscious had become conscious. And, what is more important, the subsequent integration of previously buried experience had taken place. Martha said 'I want to bring it out here.'

One of the cardinal features of the Aeolian Mode calls for further discussion at this point. In many ways, this was an insight-yielding intervention in which repressed material (anger) was liberated, correctly focused, and relocated where it belonged. However, in this example, the relocation of displaced feeling did not occur through transference interpretation of feelings invested in the therapist. The feeling was activated through the process of poetic induction when the therapist offered a mutative metaphor at the patient's point of urgency. Non-verbal communication and an appreciation of Martha's endopsychic patterning pointed towards a dynamic link between 'going blank' and buried, frozen affect. It must be remembered that other instances of dynamic change being catalysed by the Aeolian Mode may be an integral part of classical transference interpretation. But the Aeolian Mode is not confined to one particular *locus* or *modus operandi*.

This short discussion of the psychoanalytic perspective would not be complete without reference to countertransference. Yet, because the Aeolian Mode depends upon a special form of countertransference utilization, it is not easy to extract specific features here. Nevertheless, the vicariously introspective aspect of empathy had enabled the therapist to detect that Martha's buried feelings were not only of anger, but of frozen anger. Non-verbal communication may have played some part in this conscious aspect of countertransference. But, looking at countertransference in terms of the therapist's unconscious reponse to the unconscious life of the patient, we are bound to say that, in logical terms, it is almost inexplicable. This precision of countertransference attunement to aspects of the patient's experience of which he is yet unaware, remains a mystery. We may talk of unearthing feeling and relate it to frozen, unyielding earth, but this makes the metaphor too concrete. And to explain it solely in terms of intuition seems evasive. The analytic literature on 'the frozen introject' (Giovacchini 1967) is of obvious relevance here.

Organismic psychology

Prior to the therapist's intervention, Martha's inner world was in a relatively undifferentiated emotional state, whereas after it she moved towards a more differentiated one in which she could be more reflective and recall banished experience.

'A block of ice' describes the barren, adynamic condition which does not permit the gradation of perceptual and conceptual nuances. Following the therapist's intervention, such differentiation occurs and the sensory mode becomes predominantly visual: 'gouge his eyes out' – 'out of my sight' – 'Nanny's attention'. This implies that Martha is then able to use her memory in a more mature manner and accept the associated feelings of anger and jealousy. Even if Martha's subsequent perception of events is predominantly visual, it is still more variegated and gives her an enhanced flexibility of response.

NEUROPSYCHOLOGY

Although it is clear that neuropsychology is not the predominant frame of reference for this vignette, three aspects immediately invite comment. First, there is Martha's sudden silence which indicates a blocking of thought and/or speech. This is a neuropsychological intermittent functional disturbance in the flow of consciousness that impedes her word mobilization. And it does so because the pressure of her affect is so overwhelming that it cannot be consciously tolerated. This implies that her affects exist in a de-symbolized state.

Secondly, the therapist's sudden, unexpected intervention enhances Martha's state of arousal through its ikonic, mood-inducing content. Its metaphorical quality facilitates the bypassing of the repression barrier. This means that the deeply-buried aggressive impulses become conscious and are therefore accessible to introspection.

Thirdly, when Martha states that she is not surprised, this may be looked upon as a paradoxical truth which contains its contradiction. The therapist's intervention seems to raise her level of awareness, so that she knows, yet is still surprised, by the fact that she knows that she has always been frozen. Furthermore, it is in keeping with the main theme: 'You didn't change the subject.' But, prior to the therapeutic session, it was not 'a subject' which she knew she knew.

PHENOMENOLOGICAL EXISTENTIAL PSYCHOLOGY

The therapist offered Martha the fresh, untarnished novelty of an image which, in a strictly historic sense, was not overtly linked to her experience. Nevertheless, the mutative metaphor was sufficiently close to her presence in the world for some of her repressed experience to be activated. During the therapeutic session Martha's inner world had not been stationary. Movement had taken place. But she had 'gone blank'. And if she could go 'blank', then this dynamic could be harnessed for movement to take place so that she could 'go' elsewhere. The 'elsewhere' to which she could go was to 'some frozen region yet unseen, that numbed her life'. States (1978) remarks that one of the central characteristics of myth is that 'it always has "an elsewhere" at its disposal', and there are mythical and primordial overtones to this passage which engaged with archaic aspects of Martha's experience. Barthes refers to the 'benumbed look' of mythical speech, and we are here studying a fragment of a numbed life, in which mythical associative linkage de-represses, reverbalizes, and resymbolizes experience.

Heidegger (1936) refers to 'The age for which the ground fails to come', and, during anxiety, it is common for a man to find the ground is 'coming to meet him'. Part of the existential significance for Martha is that through 'going blank' she is approaching 'some frozen region yet unseen, that numbed her life'. She is moving forward to the past. Unlike Macbeth, she had not referred to 'the coming on of time' (I. 5, 9). But she is aware and is frightened of the 'coming on of place'. There is a frozen region which, though she is still approaching it, has already numbed her life. Nevertheless, she does resemble Macbeth in that a frozen region is extra hard and weight-bearing; it can be addressed as 'thou sure and firm set earth' (II. 1, 56) with extra certainty. In other words, she is approaching an area of buried, frozen experience which has already iced up relationships in her present predicament. It has also frozen, in the sense of preserving, unresolved hostility from her very distant past. And she arrives at the therapeutic session with her history-laden present (Havens 1976).

The aim of interpretive, 'uncovering' psychotherapy is closely linked with the existential significance of Martha's life. Her present relationships are impoverished, and she finds safety in being frozen. There is danger in being warm. At the same time, there is the frozen and preserved murderous heat from long ago which cripples fresh endeavour. Or it did do so, prior to this stage of therapy.

The therapeutic leverage in this instance owes its efficacy to the mutative metaphor. There is the ventilatory aspect of expressing hitherto frozen, buried feelings. There is the acquisition of insight as the unconscious becomes conscious. This new awareness is then incorporated into her current construction of reality. In other words, the buried affect of wanting to gouge her brother's eyes out is now seen for what it is, or rather was. This means that she can now have a warmer relationship with her brother.

As we try to link these complex clinical and theoretical matters, it is possible to see more than a hint of 'the pattern which connects'. And because this is so, the therapist's associative response which released Martha's buried affect can be cited as an example of the aesthetic imperative.

VIGNETTE 3.2 COMBINED GROUP AND INDIVIDUAL THERAPY
'I took perfume'

'I sometimes wanted what I took . . . but not always,' said a patient in a therapeutic group. Her anti-social behaviour had escalated from shop-lifting to multiple stabbings. Without the need of further invitation she gratuitously added:

'I took perfume.'

The therapist said nothing, but he was suddenly aware of an 'obligatory' association linking perfume to stabbing, which seemed to fit into a matrix of meaning through the phrase:

'There's the smell of the blood still.'

This powerful reverberation in the therapist's mind involved an associative leap which seemed to be too large and unwieldy to be readily incorporated into the group matrix. Even now, the recall of this session is so vivid that it seems unnatural not to write it in the first person. And perhaps an obligatory need to substitute the first for the third person intensifies the immediacy of the encounter being described.

I (M. C.) wondered if the 'smell of the blood' would be too severe a confrontation for the patient to tolerate, as it seemed to come 'out of the blue'. On balance, I decided to let the theme remain in my mind until the session ended. But it would not let me rest. Mildred, who had previously referred to her multiple 'offences against the person' on several occasions, had never spoken of blood.

Later, she apprehensively approached me in the corridor outside the group room. Yet she also seemed strangely hopeful. I asked her whether the smell of blood had ever concerned her when she relived the various incidents described as 'grievous bodily harm'. She said 'No' – with defiant certainty. And here, I thought, was an example of the Aeolian Mode leading me up the wrong path and away from the patient's inner world. But, even as I was thinking this, she added:

'The smell of blood? No, not theirs. But there *was* a smell of my own [she had indeed been cut during a struggle]. I couldn't get away from it. It smelt as though you hadn't washed for months. It was a dirty smell; especially when it was dry. The police got me away from it [the scene of the crime] quickly – *but I couldn't get away from my own blood.*'

This extraordinary fragment of dialogue taking place in a hospital corridor, in which my mistaken memory led to an 'eidetic' image of the 'scene of the crime' – together with an immediacy of affect, still lives with me. It has an almost intrusive aura of authenticity about it. It is doubly eidetic. In the words of Dickens (1849): 'I do not recall it, but see it done; for it happens again before me.' I do not recall Mildred talking to me by a hospital stair-case, but I see it done; for it happens again before me. And, as she stood there, every modality of non-verbal communication made it clear that Mildred was not recalling a struggle involving a knife, but she saw it done; for it happened again before her.

In this instance, the language of Lady Macbeth and an offender-patient in the twentieth century are almost indistinguishable. They merge into one another. Without the therapist acting upon the spur of an aesthetic imperative, at the patient's point of urgency, the creative *poiesis* would not have taken place, and Mildred's new reflective awareness would not have been brought into being. Repressed material would have remained encap-sulated as amnesic loss; and the much-needed linking of past and present experience would have been impossible.

The inability to withdraw from one's own blood is a condensed state-ment about authenticity and presence: 'What, will these hands ne'er be clean?' – 'It smelt as though you hadn't washed for months' – 'here's the smell of the blood' – 'I took perfume'.

In this vignette the Aeolian Mode induced the linking of the shoplifting of perfume with all the perfumes of Arabia. But at the moment of making the connection, I had not got as far as recalling the sweetening of 'this little hand' (*Macbeth* V. 1, 47). And I had no idea that Mildred had in fact cut her own hand or that it was her own blood which, when dry, had such a dirty smell.

This illustrates the importance of narration as it weaves together myth and history, because as Holloway (1961) observes: 'Myth is something like a potential narrative. . . . [Myths] are moulders, controllers, and sus-tainers of how men live.' They become part of the story. And without *Macbeth*, certain necessary clinical details might never have surfaced. Once again, the paradox is evident. 'Where the story is, the characters will gather.' Mildred's story was, *then, in the corridor*, and several characters gathered round as she spoke of them.

All this took place in an hour 'at work' on Monday morning. Mildred, who had not even intended to talk about shoplifting when she entered the group room, would never have considered it credible that in so short a time she would have been openly reflecting upon her inability to get away from her own blood. But the Aeolian Mode sometimes works like this. A chance happening leads to apparently unimpeded access to the inner world. That morning much hung upon Mildred's casual decision to join a relatively light-hearted discussion by adding 'I took perfume.'

73

The subsequent intermingling of 'clinical' recall and associative reverie led to the following fabric of exchange:

'I'm like a witness to my own life – like looking on – I don't feel real.'

> *'A little water clears us.'*
> 'I know you don't like to miss a bath.'

'The water was a reddy colour . . . a watery red.'

> *'Making the green one red?'*

'Memory can't be washed.[9] It's not that simple. It doesn't go like that. Medicine does nothing to memory. THE MEMORY IS STILL IN MY MIND.'

COMMENT

The individual psychopathology which lay behind repetitive assaults and the corporate dynamics of a therapeutic group of patients whose histories – in broad terms – have many common features are too complex to analyse or describe in detail. For our present purpose, it would certainly prove abortive.

Nevertheless, there is no doubt that there was a gravitational pull towards the primordiality of experience. This was activated by an aesthetic imperative which originated from previous encounters with *Macbeth*. This vignette is of particular interest because it rested upon a *mis*quotation. The therapist had linked Mildred's casual remark 'I took perfume' with the following line from *Macbeth*: 'There's the smell of blood still'; and, as with the vast majority of violent offences 'against the person', any blood present is the blood of the victim. An archetypal illustration which could carry the weight of all such assaults is, 'Who would have thought the old man to have had so much blood in him?' (*Macbeth* V. 1, 39). In this instance, there is no doubt about whose blood was being discussed.

When Mildred gave an unequivocal no in answer to the question about the smell of blood, it seemed as jarringly incompatible as the experience of inadvertently putting a car into 'reverse'. But when she suddenly remembered that it was not 'their' blood that she could smell, 'But there was the smell of my own', the original, 'correct' lines from *Macbeth* made their presence felt. There was a sense of shock and an awareness of affective precision which still evoke surprise as they are recalled.

'There's the smell of the blood still'

'*No*'

'*HERE'S the smell* of the blood still: all the perfumes of Arabia will not sweeten this little hand. Oh! oh! oh!'[10]

This vignette is so rich in didactic implications. It speaks of archetypes, tragedy, the trivial as a door to the profound, the significance of precise detail when seen against a broad associative backcloth, and so many other interesting aspects which all carry clinical weight. It was months later that an obsessional preoccupation with bathing could be seen for what it was. Nevertheless, from our point of view, it is an example of the Aeolian Mode in action; in which there was a world of difference between 'here' and 'there'. The difference leading to unthreatening access to the inner world of a heavily defended patient which would otherwise have remained sealed.

> 'Wild honey smells of open air,
> Dust of sun's ray,
> Girl's mouth violets –
> And gold of nothing.
> Mignonette smells of water,
> Love of apples.
> But – one lesson we shall not forget –
> Blood smells of blood alone.'
>
> (Anna Akhmatova 1933, quoted in
> *Nightingale Fever*, Hingley 1982)

VIGNETTE 3.3 INDIVIDUAL OR GROUP THERAPY
'Unpublish'd virtues'

'It was very good. It was almost tremendous. It was joy . . . it's a funny thing, but the better you get – the sadder you can get.'

Little did the patient realize how close he was to paraphrasing Winnicott's words (1963) on 'the capacity for concern'. There is no doubt that when a patient with a narcissistic personality disorder eventually stumbles on an experience of joy, and couples it with the awareness that 'the better you get – the sadder you can get', endopsychic change has occurred. It is probable that psychotherapy which could facilitate this change is likely to have been deep and prolonged. By the time a patient reaches a secure hospital, it is not infrequent that his offence has featured in the media. He may even have had a catastrophic phase in his life 'published' when his legal 'disposal' had been agreed. But this is all behind him when he ultimately enters therapeutic space. 'We're not here for fresh air – we've been judged already.' It is then that the therapist listens to the patient describing how he felt during and after 'the material time'; a time when numerous negative labels might have been applied: 'a beast', 'that monster'. Nevertheless, as we have previously observed, the patient often carries such strong feelings with him that he brings painful experience into therapeutic space by something 'stronger than memory'. Yet again, *David Copperfield* is there before us: 'I do not recall it, but see it done; for it happens again before me.' Incidentally, the pervasive and insidious nature of the negative labelling illustrates the crucial criminological conception of the 'controlling identity' described by Matza (1969) in *Becoming Deviant*.

A man may have many important and indeed positive attributes, but the controlling identity is that of 'a thief' or 'a killer'; worse still 'a beast', 'that monster'. Furthermore, if the patient has a depressive diathesis he may subsequently claim these attributes for himself. Should this be the case, a neglected associative response might actually deprive the patient of a facilitating reflection, rather than protecting him from an intrusive countertransference contaminant. It was in such situations that our early formulations of the Aeolian Mode began to take shape. We had a growing conviction that events of this sort could be regarded as serious tokens with psychotherapeutic implications. What we had originally regarded as contaminants, to be avoided as rapidly as possible, so that we could give our 'undivided attention' to the patient, we came to value highly. That which we had erroneously previously ignored, we gradually discovered possessed the capacity to clarify, rather than cloud, prevailing dynamics. And not only the dynamics of what the patient said, but what he was feeling as he spoke. Possibly most important of all, we may have been given a clue as to what he was feeling when he could not speak. Indeed, the feeling might explain *why* he could not speak. And, through projective identification, why *we* could not speak (see Ogden 1982).

Why should a phrase from *King Lear* incessantly force its way into my mind when I am trying to attend to the patient who is with me? Particularly, when he is reliving 'those awful days' with transparently genuine affect. Why should the phrase spoken by Cordelia as her father comes out of coma 'keep interrupting', so that I find it difficult to concentrate on what the patient is saying? But, when I take seriously what Cordelia is in fact 'saying', I hear her referring to the 'unpublish'd virtues of the earth' (*King Lear* IV. 4, 16). Suddenly, a spark jumps the gap between my clinical perception of the patient and Cordelia's insistence. Should he, in colloquial English, be invited to reflect upon the good things in his life, to talk about his '*unpublish'd* virtues'? Most of his recent encounters with police, lawyers, clinicians, and other professional interviews will have concentrated upon his disturbance, his sadness, his badness, and, maybe, his madness. One wonders how long it is since he last thought about the good experiences he has known. If such poetic induction occurs towards the end of a session, it could be because some deep echo had been sounding. The passage not only refers to 'unpublish'd virtues', but also to 'simple' remedies 'whose power will close the eye of anguish'. In this instance an aesthetic imperative exerted its effect by evoking the therapist's awareness that there was an archaic aspect to the patient's suffering. It had the quality of a transgenerational family burden, rather than that of personal pain. *Invisible Loyalties* (Boszormenyi-Nagy and Spark 1973) were undeniable. In clinical terms there was a massive need for therapeutic closure – closure indeed of the eye of anguish.

I (M.C.) have never previously used, or even thought of, the phrase 'unpublish'd virtues', even though I have been a *King Lear* addict for thirty years. I may never have cause to think of it again during a psychotherapeutic session. I emphasize this because I do not wish to give the impression that the therapist has a limited reservoir of stereotyped associations which he repeatedly surveys, to detect whether there is one which is appropriate or 'matches' the silent or stated experience of the patient. Here our approach is at variance with that advocated by Barker (1985). On the contrary, the therapist only responds to his response to the patient when the association is demanding, and so clamant that it impinges upon him so as to almost obliterate everything else. This is not an overstatement. We have learned never to use a tangential or oblique association unless its impact upon us is so powerful that we feel we will deprive the patient of something if we withhold it. But let us return to 'the eye of anguish'.

Taken out of context, this example seems naive and trivial. But, to the patient who knew that his offence had been 'publish'd' within his effective personal world, the possibility of yet having virtue which was hitherto unpublished might possibly 'close the eye of anguish'. In spite of being a rapist, he might still be a good father or a loyal friend. But such is not head-line news. There is frightening power in Matza's categorizing notion of a 'controlling identity'.

In more conventional terms, the change to a supportive phase at the end of a dynamic session is a customary way of effecting therapeutic closure. There is nothing new in this. However, the novelty may lie in the fact that the exact affective loading, the choice of appropriate wording, and the semantic *timbre*, can be more finely tuned through the process of poetic induction. The therapist is not 'using the same old phrase'. Neither is it a hackneyed, colourless cliché. And bleakening, categorizing concepts are obviated.

When the patient is so frightened of those life experiences which he has negotiated that he has needed to be protected from them by subsequent amnesia, the repression barrier may be gradually lifted through an associative response which offers him the necessary degree of safety. This recalls a line from a poem entitled 'Safety' by Rupert Brooke (1928): 'Safe though all safety's lost; safe where men fall.' Yet it is not only with the offender-patient that poetic induction offers the therapist enlarging options of response. The therapist is always in the place of privileged reception. Every therapeutic session could evoke a phrase from the first page of Marianne Moore's *The Complete Poems* (1968): 'it is a privilege to see so/much confusion'. And communication within therapeutic space is always privileged. We suggest that the 'tailor-made', associatively induced contouring of personal response to the patient militates against a stereotyped, 'theory-bound', restricted repertoire.

The following words are not from a romantic novel. They were uttered with deepest seriousness during a therapeutic session. The intensification of empathy which poetic induction had brought about was described in this way:

> 'But something else is happening. Something has stunned me. A kind of communication which I always longed for. I didn't think it was possible. *There is an experience of joy.* It must be truth.'

This is an almost exact paraphrase of the passage from *I Never Promised You a Rose Garden* (Hannah Green 1964):

> 'It was tough but true, and under the anger of it ran the tone – the tone rare anywhere, but in a mental ward like a priceless jewel – the tone of a simple respect between equals. The terror she felt at the responsibility it bore was mingled with a new feeling. *It was joy.*' [our italics]

This paradoxical conjunction of terror and joy is reminiscent of *In No Strange Land* by Francis Thompson (1859–1907): 'The drift of pinions, would we hearken, / Beats at our own clay-shutter'd doors.' This leads into a 'cry' – 'when so sad thou canst not sadder', and returns to joy. This vignette ends where it began: 'It was very good. It was almost tremendous. It was joy . . . it's a funny thing, but the better you get – the sadder you can get.'

VIGNETTE 3.4 GROUP THERAPY (IN-PATIENT)
'Skating on thin ice'

The group in question is a weekly group of offender-patients, most of whom would be dynamically regarded as borderline patients, although from a phenomenological point of view they are diagnosed as being 'psychopathic'. The majority had committed their offences during micro-psychotic episodes. David is the one truly psychotic member of the group.

The therapist enters the group room as the exciting events of the preceding evening are being discussed. All the patients have been allowed to stay up late so that they could watch the Winter Olympic Games on the television set in the day-room. This, in itself, would have been excitement enough to justify their infectious enthusiasm, but there was a double sense

78

of jubilation because the gold medal for ice-skating (dancing) had been won by the English competitors.

After listening for a few minutes to their continued exuberant recollections, one question was asked. And for the rest of the hour it became almost impossible for the therapist to find a silent gap in which to say anything! Nevertheless, there was no doubt that by the end of the session all the patients had spoken about painful memories. And they had done so at a depth which would have been unimaginable without the polyvalent, yet stabilizing, effect of a mutative metaphor.

It must be remembered that all the patients were 'offender-patients' who had taken major risks of one sort of another with their own lives, or the lives of their victims. In this instance, a metaphorical interjection, with a limitless number of possible referents, had enabled each member of the group to feel that the question was addressed to him. The question was simultaneously addressed to the group-as-a-whole by the simple visual expedient of looking at the centre of the floor:

'I wonder who would win the gold medal for *skating on thin ice?*'

It felt as though there was almost a disclosive 'rush' for the centre of the circle; as the group members were 'falling over each other' in making competitive comparisons of those critical moments in their lives when they had been on 'thin ice'.

One said the thin ice took the form of the sudden failure of all social supports: 'Family, friends, and my job all went at once.' Another implied that the outer world was stable but his inner world was not: 'My thin ice was inside me. Suddenly all my control went and I did it.'

The exigency of the present moment of disclosure within the group session was such that there was 'a thin ice' quality of risk-taking. This was because the very fact of talking about previous episodes of personal risk-taking leads to an intensified sense of vulnerability. The act of talking of previous risks is, in itself, risky. Nevertheless, 'thin ice' as a group-as-a-whole phenomenon can, when safely negotiated, endorse corporate stability. Indeed, subsequent sessions bore witness to the group's receptiveness to disclosures of previous intimacy.

In one way and another, there was a fusion of inner and outer world phenomena. This closely paralleled the intensification of an awareness of the group-as-a-whole with its corporate life, as well as the existentially intensely individual and unshareable quality of each patient's personal experience.

All the patients (except one) understood the significance of the metaphorical image of 'thin ice', which had facilitated subsequent disclosure. It exemplified two crucial attributes of the Aeolian Mode. *It invited and it did not threaten. It evoked and it did not invade.*

In many ways, the most fascinating phenomenon was the idiosyncratic response of David, who was still actively psychotic. He simply told us of the latest weather forecast in Sarajevo, where the Olympics were being held, with the implication that even though the ice might have been getting thin, the games were continuing because it was still safe enough to skate on!

At the end of the session all the patients, including David, felt that it had not only been an interesting session, it had also been helpful. Yet, looked at critically in terms of individual and corporate psychodynamics, it could be seen that while some primitive defences were relinquished others were retained, although each patient had disclosed a great deal about himself. This recalls Kermode's (1979) emphasis on the importance of 'what is concealed in what is proclaimed'. An amended and paradoxical therapeutic codicil could be added. Namely, that in this analytic group, facilitated by the mutative metaphor, much was proclaimed in what was concealed. This did not apply only to the psychotic who gave such a clear demonstration of concrete thinking. Each member proclaimed experience which would have remained concealed, had it not been for the 'skating on thin ice' mutative metaphor.

The Janusian capacity of the Aeolian Mode is evident in this vignette which demonstrates the simultaneous possibility of being synthetic and analytic. The single reflective question which the therapist 'floated' into therapeutic space had a double dynamic. It linked the discussion of topical interest, thus intensifying group coherence, with an introspective searching sequence. This led the individual members of the group to think about and describe occasions when their defences had failed.

VIGNETTE 3.5 ANOTHER IN-PATIENT THERAPEUTIC GROUP
'It's cold enough for snow outside as well'

A slow-open group of female, psychotic offender-patients assembles in the group room for the weekly session. There is a bustle of activity as tables are moved, chairs are arranged in a circle, and the group members decide where to sit. One of the patients is carrying a book entitled *Up the Garden Path* (Thelwell 1967). This was not an attention-seeking stimulus, and the book was put discreetly out of sight. But not before the therapist had a chance to see that it was a book of cartoons about gardening.

'I see Heather has brought a textbook on group therapy!'

The book was then passed round. The group members were obviously amused at the implications that psychotherapy might be nothing more than an expensive and time-consuming way of being led up the garden path.[11] Heidi suggested that the last cartoon came closest to catching the atmosphere of this particular group. This caused justified laughter and nods of agreement as each member turned to the appropriate page. This is what they saw:

From a theoretical point of view, the therapist felt that the cartoon represented a Foulkesian orientation (1964); namely, the necessity of simultaneously seeing the group-as-a-whole as well as fostering concern for the individual particularity of each member. There was no doubt that the various component members lying in the snow were part of one corporate body. Yet they each made their individual presence discernible to the therapist who had 'flown in' and was evidently concentrating upon what he saw!

Hilda: (after prolonged silent rumination about the picture) *'It's cold enough for snow outside as well.'*
Harriet: 'Yes . . . last winter we were given extra blankets and they tried to seal the windows to stop any draughts coming in.'
Helen: 'It's cold enough in my heart for snow.'

'But coldest when?'

Helen: 'It was coldest when my father died. There was snow in my heart as well . . . It's not just the coldness . . . Desolate is the word.'
Heidi: 'It was coldest and desolate for me when I was on remand. I was kept in a cold room with black pillows and black sheets.'
Hilda: 'My dog likes it in the garden when it's snowing. He buries his nose in the snow. We have a rose bush in our garden. And he likes all the snow petals coming down.'
Helen: 'Snow petals? . . . Snow balls.'

Heidi: 'Snow flakes!'

Hilda: 'Sometimes the red petals fall on the snow.'

    And . . .?'

Hilda: 'They fall on the snow.'

    'So . . .?'

Hilda: 'So there are new buds.'

Perspectival reflections on vignette 3.5

We are merging the theoretical perspectives and reviewing them con-currently in an extended discussion of this vignette. We have chosen this session because it illustrates the way in which an image can appear 'spon-taneously'. Prior to the session, it could not possibly have been predicted. It is a clearcut example of poetic appropriation (see p. 42), and it is unusual in that a group participant actually brings the image (the cartoon) with her as she walks towards her chair. The session also exemplifies the dual function of mutative metaphor, which both 'carries' the group in a supportive capacity, and 'carries it across' the boundary between concrete and abstract significance – and it does so in such a way that unconscious symbolic depth is reached. Furthermore, the metaphor also catalyses the dynamic movement for some patients, without diminishing the supportive function for the more restricted patient who is only able to think in concrete terms.

Thus, Harriet subsequently said that she thought it was a helpful session because 'we were discussing our problems'. 'Problems', for her, referred to an extra cold winter when extra blankets were needed and the staff had to seal the windows. Whereas, for Hilda it was 'cold enough for snow out-side as well'. And whether or not she was referring to snow outside her body or outside the room, there was sufficient dynamic stimulus for Helen to pick up the metaphorical implication of the outside weather, and to say that it had been 'cold enough in her heart for snow'. Finally, it should be noted that Hilda ended the group on an optimistic note. Her dog had guided her to the rose bush. And the red rose petals made a pattern on the snow. But, for her, the significance of the fallen petals was not that of a dying, disintegrating bloom but a statement that there were new buds.

The implication of life through death was evident. The petals had fallen '*so* there are new buds'. The possibility of new unfolding life in the not too distant future was an obvious therapeutic closure for this particular session in which eight offender-patients reflected upon the story of their lives. And, as the cartoon shows, even in the snow they knew that they were 'members one of another' (*Ephesians* 4, 25).

There was an irreducible here-and-nowness about this group session which took place in a warm room on a cold morning. Technically, it was a slow-open group. For some of the patients it was a *very* slow-open group, 'without limit of time'. Nevertheless, although some members had been in the group for several years, there was still the immediacy and novelty of a sudden confrontation with aspects of experience which had not been present before. The simplicity of the image ensured this. Furthermore, it was evident for each group member. And the understanding was not restricted to those who had the capacity to understand complex imagery. If it ever transpired that the image was above the patient's head, then the Aeolian Mode would justly fall into disuse and disrepute. It is not undertaken because it is 'interesting' for the therapist to play with concepts of creativity and mutative metaphor. On the contrary, it is used because it can link levels of experience for each individual patient and the group-as-a-whole. The image makes an impact because of its novelty, its simplicity, and its imminence. In terms of confrontation, the patient is unable to avoid its impact. Yet, paradoxical though it is, it also provides support. The image holds each patient, yet it securely links them together as a group. In this vignette, Harriet was at ease discussing such domestic matters as extra blankets and the need to check windows for draughts, while Helen reflected upon the loss of affective warmth when her father died.

From a phenomenological point of view, the Aeolian Mode is anti-reductive. The group session in which it was 'cold enough for snow outside as well' was not to be reduced and categorized. Not, at any rate, for the patients in the session as it *spontaneously unfolded*. This spontaneity is the guarantee of genuineness and the precision of corporate empathy. And the Aeolian Mode catalyses reflective spontaneity.

Existentially, the individual and corporate life of the group was like that of 'coming into the open' in a clearing made in a dense wood. Associative appropriation had 'let in' coldness and death, as well as the prospect of warmth and new life. One member, and therefore vicariously all members, had been able to dare to hope. And this exemplifies Yalom's inclusion of the 'instillation of hope' in his list of curative factors in group psychotherapy (1975). It also reminds us of Kierkegaard's statement that 'Hope is a passion for what is possible.' Yet, hopeful though it might be, it was still a frozen wood in which snow was in the air, because it was 'cold enough for snow outside as well'. This was a particular clearing in a particular wood. The existential significance of the irreplaceable is always evident, because the Aeolian Mode depends upon the utilization of novelty. And this is something against which habituation and stagnation are powerless and irrelevant. By definition, novelty is always new and can never be reduced to an example of something else. This group, on this morning, knew that it was 'cold enough for snow outside as well', in a way which no other group on no other morning ever could.

This group vignette so clearly exemplifies poetic appropriation because the therapist uses an image which is already spontaneously evident in the session. In this instance, it was the book of gardeners' cartoons, *Up the Garden Path*, which so well matched the severe frost and the first winter snowfall. The mutative capacity of snow-outside and snow-inside, or of frozen petals as indications of buds and further unfolding life, is so starkly self-evident that explanations are superfluous. Indeed, this is one of the hallmarks of psychotherapy undertaken within the Aeolian Mode. The vignettes 'speak for themselves'.

The poetic image always has the stamp of novelty about it, as well as a thrusting sense of almost inevitable imminence. This is perhaps reflected in the fact that both vignettes 3.1 and 3.5 occurred within the same week in November 1983, a very cold month, when frost, snow, and 'numbed life' were in the air. Indeed, there is frequently such an intense awareness of coherence and exact 'fit' that, in retrospect, it can scarcely be imagined how any other metaphor could possibly have been appropriate. The poetic image is constantly alive because of its novelty and an awareness that something has come into existence which was not there before. Though imminent, it links both present and past experience, location, and meaning. It is not a pale, dried memory.

When discussing so complex an entity as a therapeutic group, it is not appropriate to describe the individual psychopathology of each patient or the particular stage in the development of this slow-open group. Nevertheless, it is easy to see that Harriet exhibited restricted, concrete thinking. On the other hand, Hilda showed severe confusion of external and internal boundaries. Helen, who had been thought-disordered, was now functioning at a higher cognitive–affective level of psychic integration, so that she became able to use the image and link this with the metaphorical coldness of heart when her father died.

This vignette illustrates the way in which the corporate life of the group can be both supportive and analytic, and that it can be so simultaneously. Furthermore, it can function in this way for each individual member when it is facilitated and intensified through the process of poetic association. It will be noted that the therapist actually said very little, apart from his initial intervention in terms of the title of the book and the therapeutic closure. The reader may gain the impression that a book with such a title was a 'gift' to the therapist, and so it was! Nevertheless, it is our experience that, again and again, there are such 'gifts' latent in every individual and group session, if only they can be perceived and used.

Finally, we look briefly at generic psychoanalytic aspects of the group, although both individual and group phenomena could be construed from a variety of dynamic perspectives. For example, a Kleinian, a Winnicottian, a Bionian, and a Foulkesian timbre could be discerned, exemplified, and developed, depending upon the theoretical persuasion and personal proclivity of the therapist. This does not invalidate the therapeutic potential of the Aeolian Mode. It is not difficult to see that 'snow in the heart' carries echoes of frozen introjects (see p. 69). Indeed, the thought that it is 'snowing inside' is only one step cooler than Klein's well-known discussion of a patient who knew that it was 'raining inside'. Winnicott's concern about the serious playfulness in a therapeutic group is clearly evident in the enjoyment of the cartoon. And a Bionian perspective is manifested in the experience of the group-as-a-whole, which is exemplified in the depiction of the almost snow-covered man-as-a-whole. Foulkes' injunction (1964) to 'trust the group' was present from the start of the session when *Up the Garden Path* was handed round.

That the group was trusted with painful material was implicit in the linking of laughter and loss, cold and care. Ironically, the group itself was cold enough for it to be cold *'outside as well'*. A haunting verse by Yeats 'Mad as the mist and snow' (from *The Winding Stair and Other Poems*, 1933 (1950)) makes its incantational presence felt here:

> 'Bolt and bar the shutter,
> For the foul winds blow:
> Our minds are at their best this night,
> And I seem to know
> That everything outside us is
> *Mad as the mist and snow*.' [our italics]

Madness and snow. Inside and outside.

Other echoes are activated by this vignette, such as the writings of Sechehaye on *Symbolic Realization* (1951) and *I Never Promised You a Rose Garden* (Green 1964; see p. 78). The latter is an accurate association when the link is made between psychosis, the rose garden, rose petals on the snow, and the epiphany of hope. Maybe a group session such as this stands a chance of moving 'Towards the door we never opened / Into the rose-garden' (*Burnt Norton I*, T. S. Eliot 1935).

There is another strangely apposite reference, with such detailed congruity that it feels like a slightly different version of an identical scenario. Snow has covered, or will cover, everything, and *The Three Sisters* opens and closes with memory and anticipation of snow. Chekhov gives these scene-setting early words to Olga:

'It's exactly a year ago that Father died, isn't it? This very day, the fifth of May – your saint's day, Irena. I remember it was very cold and it was snowing. I felt then as if I should never survive his death . . . but this is a cold place. It's cold here.'

The play ends when Irena (her head on Olga's breast) says:

'It's autumn now, winter will soon be here and the snow will cover everything . . .'

A Russian poet closes our consideration of this theme:

'The roses are in ecstasy for ever,
Knowing no snow.'
(Afanasy Fet (1820–92). See 1982)

Postscript

By an inexplicable coincidence, the very day when a group member had the cold option of deciding whether she should talk of her father's recent death, the last words spoken during the session were: 'It's snowing.' Thus the prevailingly present story was, through Chekhov, linked to the larger story; or, through the larger story, linked to Chekhov.

VIGNETTE 3.6 INDIVIDUAL THERAPY
'This horrible fear'

In this vignette we will give description and perspectival reflection concurrently.

A 33-year-old single policeman describes an escalating sense of fear. It started from one precise focus, then became generalized, finally crystallizing as an overwhelming, focal phobia. It was felt that behind his compliant, passive demeanour there was a build-up of explosive rage, though there was little overt clinical evidence to support this. During a therapeutic session, and apparently unconnected to any previous dynamic material, the patient suddenly said:

'I have a fear of everything, and *this* horrible fear.'

How lucidly this simple language suggests the engulfing power of his fear. There is a fear of everything. And fear of 'everything' is, by definition, all-inclusive. Yet, in addition to the fear of everything, he complains of '*this* horrible fear'. It is fear of a different dimension. And it is superimposed upon a comprehensive background of fear. In the ensuing active silence, which could have been contoured by a Shakespearean injunction, 'shape thou thy silence' (*Twelfth Night* I. 2, 61), the patient added almost gratu-itously:

'There was a house full of curtains.'

At this point the Aeolian Mode was activating the therapist's receptivity to the patient's disclosure. But this, as always, is in addition to the complex response which involves not only his cognitive–affective countertransfer-ence response, but also the simultaneous attempt to understand what the patient was saying. He tried to formulate this in psychodynamic terms in order to 'shape' his silence, until an appropriately shaped interpretive response crystallized. It has already been stressed that the Aeolian Mode allows the therapist to be actively receptive, without forcing premature closure on either the patient's disclosure or his own receptivity. In this instance, it was a phrase from Dylan Thomas which flashed into his mind. It was in fact a dual stimulus, partly because the opening line of the poem is 'It was my thirtieth year to heaven.' But the activating line which had been 'oscillating with something else' – where the something else was the patient's phrase 'a house full of curtains' – was the first line of the third stanza which refers to: 'A springful of larks'.

What has the phrase 'a house full of curtains' uttered by a phobic police-man to do with the phrase 'A springful of larks' uttered by a poet? It must be admitted that this was initially baffling. Mercifully, the therapist's bewilderment was only transient, because other lines from Dylan Thomas (1952) entered the arena: 'Do not go gentle into that good night, / Old age should burn and rave at close of day; / *Rage, rage against the dying of the light*' [our italics].

It was at this point that the Aeolian Mode clarified the psychodynamics, not only of the anger and depression, but also of the existential fear of diminishing relational possibility. There was rage against the dying of the light. The patient was angry because his father was dying. The phrase that actually came into the therapist's mind was not 'Do not go gentle', but 'rage against the dying'. The response he made to the patient was:

What light seems to be fading?'

'The day, I suppose. It's autumn. The days are shortening. Another year of my life is gone and where have I got to?'

Existential way-outlessness and despair were 'obvious', but they became shot through with an almost truculent vigour: 'This is how it is . . . I take it out on myself.' There was good clinical evidence of depression taking the form of anger turned against the self. And the rage against the dying of a close relative was almost inexpressible, as was the incipient anger as a trans-ference phenomenon expressed towards the therapist. The working through of this particular anger was the main dynamic substance of the ensuing sessions.

At first sight 'I have a fear of everything, and *this* horrible fear . . . there was a house full of curtains' seemed to be far removed from 'a springfull of larks', 'do not go gentle', and 'rage'. Yet, as the session proceeded, it became clear that this was the central issue. It could well be argued that any experienced therapist would have had no difficulty in reaching exactly the same conclusion. Indeed, the clinical presentation of depression as anger turned against itself is an axiomatic tenet of basic psychodynamic theory. Nevertheless, we suggest that the Aeolian Mode can offer the therapist an enhanced fine-tuning aid, in which he can bring an accurate response to the patient. This has a paradoxical effect which, initially, seems to be working in two directions at the same time. By this, we mean that the Aeolian Mode not only gives finer precision to the therapist's response and makes it more accurate; at the same time, it accelerates the responsiveness of the patient. The patient experiences this as 'the thing itself' and not a vague approximation to his cognitive–affective point of urgency. Yet it simultaneously allows him the freedom to explore his inner world without feeling restricted by the therapist's conceptual categories.

VIGNETTE 3.7 A FUGITIVE FROM FREEDOM:
A reversed vignette: *'How free is a fugitive?'*

In the following vignette we have reversed the usual order of presentation. We have taken soundings from the field of prepared echoes before describing the 'clinical' event which activated the associative process. In this way, we hope to illustrate how associations dominated by the syncretic style, represented by the right hemisphere, are linked with sequential, digital stimuli which are 'processed' by the left hemisphere.

A poem by Robert Frost (1955) entitled 'A Leaf Treader' has the following lines at the beginning of its final stanza:

'They spoke to the fugitive in my heart as if it were leaf to leaf.
They tapped at my eyelids and touched my lips with an invitation
    to grief.'

And at the end of a chapter in *David Copperfield*, Dickens writes:

'I was thinking of all that had been said. My mind was still running on some of the expressions used. . . . But we were at home; and the trodden leaves were lying under-foot, and the autumn wind was blowing.'

Whereas there is a misty sadness in the passage from Dickens, which also carries a subtle and pervasive sense of stormy foreboding, Robert Frost describes an anthropomorphic search for escape, which also conveys an element of welcome and invitation. There is an implicit tone of resignation and acceptance in 'A Leaf Treader' which is not implicit in the desolate dampness of Dickens.

Why have these passages been described? And why are they described now? As the therapist joined a weekly offender-therapy group the following question caught his ear: *How free is a fugitive?* It is scarcely surprising that the theme of escaping is recurrent in any custodial setting. The more precise topic of distinguishing between 'escaping from' and 'escaping to', makes its appearance in one form or another, in most sessions. But because of transference distortion, and temporal translocation, the need to escape from 'the prison' or any other secure setting soon merges with the need to escape from other places of confinement, such as the home or a restricting relationship. Often this leads back to the desperate attempt to escape from a confining relationship with an over-possessive or neglecting parent; or, in the last analysis, from the cosmos or God who has a restrictive, claustrophobia-inducing grip.

The reason for presenting the above quotations before the question 'How free is a fugitive?', which emerged within the group matrix, is to illustrate the way in which the metaphor implicit in both quotations allowed an expansion and deepening of the therapist's associative responses to the original question. The ensuing theme which developed in the group was not merely one of the pros and cons of 'escaping' from an institution. On the contrary, there was an almost immediate entry into the primal experiences of fear, separation, and death.

This is another example of a phenomenon which we have repeatedly discovered when working within the Aeolian Mode. As the session unfolded, the group members explored the meaning of 'invitation' and 'grief', 'come and join us . . . welcome . . . sorrow . . . extreme sadness, but sadness due to loss'. When the members were subsequently asked whether the theme of 'invitation' and 'grief' appeared to be changing the subject, it was not only felt to be non-intrusive, on the contrary, it seemed to be intensifying the activity of the original theme (escaping and fugitive existence). Furthermore, it actually increased the depth with which it was experienced and described. In group dynamic terms, there was an intensification of *koinonia* (cared-for 'belongingness') and an augmented sensitivity within the group matrix. And, as always, there were many surprising associations which followed this phase of the session. For example, one patient described with poignant accuracy the way in which he had been abandoned by his former friends once he had got 'on the wrong side of the law'. He did not say that he had forgotten his friends, but implied they had actively moved out of the range of his memory:

'My friends have absconded from my memory.'

If we now reverse the order of presentation in this section, it will be clear that the passages from Frost and Dickens were evoked by the first words which the therapist heard as he entered the room: 'How free is a fugitive?' These associations were simply those that rose up within the therapist's mind as he tried to understand what was taking place within the minds of the individual members of the group and the group-as-a-whole. There are obviously numerous other associative possibilities. As it transpired, he felt that the theme of blown leaves and a fugitive existence would most rapidly facilitate the group's engagement with primordial themes, themes which are universally evocative. At no point did he quote from the passages he had in mind, or even refer to them. But because they 'tapped at his eyelids and touched his lips' he was sure enough that there would be an echoing and deepening response from the group. And so there was.

This particular example uses metaphor from poetry and prose. There are many other images and modalities which might have been equally effective. For example, a dead leaf might have blown in through the window, had the group been conducted during the autumn when the theme would have needed no poetic induction by the therapist. We have already described (p. 42) how the process of poetic appropriation makes use of evident and clamant images which are forcefully present for all to see, hear, or smell.

When a window in the group room is opened to allow a trapped butterfly to escape and a wasp seizes the opportunity to fly in, it scarcely calls for immense sensitivity to metaphor to see how this might be relevant to a group. Especially one in which violence, invasions, pain, and death are so closely interwoven with beauty, transience, fragility, and poignance. The group matrix can hold together people and affects so that polarities are not opposed to each other but are experienced as complementary. A stable infrastructure permits turbulent encounters and the meeting of the precarious with the powerful. Virginia Woolf (1927) takes up this theme and leads us into the chapter on metaphor:

'Beautiful and bright it should be on the surface, feathery and evanescent, one colour melting into another like the colours on a butterfly's wing; but beneath the fabric must be clamped together with bolts of iron.'

4

Metaphor: where the meanings are

'I'm standing on the edge of my days.'
'He had an uphill struggle in the swimming pool!'
>   (from a radio commentary)
>> 'Let us start a fire
>> that will cremate those fences
>> along which we
>> skirt the edge of ourselves,
>> aliens, not lifting except in
>> dreams the latch of our breast.'
>> ('The Sign', by Erika Burkart,
>>   translated by
>>   Rosemary Combridge)

'I have Cancer of the Soul'.
>> 'Heavenly Hurt, it gives us –
>> We can find no scar,
>> But internal difference,
>> Where the Meanings, are –'
>>   (Emily Dickinson, 'There's a
>>   certain slant of light')

'There are colours other than black and white –
and I think I ought to see them.'
>   (A patient's reason for starting psychotherapy)

'Minnesota remained a
Mondale island in the Reagan sea.'
>   (Commentary on a presidential election)

'Metaphor is, at its simplest, a way of proceeding from the known to
the unknown.'
>   (Nisbet 1969)

'Detecting metaphors and understanding how they are distinguished from literal uses of language is one thing, and it is important; but knowing how to use metaphors without being used by them is another thing, and may be even more important.'

(Tait in *The Myth of Metaphor*, Turbayne 1962)

Because the words metaphor and transference carry different connotational loadings, especially for the psychotherapist, it is important to remember that they actually have identical meanings (Pedder 1979). Both mean to 'carry across'; from the Greek and Latin respectively. Culture and language are pervaded by metaphors, which are found in profusion in the expressive language of psychotherapy. Because the mutative potentiality of the metaphor is a central dynamic issue in the Aeolian Mode, an entire chapter is devoted to this important topic. Lakoff and Johnson (1980) have a well-chosen title when they describe *Metaphors We Live By*. We have already furnished numerous examples of the way in which the broad span of possible referents gives the metaphor such wide therapeutic scope. Thus, 'skating on thin ice' (p. 79) simultaneously furthered the therapeutic process in both an exploratory and a supportive direction.

Because an understanding of metaphor is both intrinsic to the conception of the Aeolian Mode and essential for its dynamic efficacy, we intend to look at it in depth from various angles which impinge directly upon its clinical relevance. Important though the passage at the head of this page from *The Myth of Metaphor* is in its own right, it acquires additional significance when it is translated to a clinical setting. The psychotic patient observed to be switching on an electric iron, following a discussion in which she said she wanted to understand her problems better and get herself 'ironed out'; the borderline arsonist who 'gets on with people like a house on fire', and the non-psychotic patient who described a neighbour as 'an abyss into which other people fall', all furnish evidence of the vital clinical need for the therapist to endeavour to understand what his patient is attempting to convey. 'Detecting metaphors and understanding how they are distinguished from literal uses of language' is, as Tait says, 'important'. When it is considered in a clinical context it is infinitely more so. The clinician is kept constantly on the alert as he tries to distinguish metaphor and simile from concrete, literal uses of language. This not only carries weight in terms of diagnosis and prognosis, but may actually be a matter of life and death in a strictly literal sense.

Nevertheless, as far as the Aeolian Mode is concerned, the second part of Tait's injunction (see p. 110) also carries great weight. At the centre of the Aeolian Mode is the mutative power of metaphor, and there is therefore an ever present risk that the therapist may be 'used by them' because he has inadvertently attempted to use a metaphor in the wrong way, in the wrong place, or at the wrong time.

So great is the graphic power of metaphor that the following example from *Richard III* (II. 2, 41) needs no elaboration. The question under discussion is why children thrive when their father, upon whom they have claimed to depend for their lives, has died? The chosen wording is a vivid carrier of still-life: 'Why grow the branches when the root is gone?' The capacity of metaphor to convey so much meaning in so few words is shown in a sentence from Emily Dickinson: 'The Sailor cannot see the North, but knows the Needle can.' It illustrates economy, condensation, and clarity, as well as being inferential and beckoning.

And, from a therapeutic session with an adolescent psychotic boy whose discussion of singing merged imperceptibly into a description of the onset of auditory hallucinations. In this instance, the description of secondary sex characteristics fused with metaphor which, in turn, ushered in concrete thinking:

> 'My voice broke . . . my voice broke away . . . then the voices started.'

THE NATURE OF METAPHOR

An entry in an encyclopaedia under Metaphor (Beardsley, in Edwards 1967) is as follows:

> 'Metaphor is a linguistic phenomenon of peculiar philosophical interest and importance because its use in various domains raises puzzling questions about the nature and image of language and knowledge. The study of metaphor in its aesthetic aspects belongs to rhetoric and poetics. . . . By common definition, and by etymology, a metaphor is a transfer of meaning, both in intention and extension. The metaphorical modifier acquires a special sense in its particular context . . . and it is applied to entities different from those it usually applies to, in any of its normal senses.'

After this definition Beardsley explains the need for a theory of metaphor.

> 'An adequate theory of metaphor must explain the two properties of metaphor that are generally acknowledged to be most fundamental. First, a metaphorical attribution differs from a literal one by virtue of a certain tension between the subject and the modifier: we are alerted by something special, odd, and startling in the combination. . . . Second, a metaphorical attribution is not merely an odd conjunction, for it is intelligible.'

He then describes four theories of metaphor, which space does not allow us to include, although the fourth is particularly appropriate to the Aeolian Mode.

'This theory, the Verbal-Opposition Theory, . . . rests upon (1) a distinction between two levels of meaning, and (2) the principle that metaphor involves essentially a logical conflict of central meanings. . . . In many common words and phrases, we can roughly distinguish two sorts of meaning: (1) the central meaning, or meanings – what is called *designation* or (in Mill's sense) connotation, and may be recorded in a dictionary as standard; and (2) the marginal meaning, consisting of those properties that the word suggests or connotes (in the literary critic's sense of this term).'

Our final quotation from the encyclopaedia is on the uses of metaphor:

'The above discussion gives some indication, however sketchy, of the important roles that metaphor may play in the development of language and in poetry. Its cognitive roles are primarily two. *First*, metaphor is a convenient, extraordinarily flexible and capacious device for extending the resources of language, by creating novel senses of words for particular purposes and occasions. . . . *Second*, metaphor is a condensed shorthand, by which a great many properties can be attributed to an object at once.' [our italics]

Here are three crystal-clear examples of metaphor, one from drama, one from therapeutic space, and one from fiction.

'Look! Here comes a walking fire.'
(*King Lear* III. 4, 111)

'My parents were a couple of walking islands.'

'There remained only those rare periods of amorousness which still came to them at times but which did not last. *These were islets at which they put in for a while only to embark again upon that ocean of concealed hostility.*' [our italics]

(*The Death of Ivan Ilyich*, Tolstoy)

Stanford (1936)[12], a leading authority on metaphor, writes:

'the finest type of metaphor transcends the explicitness of paraphrase. There is some quality in the greatest metaphors which distinguishes them entirely from simile. The difference between the two is very like that between prose and poetry. Simile, like prose, is analytic, metaphor, like poetry, is synthetic; simile is extensive, metaphor intensive;

simile is logical and judicious, metaphor illogical and dogmatic; simile reasons, metaphor apprehends by intuition . . . continue the antitheses and it will appear quite a fair analogy that simile is to metaphor as prose is to poetry. . . . Metaphor defies reason and yet prevails – an incarnation of the eternal *LOGOS*.'

Risky though it may be, we cannot withhold the comment that Stanford's comparison of the characteristics of simile and metaphor have cadential qualities similar to those of the different cerebral hemispheric functions described on pages 200ff. Stanford reminds us of Aristotle's reference to the 'gift of metaphor' and that 'good metaphor depends upon the *observation and contemplation* of similarities in things'. Aristotle confesses that he 'finds in metaphor pleasures [i.e. the sudden recognition and understanding of the hidden truth] which are not to be had from simile'. Stanford continues:

'*The essence of metaphor is that a word undergoes a change or extension of meaning*. In simile nothing of this kind occurs; every word has its normal meaning and no semantic transference is incurred. This is a fundamental difference in the verbal sphere.' [our italics]

Samuels (1985) discusses the overlap between metaphor and what Jung called symbol.

'For Jung, the crucial function of a symbol was to express in a unique way a psychological fact incapable of being grasped at once by consciousness. . . . Jung distinguished between his use of symbol and what he called "signs"; these connect things that are already known. For instance, the stylized bodies on the doors of public lavatories are signs. Jung's charge against psychoanalysis was that psychoanalytic symbol interpretation made signs of symbols and hence lost the possibility of understanding their fuller meaning. . . . (M)y opinion is that Jung made too rigid a divide here and that the problem for both psychoanalysis and analytical psychology is to avoid interpreting symbols by use of some kind of lexicon. . . . Metaphor sits midway between sign and symbol for one half of metaphor is known to consciousness.'

Turner (1974) notes that 'metaphor is, in fact, metamorphic, transformative'. And he quotes Nisbet (1969): 'Metaphor is our means of effecting instantaneous fusion of two separated realms of experience into one illuminating, iconic, encapsulating image'; and then adds: 'It is likely that scientists and artists both think primordially in such images; metaphor may be the form of what M. Polanyi calls "tacit knowledge".'

In our view, the activity of metaphor can also be looked at from a neuro-psychological perspective. And this has implications for the dynamic synergism between left and right hemispheres which mediates integration of imagery, emotion, and thinking. The poetic metaphor exerts its synthesizing effect by building a bridge between the ikonic mode of the right and the linguistic mode of the left hemisphere. Thus, it also enhances the exchange between unconscious and conscious realms. Thereby it helps in the establishment of genuine insight (Theilgaard 1984).[13]

It is not easy to know where to place our reference to the work of Romanyshyn (1982), whose book *Psychological Life: From Science to Metaphor* touches our theme at so many points. But his section on 'The Metaphorical Function of Psychological Life' must have mention here.

So much for this excursion into a variety of opinions on the nature of metaphor. But before we embark[14] upon a detailed discussion of the precise way in which the Aeolian Mode rests upon the mutative capacity of metaphor and creative imagery, reference must be made to other aspects of metaphor which are cognate and cannot be ignored.

'Embarkation' is not quite a faded metaphor, that is, one which has almost lost its original meaning so that we scarcely think of it as a metaphor. Nevertheless, it serves to introduce us to the work of Abse (1971), *Speech and Reason: Language Disorder in Mental Disease*, in which he discusses not only the place of faded metaphor but also of cryptophor. The very thought of the 'carrier of hidden meaning', which is a definition of 'cryptophor', takes us at once into the centre of the field of dynamic psychotherapy, and we are on familiar ground. We attempt to make the unconscious conscious, and to gradually facilitate disclosure of hidden meaning.

Metaphor has also been studied from a psychoanalytic point of view by Rogers (1978) among others but, as Bollas (1980) wrote:

> 'It would be interesting to try to understand the logic of metaphor in object relational terms; in particular such a study might help us to understand how each metaphor is a transference in both the classic Aristotelian sense and in the Freudian manner.'

These words occur in a review of Rogers' book which has much to say about poetic imagery. However, this is with reference to the written word and does not have the connotation of *poiesis* which is central to the Aeolian Mode.

It is Lacan (1977), linking the process of signification, metaphor, and metonymy (see p. 120) with primary process phenomena, who best conveys the 'spark' and 'creative flash' of *poiesis* within the aesthetic imperative.

> 'The creative spark of the metaphor does not spring from the presentation of two images, that is, of two signifiers equally actualized.

It flashes between two signifiers one of which has taken the place of the other in the signifying chain, the occulted signifier remaining present through its (metonymic) connexion with the rest of the chain. . . . The double-triggered mechanism of metaphor is the very mechanism by which the symptom, in the analytic sense, is determined. Between the enigmatic signifier of the sexual trauma and the term that is substituted for it in an actual signifying chain there passes the spark that fixes in a symptom the signification inaccessible to the conscious subject in which that symptom may be resolved — a symptom being a metaphor in which flesh or function is taken as a signifying element.'

Brockbank (1971) points to the way in which the poet uses metaphor as a way of expressing the inexpressible. For our purposes, this is often a focal feature of the aesthetic imperative. Brockbank writes: 'What cannot be held by dogma or reached by systematic thought may be intimated to the experience of our affections through the ''fine frenzy'' of metaphor and rhythm.'

Both Wilshire (1982), who refers to being 'in the grip of the metaphor', and Turbayne (1962), who asks 'How do we avoid being victimised by metaphor so that instead of being used by it we use it?', remind us that metaphor can have a binding, restricting quality. This, too, is of importance to its application in therapeutic space. We discuss the predicament of being trapped in the metaphor in a subsequent section (pp. 110ff). Turbayne remarks that 'it is also an achievement to ''undress'' a hidden metaphor that has become part of the traditional way of allocating the facts, for this too involves breaking old associations'. We find one extended sentence of his difficult to resist. Here it is:

'We know at once that an airplane disaster may have been due to metal fatigue although the metal did not grow weary; that famine, sword, and fire may crouch for unemployment without stooping; that sleep, which knits up the ravelled sleeve of care, achieves this without the help of knitting needles; that we can be tickled by the rub of love without giggling; and that death shall have no dominion without losing a throne.'

As we start to engage with clinical aspects of metaphor, and we look again at Stanford's book (1936), we are surprised how often we have written in the margin some reference to the concrete thinking of the psychotic. Any therapist who has spent extended time in the company of the psychotic will know how frequently there is the mingling of the concrete and the abstract, the metaphorical and the literal. This, though initially baffling, has an invitational 'stretching' quality. When the therapist has been able to embrace the patient's perspectival world, as well as retaining his perceptual autonomy, the patient usually senses this and 'invites the therapist into his inner world' (Cox 1978; 1982a).

In his discussion of Aristotle's original example, the metaphor of calling a brave man a lion, Stanford refers to the necessity of looking for 'a psychological explanation . . . from the point of view of the speaker and the hearer. In the hearer's case the essential thing is *preparation*; we must understand from the context something of what is in the speaker's mind.' We have now reached the heart of the matter. Dynamic psychotherapy depends upon attempts to 'understand from the context [of both inner and outer world phenomena] something of what is in the speaker's mind'. A clinical vignette illustrates this point. A psychotic girl had explained that, of all living things, she felt closest to her toothless dog. She told the group that if she gave him one of his favourite chocolate biscuits, he would dance round in a circle on his hind legs.

'And when he had danced round once, he would dance round again . . . *because one good turn deserves another.*'

We leave the reader exploring the numerous possible connotations of this remarkable athletic achievement! It was only when the multiple implications of the phrase 'one good turn deserves another' had been grasped, that the patient felt that she had been understood. We suspect that the other psychotic patients had probably 'got there first'. But they would not have understood the wider implications of the patient's story; such as her prevailing presentation, defence organization, or the existential significance of why a toothless, biscuit-eating, dancing dog should have brought more joy to a girl than any yet experienced human endeavours.

This links with other things that Wilshire (1982) has said about metaphor in his discussion on 'Theatre as Metaphor and Play as Disclosure':

'characters enacted onstage are not verbal but physiognomic metaphors; we *see* and *feel* them to be like ourselves. . . . *The whole point of art is to put us in touch with things that are too far or too close for us to see in our ordinary offstage* life.' [our italics]

Our subsequent discussion of the precise place of metaphor in the Aeolian Mode comes under the heading of Wilshire's important words.

MUTATIVE CAPACITY OF METAPHOR

'To put us in touch with things that are too far off or too close for us to see in . . . ordinary . . . life.' These words of Wilshire's have elective affinity with Dunne's observations on The Alienated Man (1967). 'Where there is nothing and no one to stand between man and God, nothing and no one to unite man to God or to separate him from God, man is at once too close to God and too far from God.' Gertrude Patterson (1971) writes 'language must not come too close to the particular' before quoting T. S. Eliot: 'If you do not come too close, if you do not come too close, / On a summer midnight, you can hear the music' (*East Coker I*, T. S. Eliot 1940).

Set as it is between a series of vignettes which are rigorously clinical (chapter 3) and a study of 'the listening landscape' (chapter 5) which is indubitably metaphorical, this chapter on metaphor, 'where the meanings are', occupies a crucial position. In particular, this section on the mutative capacity of metaphor is the fulcrum upon which the Aeolian Mode rests. Both in significance and in location *mutative metaphors in psychotherapy* lie at the axis of our presentation.

We have given many examples of the way in which metaphor can serve as a container for feelings which are too overwhelming to be tolerated. We have also shown how it can prove to be a vehicle for carrying, mobilizing, expressing, and integrating affect and cognition in furthering the therapeutic process. Metaphor exerts its mutative effect by energizing alternative perspectival aspects of experience. This means that material which the patient has endeavoured to relinquish, avoid, or deny so that it is 'safely' classified, categorized, and 'filed away', appears again in the 'pending action' file. And this inevitably has a startling effect upon the patient. This may take the form of 'surprised relief' because the presumed intolerable was found to be acceptable. On the other hand, the discovery that there is still fire in affect embers can indicate that material, previously regarded as 'de-fused' and safe, has once again become disconcertingly insistent. For example, Ken, a 39-year-old teacher, describes how his mother always held up a much respected uncle as the ideal model of a successful man who was 'a credit to the family'. Ken was mildly dismissive of this approbation, unaware how much violent resentment he had harboured towards his mother as she sang his uncle's praises. David, another group member of about the same age, spoke of his associations after listening to what Ken was saying and making certain that he had nothing more to say:

'I held up my mother and swore at her, before I dropped her over the balcony.'

In one instance there was the metaphorical *holding up* of an ideal, whereas it was concretized in the *holding up* of a body, prior to the letting-go. Not surprisingly, the subsequent 'holding up' was at the moment of arrest.

This example shows the mutative capacity of metaphor, through which a patient realized how much suppressed anger and repressed resentment was present, through the associative linking of other aspects of *holding up*, prior to a fatal dropping.

There is a close connection between metaphorical mobility of significance and, in this instance, the presumption of concrete attribution. The therapist's interventions may make a mutative impact through the use of metaphor (recalling 'the gold medal for skating on thin ice' vignette) and this may be equally applicable to individual or group psychotherapy. Nevertheless, in the latter there is inevitably more scope for 'spontaneous' mutative associations which originate and operate within the group itself.

Core psychotherapeutic emphases converge at this point. We refer to the dynamic which is expressed in many different ways, although, ultimately, one key concept is being presented and elaborated. The patient is put in touch with things that are 'too far or too close' and this, in Malan's terms (1979), is to be put 'in touch with as much of his true feelings as he can bear'. Expressing the same thought in different words, Thompson and Kahn (1970) say 'As his endurance increases, so [the patient] is given more to endure.'

Some of the most delicate moments in psychotherapy arise when the therapist responds to a patient's initiative which is already 'deep' by taking it to an even deeper level through the use of metaphor. If such an intervention has been correctly judged then the metaphor will be mutative. If not, the patient will not make the connection. And defences prevail. Such an example arose when a man who had killed a child was embarking upon a generic 'discussion' about nature and nurture. He said:

'For example, take two children, two babies. One of whom is destined to become a neurosurgeon and the other a drug addict.'

　'or take *one* baby?'

It called for clinical discernment and 'a favourable wind' to detect whether this confrontation was too much – 'too close' for the patient to deal with. What had started out to be a discussion on life chances for two babies 'take two children' was mutated by metaphorical reflection so that 'take' meaning 'consider' became 'take' meaning 'remove'.

At heart, psychotherapy often has this quality of sailing as close to the wind as possible, so that there is the ever present risk of finding that movement ceases and progress is blocked. On the other hand, experience in the use of Aeolian initiatives, particularly in the form of the mutative metaphor, can give the therapist increasing confidence in discerning when the patient can tolerate the mutation through which 'take' (consider) becomes 'take' (remove).

Deep religious and philosophical issues may also be too far or too close, as Dunne's quotation at the head of this section implies. For this reason, metaphor has been the prime means of expressing the inexpressible since the days of antiquity. Like all good metaphors the quotation from *The Sign* by Burkart (p. 91) 'speaks for itself'. It is at once evident what the metaphorical significance of starting a fire, cremating fences, and skirting the edge of ourselves is about. It has much of the immediacy of experience disclosed within therapeutic space because the patient is often trying to describe incidents in his life which, in one sense, defy description. He is therefore bound to use words from another frame of reference which can be imported and given a richly new connotational significance. It is hard to imagine a better example than that implicit in the unusual imagery of this poem which reminds us that 'we skirt the edge of ourselves'. In some ways much of the time spent in therapeutic space consists in repetitive attempts to overcome defences which ensure that we only 'skirt the edge of ourselves', thus avoiding our central-ity. Fire is indeed one of the regular standbys for those who write about metaphor, and Abse (1971) develops the theme in this way:

'When a precise word is so far lacking to designate a novelty, another word is used. This word usually already denotes something else. A word symbol, already a symbol for a thing, a process, or a relation, is used for this new purpose, on the basis of some suggested analogy. The context makes it clear that the word is not referring to the first thing, process or relation, that this is not literally denoted; hence the word must mean something else. For example, one might say of a fire: "It flares up." One might say too: "His anger flared up." In the second use of the word *flare* we know that this does not refer to the physical flame but connotes the idea of "flaring up" as a symbol for what his anger is doing.'

Whereas Susanne Langer (1942) says 'The expression "to flare up" has acquired a wider meaning that its original use, to describe the behaviour of a flame; it can be used metaphorically to describe whatever its meaning can symbolise.' In *Speech and Reason* Abse also refers to the work of Wegener (a translation of whose *The Life of Speech* is published in the same volume with Abse's contribution on *Language Disorder in Mental Disease*) who developed the concept of the faded metaphor. Langer continues:

'[Wegener] shows that all general words are probably derived from specific appellations, by metaphorical use; so that our literal language is a very repository of "faded metaphors". Thus a man declining an invitation to dinner on the grounds that he is "tied up", implies that he has a prior engagement, not that ropes have secured him to a chair. Or again, a woman "with no axe to grind" does not imply that she has left her weapon at home.'

The numerous connotations of various aspects of fire and flame in relation to warmth and love throw light upon the faded metaphor. Indeed, the fire of love is so inherent in everyday language that it has almost lost its original meaning. It is for this reason that Burkart's injunction to 'cremate' rather than burn 'the fences along which we skirt the edge of ourselves' manages to convey the vigorous power of destruction which can lead to liberation. The faded metaphor of burning no longer conveys this proclivity to conflagration and immolation. The degree to which a metaphor has faded is obviously context-dependent. Thus the phrase 'I want to get my storm together' is a faded metaphor in the US, whereas it is not in England. On the contrary, a worn-out metaphor may come to life again, because of fresh dynamic relevance. For example, an 18-year-old bulimic girl said 'I could have eaten my parents' when they returned home earlier than expected, thus disturbing her bingeing orgy. She ended her story by saying: 'They stick in my throat.'

Although Abse's emphasis was 'This word *usually* already denotes something else' [our italics], Stanford (1936) points out: '[Metaphor] cannot exist until some meanings of words are already stereotyped. *Where there is no current sense of the word there can be no metaphor*' [our italics]. The essence of the meaning of metaphor implies 'the sense of *transference, the process of transferring a word from one object of reference to another*' [Stanford's italics].

When a patient wishes to describe his deepest experience for which there is no adequate descriptive vocabulary he must opt for metaphor, neologism, or a non-descriptive but accurate location of his intensity of feeling in some such phrase as that employed by King Lear: 'The thing itself' (III. 4, 104).

Even a symptom can have the characteristic of a metaphor; for example a political refugee, who had endured torture, denies that the experience had any lasting psychological sequelae. He maintained that the only residual symptom was a pain in his Achilles tendon, for which he received physiotherapy. He was unable to see the metaphorical connection between his emotional vulnerability and his Achilles heel. Previous torture was both 'too far' and 'too close' for him to see in his 'ordinary life' as a displaced person (see p. 214).

If he opts for metaphor he must assume that those with whom he shares therapeutic space are able to follow him, making the same jump of recognition from one frame of reference to another. If he opts for a neologism, he may be dismissed as having his own private language so that communication with others is impossible. Or the neologism may itself be perceived as a metacommunication conveying that he is, in fact, 'disturbed'; to the point of showing the clinical phenomenon of thought disorder. In their study of the discourse of schizophrenic speakers, *Crazy Talk*, Rochester and Martin (1979) write:

'To say that a speaker is incoherent is only to say that one cannot understand the speaker. So to make a statement about incoherent discourse is really to make a statement about one's own confusion as a listener. It is therefore just as appropriate to study what it is about the listener which makes him or her "confusable" as it is to study what it is about the speaker which makes him or her "confusing".'

They also say that '"talk failures" are inferences based on the *listener's* experience of confusion'. Listening and talking are two sides of an inter-actional exchange and confusion may be primary on either side. See *On Learning from the Patient* (Casement 1985).

The invitation which the psychotic offers the therapist may be solely metaphorical; it may also be concrete. We can recall an incident in which the patient not only invited us into his experience, but also invited us into his room to sit down on a non-existent chair! This sense of being welcomed by a schizophrenic generated a sense of responsive warmth (another metaphor; fading, though still 'alive') because we were aware that there could be no ulterior motive from a patient with such a fragile hold on reality. Such a personal encounter was facilitated by an awareness of being within the Aeolian Mode and responding to the patient's silence, albeit by silent physical movement.

One of the risks of writing this book is that it gives the impression of being too 'verbal'. But many of the associative cycles of affirmation which continue to move, until there is a sense of exact fit and empathic precision, are silent reflections which take place in the therapist's mind through associative reverie.

The psychotherapy of the psychoses is a vast subject in its own right. And the scope of the Aeolian Mode with such patients could almost justify a volume on its own; indeed the first published reference (Cox 1982a) described the scope of the 'associative mode' as a way of attempting to reach the schizophrenic offender-patient.

The place of metaphor in group psychotherapy is another large theme which calls for extended consideration. A good starting point would be Powell's study (1982) of a group-analytic perspective on metaphor.

The psychotherapist and the student of literature each feels that he is on home ground when discussing metaphor. Lacan (1977) has written extensively about the relationship between metaphor and symptom. Wright (1976) in a paper entitled 'Metaphor and Symptom: a Study of Integration and Its Failure', goes beyond the usual psychoanalytic approach exemplified in the writings of Arlow (1969). Thus Arlow tells us: 'Metaphor constitutes an outcropping into conscious expression of a fragment of an unconscious fantasy'; whereas Wright develops the idea that 'while *symptoms* reveal much about the *defensive* operations of the ego . . . *metaphor* reveals the ego in its *creative* operations and is a structure in whose formation the ego has fully participated'. He gives examples which elaborate and develop this theme. Having stated that 'The undoing of a symptom is in part the creation of a *metaphor* from symptom', he echoes Freud's well-known phrase 'Where id was there ego shall be.' In a sentence which is difficult to forget, Wright says 'Where symptom was there metaphor shall be.' Writing this page we (M.C.) cannot help recalling that the initial impetus to write *Compromise with Chaos* (1978) came when a patient in a therapeutic group said to another group member 'As long as you go on hiding behind your symptoms, you are nowhere near my chaos.' Towards the end of his paper Wright comments '[The analyst] takes over the facilitating function of the parent in its dual aspect and protects a developmental space against its premature closure.' Thinking of the close association between the therapeutic task and literary resources it is interesting to return to the phrase of Clemen's (1951): 'Shakespeare must bring in the image without making more words of it. "Shakespeare smuggles in the images" we might say of many passages of the tragedies in which the image is only touched upon and hinted at.' Used in this context, the word 'smuggles' is of course itself metaphorical. And Wright says that 'regressive forms have been smuggled into the ego'.

Stanford (1936) observes: 'It cannot even be conceded that metaphor is a *type* of word at all; it is a treatment of an already existing type. Current words, strange words, ornamental, coined, lengthened, curtailed, rearranged words, may each and all be metaphors when duly treated in their context. Metaphor is something above these types.' And as just quoted (p. 102), it 'cannot exist until some meanings of words are already stereotyped. Where there is no current sense of the word there can be no metaphor.'

Another book which is not primarily about psychotherapy, but which reverberates with the interplay of the cognitive–affective qualities of therapeutic space, is *This Great Stage* (Heilman 1963). This is a study of 'image and structure in *King Lear*'. It abounds in detailed analysis of patterns of imagery and modes of meaning. The power of imagery to 'push us on to another meaning' is illustrated by many examples. Referring to Brooks (1947) he comments: 'The key words which are repeated in various passages in a play have a reference not only to each passage but also to "larger meanings" that are integral parts of the whole meaning of the play.'

Ezra Pound (1934) defined 'great literature' as 'simply language charged with meaning to the utmost possible degree'. And the charge of affective meaning is the currency of exchange in therapeutic space.

One of the effects of working within the Aeolian Mode is the realization of the ways in which 'key words', used repeatedly during the process of psychotherapy, have a reference not only to each session but also to 'larger meanings' which are 'integral parts of the whole meaning' of the therapeutic process. And Ricoeur (1977) refers to the 'split reference' of metaphor to truth and fiction which, in turn, links key words to larger meanings and the clinical story to the larger story.

METAPHOR AS THERAPEUTIC RESOURCE

A patient arrives late for a group session:

> 'Sorry I'm late. I've been to the dentist. He's going to take my crown off.'

> 'How many crowns have you had?'

> 'Are you talking about teeth?'

> 'I'm talking about crowns.'

At the therapist's disposal is an entire cosmos of metaphors and images which are potentially mutative. He must not thrust his own preformed imagery upon a patient who is cautiously seeking to express the inexpressible. This is spurious, and entirely contrary to the interests of the Aeolian Mode. But neither must he withhold *poiesis* if a patient is searching for that which needs to be called into being through poetic induction. This is a threshold phenomenon of the greatest finesse. An image may be floated towards the patient to be 'bodied forth'; but only in the right dynamic location and at the right time. Discerning the optimal time for an intervention is something which may improve with experience. But the therapist is always likely to feel that his interventions could have been better located and more felicitously timed. Energy spent in discerning the moment of *kairos* is never wasted. It is *the* moment in which to speak or to be silent. Furthermore, if it is genuinely kairotic, the patient will also be aware that it is *the* moment, and he will look no further for the thing itself.

Metaphor is particularly suitable for conveying pre-conceptual experience, especially that related to the body. For example, in patients with psychosomatic disturbances the metaphor can facilitate the transformation of kinaesthetic experience to other representational systems. And this aspect of metaphors takes us back to the early pages of this book (p. 9) and Hobson's detailed exploration (1985) of the significance of metaphors through which the body 'speaks'.

It is not surprising that, in addition to being a therapeutic resource, metaphor is also a *supervisory resource*. Indeed, Anne Alonso, in her timely study of *The Quiet Profession: Supervisors of Psychotherapy* (1985), lists 'developing the capacity to work in the metaphor of the transference' as one of the 'supervisory functions'.

We now move further into the study of metaphor which is relevant to our purposes. Before doing so, we recall that, although Shakespeare sometimes 'smuggles in the images', at other times he does the exact opposite. Sometimes his images forcefully and overtly invade our territory and occupy our attention. Such powerful metaphors are almost overwhelming and could be legitimately described as militant metaphors.

> 'There may be in the cup
> A spider steep'd, and one may drink, depart,
> And yet partake no venom (for his knowledge
> Is not infected); but if one present
> Th' abhorr'd ingredient to his eye, make known
> How he hath drunk, he cracks his gorge, his sides,
> With violent hefts. I have drunk, and seen the spider.'
>
> (*A Winter's Tale* II. 1, 39)

This passage illustrates Melville's words about Shakespeare: 'those deep faraway things in him; those occasional flashings forth of the intuitive Truth in him; those short, quick probings at the very axis of reality; – these are the things that make Shakespeare, Shakespeare' (Sedgwick 1944). There are the links between metaphor's therapeutic capacity and its inevitable involvement in religious language. Both require a cognitive–affective 'carrier'. Janet Soskice (1985) refers to 'chronicles of experience, armouries of metaphor, and purveyors of an interpretive tradition' – a sequence which invites integration of intrapsychic and transcendental phenomena.

FADED METAPHOR AND CRYPTOPHOR

A clear distinction needs to be made between the faded metaphor and cryptophor. We have already referred to Wegener's original description of the concept of the faded metaphor and Langer's subsequent elaboration (pp. 101–2). The faded metaphor is easy to understand. Our day-to-day language is loaded with faded metaphors; by way of example, we have already illustrated our intention of 'embarking' on a discussion of metaphor as we stand upon the *terra firma* of our city offices. We need to be reminded of the existence of faded metaphor before we approach the topic of cryptophor, which is of significance in all those psychotherapeutic approaches concerned with 'uncovering' buried meaning and feeling.

We have noted that the word 'metaphor' comes from Greek and means 'to carry across', whereas 'cryptophor' means 'to carry (hidden) meaning'. The faded metaphor is perceived as pertaining to the field itself, rather than being 'imported' to convey a fresh meaning.

It is essential for the therapist to understand the many faces of metaphor if he is to work effectively. But the call for the fullest possible awareness of the potential place of cryptophor in therapeutic space is even more important. There are many senses in which hidden meaning may be carried both by non-verbal means ('his eyes were crammed with all his life') and in the many hints and glimpses of potential significance which lie 'at the edge' of direct verbal disclosures. In his discussion of language in schizophrenia, Abse (1971) writes:

'When the ratio of primary to secondary process is high, symbolism takes the form we have designated as cryptoforic, based on its usual exhibition in dreaming consciousness and the need, from the viewpoint of ordinary waking consciousness, for its decipherment. . . . Cryptoforic symbolism depends on "thing-identity", with later one thing being repressively detached from the other and achieving conscious representation only through the recapture of some of the original interest in what is expressed. So the visual symbolic elements of dream (e.g. snake, jewels, caves) have lost one pole of reference in the waking consciousness but retain considerable affective importance.'

Although it sounds esoteric and detached from mainstream psychotherapeutic practice, the 'decipherment' of cryptophoric material is in fact a central task which confronts the therapist. And when the patient is psychotic, such cryptophoric statements of experience often have a concrete symbolic embodiment. Thus, when a psychotic patient asks

'What did the old oak tree say to the watercress?'

there is an immediate awareness that, far from being a light-hearted diversion from the serious purpose of the therapeutic group in which it was uttered, it carries an investiture of almost solemn and overwhelming significance for the patient who asked it. Indeed, the answer which the questioner himself provided spoke of the proximity of universal death for both the strong and the weak, the old and the young. His answer to his own question was

'I'll bend down and crush you . . . Then we'll both be dead.'

Many dreams have cryptophoric symbolic significance. And unless they can be satisfactorily deciphered, the patient who has cautiously disclosed such personal details may continue to feel fear because he is bewildered by his own experience.

Dynamic psychotherapy offers the patient alternative frames of reference in which to see his predicament and to explore his feelings. Modification of the conceptual field can actually change what the patient experiences.

To take a simple and previously quoted example (in Cox 1978), one group member complaining about the awful countryside through which the Thames flowed, provoked the reply 'yes, but think of all the history it flows through'. This made the 'geographical environmentalist' almost catch her breath, because it was clear that she had not considered the long context of time through which the river flowed. There were many cryptophoric aspects of her own experience buried in this discussion about the river which needed to be deciphered. One of the questions which inevitably arises in connection with rivers, estuaries, and the open sea is related to the fear of the loss of individual identity and almost 'drowning' in the ocean; compared with the opportunity of joining a larger life and relinquishing earlier feelings of being cut off from the 'mainstream of life' (it seems impossible to avoid metaphor when writing about metaphor!). This illustrates the point that when the metaphor has become so deeply embedded in our culture that we fail to notice it, it has indeed faded.

Numerous interspersed examples of metaphoric statements have already been given. Here they cluster together:

'She is an abyss into which other people fall.'
'I love gnawing on pain.'
'I want to put my storm together.'
'The antiques are going begging.'
'I heard tip-toe talking.'
'I'm standing on a deeper razor-edge.'

This last has a double connotation. There is the sense of precariously balancing on a razor edge; but the balance is of something 'deeper' in life than a fence. There is also the decisively incisional aspect; with all the implications that 'cutting' carries.

In *The Emerging Goddess* (1979), Rothenberg's study of 'the creative process in art, science, and other fields', we read: 'On the basis of clinical evidence, linguistic metaphors invariably have unconscious significance and it is reasonable to assume that other types of metaphors also have an unconscious significance in art. Metaphors represent and embody obliterated boundaries and they thereby evoke the boundaryless unconscious world.' This leads us to the significance of metaphors other than linguistic metaphors. Creative arts and the many forms of expressive therapy may all use non-linguistic metaphors which still, true to their etymological origins, 'carry [meaning] across'. And, as far as therapy is concerned, the deeper the psychopathology, where experience is beyond the containing capacity of language, the more are non-linguistic metaphors in the ascendant. For obvious reasons this is most clearly seen at the psychotic end of the dynamic spectrum. We have noted the way in which touch and movement often reach the isolated schizophrenic who is 'out of touch' with others at a verbal level but can speak to them through gesture and posture. Even the very act of describing this complex interaction employs a double metaphor!

Finally, it must be noted that the widespread use of metaphor in the 'personal' language of psychotherapy is related to, but cardinally distinct from, its particular place within the Aeolian Mode. Here the metaphor is mutative and actively catalyses dynamic change, rather than describing changes that have already taken place. Thus the words of the Duchess in *Richard II*, though metaphorical, are not dynamically mutative even though they attempt to induce speech: 'Thine eye begins to speak, . . . / Set thy tongue there' (*Richard II* V. 3, 124).

Similarly, the previously cited example (p. 94) 'My parents were a couple of walking islands' is not mutative *per se*, because it was not followed up. Had the question 'What kind of sea were they in?' followed, it might have become so. Otherwise it remains a powerful description. But no more than that.

Having reviewed the literature on the depth and timing of interpretation, Hammer (1968) continues:

> 'In terms of depth there is more or less agreement that the surface of the unconscious is the level to be sought. One communicates to the patient what the patient is *almost* ready to see for himself, that which is just outside awareness. . . . Thus, by drawing the near, but unseen, closer to its ultimate elucidation, we put within the patient's grasp that which is just beyond it.'

We are at the point of apparent paradoxical collision here. Hammer, representing a classical psychoanalytic approach, refers to interpretation and 'the surface of the unconscious . . . what the patient is *almost* ready to see for himself', so that he can 'grasp that which is *just* beyond it'. The use of metaphor within the Aeolian Mode as a mutative agent, through the processes of poetic appropriation and poetic induction, seems to have the capacity to 'touch the depths before the surface is stirred'. Its efficacy, clinically evident on so many occasions, has something to do with the patient being reached from *within*, rather than entered from without. Elsewhere Hammer (1978) has said that 'metaphors are first cousin to images'. And this comment takes us back to Bachelard (op. cit.) and anticipates chapter 5.

METAPHOR AS TRAP: METAPHOR AS HIDING-PLACE

Both the therapist and the patient share the risks of being trapped by a metaphor, but they can also remain hidden and use the metaphor as a protective screening device. We have chosen to give an example of a therapist's analytic perspectival world which carries the risk of being entrapped, followed by a micro-vignette of a patient who used the metaphor as a safe hiding-place.

The therapist 'trapped' in the metaphor

Because of metaphor's potential for versatility the therapist runs the risk of being trapped by it. For example, when an analytically orientated therapist hears a man describing a fantasy in which he has a long, thin key which will not stay sufficiently stiff for him to insert it into the lock to which it belongs, it is almost impossible not to think of metaphorical significance and the psychosexual dynamics of impotence. It requires a shift in the therapist's thinking to accept the fact that the patient is within a secure institution, is planning an escape, and is actually describing a key that had been manufactured in insufficiently solid material. Likewise, when a promiscuous young woman refers to something which 'goes stiff when you hold it in a certain way', it calls for perceptual revision to discover that she is describing a wooden, segmented, imitation snake. A phallic symbol it may be. But she *was* describing a snake, whatever other implications there may have been. To quote Rothenberg (1979) again: 'Metaphors represent and embody obliterated boundaries and they thereby invoke the boundaryless unconscious world.'

Particular finesse is required of the therapist when many of the words used by the patient, and by psychoanalytic and forensic colleagues, have different yet closely interrelated meanings. We are referring to such words as 'boundary', 'identity', 'holding', 'association', and 'security'. From each perspective there is an accepted literal connotation and a metaphorical one. Thus, for the therapist, security may refer to satisfactory early emotional bonding which leads to endopsychic stability, whereas to the forensic expert it carries connotations of secure perimeters, high walls, and searchlights. Yet both are important in offender-therapy (Cox 1986). Indeed, metaphor is so central in the psychoanalytic world that it is easy to forget that even the language of 'defence' is a metaphor Freud chose to use. We wonder how things would have changed if, instead of the military metaphor, Freud had used, for example, the metaphor of music in terms of discord, resolution, harmony, counterpoint, and so on.

There are dangers in working dynamically within the metaphor. A patient expresses this lucidly: 'I get carried away on metaphors. The

110

metaphor then begins to take control. Then you become obsessed with the image. The metaphors and images become the things themselves.'

Barker (1985) in *Using Metaphors in Psychotherapy* refers to Lankton and Lankton's (1983) concept of 'multiple embedded metaphors'. This is an appropriate place to mention the possibility of being embedded in a metaphor, because 'embedded' could imply either being trapped or hiding.

Susan Sontag (1978) makes the important point that illness is not a metaphor. In *Illness as Metaphor* she criticizes the description of social events as 'cancers' in society, or the attitude which equates tuberculosis with death. And there is much truth in these strictures. We are aware of the metaphorical weight that AIDS currently carries. Nevertheless, the situation is reversed if we consider *metaphor as illness*, and it can be just this if the patient is trapped by metaphor; *in extremis*, psychotic confusion of the concrete and the metaphorical can have disastrous consequences. And the clinician whose task is is to distinguish a concrete from a metaphorical statement has an awesome responsibility in relation to the patient and the society within which he lives. Awesome, because they call for radically different trajectories of management. Consider a man who 'kills' a rival with a savage book review, and one who 'kills' a rival with a knife.[15]

The patient 'hiding' in the metaphor

That a patient can 'hide' in a metaphor means that it can have a supportive, containing function, because he can 'say' how he feels, or what he did, without 'really saying' it. And this is one of the cardinal psychoanalytic objections to the use of metaphor, unless it is truly mutative, confrontational, and insight inducing. Thus, an aggressive psychopath may say: 'I knew the fuse had been lit, my finger was on the trigger of my aggression, the time had come to face the music, the chips were down, I could contain it no more . . . so I blew my top. I sent him flying into the middle of next week and I certainly pulled him down a peg or two . . . I can tell you.'

Whereas such a circuitous course of pseudo-disclosure is relatively easy for a therapist to confront in individual therapy, such a string of avoidance metaphors can prove provocative and almost intolerable in a therapeutic group. In one group session, a patient who had hitherto been protected by a seemingly endless stream of metaphorical disclosures about a series of violent episodes culminating in his arrest, so incensed a usually placid schizophrenic that he was finally confronted in unambiguously direct terms: 'I don't understand all these images . . . *I* killed a 68-year-old man . . . What did *you* do?' The questioner subsequently offered this acute observation: 'You used an analogy to make things more complicated than they need to be, as a protection.'

111

After a confrontation of this calibre, even the most sophisticated meta-phoric camouflage makes further psychopathic manoeuvring impossible. The direct question: 'What did *you* do?' following the statement '*I* killed a 68-year-old man' makes a direct and simple answer mandatory. Anything else is manifestly an avoidance. In this instance, the very fact that the patient had originally been protected by the elaborate camouflage of meta-phoric avoidance ultimately made him more vulnerable, so that the chal-lenges from the other members of the group were like guided missiles. Thus the patient who tried to hide within the metaphor was eventually trapped in his own trap. On many occasions, however, the metaphor offers a haven, an asylum for those whose experience is too sharp to disclose – yet too painful to contain. Emily Dickinson describes the protective disguise of poetic obliquity in this way:

'Tell all the Truth but tell it slant –
Success in Circuit lies'

Cynthia Chaliff (1973) observes: 'Her technique is to render the essence of a feeling, the pattern which all manifestations of it will follow, whatever the cause.' And this carries numerous Aeolian implications. The following fragment from Emily Dickinson (quoted in Chaliff) can serve to convey the angular – precise yet unlocated – language of many patients at the margin of reality:

''Tis a dangerous moment for any one when the meaning goes out of things and Life stands straight – and punctual – and yet no content comes. Yet such moments are. If we survive them they expand us, if we do not, but that is Death, whose if is everlasting.'

The psychotic patient 'at the margin of reality' often makes therapeutic space bewilderingly condensed with disclosures. These may be metaphori-cal and/or they may be concrete. Thus the statement 'things keep flying back from nowhere' may refer to memories, bricks, or even trees. At junc-tures such as these, the therapist becomes aware that the discrimination between paranoid projection and existential distress calls for great vigilance. The Aeolian Mode may then help to intensify the therapist's understanding of a patient as metaphor slips imperceptibly into paranoid 'reality'. Clinical experience can be extended and sharpened by descriptive passages from fiction:

'Early in the morning, before sunrise, some workmen came to the landlady's apartment. Ivan Dmitrich knew perfectly well they had come to reset the stove in the kitchen, but fear prompted him to think they were policemen in disguise. He stealthily crept out of the apartment without stopping to put on his hat and coat and, terror-stricken, ran down the street. Barking dogs tore after him, somewhere behind him a man shouted, the wind whistled in his ears, and it seemed to Ivan Dmitrich that *all the violence in the world had gathered together in pursuit of him.*' [our italics]

(*Ward Six*, Chekhov)

'NARRATOR: And without pausing for a moment to reflect upon the course he was taking, he fled away with surprising swiftness, borne upon such wings as only fear can wear (*Smike is in a spot running. Behind him, through the darkness, we see, as a fantasy, a nightmare vision of Dotheboys Hall: Mrs Squeers, ringing her bell, Mr Squeers with his cane, Wackford laughing, Fanny, the Boys. We hear lines too,* **echoed and distorted:** *"And a pretty thing it is". "O.U.T.C.A.S.T.". "Forsaken". "Homeless". "In here, you haven't finished". "I'll flog you within an inch of your life". And gradually,* **the noises coalesce,** *and become the swishes of a cane, growing louder and louder. Smike puts his hands to his ears. The sounds grow even louder: they're inside his head. Finally, the nightmare fades, Smike stops, takes his hands from his ears, and there is silence. An owl hoots. Silence.*) [our emphasis]

'NARRATORS:
And it was not until the darkness and quiet of a country road
    recalled him to the world outside himself,
And the starry sky above him warned him of the rapid flight of
    time,
That, covered with dust and panting for breath, he stopped to
    listen and look about him.
All was still and silent.'

(*The Life and Adventures of Nicholas Nickleby*, Dickens,
adapted for the stage by Edgar 1982)

Both passages have caught the ambience of micropsychotic paranoid episodes – 'all the violence in the world had gathered together in pursuit', 'the noises coalesce' – as they might originally develop and then be relived during therapeutic sessions. It is to be hoped that before the patient leaves therapeutic space, he will have been 'recalled . . . to the world outside himself'.

PARONOMASIA, DEICTIC STRESS, AND RELATED PHENOMENA

Coming under the familiar heading of metaphor, paronomasia may seem like a strange intruder. But it has been included for good reasons. The term is probably unfamiliar to the majority of psychotherapists. We are therefore using it to stand vicariously for the many uses of language within the fabric of therapeutic exchange. It represents the options open to the therapist at numerous choice-points in his dialogue with the patient. Alternative or changing verbal lights may enhance the possibility of other ways of looking at things. It is, in short, another manifestation of *poiesis*. Although paronomasia does not fall into the conventional category of 'interpretation', it frequently enables sharper distinctions to be made. On the other hand, it may provide a necessary degree of obliquity and shrouding for the patient whose perception is rigidly controlled in 'either/or' categories.

Paronomasia

Paronomasia is playing on words which sound alike. It is a pun. But in contrast to the vernacular and widespread use of pun, far from having a light-hearted or flippant implication, it is best understood as implying 'beyond the meaning' or beyond the name which is altered slightly in naming. It is interesting to note that in 1890 the *Saturday Review* referred to 'the playful paronomasian method of the poet'.

As this book is about a mode of dynamic psychotherapy, it would not be appropriate to look at various figures of speech from a strictly semantic point of view. However, word reversals and double meanings are intensely active within therapeutic space: no matter whether it is that of individual psychotherapy or the complicated reverberating matrix of a therapeutic group. Nevertheless, because the dynamic flux of meaning and nuance is of such vital importance in the rich texture of verbal exchange between the patient and the therapist, we provide a few examples which are congruous with the Aeolian Mode. They link *poiesis* with a specific genre of aesthetic imperatives.

1. *'A stable.'* Brian is a heavily-defended industrialist who energetically participates in numerous social events. He somewhat painfully acknowledges this as being his method of avoiding deep feelings. He is just beginning to regret that he 'cannot remember' dreams. There is nothing in his life to give him gyroscopic stability in external turbulence.

'I've actually got a dream to tell you . . . or at least a tiny bit of a dream.'

'A bit of a dream seems a good beginning.'

'I'm leading some kind of animal . . . a horse, yes . . . a horse and I'm looking for somewhere to put it.'

'A stable?'

'Yes . . . that's it. A stable.'

'A stable what, Brian?'

[Energetically, speaking more quickly and looking excited] 'Yes . . . that's *it*. Stability. That's what I've always needed and never had. I spend the time rushing around but I'm always looking for something certain. I've never really known anything stable.'

This paronomastic intervention was that of turning a noun, 'stable' into a word adjectival of something else, 'a stable what?'. This is inevitably language-bound. It was 'effective' because it facilitated dream reflection and subsequent analysis. A Shakespearean example of a noun becoming adjectival ('deer' to 'dear') comes from *King Henry VI* Part I (IV. 2, 54):

> 'If we be English deer, be then in blood;
> Not rascal-like, to fall down with a pinch,
> But rather moody-mad and desperate stags,
> Turn on the bloody hounds with heads of steel,
> And make the cowards stand aloof at bay:
> Sell every man his life as dear as mine,
> And they shall find dear deer of us, my friends.'

2. *'I always knew mum would give me a good hiding.'* In this composite disclosure with multiple meanings and a complementary affective loading, the patient might have been referring to the fact that his mother would always thrash him. Or, when 'on the run' from the police, she would always ensure that he was safely hidden in the loft or the basement. In fact, this particular offender-patient meant both.

3. *'I'm running out of time.'* This phrase may mean many things. There may be 'meaning beyond the meaning'. It can mean that there is not much time left; in the sense that time is running out, just as oxygen or heating oil may soon be used up. On the other hand, the psychotic may feel that he is not merely walking out of time, but is actually leaving time faster than his therapist, who cannot keep up with him. It may also be a prosaic description of a man who is 'marching to a different drummer' except that he has broken ranks and is actually running 'out of time'. Numerous other potential significances can be discerned. And when this sentence finds its way into therapeutic space, the therapist needs augmented perception as he endeavours to understand not merely what the sentence connotes, but how many of the above connotations may be simultaneously relevant. Each may contribute to the disclosure.

4. *'He was dead quiet.'* It is not surprising that the arena of offender-therapy often has some such phrase at its centre. It may be literally true. It may be metaphorically true. It may have new paronomastic overtones.

115

Once again, we are aware that the preceding paragraph may sound 'clever'. We may be 'charged' with the fact that we are reading *more* into the situation that the patient intends. But we hope to avoid the opposite risk, namely, that we actually read *less* than the patient wishes. Because, if this proves to be so, the patient so often feels that we cannot 'take' the experience which he is describing. We have looked at such phenomena elsewhere (Cox 1982a, 1983). How could the two ensuing statements with multiple levels of significance ever be taken solely at 'face' value?

'I just went on killing her. It never occurred to me that she'd die.'

'She said nothing. So I killed her. Then nothing was said.'

5. *'Last weekend everything came to a head.'* Escalating family tension – including the threat of suicide by the use of a pistol held against the temple – was described thus. It was true as a metaphor. And ominously literal.

Deictic stress

The index finger is the pointing finger. Deixis is the Greek word for 'pointing' or 'indicating'. It is of pervasive significance in all human communication. Every discussion, ranging from formal rhetoric and legal debate to casual chat and domestic dialogue depends upon the emphasis placed upon words within an overall pattern. This emphasis is the deictic stress. We can only mention it briefly here, though it is a major issue in linguistics (see *Pragmatics*, Levinson 1983). In written dialogue there is a limited repertoire of indications, such as punctuation, italics and underlining through which deictic stress can be implied. Kenner (1983) describes how the Irish playwright J. M. Synge wrote very slowly, on a primitive typewriter which involved rotation of the printwheel before it was slammed forward. He was meticulous about punctuation. Synge typed: 'Good evening kindly, stranger.' But a London printer's version was: 'Good evening, kindly stranger.' A patient describing his experience is rarely less meticulous than Synge. He expects what he says, and the emphasis he places on his words ('punctuation'), to reflect what he feels. When it is ambiguous, therapeutic empathic skill is stretched to the limit.

The significance of deictic stress and its affective context is always evident in a therapeutic setting. But no less so upon the stage. Horatio's injunction to the ghost is a good case in point: *'Stay, illusion!'* (*Hamlet* I. 1, 127). Just two words, a comma and an exclamation mark – but they serve us well as carriers of the significance of language and the power of ambiguity. And the Aeolian Mode depends upon both. This is because it bridges the 'given' language of literature, and the 'being given' language born in therapeutic dialogue. It enables the patient to tell his story; even that part of his story which had previously been unconscious and therefore held from him. It also allows him to hear, through dream and fantasy, those stories so like his own which he needs to hear. They remind him that though he is not alone, yet his story remains his in all its particularity. Those larger stories in which clinical history merges with fable and myth will be told and gradually heard, even if the telling is by no appointed story-teller. And, paradoxical though it initially appears, the larger the story, the more implicatory does the detailed deictic stress become. This is because it can point to 'other things'. Equally well, it can tame and domesticate the potentially primordial. It is all a question of 'how' what is said, is said.

Man needs to speak about himself. And he needs to hear of other stories which engage with his own. Yet because much of his listening is distorted by previous encounters, psychotherapy often appears to concentrate upon reducing the sinister effects of damaged self-esteem and perceptual disturbance. Important though this 'undoing' aspect of therapy is, there are also affirmative anchorings of a place within a larger story, which is reflected in fable and carried by myth.

Commentaries upon the implications of Horatio's words addressed to the ghost, 'Stay, illusion!', are not unanimous. Both words have more than one meaning, so that dogmatic assertions about what they 'must' mean are out of court. Their significance initially baffles us. They are imperative and aesthetic; that is, they are a response to the pattern which connects. And they remind us of the precarious position in which we are placed as we try to understand an unfolding clinical history. It is unusual to give directions to an illusion, except in psychotic constructions of reality. And, perplexed though he was, Horatio remained 'orientated in time and place'.

Language is brought to life in speech through appreciation of deictic stressing. It is always accompanied by non-verbal communication. And the actor playing Horatio has a range of possible options open to him. He may hold his hands in front of him to prevent the ghost coming closer. He may beckon or even try to hold the 'illusion', as though he were a welcome guest who was leaving too soon. His hands may not move, but his facial and verbal expression will 'speak' somewhere along a continuum between 'Stay where you are – don't come any closer' and 'Stay with us – please don't leave us yet'. The complexity of the situation is compounded by the fact that Horatio wishes to talk with that of which he is afraid. And this is an exact paradigm of an inescapable phase in all psychotherapy. No patient can avoid talking with, and ultimately appropriating, that part of himself of which he is afraid. And he most fears that which may or may not be real.

117

The psychotic is usually so certain of 'the voices', that their reality is not questioned. But we are all most vulnerable at the point where reality and illusion meet.

Deictic stress applies not only to the stressing of particular words or syllables, but to the significance of inflection and the duration of pauses. And it is relevant in vernacular 'chat', as well as in portentous disclosure. Thus the sentence

'The lady from next door came in to help me undress.'

takes on an entirely different significance when the words 'the Christmas tree' are added. 'Undressing the Christmas tree' being the Swedish idiom for 'taking the decorations off'. There was no ambiguity evident when the end of the sentence arrived!

'The lady from next door came in to help me undress . . . the Christmas tree.'

The therapist is never quite sure how long the '. . . . .' is going to be! And this takes us back to the perennial significance of silence. Another generic example is furnished by an offender-patient who had already killed once and was discussing the possibility of killing again.

'I would never kill anyone.'

Here the deictic stress makes all the difference, depending upon which word in this important statement carries the stress. If the reader reads the words aloud and in each reading changes the stressed word many different colours emerge. During the therapeutic session in question the patient stressed the word *anyone*. Seminar discussion on this issue tends to circle around the theme of the patient being 'so safe' that *no one* would be killed. The patient was actually reassuring the therapist that *he* (the therapist) was safe. *He* would not be killed. And the implication was '*you* are safe; but let me get *him* within my sights and I would pull the trigger'.

It would be an important omission to leave the theme of deictic stress without reference to the work of Kristeva (1982; see also Moi 1986). Although much of her analysis is textual it has indubitable relevance to the spoken word, reaching its sharpest focus in the deictic stressing which takes place during a therapeutic session. Space only permits a few selected quotations which will surely invite further exploration. She refers to the 'successive surges of the intonational curve'; '*Suspensive intonation* stresses incompletion and invites the addressee to include himself in the daydream. The *exclamatory intonation* shows the enthusiasm, the surprise, the fascination of the speaker. . . . Enunciation devices, usually repressed, by means of which subject and addressee, in their mutual combat and fascination, discover logical . . . spatial . . . and intonational means of revealing themselves in the statement.' In her structural analysis of Céline's prose, Kristeva points out how an entirely different and more subjective involvement is evoked within the reader by the use of 'three dots' rather than a comma: '. . . thus isolated, the constituent *loses its identity* as object phrase, for instance, and while it does not gain a truly autonomous value it still floats in a syntactic irresolution that opens a path to various logical and semantic connotations, in short, to daydreaming.' This detailed literary material may seem to be academic, 'small print' and far removed from the therapist's direct encounter with his patient. But this is only an initial impression. On reflection, it will be seen to be directly related to dynamic psychotherapy; and to the Aeolian Mode in particular. It is not only to the theme of daydreaming, primary process, stream of consciousness flow that we refer.

Deictic stress serves as a guide. And it is of greatest relevance as a pointer towards unconscious phenomena which do 'not quite surface', even as slips of the tongue, but remain incipient and partially concealed as *errors of intended emphasis*. It is in such detailed listening to what the patient is saying, and not quite yet saying, that the therapist's awareness of the phenomenon of deictic stress can help him. And the various writings of Kristeva (1980; 1982; 1984) illuminate the significance of selective stressing *par excellence*. A micro-vignette may anchor this observation still further. A group member arrived ten minutes late for the morning session. As I (M.C.) opened the door to let him in, closing it again behind him, and returning to my seat, I must have been distracted from the disclosure sequence for perhaps thirty seconds. Certainly less than a minute. But when I sat down, I was baffled at what appeared to be a complete change of theme. I remarked:

'I seem to have missed something important.'

And the girl who was speaking said:

'Yes, you have . . . a comma. I had said "I don't understand, myself".'

It was to do with the deictic stress which changed the significance of what was being said. There are several potential significances to the sentence: 'I don't understand myself', depending upon the emphasis, the punctuation, and the 'intonational surge', to use Kristeva's phrase, of the bridging between 'understand' and 'myself'.

A final example comes from a non-forensic therapeutic session. The words can speak for themselves: 'There isn't anyone about to die in my family.' The meaning is ambiguous until the therapist clarifies where the stress and the 'punctuation' lie. It might mean 'there isn't anyone, . . . about to die in my family'. On the other hand, it might mean 'there isn't anyone about to die, . . . in my family'. Or, 'there isn't anyone about . . . to die in my family'.

This example of differential deictic stress illustrates the sharpening of disclosive significance which is present potentially in almost every therapeutic session.

Sometimes the dynamic emphasis of a session has been changed when deictic stress is relocated. This is best illustrated by homophones:

'I always played apart?'

       A part? . . . Apart?

'Agenda'

       'A gender?'

'I shall be around'

       'A round what?'

'I feel I'm being followed.' [Fact? Paranoid anxiety?]

'I feel I'm being followed . . . by bad luck.' [An ordinary figure of speech]

The smallest moderation of inflection can exert a profound alteration in significance. It is for this reason that paronomasia and deictic stress have been smuggled into the book under the cloak of metaphor. Their impact sometimes depends upon metaphor but in most instances there is no direct connection. Nevertheless they are often decisive in locating 'Where the Meanings, are – '. And one of the strengths of the Aeolian Mode is that it enlarges the therapist's range of reflective choice-points. In this way the capacity to respond to the patient's particularity is augmented. This is congruous with Leighton's injunction in *My Name is Legion* (1959): 'Let us have done with "for instance" and begin with "instance".'

We are closing this section with an instance which is as simple as it is powerful. A furtive, frightened, suspicious – almost paranoid – girl said:

'I can't talk to them. . . . They know all about me.'

       'But if they knew *all* about you?'

'If they knew *all* about me, then they'd understand.'

Metonymy

Metonymy has a referential function and allows one entity to stand for another. More particularly, it substitutes the name of an attribute for that of the thing itself. And Shakespeare gives us a good example when Antony addresses Cleopatra as 'Egypt': 'I am dying, Egypt, dying.' (IV. 13, 18); 'O! Whither hast thou led me, Egypt?' (III. 9, 51).

A special kind of metonymy is the *pars pro toto*. 'She's just a pretty face.' And a particularly sombre example of metonymy, which is not uncommon in the disclosive world of a subsequently reflective homicide, is:

'I went into the room and saw THE TARGET DOING HER HAIR.'

It should be noted that this actually exemplifies *toto pro pars*.

It seems wrong to give brief attention to a theme of such obvious forensic and psychotherapeutic weight. Nevertheless, when a patient sees 'the target doing her hair' the therapist will be aware of a rich texture of potential interventions.

We have looked at metaphor from several angles and we return to the 'internal difference, Where the Meanings, are – ', and to the curious fact that metaphor and transference are synonymous in different languages. Having drawn attention to some of the hazards of metaphor-transference in psychotherapy, it is important that we end this chapter on a positive note. Metaphor undoubtedly carries massive therapeutic potential.

A 26-year-old postgraduate geology student was able to talk of panic attacks and frenzied assaults when she knew 'There was a definite *shift along the fault-line*'. Her capacity to reflect upon the time in her life when 'the fault occurred' gave her a means of exploring 'a very early fault' (echoes of *The Basic Fault*, Balint 1968), and of subsequently claiming that it was her 'fault'. At this point projective defences were relinquished and she was progressively able to tolerate feelings she had previously denied or displaced. In this instance, her statement that 'A fault is a line of weakness in the structure' proved to be a dynamic fulcrum. The simplicity of the metaphor which linked developmental layers of the mind with geological strata speaks for itself, so that 'explanation' is superfluous.

'Even at the turning'

We have made many references to metaphor's capacity to sustain several different referents simultaneously. It can point to more than one meaning at the same time. This may occur in prose or poetry, although, from our point of view, it is of particular importance in therapeutic space. Thus a patient may be 'saying several things' at once. Metaphor can therefore 'hold a patient steady' – a gyroscopic function – while his environment changes.

Nevertheless, we have not sufficiently stressed metaphor's capacity to 'hold things steady' while the patient changes. To put this in a nutshell, we could say that metaphor has a double therapeutic potential. First, it can broaden the sweep of what is being described – because it can carry several 'meanings', each of which is legitimate. Secondly, while endopsychic movement is taking place – such as during the relinquishment of primitive defences – the 'double focus' allows a patient to be 'held steady'. He does not need to 'change the subject' when, for example, paranoid ideation ceases, or suicidal intention subsides. This means that the patient still feels 'at home' in the language whose referent has changed. Though 'novel', the topic remains familiar. Thus, a schizophrenic who tried to leave the ward with his bed on his back – having read 'Take up thy bed and walk' (*Matthew* 9, 6) was able to focus on the implication of what new life might mean for him.

Again, dreams of 'digging square holes in the sea in order to make a grave' are 'saying' many things. And fantasies of 'swimming beyond' the lighthouse 'or the breakwater' are modified when associated with Conrad's mutative description of a suicide attempt (*The Planter of Malata*):

'For to whom could it have occurred that a man would set out calmly to *swim beyond the confines of life* – with a steady stroke – his eyes fixed on a star.' [our italics]

To swim beyond – *not* the lighthouse, *not* the breakwater – but beyond the 'confines of life' – gives new expressive possibility even though, and may be *because*, it implies engagement with death. The metaphor changes a distance for swimming to a distance from existence; and the capacity to talk of confrontation with the possibility of death in such detail may free the patient from too literal an encounter. But, as always in psychotherapy, this mutation is only possible and effective when feeling is at its height, its point of urgency; to recall Virginia Woolf, only when the patient is prepared for the sight of himself. Tidal images have great therapeutic potential and archaic, poetic diction is often active at liminal turning points. Falstaff died 'even at the turning o' the tide' – a circumstantial detail with metaphorical overtones (*King Henry V* II. 3; 13).

Clinical disclosure abounds in similar incidents: 'Dad died at 10.15 p.m. – *at the break in the news*.'

'The Turning Tide' approaches and recedes from 'The Listening Landscape' at 'The Reasonable Shore' (*The Tempest* V. 1, 81), which some have seen as the conscious threshold of 'reason'. It brings us to imagery and recalls Shakespeare's Aeolian Mode (see p. xxii).

5

The listening landscape:
swarming shadows

IMAGERY AND PERCEPTION

'Those masterful images because complete
    Grew in pure mind, but out of what began?'
        ('The Circus Animals' Desertion' in *Last
            Poems 1936–39*, W. B. Yeats 1950)

'To tell a story is often to make images . . .
We cannot take a step in life or literature without using an image. . . .
Not only does each image tell its singular story, but that story invokes
another.'

(*Tellers and Listeners*, Barbara Hardy 1975)

'The Possible's slow fuse is lit
    By the Imagination.'

(Emily Dickinson)

No theme is more integral to the Aeolian Mode than that of imagery. Indeed,
the preceding discussion about the dynamic components and the therapeutic
initiatives depends upon the coherence between different capacities of the
image. And the ensuing discussion about the interrelationship between the
three theoretical foundations of the Aeolian Mode also studies the integrated
potentiality of imagery. Nevertheless, in this chapter, imagery is the central
focus and is not adjectival or subordinate to a broader theme.

This section is 'imagery *and* perception' because one cannot exist
without the other. It is impossible to deal exhaustively with two such large
topics and we are strictly limiting this presentation to those aspects of
imagery and perception which are necessary for our purposes.

Whereas it is customary to draw a distinction between *percept* and *image*,
the former relying on sensory input representing the outer world, and the

latter being an inner world construct in the absence of external stimuli, it is important to remember that this discrimination is not absolute. A percept is never a replica of the world, because perception is an active, selective and adaptive process. As Woodworth (1938) told us, 'We not only see, but we look for; not only hear, but we listen to'. Thus perception takes place in a tuned organism, and the process itself is influenced by memory and categorizing principles. As Holt (1972) points out, 'We do not simply see, we recognise what we see.'

Both percept and image may be related to any sense modality, but the majority of studies have concentrated upon visual experience and visual imagery. This may be linked to the degree of linguistic representation of the sensory mode. We see, look, regard, behold, study, perceive, glance, eye, survey, scan, inspect, watch, observe, stare, discern, gaze, gloat, notice, inspect, or recognize. There is infinite variety in each activity which may be elaborated by a whole keyboard of adjectival modifiers. And we have sight, vision, spectacle, view, survey, foresight, perspective, and outlook.

Bruner and Postman (1949) use the term 'perceptual expectancy' in their exploration of the way in which anticipation interacts with percepts in some kind of staging centre, in which the sensory input is matched with a hypothesis. All this points to the fact that it is impossible to draw a sharp line of demarcation between the two concepts of percept and image. And, though both are enmeshed in a continuum, there is usually sufficient polarization between the external and the internal world for the preservation of 'reality testing'. In the psychopathology of the psychotic, this reality testing is lost. In some of the deeper aspects of empathy (see p. 170) it is relinquished by the therapist as he engages with the fragmented psychotic, for whom trusting is a risky undertaking. It is of critical significance, although it sounds contradictory, that such voluntary relinquishment of reality testing on the part of the therapist is partial and reversible, and always at his executive discretion. Without this phenomenon the psychotic may never be 'reached'. If it ever becomes more than partial and reversible for the therapist there are dire consequences because he, too, has then lost touch with reality. There are many passages in this book in which we discuss the part the Aeolian Mode can play in facilitating dynamic psychotherapy with the psychotic patient. In the vignettes cited much depends upon the integration of percept and image, because they determine how the therapist 'reads' the world which the patient is also 'reading'.

Having said all this, objectivity is always relative. And even though Husserl asked us to perceive the world, having 'our prejudices placed in parenthesis', his suggestion, at best, merely serves to discipline our subjectivity. The paradox remains. Both the solipsistic view – the apprehension that one's own ego is the only one existing – and the one advocated by naive realism – that identity exists between physical and experiential worlds – are equally absurd. It is a question of balance. We tend to presume that our appreciation of the outer world corresponds exactly to its factual nature: thus the sourness of vinegar, the colourglow and fragrance of flowers, the softness of fur are all spontaneously experienced as being inherent in the objects themselves (Theilgaard 1968).

> 'but you are the music / While the music lasts.'
> (T. S. Eliot, *The Dry Salvages V* 1941)

All this can be epitomized and focused in the statement: We are not passive onlookers, but active participants; we are not told what to experience, but we create the experience itself.

The words of Barbara Hardy at the head of the chapter make this abundantly clear: 'We cannot take a step in life or literature without using an image.' And the Aeolian Mode is, in more than one sense, a process which enables the patient to 'take a step in life'. But it is a step which the patient has hitherto been unable to make. This may be because of his intrinsically restricting and heavily defended personality structure. It may be because he lacked the facilitating environment. It is usually a combination of both which prevents further progress and leads to the exploration of therapeutic possibilities. As we have repeatedly emphasized, the Aeolian Mode is particularly appropriate with those patients for whom conventional therapeutic endeavours seem less than satisfactory. The heavily defended psychopath and the psychotic patient seem to respond because their perception of the inner and outer world is made more flexible and encouraging through the use of image and the mutative metaphor. We cannot disentangle the linking of metaphor and image because, for our purposes, we use images of every modality for 'carrying meaning across', so that the patient can perceive things in a new way.

Images can be classified in many ways. Thus they can be related to specific sensory modalities or categorized in terms of their degree of primordiality. However, such categorization does not bring us closer to an understanding of the nature of imagery. Uncertainties and ambiguities are unavoidable. We are in a constantly changing interaction with our environment. And this interaction takes place at various levels. As Rose (1980) says, 'The imagination is a pause between uncertainties.' And Freud in *The Ego and the Id* (1923) writes:

> 'We must not . . . forget the importance of optical mnemic residues, when they are of *things*, or . . . deny that it is possible for thought-processes to become conscious through a reversion to visual residues. . . .

Thinking in pictures . . . stands nearer to unconscious processes than
does thinking in words, and it is unquestionably older than the latter
both ontogenetically and phylogenetically.'

(p. 21. See also p. 200 below)

There is always the risk that attempts to categorize the process of forming images will obscure its significance. Armstrong (1946) in his analysis of
Shakespeare's imagery writes: 'To treat Shakespeare's words simply as
stimulus words in relation to others is to disregard the psychological
intricacies of association. . . . The attempt to classify psychological processes into static logical categories is foredoomed to failure. It is seeking the
living amongst the dead.' Whereas Jung (1964) says, 'Because there are
innumerable things beyond the range of human understanding, we constantly use symbolic terms to represent concepts that we cannot define or
fully comprehend.' And this brings us to Bruner's statement (1980): 'We
have ways of using imagination to understand what can never be fully
understood.'

This, in turn, introduces us to the major theme of the images of the
dream, which must, unfortunately, remain at the periphery of our discussion. Freud's unforgettable words (1900) about the 'navel' of the
dream, 'the spot where it reaches down into the unknown', are congruous
with Bruner's statement about that which 'can never be fully understood'.
There are also reverberative echoes from the bewildered world of the
psychotic and from the tight defensive protection of the psychopath. In
various ways, they are often painfully aware of what can never be fully
understood, though they deal with this pain in different ways. For both
groups the Aeolian Mode seems to go some way towards bridging the gulf
between that which can be understood and that which is beyond understanding.

Ultimately, we all acknowledge that the depths of the nocturnal dream
are an ontological mystery, though they are vibrant with creative images.
And the story told by the dream is often more vivid than that evoked by the
waking perception of the outer world. And, without doubt, it is more
strange than the everyday world because no editorial scissors have cut away
the inconsequential. There is a direct link between the story told by the
dream, the story which the patient needs to tell, and his immersion in the
larger story which encompasses the story of our lives. It also links the
archetypal and the accidental, the fable and the story. Hoffman (1967)
writes: 'The story must redeem the fable from abstraction. When there is
no historical reality in which the fable is both concealed and revealed, no
tactile world, no solid landscape, no living characters nor believable
chimaeras, in short no story, there is only the fable.'

In a subsequent passage Hoffman comments that the poet Muir 'is a patient extractor of meaning from event, not an imposer of willed unity upon experienced chaos'. Through the Aeolian Mode, the linking of the perceived world and the activity of the image enables the patient to move towards the integration of extracting meaning from event, while not ignoring experienced chaos. Indeed, many of our patients not only experience chaos, they have caused chaos in the outer world and, in many cases, in the inner world of those with whom they have to do. It was no accident that our (M.C.) previous discussion of this theme was under the heading of *Compromise with Chaos* (1978).

Dreaming has been the most studied subject within the field of imagery. This is one of the reasons why we do not concentrate on dream-imagery in this chapter. Another is the fact that the sleeper crosses a frontier. His state of consciousness alters and he is more a spectator than a participant when he relates his dream. When recounting a dream, he feels less 'responsibility' for it than when talking of his waking reverie. But, though less responsible, he feels more involved in his dream world, even when it is *terra incognita*. In the words of Bachelard (op. cit.): 'For every dream which we recount upon the light of day, there are many whose thread we have lost.'

These latent, forgotten dreams do not belong to the introspective sphere but to the realm of the representational. In his classic description of the difference between latent and manifest content in the dream, Freud (1900) described four mechanisms: displacement, condensation, concretization, and secondary elaboration. Thus the dream utilizes mechanisms characteristic of primary-process thinking and this has the closest link to the phenomena of psychopathology, and also to those of creative, artistic imagery. Kris *et al.* (1964) make a new equation between art and dream; the ambiguity found in art, particularly poetry, is like the overdetermination Freud found in dream-work. Kant declared that 'The madman is a woken dreamer', and Wundt maintained that 'In dreaming we experience all the phenomena which meet us in the world of the insane.' 'Dreams and art are not merely linked because they fulfil wishes, but because both have to make use of strategies in order to overcome the resistance of consciousness' (Wright 1984).

Whereas Elizabeth Wright refers to the 'strategies' of dreams and art, Ella Freeman Sharpe (1937) refers to their context. Meltzer (1984) comments as follows:

'Her [Sharpe's] central creative contribution to the theory of dreams was to point out the mountains of evidence that dreams utilize what she chose to call the "poetic diction" of lyric poetry. By this she meant that dreams employ the many devices of simile, metaphor, alliteration, onomatopoeia etc. by which the language of poetry achieves its evocative capacity.'

Our survey of the relevance of imagery to the Aeolian Mode is cursory and incomplete. It is closely linked to psychopathology and the other kind of disturbance of the *status quo* which comes under the heading creativity. And, at root, this is part of the process of *poiesis*. As with the other phenomena we are discussing, imagery and perception find their most acute relevance for the Aeolian Mode at the point where *poiesis*, the aesthetic imperative, and the point of urgency converge.

Theoretical aspects

The term 'imagery' is used in many ways. It has been applied to both conscious and unconscious constructs, to the product as well as the process in the realms of philosophy, psychology, and neurophysiology. It is here that we are confronted with the inevitable epistemological dilemma related to the body–mind problem. This is brought into sharp relief in a brief dialogue described by Claudel (1978) to which we refer in connection with *the larger story* (p. 242):

'Did you mean this world? Or is there another?'
'There are two of them and I tell you there is only one of them and it is enough.'

This reflects an acceptable monistic position. But it also serves as a signpost pointing towards the different manifestations of organismic processes which constitute a whole. And it is the range of manifestations which call for divergent theoretical constructs. These, in turn, are shaped by various scientific disciplines (Theilgaard 1968). The crux of the matter is the level of emergence. But this does not necessarily imply a plunge into dualism, though it calls for the clarification of terms and concepts so that we can distinguish between neural processes and phenomenological events. This is elaborated by Holt (1972), whose definition serves our purposes: '"Percept" or "image" is used when we are speaking about a phenomenal content of a sensory or quasi-sensory nature. "Presentation" is applied when it is a case of the same meaning as mediated by or encoded in a brain process without awareness.'

He underlines the important implications of this distinction: 'the functional equivalent of a mental image can be formed and processed extensively with other encoded information without awareness.' These image-formation processes have a transactional relationship with processes which also represent emotions. It should be emphasized that the weight of our discussion is upon the experiential not the experimental side of imagery.

128

Bachelard, a philosopher of science with a life-long interest in rational processes, tried to apply objective methods in his study of poetic imagery. The outcome of his endeavours led him towards phenomenology. He saw this as being the only method for mediating and reflecting the essential validity of imagery. Initially, he attempted to separate subject and object, though he subsequently realized that they converged and coalesced in an expansive, creative union. Viewed in this way, the web of imagery is closely woven and does not lend itself to objective, scientific analysis. The customary scientific procedure of labelling and categorizing, essential though it is for other purposes, is inappropriate for studying the prime importance of imagery within the Aeolian Mode.

Heidegger referred to the sphere surrounding our thoughts in his discussion of the importance of being aware of our horizons. And Husserl made the significance of variable horizons a major topic. However opaque and difficult this may be, it extends our understanding of the depth of experience. 'It is not an objective world of fact, but a subjective world of meaning' (Theilgaard 1980). As Steiner (1978) has said: 'The drive towards objective contemplation, logical analysis, scientific classification, which cuts us off from being, presses on the Western intellect.'

It should be noted that the unification of experience is more pronounced in early childhood. It is then that a primordial functional unity seems to exist in both the sensory and the imaginative field. To the very small child there is no separation between the inner and the outer world. It is 'a buzzing, booming confusion' (W. James 1890). And, as Werner (1948) indicates, there is a high degree of unity between subject and object which is mediated by the motor–affective reactivity of the child. This leads to a dynamic way of experiencing the world. The immediate surroundings and the distant horizon are seen as a world not far removed from that of fairy tales and magic, and the borders between reality, play, fantasy, and dream become fused. This integrated sensory–motor–emotional mode of reaction makes for a close connection between the child and his environment, which results in a far more dynamic, vivaciously intensive way of experiencing the world; a manner of experiencing far removed from the 'objective', factual, and static style of the adult. Werner has referred to this undifferentiated process as being syncretic, diffuse, labile, and rigid, whereas the differentiated style is discrete, articulated, stable, and flexible. This implies that the image, originally occurring in the child's sensory sphere of feeling and fantasy, gradually changes its functional characteristic. It slowly loses sensitivity, colour, vivacity, and globality. And, as it does so, it bleakens, congeals, and sometimes petrifies. Indeed, the degree of petrification may become so extreme that it is a central feature in the restricted, concrete thinking which is clinically evident in major psychopathology. Nevertheless, the healthy

129

adult maintains the capacity for dynamic experience of the world around him, because there has been a progressive balancing between the subject who perceives and that which is perceived. Emotion can sometimes be so strong that it leads to a condensation of implied significance into a single image. This accounts for the syncretic character of certain images which may be found in the gross disturbance of psychopathology or in the heightened capacity for creativity.

SYNAESTHESIA

This syncretism is sometimes evident as synaesthetic experience. This occurs when one specific stimulus arouses not only the corresponding sensation, but also evokes images belonging to other sensory modalities. Literature abounds in examples of this confluence, which gives the image both novelty and richness.

> 'sehe mit fühlenden Aug',
> fühle mit sehenden Hand.'
> ('Look with feeling eyes,
> Feel with looking hand.')
> (*Römische Elegien*, Goethe)
>
> 'Look with thine ears'
> (*King Lear* IV. 6, 149)

'The smell took the shape of my father.'

The fusion of the senses into one identity is also revealed by the statement of a schizophrenic patient (quoted by Schilder 1914):

> 'When I say red, that means a concept which can be expressed in colour, music, feeling, thinking and in nature. And when this idea is expressed in any one way, the other forms of the idea are felt to be there too. Hence, man has not five senses but only one.'

A three-year-old said: 'The leaves smell nice and yellow.' And Emily Dickinson wrote: 'Let no Sunrise' yellow noise / Interrupt this Ground' in a short poem about the grave, 'Ample make this Bed'.

PHYSIOGNOMIC PERCEPTION

Physiognomic experience is the name given to the dynamic perception of objects, based on the fact that they are predominantly perceived through the motor and emotional attitude of the observer. Things perceived in this mode may appear 'animate', and they seem to express a degree of inner life, even though they are actually lifeless (Werner 1948).

This way of perceiving is an indication of nearness, and it is radically different from the more everyday organization in which things are categorized according to their technical and factual qualities. When a two-year-old child, walking with his mother in the autumn forest, sees falling leaves and says 'look, the trees are crying', it is an indication of his physiognomic understanding of the world.

The physiognomic quality is vividly illustrated when a schizophrenic patient, anxiously looking at a swinging door, says: 'The door is devouring me.' Or again, the moon is endowed with feeling: 'It is a very troubled moon.' Kandinsky (1913) writes in his biography: 'On my palette sit high, round raindrops, puckishly flirting with each other, swaying and trembling. Unexpectedly they unite and suddenly become shy threads, which disappear among the colours.'

Discussing e. e. cummings' capacity to capture the *mot juste* and to communicate atmosphere, Norman (1958) quotes and comments as follows:

> ' "beyond the brittle towns asleep
> i look where stealing needles of foam
> in the last light
> thread the creeping shores"

Here, "stealing," "thread," and "creeping" are used with precision; but it is when he selects the word to describe what the sea itself does that he achieves a master stroke – the sea

> "*pours* its eyeless miles".'

Ejler Bille (1975) asks:

'Has the rain a face? Is it reflected in the blackberry bushes and in the ripe apples?'

And Morgenstern comments:

'Die Möven sehen allen aus als ob sie Emma heissen.' 'The seagulls all look as if their name is Emma.')

> 'Art thou not, fatal vision, sensible
> To feeling, as to sight? or art thou but
> A dagger of the mind, a false creation,
> Proceeding from the heat-oppressed brain?'
> (*Macbeth* II. 1, 36)

> 'And now, while the trees stand watching . . .'
> ('The Combat', Muir 1960)

> The sky with all its clustered eyes
> Grows still with watching me.'
> ('Ballad of Hector in Hades', Muir 1960)

Anthropomorphism develops out of physiognomic perception: 'good ground be pitiful and hurt me not' (*King John* V. 3, 20). Pity is a higher affect state.

Lehmann (1913) described 'threatening clouds', 'friendly landscapes', and 'majestic mountains'. He analysed the extent to which these moods depend upon associations and previous experience. He found 'that the response to the natural world depended upon the reproduction of kinaesthetic sensations'.

Although the physiognomic experience is often visual, it may involve any of the sensory modalities: auditory, tactile, olfactory, gustatory, or kinaesthetic. Kinaesthetic imagery occurs in music, dance, and poetry. And kinaesthetic sensation plays an important role in empathy (see chapter 6). 'some say, the earth / Was feverous, and did shake' (*Macbeth* II. 3, 58). The natural world, when known physiognomically, is 'alive'. And the experience may become part of purely magical, animistic–daemonic, poetic–symbolic, empathic–sympathetic or religious–theistic viewpoints.

Our very first experiences concern the body.

> 'It serves as a general schema for the articulation of the world as a whole. . . . As the child's knowledge of the non-bodily world expands, it relates itself automatically to that which has already been experienced in the bodily world. We establish life-long symbolic connections between our own body and the outside world.'
>
> (Rose 1980)

The tendency to impregnate the outer world with the human form is universal. It is most pronounced in childhood. It is widespread in psychic regression due to mental illness and is actively fostered by the creative artist. Ignatieff (1984) refers to Lear's claim that he deserves to live: 'When there is no family, no tribe, no state, no city to hear it, only the storm hears it.'

The ontogenesis of imagery

The early experiences of childhood have the greatest impact on the formation of subsequent cognitive styles and personality functions. And this implies that the amalgamation of body images with features of the outer world provides a vehicle for subsequent therapeutic intervention. It becomes vividly evident as language develops, particularly so when abstraction and conceptualization predominate over the concrete, functional aspects of language. Words then tend to replace images. Nevertheless, the total absence of the capacity for imagery is rare, and for the memory-image it is virtually unknown. Anthropologists describe the amazing sensory memory of primitive man. This is similar to that of the child, in that there is no sharp demarcation between percept and memory, whereas civilized man tends to use images as an *aide-mémoire*. These add life to words which may be 'faded poor souvenirs'. This linking takes place at the verbal-conceptual level of memory function.

From a therapeutic perspective, it is important to be aware of the ikonic, non-verbal nature of very early experience. As anamnesis reaches further back to the earlier realms of the patient's experience, it goes beyond the range of words until it reaches the unitary, global experience of early childhood. We have discussed numerous instances where the patient is trying to describe primordial experience for which there are no words and which, paradoxically, may be 'earlier than memory'. Again, in the early inspirational phases of creative imagination, imagery is often of a non-verbal nature. And this applies whether such creativity is that of the artist or the scientist. On 14 March 1830, Goethe told Eckermann of the way in which his ballades originally existed in a pre-verbal state:

'Ich hatte sie alle schon seit vielen Jahren im Kopf, sie beschäftigten meinen Geist als anmutige Bilder, als schöne Traüme, die kamen und gingen, und womit die Phantasie mich spielend beglüchte.'

'For many years I already had them all in my head, they occupied my spirit as graceful pictures, as beautiful dreams, which came and went, and by which the fantasy made me playfully happy.'

We also know that scientists sometimes generate their ideas from visual non-verbal images, which are subsequently developed into hypotheses through metaphorical elaboration. Niels Bohr held that language is limited and that no concept is large enough to contain reality. He said that a truth, the opposite of which is an untruth, is a superficial truth. Deep truths are characterized by the fact that their opposites are other deep truths.

With increasing age there is both a quantitative and a qualitative change in the individual's imaginative capacity. But this does not imply that the adult ever outgrows this need. Indeed, it is life-long. It is a necessary component of the adult's logical and creative ability, although, in order to fulfil its role, the novelty, freshness, and vivacity of imagery must be retained so that the adult achieves the greatest versatility of approach. Such flexibility enhances his capacity to keep close to experience and not to retreat into the distancing of intellectualization. The imagination tends to bleaken in adult life, and rigid categories may reduce perceptual sensitivity. The sense of wonder is diminished and gratitude for experience itself may fail. We do not 'dwell' in experience, which is quickly 'filed away'.

'Perpetual vigilance needs to be exercised to keep such truths freed from "verbal invasion", or from becoming clichés!' (Coulson 1981). The antecedent level is not lost on the way during development. It remains an integral part of a more complex organization, in which more advanced processes predominate. And analogical processes at different steps on the developmental ladder can be integrated and work in harmony with each other. The creation of dynamic images takes place in the antechamber between consciousness and unconsciousness. And they are more likely to occur spontaneously than when purposefully sought. Thus, when a name is on the tip of the tongue, it is more readily mobilized when one relaxes.

Freud (1914b; 1923) drew a close connection between visual imagery (*Vorstellung*) and primary process phenomena. The dual functioning of the mind is sharply distinguishable only from a hypothetical viewpoint. In the actuality of experience there is always intermingling of the primary and secondary processes. In the former, time is perceived as enduringly constant, and space is inhabited by fused objects. Feelings and action-oriented impulses prevail. The secondary process, on the other hand, deals with time as distinct, sequential, changing moments and space is inhabited by circumscribed, clearly categorized objects. Logical, linear thinking reigns supreme.

There are many gradations between conscious and unconscious ways of experiencing, though they take place concurrently. As Rose (1980) has pointed out: 'parallel chains of unconscious imagery proceed *pari passu* beneath conscious experience'. Kragh and Smith's experiments (1970) concerning the ontogenesis of perception, in which marginal and focal perceptions were studied tachistoscopically, corroborated this notion of the unconscious accompaniment of conscious images. Yet even this dual system of data processing cannot entirely deal with the complexity of the outer and inner space. Uncertainties and ambiguities are unavoidable. It is difficult to imagine a better example of perceptual perplexity than that of the patient who said: 'I can't see my face. I can't trust my reflection. And what else is there?' Although an image may have a generalized content, it may also express special nuances – which cannot be communicated in the abstract formulations of generalized thought.

The condensed imagery reflects conceptual plurivalence. This ensures the multiplicity of meanings, yet it sometimes also creates feelings of great certainty and conviction. These are exemplified in the Eureka experience which is *Swifter than Reason* (Day 1963). This is analogous to those instances of scientific discovery when a problem, hitherto insoluble, is suddenly solved. It is as if the accidental turning of a kaleidoscope caused all the disparate and perplexing components to fall together into a new coherent pattern. Watson (1986) implies this when he refers to 'The paradox of probability, the conjuring of certainty out of collections of random and unrelated events'. He suggests 'some principle that transcends cause-and-effect, some kind of form, a sort of harmony that chimes through the universe'. This is an unmistakable echo of Bateson's phrase (1979), 'the pattern which connects'.

The baffling question, 'And what else is there?', was followed by an assertion: 'You are part of what has happened – I steady myself against you.' The patient is a seeker. The therapist, too.

> 'Have you, lost seeker, found?'
> ('On a Deserted Shore', Kathleen Raine 1981)

Symbol

> 'And thou art wrapp'd and swath'd around in dreams,
> Dreams that are true, yet enigmatical;
> For the belongings of thy present state,
> Save through such symbols come not home to thee.'[16]
>
> (*Dream of Gerontius*,
> John Henry Newman 1801–1890)

Therapy undertaken in the Aeolian Mode gravitates towards primordial imagery. But it has a double goal, because it aims to integrate the images with true symbolic expression. This means that, although it exists in its own right, it also points beyond itself to something else.

A symbol is sometimes given a wider connotation – as something standing for or representing something else, by denoting, depicting, or exemplifying it. Viewed in this way, it makes every ikonic content, every word symbolic. We use it here in a more limited sense. For our present purposes, a symbol is seen as an integration of imagination and linguistic processes which differ from those representing spontaneous perception of the visible environment. The symbol carries an affective loading, and symbolic expression integrates two modes which reflect processes linked to the duality of the brain. 'Symbolizing is an activity, which appears when the consciousness reaches a high level of functional integration' (Fossi 1985).

Furthermore, the integration of insight and 'articulation' is an important component of psychotherapy. Rothenberg (1983) makes this point when he writes: 'The creative aspect of therapy is a process of integrating rather than simply combining or reconciling.' As a prerequisite for a symbol to 'stand in for something else', the individual needs to have experienced a sense of loss. In Kleinian terms, this means that, for symbols to be effective, the patient needs to have reached the depressive position. But a symbol can equally well stand as an emblem of the larger story within which we live out the story of our lives. In other words, it can evoke and invite – not on the basis of what man may have lost, but on what he senses there might be.

135

Goethe observed: 'In the symbol, the particular represents the general – as a living and momentary revelation of the inscrutable' (see Cirlot 1962). Ogden (1985) states: 'symbolic function is a direct consequence of the capacity to maintain psychological dialectics, and the psychopathology of symbolization is based on specific forms of failure to create or maintain these dialectics'. He also refers to Winnicott's view that it is within potential space that symbols originate. In the absence of potential space, there is only fantasy. Within potential space imagination can develop.

The symbol is not a subordination of the image to the word. It is a refreshing, vibrating rivalry complementing experience and giving emotional resonance. Symbols reconcile inner forces which are not evident in the province of discursive logic. The evocation of the image makes the experience particular and substantial. This synthesizing power is seen in the poetic image as a mingling of the concrete and the abstract. By thus linking these concrete images, characteristic of childhood, with the abstract concepts of adulthood, the creative process both affirms and gives substance to the image. Coleridge speaks of the faculty of imagination as

'that reconciling and mediating power, which incorporating the Reason in Images of the Sense, and organizing (as it were) the flux of the Sense by the permanence and self-circling energies of the Reason, gives birth to a system of symbols, harmonious in themselves, and consubstantial with the truths, of which they are conductors'.

(In Coburn 1972)

It is a reconciliation of opposites and of contrasting qualities:

'sameness and difference; general and concrete; idea and image; the individual and the representative; novelty and familiarity; emotion and order; judgment and feeling; the natural and the artificial; the poet and his poem'

(Barth 1977)

which blend into coherent experience. The poetic imagination fuses disparate phenomena into a new gestalt. In Coleridge's words, 'It dissolves, diffuses, dissipates in order to re-create' (*Biographica Literaria*). He says that imagination 'fuses' whereas 'fancy' – which is not the symbol-making faculty – merely 'aggregates' (in Shawcross 1907).

Symbols can coalesce and be recombined. Holland (1985) writes: 'In the act of symbolizing . . . we undo boundaries in order to discover them and in discovering boundaries we create them again.' Floating fantasies are fashioned into ordered patterns. 'To escape from being at the mercy of fantasy, some measure of symbolic control has to be achieved' (Wright 1984).

136

Chance alone is not necessarily creative. It is the unmasking and dynamic re-combination of images and symbols which makes it so:

'If an image that is *present* does not make us think of an image that is *absent*, if one occasional image does not set going a whole host of wandering images, an explosion of images, there is no imagination. There is perception, a memory of perception, a familiar memory, the customary colors and shapes . . . Within the human psyche it is the experience of opening, the experience even, of *novelty*.'

These are Bachelard's words from his 1943 publication *L'Air et les Songes*, translated by Forsyth (1971). We inevitably connect them with our first quotation from Bachelard. At the same time, they further demonstrate his emphasis on novelty and *poiesis*. Forsyth himself writes:

'With Bachelard we are watching the very first stages of the imagining process, we are back at the roots of being; we are studying not the formal synthesizing imagination but the imagination of matter, which is always fresh.'

Barth (1977) says:

'Symbol reveals the deepest mysteries of human life but respects their ultimate resistance to revelation. Symbol leaves the mysteries as it finds them, awesome, compelling, radiant with darkness and with light.'

There is indeed a merging of symbol and image, when each is considered in the radiant darkness and the dark light of psychic life. Similarly, though 'moving images' are described in the literature, that which is firmly and 'immovably' grounded may be more psychologically mobile than the image which is a 'drifting, homeless, expatriated thing' (see Patterson 1971). The therapeutic potentiality of an image depends not only upon its capacity to surprise and its dynamic freshness, it also utilizes its inherent synthesizing power. The active organizing principle acts below the level of consciousness and is linked with emotion. It also enables the echoes of the past to reverberate: 'Through the brilliance of an image, the distant past resounds with echoes' (Bachelard, op. cit.).

The symbolic image is generated by the integration of the dual processes of the mind. It depends upon dynamic synergism between the left and right cerebral hemispheres (p. 200). It is the optimal balancing of imagery, emotion, and thought which facilitates the creative process. If a stream of images invades and dominates the field of thinking, the ensuing impressions are chaotic and wild. If thinking is drained of ikonic content, the result is alienated, insipid intellectualization. The most highly connotative language is that of poetry, which is rich in metaphor, imagery, and symbol (see chapter 4).

As Bowra (1951) reminds us: 'there is still a place for poetry because it does something that nothing else can do.'

'I'm blind because I see too much, so I study by a dark lamp.'

(see p. 40)

This is the poetic, archaic language of a chronic schizophrenic. And it does several things that nothing else can do.

In his discussion of 'Interpretations Couched in the Poetic Style', Hammer (1978) describes the ethos of a poetic style of interpretation:

'In addition to the issues of content, timing and depth of interpretation in the service of enabling insight, recall, or deepening of the analytic regression, we might consider the more intangible manner, or style, in which the interpretation is offered . . . when interpreting, the analyst often subordinates image to idea, so that what emerges is treatise, polemic or catechism – anything but revelation or a deeper vision. In contrast, in poetry we experience the most effective, the most concentrated and emotionally texted communication man has as yet devised. It is through richly layered imagery that the poet works to create those fusions of echoed meanings that can set off landslides of resonating association to the readers.'

In 1879 Gerard Manley Hopkins wrote that 'the poetical language of an age should be current language heightened, to any degree, heightened and unlike itself, but not . . . an obsolete one'. He also observed that 'Poetry is in fact speech only employed to carry the inscape of speech *for the inscape's sake* – and therefore the inscape must be dwelt on' [our italics] (see Milroy 1977).

'I'm blind because I see too much, so I study by a dark lamp.' This opaque-yet-luminous proclamation is, we suggest, 'current language heightened' and it is certainly not obsolete. And, spoken as it was by someone with very tenuous links with any other human being, it was 'carrying the inscape of speech for the inscape's sake'. It could in fact do nothing other. External world phenomena and 'reality' were known to be unreliable. Relationships always failed. The inscape provided the only horizon. But too much had been seen. And it was safer to study by a dark lamp. This seems a fitting threshold at which to encounter the pull of the primordial.

ARCHAIC LANGUAGE

'We journey from the narrow place through the perilous place to the safe place.'

(*Barbarous Knowledge*, Hoffman 1967)

'[This] will close the eye of anguish.'

(*King Lear* IV. 4, 14)

'The pristine archaic themes remain standing like monumental ruins.'

(Santillana and von Dechend 1977)

'But I woke in an old ruin that the winds howled through'

(W. B. Yeats 'The Curse of Cromwell' in
Last Poems 1936–39 (see Yeats 1950))

'It is the other rivers that lie
Lower, that touch us only in dreams
That never surface.'

('Rising Damp', Ursula Fanthorpe 1982)

'Either the Darkness alters –
Or something in the sight
Adjusts itself to Midnight.'

(Emily Dickinson)

'a language which drops any of its sources grows thinner, loses a dimension, or suffers a diminished range of reference.'

(Coulson 1981)

Archaic language is easy to recognize. But it is not easy to define. It is not necessarily 'old', in the sense of being written in the remote past, or even in antiquity. It is not identical with the language of the primary process, in a psychoanalytic sense, though it is closely related to it. Similarly, although it has some of the qualities of infantile forms of language, it is still demarcated from them. It tends to be condensed, concise, direct, forceful, vivid, inferential, and it is affect-laden. Its equivalents are found in Greek myth, the Old Testament, the Nordic sagas, and Havamal. Prickett (1986) writes: 'the language of Shakespeare and the Authorized Version of the Bible is not a dead language in the late twentieth century. . . . It is archaic, but still present to us as a current linguistic idiom; *in use* every day in churches and theatres, taught and discussed in schools, seminaries, and universities, broadcast in some form almost every day on radio and television. It is not the language of ordinary colloquial speech, but then, *it never was.*' Kathleen Raine (1967) refers to the 'archaic splendour' of Edwin Muir's poetry, and the force of 'imaginative simplification'.

For our purposes, its predominant attribute is that it is heavy with affective loading and, as such, it carries existential weight. It also has a quality which is elusive when it comes to description, and which synonyms do not quite 'fit'. The adjective which comes closest as a description of language as it is used in therapeutic space is the word *Nobilmente*, chosen by Elgar for the Andante of his First Symphony. There seems to be no exact translation but it has implications of seriousness, nobility, dignity, and 'circumstance'.

139

As with all attempts to delineate characteristics of the language of deep feeling, there is a risk of being vague and 'romantic', or reductive and categorizing. Once again, it is the active process of *poiesis* which ensures its validity, though, in this instance, we are using the term to embrace the language of poetry itself. In his lecture of 1933 on 'The Name and Nature of Poetry', A. E. Housman, referring to the physical effect induced by 'mere words', says:

'because they are poetry, and *find their way to something in man which is obscure and latent, something older than the present organisation of his nature,* like the patches of fen which still linger here and there in the drained lands of Cambridgeshire'. [our italics; see also p. 64]

It is impossible to improve on Housman's words as a description of the significance of archaic language for the Aeolian Mode. As the therapist listens to what the patient is saying, he discerns content, cadence, and loading which 'find their way to something . . . which is obscure and latent, something older than the present organisation' of his patient's personality. And patients themselves often recognize this 'special kind of language' which they find themselves using at certain times.

'It's a legacy. I have it because the purpose is still there. It's how we used to think when we were very alone; when we were trees; and when we were rocks.'

'You called me back into being when you began to speak of these things.'

'These things?'

'Yes . . . original things. You see, I'm speaking in verbal, categorizing language; but they're in another language. They may be the "from" that everything comes from. The unconscious is more real; it's more enduring; and it has endured me.'

'The feelings come to me with something stronger than memory. There is something familiar; not familiar in that you've heard the exact words before. It's as though you are describing an experience which is yours, and yet you didn't know you'd had it.'

'It is familiar because it was there before you were.'

Following this reflective reverie, this patient said that there was a primeval quality to such feelings and language. And there is no doubt that he was in touch with the primordiality of such experience.

In the book of Job (8, 9) we read: 'For we are but of yesterday, and know nothing, because our days upon earth are a shadow.' But in this passage 'yesterday' refers to the brevity of life, and it illustrates the latent energy of archaic language. This is because it links feelings in the immediate present with the extended personal past which, in turn, merges with a transgenerational burden of significance.

Just as 'poetry is not the thing said but a way of saying it' (see p. 64), so archaic language is a way of weighting words with the cadence of earlier destinies. Although the actual words are often in basic English, they seem to carry meaningful congruity with all epochs of the patient's life. There is often a blurring of tenses, so that it is hard to detect whether the experience is still continuing, or whether it has been outlived. This should not surprise us, because the unconscious is timeless. But there are also blendings of incipience and fruition. This is exemplified by a phrase at the end of Tolstoy's short story *Hadji Murat*. As his death began to make its presence felt, we read that 'It all seemed so insignificant compared to *what was now beginning and had already begun* for him' [our italics].

Had this been described in therapeutic space by Hadji himself, it would certainly count as archaic language. But all dynamic therapy shows this phenomenon when the patient encounters his hidden experience. A man whose dead victim was lying on his back on the floor said:

'I was staring at him.
And he was staring at nothing.'

These archaic disclosures are true as accounts of current experience, but they seem to ring even more true as epiphanies of earlier experience which, until recently, has been lost. Thus 'I was staring at him' was an accurate account of the forensic event, but it subsequently echoed with transferred experience which the patient had wanted to forget. He had been ignored in childhood. The archaic transformation leads to the following 'reading':

'I was staring at my Dad.
And Dad was staring at me . . . at nothing.'

It was a demonstration of very low self-esteem.

The opening of this section closes by drawing attention to the affective and linguistic echo between the language called into being with fear and perplexity in therapeutic space, and that of formal poetry.

A slumber did my spirit seal;
I had no human fears:
She seem'd a thing that could not feel
The touch of earthly years.

No motion has she now, no force;
She neither hears nor sees;
Roll'd round in earth's diurnal course,
With rocks, and stones, and trees.
                    (Wordsworth 1770–1850)

Archaic language in therapeutic space

As the patient's story unfolds, the pull of the primordial is often felt. This is usually evident when he begins to employ archaic language to describe that which must declare its presence. But sometimes the primordial appears as a countertransference phenomenon. This occurs when the therapist finds that archaic echoes are evoked by trigger stimuli in the patient's colloquial, vernacular style of disclosure. It was exemplified in vignette 1.1 where the patient's anticipatory anxiety evoked primordial apprehension of 'crossing the Jordan'.

Foulkes (1964) has drawn attention to the various levels which can be discerned in a therapeutic group. He refers to the current, the transference, the projective, and the primordial level. 'This fourth level is the one in which primordial images occur according to the concepts of Freud and those particularly formulated by Jung concerning the existence of a collective unconscious.' For our purposes it is important to note that primordial images are often described in archaic language. But the earliest images of all may be detected in the contouring of an archaic quality of silence. Primordial reverberations may echo in the group matrix. But they may energize the 'group in the mind' of a patient in individual therapy. 'Of all my dead it's you who come to me unfinished' (see p. 145).

The closer the language of psychotherapy comes to having a cognitive–affective expressive function, the more it assumes archaic characteristics. Though there are exceptions to this rule, the therapist often finds that the first hint that his patient is on the brink of disclosing deep material is when the vernacular is seasoned with the archaic. And, ultimately, the archaic may predominate.

We can guess, we can infer, but we cannot explain with any certainty why archaic language is so frequently invoked to carry our deepest feelings. Yet it is so. And this phenomenon is independent of formal education and degree of literacy. It may have something to do with the point at which 'everyday language' breaks, because too much is expected of it. It may also have something to do with those transgenerational existential debts (Boszormenyi-Nagy and Spark 1973) which continue to influence the experience of subsequent generations. Such debts are often better expressed in language which is timeless for each language generation. It may be a debt of gratitude to life, a debt of taking life for granted or a debt evident as some other invisible loyalty. Sometimes it appears that affect 'skips' a generation or so puzzles it recipients. 'Modern English, excellent though it is as a means of *communication*, is much less suitable as a medium of *expression*' (Latham-Koenig 1984). This pull of the primordial is clamantly evident in the disclosive and expressive language of psychotherapy. It often erupts abruptly because it is called upon to convey the deepest feelings about loving or hating, living or dying. It may occur during a relived 'description' of earlier joy or sorrow. But it almost always clothes a transference-intensified perception of the world, and, in particular, that precise presence of a significant other in the world through the vicarious presence of the therapist. Such archaic language may describe the basic experiences of being full or being empty, of being hot or being cold, of being held or being abandoned. More complicated affects are frequently finely tuned through the invocation of archaic expression. Thus prophetic assurance or catastrophic abandonment are given the measure of proclamation or degree of primitive 'howling' they justify.

Latham-Koenig continues, 'It is almost as if, when man comes into contact with the divine, his language tends to break away from ordinary colloquial speech.' It is certainly true that archaic language is used in the language of worship, and many prayers are heavily endowed with this archaic loading. Again it is instantly identified, but hard to analyse. It is not just 'old English'. Man is 'set in the midst of so many and great dangers'. He asks to 'have a right judgement in all things' and addresses God in this way: 'O Father of lights, with whom there is no variableness, nor shadow of turning'. It seems to be a matter of cadence and the indubitable significance of what is being said. But other than rational factors contribute to the sense of the primordial which many schizophrenics have, who have had no chance of learning such language by 'contagion'. 'The world's a dying ember' is one such example. 'A dark lamp' is another. Archaic language is equally at home, and equally essential, at the opposite pole of experience. The diabolical, the menacing, and every kind of threat of alienation, or loss of authenticity, may call for the archaic (see p. xxviii).

Prolonged experience of being in the presence of numerous 'disturbed' psychotics furnishes undeniable evidence of the resort to archaic expression. This is often almost inexplicable in terms of the patient's formal education and previous experience of language.

'The world's a dying ember.
That's my estimation of the world.'

Such an unheralded commentary on 'the world' is perhaps expected from his fool, or even King Lear himself. It is in the same key as his estimation of the world: 'I think the world's asleep' (*King Lear* I. 4, 48). But, as an unsolicited, spontaneous utterance from a chronic schizophrenic, during an extended silence in a group therapy session, it places 'a radiant obstacle in the path of the obvious', to borrow Steiner's discussion of Heidegger and astonishment. It astonishes us, too, and makes any professional attempt to categorize psychotic speech seem trivial. How does such a patient have access to this degree of reflective acuity and yet command a matching expressive fidelity? Her usual preoccupation is with basic biological needs, which are described in brief, truncated, frequently monosyllabic utterances: 'I'm hot. I'm cold. I'm wet. I'm hungry. I'm thirsty. It's cold.' Her bodily sensations preoccupy her, and delusion and hallucination frequently make their presence felt: 'There is a sizzling sound on my left shoulder.'

We suggest that her words have such a powerful impact upon us because their primordiality touches our depths. As Halliburton (1981) reminds us: 'If one is primordial enough . . . the possibilities are actualized.' These words reach us through their archaic resonance. *Poiesis* has occurred. We know that 'a dying ember' is saying that the fire has lost its heat. But we also know that it is saying more than this. There is an inference of cosmic cooling. She is saying something more all-embracing and unavoidable than *a* fire has lost its heat. There can be no other warmth on earth, because the world — all of it — is cooling. The embers are no longer glowing. The world is a dying ember. And the world is both around us and within. My inner world is cooling too. My warmth is not being replenished.

Furthermore, there is no panic, no cataclysmic sense of urgency. That the world is a dying ember is neither her dread nor her nightmare. It is her sober estimation. She had never been known to use such a word as 'estimation' before. And she may never do so again. But all the staff who heard this remarkable utterance wondered where such knowledge and such expression had come from. It exemplified that prophetic quality which Siirala (1961) has described. And it was certainly archaic. It may well have owed its origin to a transgenerational existential debt. And the following words were these:

> 'It was the end of the world when I first came here. I couldn't see anything. I couldn't feel anything. Me and my brother were dying embers. We didn't even know our addresses.'

Literary references may illuminate this theme of transgenerational obligation which, not surprisingly, often has archaic connotations:

> ' "It is easy," I was crying,
> "for you to tremble, for you to enthral me,
> as the dead draw the dying" .'
>
> (Wolfe 1928)

'The dead may pass
their serious burdens to the living.'

(Porter 1978)

'This news is mortal to the queen; look down
And see what death is doing'

(*The Winter's Tale* III. 2, 148)

'Of all my dead it's you who come to me unfinished.'

(Adrienne Rich 1978)

'She danced into the lonely churchyard, but the dead were not dancing; they had more important things to do.'

(Hans Andersen, translated by Vera Gissing 1979)

'Now he is dead, but he still allows me no escape. He will haunt me to
my grave.'

(*Bleak House*, Dickens)

'And if he comes that close, then through him those dead voices may
speak, the only voices, as Kierkegaard says, which are impossible to
silence.'

(Rupp 1969)

'The dead need no advice.'

(Bernard Levin, *The Times* 22 December 1986)

Any discussion about archaic language involves an interweaving of content
and cadence. It will be recalled that the initial contact with the primordial
as a countertransference phenomenon in vignette 1.1 was not only the
cadence 'How wilt thou do in the swelling of the Jordan?' but also the
content which, in turn, led to the 'other rivers that lie lower'. This is
discussed in the penultimate paragraph of this chapter.

At this point we are aware of a confluence of various themes which
permeate the book. Archaic language as a genre is important in its own
right. And we have frequently stressed the therapeutic significance of the
process of *poiesis* and also of poetic language. But poetic language is not
necessarily archaic. And both are significant as bearers of allusion (see
p. 152). In this section, however, we are concentrating our attention upon
the frequent adoption of the archaic, which carries with it a penumbra
which is both mysterious and compelling.

When the patient is unable to express that 'uprush of feeling' in
'everyday' words, he often invokes archaic imagery. This occurs when
an aptly timed interpretation links inexplicable present experience and
unbinds the restrictive legacies of the past. Such an intervention is then a

truly cognitive–affective event. And the cathartic component of supportive therapy may be stamped by an equally powerful and archaically expressed affective thrust; though, in this case, the buried past remains buried.

The holding function of analytically orientated therapy brings us close to Modell's discussion (1976) of an important theme. And we (Cox 1986) have explored the holding function of dynamic psychotherapy in a 'holding', custodial context. But there is an even wider connotation of the holding function of therapy, when a patient recalls the words 'With faith I plunge me in this sea' (Charles Wesley) – and then adds that 'the sea is the unconscious, the unknown, and the unimaginable'. But it is an unfamiliar sea entered with 'faith . . . but it's *your* faith'. 'Faith', here, might be extrapolated to a wider theological frame of reference, but in this specific instance it referred to trust that, though risky, therapeutic space was not an alien abyss. The space in which the patient was exploring his inner world was *therapeutic* space, and depth was trusted to prove to be ultimately affirmative. It does not seem unreasonable to invoke Erikson's concept (1950) of basic trust here, when a patient is reliving experience in which trusting has hitherto been groundless.

The pull of the primordial is present in day-to-day conversation, in therapeutic sessions, and in the wordless moments of drama. This is brought into sharp focus when one of the earlier, 'verbal' speeches of King Lear is set beside the primordial cry of anguish as he enters 'with Cordelia dead in his arms':

'Howl, howl, howl!'
(*King Lear*
V. 3, 256)

And no one is a stranger to silent, internal, inaudible howling. Primordial preverbal pain. Archaic anguish. States (1978) refers to 'a depth that articulation would only violate'. And the therapist is then a silent witness of soundless depth.

We have included this section because it is our experience that the deeper the feeling the patient wishes to express, the more is the affective loading of his speech coloured by what, *for him*, is archaic language. The words 'for him' are in italics because it is self-evident that the precise language chosen by a patient, at his point of urgency, inevitably depends not only upon his cultural background, but also upon a wide range of influences which impinge upon his linguistic and expressive possibilities. Nevertheless, it seems clear that the affective loading of language is linked with a return to earlier dialects, or even other languages, which were the patient's 'mother tongue' at an earlier phase of his life. It is therefore technically a regressive phenomenon, but it is not necessarily a defensive one. Indeed, it is often the exact opposite of defence; because a patient is able to express feelings which were originally defended against. Linked with this is the well-known phenomenon that the dialect, and manner of speaking, in which a man loses his temper, or makes love, frequently reflects the dialect of his earlier life, rather than of his present-day social context. Thus a 'Geordie' may 'howl' as a Devonian, or *vice versa*.

It comes as no surprise that there are similarities between this particular aspect of *poiesis* in disclosure within therapeutic space and the language of literature chosen for the *poiesis* of 'poetry'. Thus Tillyard (1934) writes: 'The importance to mankind of expressing, of airing these primal feelings is great. Poetical obliquity is one of the chief instruments of this process.' In a subsequent passage he refers to the need to 'preserve antique ways of feeling'. It is interesting to note that, whereas this is a specialized aspect of poetic studies, 'poetical obliquity' can be discerned in every therapeutic session.

The pull of the primordial

There are certain phrases which seem naturally and inevitably to cluster together. They all denote movement. There is the pull of the primordial. There is the experience described by States (1978) where he refers to the ' "uprush of feeling" that takes place when you suddenly, or gradually, perceive that the text you are reading is in some devious or hidden sense "oscillating" (as Kierkegaard says) with something else, being in effect foreordained, though the point of ordination is nowhere to be seen'. For our purposes 'the text' represents the patient's unfolding story. But during psychotherapy the reverse is true, because the 'point of ordination' is abundantly evident as a transference phenomenon. It is the working through of the 'oscillation with something else' which is the central task in psychotherapy. This is an amalgamation of experience gleaned over many years:

'I need archaic language to put it in.'

　　'Why?'

'It's not the language one speaks every day – it's so trampled on. The archaic and poetic is "what else there is". It hints at things. It puts it at a distance . . . it is as though someone else is saying it. It is far away. It hangs about a bit. It lingers. It's got a stillness around it.'
'It puts it at a depth. It feels like it has more than a subjective feeling. It is carrying messages between people who would otherwise be isolated.'
'It doesn't mean more, but it's more readily understood.'

'It takes you back further than your own early life.'

'It helps one to get behind things. What did ancestors think they foresaw? They were looking forward to it.'

'It helps to look forward to the past from a more remote past.'

'It feels both more and less precise. It expresses feelings more "washed", i.e. more clearly.'

'It sets it apart from your own daily life.'

'It can make the experience it conveys a "new one", i.e. it keeps it alive.'

The paradoxical component here is striking. We are told of things 'that cannot be and that are' – 'and that which speaks out of the oldest twilight' (Chesterton). And the pull of the primordial could not be more clearly stated than in the phrase, 'It takes you back further than your own early life.' Here myth and the language of myth are unmistakably present. Unfortunately, mythopoiesis, a world in itself, can only receive passing mention. But the two basic perspectives, the historic and the recurrent, which Slochower (1970) describes, merit attention. The Aeolian Mode may, at any moment, invoke the aid of *poiesis*, so that the perennial myth is constantly made fresh in each personal story. 'Myth has cast a spell on the very ages which denied or opposed it. Like the severed head of Orpheus, it "goes on singing even in death and from afar"' (Jung and Kerenyi 1951). The field of forensic psychotherapy is heavily loaded with clinical legacies of myth. Oedipus and Icarus must stand as emblems for their twentieth-century peers. But in the practice of offender-therapy, the 'severed head' may not be merely that of antiquity. Nor of metaphor.

In fact, it was through the difficulty of trying to establish psychotherapeutic contact with patients whose inner worlds were almost inaccessible because their histories included the severing of heads, that we realized afresh that orthodox analytic approaches could not always take us the whole way. It was from this experience that our use of the image and the mutative metaphor gradually crystallized. Hoffmann (1967), describing Muir's *donnée*, says: 'We each fall anew from Eden and retrace the long voyage through the narrow place and the perilous place in search of the sufficient place.'

Our technical language in forensic 'case conferences' may use different terminology, but the mythical roots of a homicidal psychopath are often vividly evident in his 'clinical' story. We find him entering the perilous, via the narrow, in search of that which is sufficient. And therapeutic space may afford him temporary dynamic asylum, *en route* to the discovery of his developing *inner* sufficiency. Thanks to Bachelard (op. cit.) we realized that it was possible to 'reach the depths before stirring the surface' even with patients whose destructive activities had been so extreme. But, in these current clinical encounters, there was no singing in death or from afar.

Another reflective comment upon archaic language was as follows:

'What goes with it is an unresolved feeling. It comes with the assurance of many meanings. Something has been said by many people before – but the meaning is the least important thing about it. *It's the atmosphere of it*. It can mean a variety of things. *It lingers*. It is like a child looking at grown-up ''connected hand-writing''. You know it means something.'

These reflections followed a discussion of the power that was inherent in the phrase: 'Entreat me not to leave thee' (*Ruth* 1, 16) when it is set beside a modern translation, 'Do not urge me to go back and desert you.' The former has cadence, coherence, completeness, and compactness. But its strength lies in the intensity and depth of the feeling it carries.

As this book is primarily about the mutative aspects of metaphor and imagery through poetic appropriation and poetic induction, we will draw this section to a close by linking several references. The first originates within therapeutic space, the others come from literature:

'He went into the house and the shadows followed him . . . all these feelings came upon me. They are more ''upon'' me than really within me. I am meaning something else but I don't know what it is.'

'sin and love and fear are just sounds that people who have never sinned nor loved nor feared have for what they never had and cannot have until they forget the words . . . hearing the dark voicelessness in which the words are the deeds, and the other words that are not deeds, that are just the gaps in people's lacks, coming down like the cries of the geese out of the wild darkness in the old terrible nights, fumbling at the deeds like orphans to whom are pointed out in a crowd two faces and told, That is your father, your mother . . . Then it was over. Over in the sense that he was gone and I knew that, see him again though I would, I would never again see him coming swift and secret to me in the woods dressed in sin like a gallant garment already blowing aside with the speed of his secret coming.'

(*As I Lay Dying*, William Faulkner 1935)

'But, sometimes, when I took her up, and felt that she was lighter in my arms, a dead blank *feeling came upon me*, as if I were approaching to some frozen region yet unseen, that numbed my life. I avoided the recognition of this feeling by any name.' [our italics]

(*David Copperfield*, Charles Dickens, see p. 66)

149

Like all dynamic psychotherapy, the Aeolian Mode attempts to put the patient in touch with those areas of his affective life which have been banished from his horizon of awareness. And such a dismissal may be through an unconscious defence mechanism or through deliberate avoidance. In either case, the experience is inaccessible to intentional recall.

The pull of the primordial, the invocation of archaic language, and the sense of 'oscillation with something else' have a dual impetus which the patient senses. There is both a distancing and an intensification of proximity. The archaic heightens a sense of pervasiveness and therefore departicularization. Yet, at the same time, there is a primordial sense of personal privacy. This is a paradox which we do not wish to resolve. It is Janusian and firmly faces both ways. But that is part of the essence of the experience which often brings patients to therapy, and of all men as they search for their own 'earlier destinies' (Kenner 1948). And such destinies are enshrined in myth.

In comparison with images, myths tend to house more unconsciously determined material, memories from earlier periods and primary process associations. They deal with material as symbolic, rather than literal and reality-bound. Like drama, myths invite the suspension of belief and of the rules of logic, social convention, and conscience. For these reasons, regression that follows mythical interpretation is likely to have creative potential (Victor 1978).

Taking an almost quantum leap of time from Greek mythology, via the Old Testament, to the *New York Times* (14 January 1979), we find a phrase that aptly describes the way in which experience may be kept at bay. At least until it is rendered increasingly tolerable through psychotherapy. Our attention therefore moves from the mythical, archaic singing of the severed head of Orpheus to clinical realities of the twentieth century. The *New York Times* carries this sentence – a sentence already mentioned twice (pp. 19 and 32) because it is enfeebled by paraphrase, though its point still needs to be made:

> '[They] sort of "break down" formally in a way that suggests that something behind the text was almost too hot to handle!'

Deep feeling may not quite surface because there is something behind which is 'almost too hot to handle', so that 'everyday' language cannot hold it. It is not surprising that ultimate questions about experiences which are 'too hot to handle' – even in psychotherapy – lead us towards theology on the one hand, and *Barbarous Knowledge* (Hoffmann 1967) on the other. Tillich (1966) in *On the Boundary* wrote: 'One must stand between the archaic and contemporary . . . to recapture, on the boundary, the original archetypal language.' This takes us back to the linking of the current and the archaic with which this section started. In 'Rising Damp' Ursula Fan-thorpe (1982) refers to the underground rivers of London by name, and then follows this powerful stanza:

> It is the other rivers that lie
> Lower, that touch us only in dreams
> That never surface. We feel their tug
> As a dowser's rod bends to the source below.

In our view, this is also true of the 'tug' we feel at the archaic pull of the primordial as a patient tells his story. The phrase 'the other rivers' is one which evocatively and precisely has the quality of *poiesis*. For each of us there are personal 'other rivers'. But there are also generic, archetypal, and pervasive 'other rivers'. And, once again, the older they are, the more personal and more universal they become.

Bodkin (1934), writing over fifty years ago, quotes a passage from Gilbert Murray which is up to date because it refers to feelings 'thousands of years' old.

> 'Gilbert Murray [1927] apologizes for the metaphor of which he can-not keep clear when he says that such stories and situations are ''deeply implanted in the memory of the race, stamped as it were upon our physical organism''. . . . We say that such themes ''are strange to us. Yet there is that within us which leaps at the sight of them, a cry of the blood which tells us we have known them always''. . . . And again: ''In plays like *Hamlet* or the *Agamemnon* or the *Electra* we have certainly fine and flexible character-study, a varied and well-wrought story, a full command of the technical instruments of the poet and the dramatist; but we have also, I suspect, *a strange, unanalysed vibration below the surface*, an undercurrent of desires and fears and passions, long slumbering yet eternally familiar, which have for thousands of years lain near the root of our most intimate emotions and been wrought into the fabric of our most magical dreams. How far into past ages this stream may reach back, I dare not even surmise.''' [our italics]

Such archaic description has close affinities to the physiognomic perception of listening landscapes and the 'urgent country' near Rocamadour. Church (1957) describes 'the village of stone and sunshine in that urgent country where nature still has something of terror close beneath the surface. But is not that too a characteristic of the world of dream?'

The final line of the poem is in no doubt about 'the other rivers that lie lower'. It is a fitting conclusion to a section on archaic language and the pull of the primordial:

> *'Phlegethon, Acheron, Lethe, Styx.'*

But in a book with a strongly applied clinical *raison d'être*, it seems appropriate to end with words from therapeutic space. Painful memory provoked by a casual comment was described as follows:

'Unwittingly, he rings an old bell.'

And the patient is aware of a defensive paradox when his apprehension, evident in 'I talk of old times and dilute what I'm trying to say', is set against: 'The primordial is over-layered: – it takes quite a time to strip off the layers.' But the pull of the primordial can do just this.

Both old bells and archaic language are used to warn, to invite, and to announce. They can confront. And they can support.

ALLUSION

'Allusiveness makes the reader work – and perhaps also play. . . . Allusion creates a particularity and keeps abstraction fresh.'

(Barbara Hardy 1975)

The dictionary defines 'allusion' as a 'covert, implied or indirect reference'. Its origin is from the Latin *ludere* which means 'to play'. As Winnicott (1971) and Garland (1981) remind us, playing is the serious work of the growing child and the growing child-within-the-adult during psychotherapy. And a therapeutic group provides 'play space' for sober citizens to re-enjoy the forgotten pleasures of creative exploration.

It is widely acknowledged that accurate empathy is one of the essential ingredients in an effective therapeutic alliance. An important contributory factor in such 'effective' empathy is the recognition of covert and oblique references. And the clinician knows of the numerous clues which the non-verbal communication of gesture, posture, and expression convey. Here are a few reminders:

'His eyes were crammed with all his life'
(*All the Days of his Dying*,
Marlena Frick 1972)

'The King is angry: see, he gnaws his lip.'
(*Richard III* IV. 2, 26)

'When he smiled, he didn't smile.'

'my words were uttered in no ordinary manner; my forehead, cheeks, eyes, colour, tone of voice cried out, more clearly than the words I spake.'

(Augustine)

'That look told Ivan Ilyich everything . . . that movement confirmed everything.'

(*The Death of Ivan Ilyich*, Tolstoy)

'He speaketh with his feet,
He teacheth with his fingers.'

(Proverbs 6.13)

'Thine eye begins to speak
Set thy tongue there.'

(*Richard II* V. 3, 12)

'Speak that I may see thee.'

('Discoveries', Ben Jonson)

'There was speech in their dumbness,
Language in their very gesture'

(*The Winter's Tale* V. 2, 13)

'Thou tremblest, and the whiteness in thy cheek
Is apter than thy tongue to tell thy errand'

(*Henry IV Part II* I. 1, 68)

Accurate empathy depends not only upon the perception and reception of the overt, but the detection through an 'echo-sounding' response of the covert. Virginia Woolf, a writer with a particularly rich tapestry of allusions, wrote in *A Room of One's Own*: 'Great poets do not die; they are continuing presences.' And Beverly Schlack (1979) devoted a whole volume to the study of her use of literary allusions in *Continuing Presences*. This is a spur to the therapist's attentiveness to those oblique, half-heard echoes which orchestrate and harmonize the single melodic line of the spoken word. These are as relevant in clinical work as they are in *A Room of One's Own* – or any other work of fiction. And they are no less significant in the inner world disclosure of the psychopathic killer, as they are in that of the depressed academic. They are *always* important. Psychotherapy undertaken in the Aeolian Mode draws upon those indirect, allusive messages which, when once detected, are seen to lie thick upon the ground.

Inferential 'marginalia' frequently carry autonomous existential weight. By this we mean that they are not necessarily, or solely, restricted to providing evidence of 'defence organization'. They may be a link with wider frames of reference than the categorizing implications of 'personality structure'. Shared, allusive frames of reference are part of a common cultural heritage. But it must be immediately emphasized that this is not necessarily related to 'university studies in literature' or familiarity with the genre of Virgina Woolf. It is equally, and often more pervasively, related to the titles of pop songs, fairy tales, myths, media advertising slogans, or other aspects of current affairs and public life.

The reader will now come across two quotations. It is likely that the first will be regarded as so well known that it is almost patronizing to ask for any associated wording. Whereas the second may ring allusive, though indistinct, bells. Or none at all.

> 'To be, or not . . .'
> (*Hamlet* III. 1, 56)

We suggest that few readers will be unable to complete the line!

At the end of the Clark Lectures, given in Cambridge in 1946, on *The Poetic Image*, C. Day Lewis (1947) said:

> 'It is still your task to show men fear in a handful of dust and *eternity in a grain of sand*.' [our italics]

It is probable that the phrase 'eternity in a grain of sand' will provoke the ringing of a distant bell of familiarity. But the reader may well be disturbed, because it does not quite fit into what he thought was a relatively familiar quotation about 'a grain of sand'. It may be argued that in this instance a poet is giving a lecture on the poetic image to an audience which would expect poetic allusions. Nevertheless, we still experience a slightly uneasy feeling that there is something here which is wrong. It is familiar, yet not familiar. And a therapist often has a similar feeling as he listens to what his patient is saying. There is an allusive quality because we are aware of an indirect and oblique reference which we cannot quite bring into focus. In fact, C. Day Lewis was deliberately condensing and distorting some lines from William Blake:

> 'To see a World in a Grain of Sand,
> And a Heaven in a Wild Flower,
> Hold Infinity in the palm of your hand,
> And Eternity in an hour.'
> (*Auguries of Innocence* 1)

It is here that the impossibility of the 'impossible profession' begins to bite. It is difficult enough for the therapist to engage accurately with the manifest content of what the patient says. And it is clearly impossible for him to be able to follow all those allusive references which a common cultural heritage yields. But it is doubly impossible to follow fully those secret and deliberately hidden allusions which come, not from the common cultural heritage, but from a particular personal past. Idiosyncratic though they are, they still colour both the conscious and the unconscious aspects of speech.

Nevertheless, it is the therapist's capacity to 'tune in' to the particular personal past of the patient which is of decisive significance. The degree of empathy, which is sufficiently firm to take the full weight of disclosure, is often indicated by the patient's appreciation that his allusive inferences have not gone unnoticed. This is of importance when psychotherapy is undertaken with neurotic patients. It is not only more difficult, but it is also far more necessary if the psychotic is to be able to trust a therapist with his idiosyncratic frame of reference. With no other patient population is Husserl's concept of the 'perspectival world' more important than when working with the psychotic. The therapist needs to share it partially, reversibly, and temporarily. Reverting to the words of a psychotic patient, which have already been looked at from several points of view (Cox 1978), we are encountered by language which is concentrated and allusively dense.

'I'm blind because I see too much, so I study by a dark lamp.' [see pp. 40 and 138]

There may well be allusive implications in the phrase 'a dark lamp' which still remain hidden. Because of this, the empathic bond, so crucial when in the presence of the psychotic, may be even more fragile than is necessary. This points to the conclusion that no therapist will ever be able to understand all the allusive implications of his patient's account of experience. He may have the full armamentarium of professional training and the advantage of a psychodynamic perspective, yet he still remains challenged by the full range of human experience, in the face of which poetic images offer cautious glimpses, far removed from spurious certainties. In Brockbank's words (1976): '"Have I caught thee?", we ourselves ask of the play [*King Lear*], wondering what haunts its elusive speculations, what we are meant wholly to see and what we are merely to glimpse.'

This salutary reminder from the realm of literary criticism is one which the clinician needs. Some 'clinical' events cannot be 'wholly seen'. Once again, we find ourselves asking exactly what a 'dark lamp' is. It certainly meant something exact to the person who said it.

This section on the enhanced poverty of therapeutic exchange which can result from unrecognized allusion, is of importance in all dynamic psychotherapy. Yet the Aeolian Mode places great emphasis on allusion because, without it, the associative penumbra is inevitably depleted. This invokes an association from Pirandello (1921): 'the shadows were swarming with us'.

When a therapist is working within the Aeolian Mode the shadows are indeed swarming with allusive potential. And, lest the therapist should be distracted by their presence, he needs to concentrate upon the psychodynamics viewed from a conventional analytic perspective. If the shadows are to be regarded as swarming with useful associative material, and not with distracting contaminants, then the therapist must be as equally aware of the patient's personality structure, defence organization, and libidinal orientation, as he is when the web of allusion confronts him in such phrases as 'To be, . . .' 'eternity in a grain of sand', or 'a dark lamp'.

The shock of unintended allusion

VIGNETTE 5.1 (GROUP THERAPY SETTING)
'a telephone directory?'

TOM: 'I had a dream that I saw you [the therapist] in a long blue cloak and a black boater [straw hat] vanishing into the distance.'

'What did you feel, Tom?'

'Nothing. I didn't *feel* anything.'

'Nothing?'

'Nothing. I was just an observer.'

[Thinking of the most mundane and inert object possible]
'As interesting as a telephone directory?'

BOB: [hitherto uninvolved and 'miles away' – suddenly excited, making mercurial movements of arms and legs]: 'How *could* you mention telephone directories – and on Derby Day, of all days!'

The therapist could not possibly have known of the previous connection between Bob and telephone directories. Bob subsequently told the group that his last crime had involved a phone box on Derby Day. During his last day 'at large' telephone directories had been of crucial significance. Was this 'mere coincidence'? Or synchronicity? Or intuition? Or the stochastic principle? The therapist had intended to choose the most 'neutral' item he could think of. His unintentional, 'casual' allusion had proved to be of almost depth-charge proportions for Bob, whose unexpected memories came flooding back.

No conversation is ever safe from such phenomena; and a therapeutic matrix least of all. Unwittingly, the therapist may ring old, forgotten bells. In a therapeutic group any one may sound such an alarm. Fortunately, no form of professional training in psychotherapy can confer immunity from the spur of the unintended allusion. This 'anything may happen at any moment' quality keeps the members on corporate 'tip-toe' and associative reverberations in the air.

'Now a thing was secretly brought to me, and mine ear received a little thereof.'

(Job 4.12)

'Convincing circumstantial detail is likely to have an enlivening effect: the dead, revived, gather round with their lives in our heads.'
(Cunningham 1979)

Sometimes patients use language which, initially, appears to be unremarkable. But closer attention reveals other levels of meaning which are both ambiguous and condensed. And its very concentration lends it a peculiarly rich, allusive quality. For example:

'Nothing was very much there.'
'Nothing is really finished.'
'I talk about old times and dilute what I'm trying to say.'
'What is within me encompasses me.'
'I was always playing apart.' [an isolated childhood?]

and its homophone:

'I was always playing a part.' [lack of authenticity?]

Other passages are lyrical and 'prophetic', using the latter word in the strict sense of *saying* 'how things *are*' – not 'how they *will be*'.

'But the darkness comes over and gets me. The darkness plunges over and into and around me, it dismembers me and takes me all to pieces. I take the fundamental truth of all things and lay it alongside my little life here. You can't dis-spell your own darkness.'

There are allusive triggers in this reflective passage, though each reader will probably find a different inner echo to word and cadence, affect and image.

In *The Language Poets Use*, Winifred Nowottny (1962) refers to literary allusions which 'almost shriek for admittance', in her discussions of a poem by Dylan Thomas. And, different though our interest with *poiesis* may be, her questions about allusion are equally pressing if we are fully to appreciate what a patient is *saying – not saying – almost saying*. She asks 'How is allusiveness to be established? Even if it is established, what does it mean?. . . . what limits are to be set to the relevance of the allusion . . . to the concerns of the poem [*clinical disclosure*] in which it is included?' [our italics]. 'Does the allusion consist only of the lines that enable us to identify it, or is the immediate context of the allusion relevant?' If these questions are now read again and linked to a therapeutic session, it will be evident how complex is the 'unravelling' aspect of therapy.

'He just kept on dying and dying and dying and never actually died.'

'I just went on killing her. It never occurred to me that she'd die.'

The quotation from *All the Days of his Dying* on page 152 is one of numerous possible allusive links to the sequential discontinuing stages of dying which feature in these disclosures. Exactly how allusion makes its imprint on those within therapeutic space, and how it influences the timing and texture of the therapist's response, is too large a question to try to answer here. But, whenever it is ignored, the therapist knows that he may be failing to follow a vital clue to crucial aspects of the patient's inner world.

Barbara Herrnstein Smith (1968) studies closural allusions in *Poetic Closure*. She refers to phenomena which are 'more specific than "association"' – and goes on to describe the '"kinaesthetic image"': not a picture of the event from the outside, as it were, but a sense of what it feels like to be engaged in it' (see p. 173). This brings us back to the dynamic components of the Aeolian Mode. It so clearly joins the *poiesis* of poetry to that of psychotherapy. And it links them both to the aesthetic and the kinaesthetic imperatives which all focus at the patient's point of urgency. It is to the gravitational 'pull of the primordial' that all these converging forces respond. It is not only 'great poets' who are continuing presences. All those who have ever been present continue to exert a 'presence' which may, or may not, feature in consciousness.

PARADOX

'The things that cannot be and that are'

(G. K. Chesterton)

'It is localized everywhere.' [see p. 247, and note 16 on p. 254]
'I bombarded him gently with my life.'
'Oh – I feel so cold. But not fire-cold.'
'First death, then life.' [Kierkegaard]
'I bought a coat five sizes too big. Yet it fits.'

Among the dictionary entries for 'paradox' we find: 'a statement seemingly self-contradictory or absurd, though possibly well-founded or essentially true'. Though the theme of paradox surfaces at many places in these pages, the references to paradox are usually adjectival of something else. But here the paradox is 'the thing itself'. And Edwin Muir (1960) gives us a paradox which can stand as a thematic emblem for the one story, and the one story only, that each man must tell:

'What I shall never know
I must make known.'

('The Poet')

It is almost a mirror image of two lines by Sackville-West (1926):

158

I tell the things I know, the things I knew
Before I knew them, immemorially.'   ('Winter')

Whereas the many faces of metaphor and archaic language have been studied extensively, our approach to paradox is circumscribed because the *Bachelardian paradox* is inherent in the Aeolian Mode. And the brief vignettes show this paradox at work. Patients are exploring deep feelings while their surfaces remain intact. Paradox is clearly evident in mixed metaphors which are logically impossible, though they have incontrovertible affective lucidity. For example, we 'know' what a patient means when he says: 'I'm high and dry. And totally at sea.'

The Aeolian Mode, and its many ramifications into myth and metaphor, imagery and poiesis, stem from Bachelard's baffling and central paradox. Initially it appears to be widely at variance with the direction of classical analytical momentum. Greenson (1967) emphasizes the orthodox injunction: 'begin every interpretation from the surface'. And when Bachelard's statement is set alongside this, a polarity is at once evident.

But if this orientation is accepted, not only as an aesthetic observation but also as a therapeutic response, then paradox is undeniably at the heart of the matter. It implies that exploratory, analytically orientated psychotherapy can start where it is usually regarded as ending – a race where the competitors are under starter's orders at the finishing tape.

Converging divergence

It is frustrating, annoying, and counterproductive if a therapist thrusts an image, a metaphor, or a paradox into a silence in which the patient is creatively reflective. Should the Aeolian Mode be responsible for such an ill-placed intervention it is a contaminating travesty and is in no way therapeutic. It is for this reason that we have been at pains to stress that the Aeolian Mode comes into its own with the patient for whom intrinsic personality structure or prolonged incarceration has resulted in a sense of apathy, fear, and lack of creative reflection. It offers fresh alignments to patients for whom there is a poverty of novelty so that no fresh 'wind of healing' blows across them (see p. 10).

A patient who had been in individual therapy for many years spoke of terminating the therapeutic contract in this way: 'I wanted to finish it in some way . . . but I couldn't.' He is taken by surprise when his request for closure is followed by the therapist's paradoxical invitation to explore more deeply. A phrase from *Antony and Cleopatra* (V. 2, 193) was in his mind, but this is what he said: 'What kind of darkness are you ready for?' ('Finish, good lady – the bright day is done, and we are for the *dark*' [our italics] was the Aeolian trigger.) He felt the patient was trying to avoid deeper (darker) therapy by saying the time had come to finish it.

159

'I am already in darkness. Hmm . . . I wanted to talk about devil worship . . . about selling my soul to the devil.' The therapist recalled a book on *Darkness and Devils* (Murphy 1984) about *King Lear*, and the following line was activated: 'Nero is an angler in the Lake of Darkness' (*King Lear* III. 6, 6).

This is an example of poetic induction which illustrates that the Aeolian Mode does not depend on the patient's knowledge of *King Lear*. The therapist did not know whether the patient had ever read or indeed heard of *King Lear*. And he still does not know.

Poetic induction was blended with empathy built up over years with many episodes of testing, almost to breaking point. This exemplifies the way in which literature can enlarge the therapist's 'broad general sympathy with life and people', so that the aesthetic imperative enables a patient to dwell in that degree of darkness which he had previously tried to avoid. The therapist introduced 'darkness'. Without this introduction the dialogue would have remained more defended and superficial. The potential psychosexual implications of a fishing rod, and angling in darkness, gave the patient the possibility of exploring repressed sexual material. Like the fish, it might 'surface' and be seen for what it is.

The power of paradox – the 'seemingly self-contradictory' – is that the expressed wish to finish was turned into the finish of finishing, so that the disclosive flow continued.

This clinical illustration comes from the reflections of an offender-patient. He was reliving the experience in which he had 'finished' the life of his victim and was contemplating finishing his own life. In psychoanalytic terms his id-derivatives had been powerfully active, causing catastrophic social turbulence. And the instability of his intrapsychic life was again intensifying. To 'finish things' and to 'finish it all' was in the air. So was darkness and the theme of 'deeds of darkness'. But he was confused about what there might be in the darkness which, in turn, could frighten him. He was, in some senses, 'an angler in the lake of darkness', terrified of what he might catch. There was a sufficiently firm degree of empathic bonding between the patient and the therapist for them to be aware that they were each 'fishing'. The immediate future of disclosure was uncertain for them both. It was not a question of the therapist 'fishing' or trawling in the patient's 'lake of darkness'. Nor was the patient fishing alone. It was a collaborative effort which was therefore safer and more readily undertaken. There is clearly a direct link in this example between poetic induction and activity in the depth preceding the stirring of the surface (Bachelard op. cit.).

The paradox relates to both timing and depth. Just at the moment when therapy might have ended, a further long trajectory in the therapeutic journey began. And just at the point when the patient opted for with-drawal to talk of superficial things, he found himself trying to understand his deeds of darkness – as one might embark in hope and fear on a fishing expedition on a lake of darkness.

Within the Aeolian Mode paradox depends upon *poiesis*. It is not a trivial replica of reality, a reflection of past experience, or a floating image. 'The paradox is more than a truth standing on its head. The paradox is a deep truth. . . . The opposite of a deep truth is another deep truth' (Bohr, see Blædel 1985). And Emily Dickinson refers to harmonious dissonance, rich poverty, comforting danger, joyous grief, luminous darkness, and peaceful tempest.

Paradox – as it is used in the Aeolian Mode – usually has a startling quality, which both perplexes and lowers the patient's tension. And often it is the patient – particularly the psychotic – who says paradoxical things which intrigue, delight, and yet give the impression of 'hitting below the belt'. For example, 'You don't look your age. How old are you?' and 'I've forgotten your name, but it's not your fault', were both observations 'born' in a therapeutic group.

A few associations on the capacity of paradox to astonish are irresistible:

'We are perpetually surprised'

(Leishman and Spender (1939) on Rilke)

'Martin Heidegger is the great master of astonishment, the man whose amazement before the blank fact that we *are* instead of *not being*, has put a radiant obstacle in the path of the obvious.'

(Steiner 1978)

A previously quoted passage (p. 147) is now set in a larger context:

[There is] the fundamentally creative nature of myth-seeing – that mystery or "uprush of feeling" that takes place when you suddenly, or gradually, perceive the text you are reading [*or the clinical history you are hearing*] is in some devious or hidden sense "oscillating" [as Kierkegaard says] with something else, being in effect foreordained, though the point of ordination is nowhere to be seen . . . One of the central characteristics of myth is that . . . it always has "an else-where" at its disposal. . . . The point is not what one can make of the image but that such pockets of emptiness are never reliability insig-nificant.'

(*The Shape of Paradox*, States 1978, our italics)

Paradox is an elusive and persuasive topic which could take us into many interesting byways. But, for our purposes, it is almost invariably linked to the metaphorical motion of gaining access, entering, invading, and being received. In particular, the paradox of gaining entry from a starting point deep within, means that the patient's threshold of awareness is crossed from inside rather than outside. It is not a question of invading from without, but of discovering the self as a 'place of safety'.

Paradox implies a reconciliation of qualities which initially appear to be in opposition and mutually discordant. And the formulation of a creative paradox is in itself an act of *poiesis*. In the Aeolian Mode, Bohr's 'deep truth' of paradox is contained in the seemingly absurd statement that analytic work can start deep, without the patient intensifying his forces of resistance. Yet – and this is the eye of the paradox – we hope to demonstrate that the patient's defences can be gently 'dismantled' from within, rather than broken through from without; and that he actually encourages another to let down his drawbridge for him, rather than ensure that his allies deepen the moat and build the walls higher. This description has slipped into the military metaphor of attack and defence, which was that chosen by Freud. Though it must never be forgotten that it is only a metaphor.

Paradoxical attentiveness

Books with titles like *Not that it Matters* or *If I May* (A. A. Milne) exert an almost irresistible force on even a casual reader. Others entitled *On Nothing and Kindred Subjects*, *On Anything*, *On Something*, *This and That and the Other*, or simply *On* (H. Belloc), induce the same magnetic pull. This is because we have no idea of the contents until we open the book. Other members of the family are: *Generally Speaking*, *All Things Considered*, and *Tremendous Trifles* (G. K. Chesterton). Our curiosity is aroused. The authors want to tell us something. Why have we included the titles of short stories and essays in a book which is 'clinically based'?

The answer is a simple one. We shall use *Not that it Matters* as a representative, because it has somehow caught the essence of the therapist's paradoxical attentiveness. It is exploratory, free-floating, discerning, and affectionate. The therapist tries to attend to everything. Yet, at the same time, to nothing in particular. Not that it matters. These essays and short stories were all written within a few years of each other, early this century – though they were recently joined by a posthumous collection of essays entitled *Of This and Other Worlds* (C. S. Lewis). They remain contemporary as oblique reminders of a serious search for significance.

They convey the therapist's Janusian style of 'searching', yet 'waiting to receive'. He is attuned to the patient's inner and outer world. Or the other way around. Not that it matters.

This indirect attentiveness to the inner world of the patient, evident in what he says, what he cannot say, and what he is on the brink of saying, reminds us that: 'Pockets of emptiness are never reliably insignificant' (States 1978). But Polonius was there long ago:

> 'With windlesses and with assays of bias,
> By indirections find directions out.'
> *(Hamlet* II. 1, 64)

As mutative agents in the Aeolian Mode, metaphor and paradox are closely related, and to be efficacious they often depend upon each other. All this is focused upon the choice of that metaphor which is appropriate because it emerges *de novo* in the very fabric which is being woven in the therapeutic session. Three examples follow:

The paradox of 'outside calls' from inside: Molly, whose description of a previous job was almost a metaphor of her own clinical denial and disconnectedness, said:

'I used to be a telephonist at an office switchboard. When I got anxious I pulled the wires out. I cut off the boss! I felt cut off and everyone was trying to get through to me.'

Her history was punctuated by auditory hallucinations, barely internalized injunctions, and partial introjects:

'I always cut off outside calls.'
'I never cut off inside calls.'

She was carefully distinguishing between 'inside' and 'outside' calls, that is to say 'thoughts' and what she 'heard', and between human contact and auditory hallucinations. And it is interesting to note that the punitive, authoritarian 'boss' was safely distanced as an 'outside call'. The metaphor enabled her to talk in such a way that she bypassed her defences, although her affect was not inappropriate. Little by little, endopsychic change – in the depths – ensued. There was less denial, less projection, and a greater stability of object relationships. The therapist's task was to utilize the double metaphorical description of her job as a telephonist and the implicit account of her 'mental state'. Supportive therapy consisted in monitoring the theme in the 'switchboard mode'.

In this instance, the Aeolian Mode had allowed her to 'call into being that which was not there before'; namely, an appropriately safe way of carrying into consciousness feelings which were previously too frightening to contemplate. Her anxiety was safely encountered in the depth and, in the presence of the therapist, she brought what had hitherto disturbed her to the surface in terms of a benign image. The Aeolian Mode places high emphasis on the freshly-minted accounts of experience used by the patient. It does not adopt a faded or tired metaphor. It is not second-hand language. It does not use technical terms which, though still reasonably fresh, lose their vitality so quickly. Words such as 'resonance' and 'mirroring' are, even now, beginning to fade. We sometimes use the words of the patient (see pp. 42–3). We sometimes introduce images which are elaborated by the patient.

The paradox of killing though denying death: 'I just went on killing her, it never occurred to me she'd die!' Killing was a discrete, dissociated activity – in no way connected with a death which took place close at hand. Aeolian imagery brought both activities slowly to the same focal point, so that the patient could deal with his murderous impulses. Psychotic utterances always make us question our conceptual frames. For example: 'Death sometimes kills'; 'I've been decapitated to death.'

The paradox of a patient surprising himself: Dick, a psychopath, who had difficulty in expressing personal feelings, was anxiously watching a bee-keeper endeavouring to take a swarm of bees which had alighted on a wall immediately outside the group room. Reflecting upon the degree of courage necessary to undertake such an activity, the patient said: 'Bees are OK, they don't sting if you understand them.' The therapist's comment, 'I wonder if people are like that?' led to an immediate response not only from Dick but from other members of the group.

The bee 'theme' had initiated detailed disclosure about Dick's previous violent offences which, hitherto, he had been almost unable to mention. Stimulated by the therapist's question he replied, with scarcely time to breathe,

> 'I did. I certainly was. I stung because I was not understood. I stabbed and I attacked and . . .'

A competitive clash to obtain 'speaking space' followed hard upon Dick's description of the way in which he had 'stung' those who frightened him.

These paradoxes seem to be resolved when it is recalled that the deepest memories are repressed, not as words, but as affect-loaded images. Therefore the evocative power of the metaphor 'permits multiple perspectives, even contradictory trends in the psyche . . . one thing is not necessarily more important than another. Psychological plurality and a tolerance of ambivalence are fostered' (Samuels 1985).

Nevertheless, in this instance, as in every group vignette cited, the therapist endeavoured to understand Dick's defensive organization, as well as the reverberating timbre of the group matrix. Behind the intervention lay coherence between three dynamic components. 'I wonder if people are like that?' linked the urge to act because of maximal 'fit' of: metaphor, mood, and endopsychic patterning (aesthetic imperative); the novelty of the image which called something into being (*poiesis*); and Dick's need to face his own music which was impossible to resist (point of urgency).

Both the 'switchboard' and the 'stinging' vignettes illustrate the way in which dynamic material can be released when metaphor retains the patient's 'copyright'. But he does not limit its significance for other members of the group. The 'stinging' was primarily at Dick's point of urgency, though it drew others into its disclosure wake.

Paradox is inherent in all life-through-death experiences. St John of the Cross writes 'I must die because I do not die', though the final stanza affirms 'I live because I've ceased to die.'

Therapeutic space receives many such anomalous and ambiguous statements, although 'I just went on killing her, it never occurred to me she'd die' is paradigmatic. Oscar Wilde (1898) referred to a judicial hanging in this way:

> 'He had but killed a thing that lived,
> Whilst they had killed the dead.'
> ('The Ballad of Reading Gaol')

Yet the Bachelardian paradox remains. Even with such destructive acts, the depth can be touched before the surface is stirred. This is one way of approaching the inner world which is afraid to be known through any kind of invasion. Poetic induction enables something to be called into being which is ego-syntonic and does not provoke rejection.

Oscar Wilde again, in an evocative passage with archaic elements which opens with a double paradox:

> 'All trials are trials for one's life, just as all sentences are sentences of death; and three times have I been tried . . . Society, as we have constituted it, will have no place for me, [17] has none to offer; but Nature, whose sweet rains fall on unjust and just alike, will have clefts in the rocks where I may hide, and secret valleys in whose silence I may weep undisturbed. She will hang the night with stars so that I may walk abroad in the darkness without stumbling, and send the wind over my footprints so that none may track me to my hurt: she will cleanse me in great waters, and with bitter herbs make me whole.'
>
> ('De Profundis' 1949)

The supportive quality of therapeutic space sometimes has this balsamic effect. Paradox is profound when devastated man makes known what he has never yet known. And it often colours that familiar phase of psychotherapy in which a patient discovers that he cannot forget what he cannot remember.

The offender-patient may 'repeat' an offence he has 'never done before'. He thus brings himself in line with Edwin Muir's (1960) observation: 'Nothing yet was ever done/Till it was done again' (Twice-done, Once-done).

Paradox can be evident as clinical ambivalence, such as that shown by a man who cannot relinquish what he does not want to keep. Aeolian *poiesis* can sustain the presentation of paradox, and induce the possibility of process, for a patient hitherto 'locked' in paradoxical binding.

INTIMATIONS OF INTIMACY

'"But when we sit together, close," said Bernard, "we melt into each other with phrases. We are edged with mist. We make an unsubstantial territory."'

(*The Waves*, Virginia Woolf 1931)

The title of this section draws attention to the dual connotation of the word 'intimate'. The adjective 'intimate' means profound, inmost nature, essential, intrinsic, closely connected, or familiar; whereas the noun 'an intimate' refers to a close friend, though the verb 'to be intimate' carries more than a sexual allusion. It implies sexual contact. Nevertheless, the verb 'to intimate' means to make known formally, to communicate by any means, however indirect . . . to signify, to suggest, to indicate, to imply, to hint, to mention indirectly or in passing.

Intimacy is the 'quality or condition of being intimate', and though it was once a euphemism for illicit sexual intercourse, it is now the word chosen to cover the many nuances implicit in a sexual relationship. This is in contradistinction to the psycho-physiological aspects of sexuality, such as orgasm and its build-up and sequelae.

Psychodynamic responses to the topic of intimacy run the risk of jumping too quickly to such distancing categorization as, for example, the '*vagina dentata*'. But there is an opposite risk of romanticizing sexual performance, so that the therapist relinquishes his hovering yet analytic attentiveness.

Like his patient, the therapist is a sexual being, whose basic drives may be frustrated, deflected, or satisfied. His ability to retain a free-floating attitude – part of his overall countertransference response – will depend upon his personality structure, his life experience, and his professional training and skill.

Having said all this, to be present with a patient who is disclosing intimate material makes demands upon the therapist. He endeavours to avoid being voyeuristic on the one hand, or defensively diversionary on the other. Intimacy is linked with allusion and paradox for the reasons which follow.

Sexual allusion plays a major part in both individual life and that of the community. Fashion, advertising, and humour are all coloured by sexual inference. The language of religion and the response to music and art are steeped in allusive reference to intimacy. And one of the greatest challenges which actors have to face is how to convey a sense of intimacy to the back of a large auditorium.

Paradox is close to intimacy, because to be truly intimate implies that a person is most himself. An individual needs to have a firm sense of his personal boundaries if he is to be free enough to dare to lose them during orgasmic fusion. *Poiesis* has more than the biological connotation of 'giving birth'. The capacity to be playful, when most deeply serious, is part of the creative paradox of the shared life of intimacy. A specific reminder of the paradoxical fact that intimacy can simultaneously satisfy and yet be provocative is given in Enobarbus' description of Cleopatra: 'She makes hungry where most she satisfies' (*Antony and Cleopatra* II. 2, 236).

The Aeolian Mode allows the therapist to acquire sharper discriminative attentiveness to disclosures about intimacy, such as 'bedroom talk' or death-bed utterances. The many meanings of 'love' and the numerous implications of 'I love you' scarcely need elaboration. King Lear's 'Let copulation thrive' (IV. 6, 114) is worlds away from the overtly erotic language of Éluard (1968): 'And the door of time opens between your legs / The flower of summer nights at the lips of lightning'. A recently published poem by a schizophrenic patient asks:

> 'shall I make love to you in timeless space
> your womb the universe my sperm the stars'
>
> (Robinson 1981)

There are numerous other passages of literature in which the intimations of intimacy are far more evocative, because they are more opaque and because they fulfil Bachelard's criteria of the truly poetic image. We have in mind the stanza by John Donne (1572–1631) from 'Hymne to God, my God, in my Sicknesse', which carries implications of the many faces of intimacy.

> 'Since I am comming to that Holy roome,
> Where, with thy Quire of Saints for evermore,
> I shall be made thy Musique; As I come
> I tune the Instrument here at the dore,
> And what I must doe then, thinke here before.'

It is inevitable that the language of mysticism and reflective religious reverie should share affective sonorities with those other aspects of ecstasy subsumed under the heading 'intimacy'. But the wider title 'intimations of intimacy' was chosen because the deepest human experiences will always outstrip the capacity of language to describe them. Language reaches its limits, and the subject will assert that, whatever 'the words say', the experience was 'more than that'.

It is not only in sexual orgasm that individual boundaries are relinquished. The capacity to be, feel, think, or pray together – in speech or silence – is a heightened form of intimacy. And the sharing of 'unedited' dream fragments, daydreams, and reveries implies a depth of mutual trust in which disclosure augments intimacy.

At the heart of corporate religious experience and in the reluctant, or welcomed, 'letting go' of life as death approaches, previously guarded boundaries are sometimes abandoned. And how this transition is accomplished is, most certainly, an indication of an individual's capacity for intimacy. Death may be greeted as 'Sister Death', or feared as 'Death's cold hand' begins to close. Thomas, in *Murder in the Cathedral* (T. S. Eliot 1935) says, 'I am not in danger: only near to death.' And St John of the Cross in the words just quoted, draws our attention to dying and ceasing to die. And life through death – integration and authenticity through relinquishment and letting go – is an expression of intimacy.

Other aspects of intimacy, such as parental love for children, evoke a rich field of prepared echoes. Without deliberate searching, the following sentence presented itself: 'Like as a mother comforteth her children, so will I comfort you' (*Isaiah* 66, 13).

The language of music springs to mind when writing about intimacy, because even the words of poetry seem no more than 'a raid on the inarticulate' (*East Coker V* T. S. Eliot, 1940). Nevertheless, a passage from *Romeo and Juliet* can serve as a reminder of the way in which an ethos of intimacy is better conveyed by poetry than any other verbal mode.

> 'Come gentle night, come loving black-brow'd night,
> Give me my Romeo; and when I shall die
> Take him and cut him out in little stars,
> And he will make the face of heaven so fine
> That all the world will be in love with night,
> And pay no worship to the garish sun.'
>
> (III. 2, 20)

We may reach no further than 'intimations of intimacy'. Because, though it may be mentioned overtly and directly, it is often referred to by oblique inference, in an indirect fashion, or 'in passing'. Intimacy is merely hinted at, because the patient is 'too naked' to make direct reference to intimate material in the full glare of an interrogative interview. Even during the course of prolonged psychotherapy it needs to be remembered that intimate matters remain intimate. If this is not so, the patient is 'overexposed' in several senses. It is for this reason that the subsequent chapter deals with the crucial topic of empathy, for without the therapist's empathic attentiveness the patient is rarely able to discuss intimate details – unless, that is, he has an exhibitionistic narcissistic personality and almost 'forces' accounts of extreme intimacy on to the therapist. This is in fact part of the ongoing clinical appraisal which takes place in all psychotherapy.

In such circumstances, the therapist will then be looking for other evidence of genuine intimacy, because true intimacy is never easy to disclose. *En passant*, it should be noted that many sex-offenders fall into this category (Cox 1979). We have described the phenomenon of pseudo-disclosure which is so frequently found when a psychopath tells that part of his story which may deal with topics usually regarded as 'intimate'. In this event, the therapist waits until that which is genuinely intimate declares itself. This usually becomes evident in the abrupt ending of 'easy speech'. Having said that true intimacy is often mentioned indirectly or in passing, we are back to 'not that it matters' (p. 162), because an intimation of intimacy will make its presence felt within therapeutic space one way or another. Furthermore, if it does not do so, defensiveness has succeeded and Aeolian responsiveness has failed. This must be so, because the absence of intimacy implies that the patient has been avoiding something which needs to be faced. Or rejoiced in.

6

Attunement

'Beautiful and bright it should be on the surface, feathery and evanescent, one colour melting into another like the colours on a butterfly's wing; but beneath the fabric must be clamped together with bolts of iron. It was to be a thing you could ruffle with your breath; and a thing you could not dislodge with a team of horses.'

(*To the Lighthouse*, Virginia Woolf 1927)

The three sections of this chapter deal with different aspects of the important topic of attunement. Attunement being the 'setting' of an instrument so that it is maximally receptive. It is therefore a cardinal feature of the Aeolian Mode which depends upon precisely this faculty.

Empathy, defined by Kohut (1959) as 'vicarious introspection', implies affective resonance and a partial, temporary fusion of perspectival worlds. The empathic process is furthered by the therapist's concentration upon waiting and witnessing. These activities facilitate the development of that trust, without which neither transference phenomena, nor the patient's supportive confidence, can gain a foothold.

Finally, the Rorschach approach enables the patient's inner world to be safely explored through the non-intrusive, evocative promptings of ambiguous stimuli. In this instance, attunement achieves the paradoxical effect of showing how far the patient is in tune with himself. It reminds us of Malan's reference (1979) to the degree to which a patient is in touch with his true feelings.

Because empathy is the most significant and pervasive aspect of attunement we tackle this first.

EMPATHY

Shortly after returning from a holiday with his parents, a young schizophrenic patient remarked that he had left his left arm in Italy. His casual

170

speech, his expression, and his gestures would have been more appropriate for describing the loss of an old second-hand umbrella.

When such a remark is made in a therapeutic setting, the therapist is instantly aware of the challenge to his empathic abilities. By a theoretical *tour de force*, and by juggling with hypothetical constructs (such as 'part-object') and phenomenological descriptions (such as 'Italy' and 'left'), he might be able to find some kind of an *explanation*. Such a causal explanation would be unlikely to secure an *understanding*, and the patient will probably feel an increased sense of distance rather than receptive proximity.

Empathy occupies an increasingly important place in psychological literature. However, it is often dealt with in an elusive or nebulous fashion. Although its importance in psychotherapy and creativity has long been recognized, very few systematic attempts have been made to elucidate it. Few writers go beyond an almost wistful contemplation of this phenomenon. Yet it remains paradoxical that empathy is both natural and obvious, and, at the same time, inexplicable.

In view of the many angles from which the topic of 'empathy' has been approached, we now provide a brief survey of those attempted definitions which are of particular relevance for the Aeolian Mode.

Rapaport (1951) attests that 'though empathy and intuition certainly are the archetypes of our knowledge about our fellow human beings, their nature is still a closed book to us'. And in his book with the paradigmatic title *Listening with the Third Ear* (1948) Reik writes that 'empathy' is used to describe psychological understanding, but often without expounding what is meant. He also criticizes those approaches which regard empathy as an instrumental asset.

Attempts to define and clarify the concept have only met with limited success. This may be due to the very nature of the underlying process, which is preverbal, preconscious, and unique. As a phenomenon it is so different from, and so much more than, reason, that reason can never comprehend it.

This distinction is underlined in a more formal 'glossary' definition where empathy is regarded as 'an emotional knowing of another human being, rather than an intellectual understanding'.

Empathy as a means of dynamic transposition has been studied by several authors. Rosalind Dymond (1949) sees empathy as 'the imaginative transposing of one self into the thinking, feeling and acting of another, and so structuring the world as he does'. And Bugentan (1965) writes: 'When I am most able to attend to my patient in a way that is creative, I listen to him, and experience total presentation of himself in a fashion which subjectively gives me the experience of participation with him in his telling of himself.'

Benedetti (1976) finds that the instrument which enables us to come into touch with the great images of the unconscious of the patient is our capacity to become caught by them, without being divided by them as the patient is, and to tell the patient what they mean to us. We show him the impact of his symbols upon us. We do not clarify the unconscious of the patient, but we try to integrate it into ours.

We (M.C. 1978) have extended 'vicarious introspection' to embrace the capacity of looking *out* of the patient, which brings us close to Husserl's understanding of reaching 'the perspectival world' of the other.

A salient feature of empathy thus seems to be a way of understanding in which the feelings of each participant merge. This implies that the therapist's capacity to attain a deeper understanding applies not only to the patient, but also to himself. It is therefore an interactional phenomenon involving enhanced, mutual patterning.

Joyce McDougall (1978) states: 'in spite of all the well-known pitfalls of countertransference affect, I am obliged to suppose that these "signs" in the analyst are more than the unique reflection of his own inner emotional state, or his unconscious reactions to the patient's monologue, and that we are dealing with a primitive communication, not decodable in the usual way'. It is therefore clear that she regards this form of communication as an original or fundamental transference.

Some authors view the reciprocity characterizing the empathic process as a 'temporary identification' (Fenichel 1953) or an identification in fantasy (Schafer 1959). But the latter also stresses the temporal aspect by pointing out that it is not a permanent identification. The therapist maintains his own sense of individuality at the same time as he 'feels as one' with the patient. This is concordant with Ogden's statement (1985): 'Empathy is a psychological process (as well as a form of object relatedness) that occurs within the context of a dialectic of being and not-being the other.'

The dynamics of empathy

There are conscious and unconscious modes of understanding which have categorizing and symbolic implications respectively. While the former tends to make a phenomenon umambiguous, the latter embraces a multiplicity of meanings, indicating that 'the web is closely woven'. Such a web defies objective, scientific analysis. An abstract, categorizing procedure makes us cling to what is clear and evident, though our grasp may be shallow and have little purchase. On the other hand, if our attention is turned to the horizon, we engage with deeper levels of experience.

Whereas analytic thought and logical reasoning are based upon a detailed, clearly defined relationship between two elements at a given time, the intuitive process has more undifferentiated, global characteristics. According to Hardy (1975), Proust describes intuition as the literary equivalent of experiment in which the work of intelligence succeeds, rather than precedes, creative work. Empathy is a synthetic function, in that the process involves a holistic understanding of a given situation or of a psychological reality. This is unlike the analytical approach which works from the part to the whole. It has a gestalt quality, and it is therefore closely allied to the gestalt psychological and organismic theories. But the very fact that the nature of this process is global makes it difficult to study. Like the perception of familiar objects, empathic understanding starts with an anticipatory set. And, as in perception, our 'reception' cannot be objective or 'correct', in any absolute sense. The more we are able to put our prejudices in parenthesis, the more we abstain from a rational response, and the more we remain open and receptive to what might be taking place within the other person, the greater is the chance that he may be encountered in his entirety.

Kinaesthetic empathy

The empathic way of experiencing has much in common with the *physiognomic mode of perception* (see p. 130). Both are preconscious, holistic, primary processes, involving emotions. And they are brought alive through the activation of *kinaesthetic activity*. The difficulties in accounting for empathic, synthetic, creative activity may be partly due to its relationship to the right hemisphere, in which non-verbal processes predominate.

Titchener (1908) was among the first to recognize the role of kinaesthesis in endowing experience with a meaningful coherence. Rommetveit (1968) notes the specificity of the interrelationship between conditioning feelings and cognitive events with respect to 'words'. He argues that when a child learns a word he also comes to associate a particular 'organismic state' or a complex affective–sensory–motor pattern with that word. This state may persist as a kinaesthetic component of the adult's word aura.

The primacy of the kinaesthetic sense underlines its importance in therapy. At a time in development when archaic fantasies are stored at a presymbolic level, the kinaesthetic sense may be the only channel by which tension is released. And later, when 'flesh becomes word' it still constitutes an important component in the endopsychic structuring of unconscious fantasies.

Concerned as we are with symbolization and psychic significance, we tend to overlook the relationship between psychological and somatic processes. However, it is impossible to ignore this duality when confronted by psychosomatic illness. In these instances, where 'the body does its own thinking' (McDougall 1974), our empathy is challenged. Unlike the hysterical personality whose symptoms carry a symbolic message, the patient with a psychosomatic disturbance tends to have his decisive experience coded at a preverbal level. It is for this reason that the therapist's kinaesthetic sense increases empathic possibilities with such patients, who are otherwise difficult to reach. It is when symbolic functioning fails that the projective aspects of empathy assume greater significance.

Kinaesthetic empathy and literary imagery

Slatoff's study (1960) of William Faulkner underlines the importance of *kinaesthetic empathy*. And the clinician can learn from his close scrutiny of 'movements, quiescences, turbulences, tensions, releases, writhings, and strainings of . . . [the] inmost self'. Slatoff continues:

> 'We can say that he produces these deep inner movements and tensions largely by his persistent and many-pronged stimulation of the kinesthetic and visceral senses, but we must understand that the phrase "kinesthetic and visceral senses" is inadequate here and that there is undoubtedly a profound kinship between the responses we call "kinesthetic" and "visceral" and our fundamental sense of life and of our own being; certainly there is a deep kinship between those responses and the experiences of the kind of inmost self Faulkner assumes. We must understand, also, that empathy is largely dependent upon such motor and visceral responses.'

Slatoff gives numerous examples of Faulkner's preoccupation with movement and stillness, such as: 'Without ceasing to run she appeared to pause . . . Yet still the rider leaned forward in the arrested saddle, in the attitude. of terrific speed . . . Moving sitting still . . . We just stood there − I motionless in the attitude and action of running, she rigid in that furious immobility.'

This attention to the movement and stillness itself, and to its description, has captured many aspects of kinaesthetic empathy which may permeate therapeutic space. The therapist interested in Aeolian initiatives will find *Quest for Failure: a Study of William Faulkner* intrinsically interesting and a rich source of associative material.

Kinaesthetic empathy, music, and dance

The theme of 'the dance' could equally well come under the heading of body metaphors and the metaphorical aspect of man's shape, movement, and participatory capacity in social life. For our purposes, however, it fits most easily in association with kinaesthetic empathy. It is too large a topic to explore in detail, but likewise it is too important to ignore. There are particular Aeolian associations in *The Universal Drum* in which Audrey Rodgers (1979) looks at the place of dance imagery in the work of several American poets. Writing of William Carlos Williams, the author refers to the polarities of Williams' experience and continues: 'The poems . . . introduce the ritual movement from death to rebirth as the poet seeks, through the dance of the mind, to advance from stasis to creativity.' The book sparkles with such phrases as 'the certainty of music' . . . 'only the dance is sure' . . . 'into the other dance'.

The book ends by bringing together many themes which will find echoes throughout these pages. 'An image, however brilliant, is part of a poetic whole encompassing scaffold, language, and rhythm'; 'the dance image is successful only when the harmonising imagination of the poet brings all other poetic components to bear upon his experience'. And this takes us directly to the focal point of the Aeolian Mode because we are concerned to bring 'all other poetic components to bear upon his [the patient's] experience'. We could expand this statement into a field of wider clinical relevance by saying that 'poetic components', for us, imply the broad spectrum of *poiesis* rather than the narrower, but equally legitimate, conventional understanding of that which is 'poetic'. A line from Yeats points towards the theme of 'the larger story' with which this book ends. It poses a baffling question about the nature of empathy and the Dance of the Mind.

'How can we know the dancer from the dance?'

Mellers (1980) in *Bach and the Dance of God* writes: 'The dance-songs of primitive peoples depend on the rhythms of the human body and on the 'sensual speech' that relates us to Nature. . . . One may suspect that his [Bach's] appeal is almost primeval, for in his music one is seldom totally divorced from a motor rhythm which, like that of 'primitive' musics, is regular, reiterated, non-developing: as unremittent as the turning earth, as continuous as the surging sea.' And such 'motor rhythms' can be integral aspects of kinaesthetic empathy. Liturgical dance links symbolic functioning, projection, and corporate primordiality in the Dance of the Soul.

Schachtel (1950) writes: 'In every act of kinaesthetic and other empathy there is an element of projection. Thus, his personal kinaesthetic or other feeling, aroused by what he sees, is projected onto the person or object seen and merges completely, without the subject being aware of it, with the percept of the person or object empathically perceived.' Empathic projection, therefore, may be thought of as a two-way channel of empathy and projection, which allows the therapist to use his body as an intuitive processor.

Kinaesthetic empathy is vividly evident in the following vignette.

During a group session in early August Stella is describing a phase in her life when she avoided all social contacts and retreated into her flat.

'I got tons and tons of food, locked the door, drew the curtains, and took the phone off the hook. I didn't want to meet anyone. Lots of people wanted to see me but they only wanted to talk to me about their problems. I'd had enough.'

Stella's description was interrupted by an unexpected whining–mumbling sound emanating from Betty who had pursed lips, held her arms very tightly, and shook rhythmically. So profound was this sudden change of posture, gesture, and respiration that one of the nurses said it looked like rigor, or some kind of fit. Betty, who had been intently following everything Stella had said though she had remained silent up to this point, suddenly exclaimed: 'That's just what I did.'

Later that day Betty wanted to discuss the events that transpired during the group session. She said 'I was terribly cold THEN', but the 'THEN' in question, was not the 'then' of the recent group session on an August morning, but the 'then' of ten years ago when she had done just what Stella described.

'It wasn't cold outside. But it was cold in my room and cold in me. I wasn't well. Although it was warm I had a hot-water bottle and kept warm in bed. The cupboard was full of food but it was so cold that I didn't want to get out of bed to cross the room to get the food. I didn't eat for days. I lost lots of weight.'

It was not easy to disentangle the literal and metaphorical significance of being cold. Perhaps she was physically cold. She was certainly cold in the sense of being shut off from warm relationships. She was alone. Coldness has been explored in several places. And, though there are associative possibilities of coldness from *The Three Sisters* or *King Lear*, among others, neither of these proved to be an aesthetic imperative on this occasion. The clue to understanding Betty's world and her linking of current and past events lay, in this instance, not in an aesthetic imperative but in the unmistakable evidence provided by kinaesthetic empathy. As Stella was speaking, Betty identified part of her own life in what Stella was describing. But she also conveyed to Stella that she, too, knew of the need to withdraw, the draining of warmth of all kinds, and the necessity to make provision for a self-imposed siege.

The most striking feature about this incident was the kinaesthetic aspect which occurred alongside Betty's memory of a time in her life when she had been very cold. Her kinaesthetic response in the form of shivering was not only visible, it was actually audible. And it was the *sound of her coldness* which first drew the therapist's attention away from her present involvement in the group, to the reliving of previous experience. Once again, this illustrates David Copperfield's words: 'I do not recall it, but see it done; for it happens again before me.' This example of kinaesthetic empathy was between two members of a therapeutic group, but no therapist/counsellor will have any difficulty in recalling occasions during therapeutic sessions when he himself has first-hand evidence of kinaesthetic empathy. It may take many forms; from overt 'symptoms', such as nausea or sweating, to curious subjective feelings which do not come into the canon of organic medical orthodoxy, but which are real nevertheless.

The crucial point to observe about this empathic bonding is that pronounced shivering took place during Stella's 'remembering' on an August morning; because something 'stronger than memory' had taken Betty back ten years, to a time when she withdrew from a life which was withdrawing from her. She shivered then. And she shivered again in August because Stella's experience had been hers too.

Ogden (1982) writes of the way in which the therapist allows himself to be partially moulded by this interpersonal pressure and yet is still able to observe these changes in himself. He thus has access to a rich source of data about the patient's internal world. A source comprising induced thoughts and feelings, all of which are experientially alive, vivid, and immediate. Yet, as Ogden points out, they are also extremely elusive. They are difficult to formulate verbally because the experience is in the form of an enactment, in which the therapist himself participates.

The capacity to empathize can be facilitated by the use of metaphor, analogy, and paradox. These are all integral agents for change in the Aeolean Mode.

And 'poetry itself', in the exact words of Haefele (1962), 'is so meaningful because it establishes relations between the abstract and the concrete. Poetry equates abstractions and ideals to simple acts and percepts. It requires the "almost seeing and feeling" of concrete things first.' The feeling aspect is also stressed by Rothenberg (1979): 'In other words the particular phrases, images, ideas or poetic metaphors which constitute inspirations and inceptions of poems are themselves metaphors for personal conflicts. The personal importance of these phrases is felt, not conceived.'

Analogical language has its roots in an archaic era, although it also has a more generalized validity. It has a greater capacity than an abstract, more recently developed digital mode of verbal communication. In creative adults this *multimodal way of processing* is often regarded as a regression. But we view this mode as embracing the whole spectrum of experience from primitive styles of processing to the most highly developed.

When Shakespeare uses an image, an analogy, or a metaphor, he evokes ideas and feelings which astonish and hold us. He enables 'Being [to] sparkle as Being!' (Sartre 1950).

> 'my cloud of dignity
> Is held from falling with so weak a wind
> That it will quickly drop: my day is dim.'
> (*King Henry IV Part I* IV. 5, 99)

We have already referred to Clemen's comments (1951): 'We observe as characteristic features of this passage the following: mingling of the concrete and the abstract, concentration of content, ambiguity, connection of the parts by association and suggestiveness.' And we may add: the movement and the kinaesthetic colouring.

Deep empathic exchange might ensue if a recently bereaved patient, feeling that his flag was at half-mast, detected that the therapist had sensed that his day was 'dim'; because there was 'so weak a wind' of current affairs to keep his life unfurled. But empathy of this intensity might 'need' few spoken words – or depend upon none at all.

Empathy depends upon the therapist's capacity for holistic perception. This is usually regarded as being within the province of the right cerebral hemisphere (see p. 200 on neuropsychology). Successful empathy results in tension-reduction. This depends upon subliminal perception, kinaesthetics, and feelings which are often almost incommunicable. Although empathy is necessarily subjective, it is not, *ipso facto*, inaccurate. On the contrary, it is often accurate, particular, and honed to a fine degree of precision. Yet this sense of exact 'fit' is often known only to those involved. It is evident to a far lesser degree to the disinterested observer. The Aeolean Mode 'jumps the gap' here, and through *poiesis* it transforms the emotional set into words and makes the inexpressible expressible.

In this section we have tried to explore empathy from several synergistic perspectives. As we move from one representational system to another – from language to imagery, or from visual to auditory images – we are alongside the patient in his search for presymbolic memories. Paradoxical though it seems, we reach the patient's abstract world through the concrete. As Maycock (1963) said of Chesterton's attitude to life: 'It is always the particular thing that is closest to the thing that passes understanding.'

We encourage the patient to stay in his experience. But it is experience recentred through being transposed to a more archaic context. This was illustrated in our first example (p. 8), when 'fire and ice' conveyed depth, which 'positive and negative feelings' did not. Thus the experience was moved from the 'background' to the 'foreground', and a more affirmative contrast resulted.

Memories are not always retained in language. They may be held as an emotional set in a wordless state, which is both primitive and uncoded. This undifferentiated, cross-modal and physiognomic mode of retention may be reached, engaged with, and transmuted through empathic facilitation.

Further mention must be made of the power of novelty. It seems to integrate the impact of the creative, the analytic, and the capacity for empathy. That empathy is related to novelty initially appears to be paradoxical, until it is realized that accurate empathy depends upon precise phenomenology. The latter being defined by Spiegelberg (1972) – following Rubin (1915) – as 'a turning away from concepts and theories toward the directly presented in its subjective fullness'. But if empathy is to be of the highest attunement possible, then however familiar the subject may be, there still needs to be detected in the familiar that which is novel: that which is not familiar. Thus, in the last resort empathy, upon which all psychotherapeutic endeavours depend, itself calls for attentive discernment of that which is ever new. The trusting of intuition – when integrated with other 'clinical' modes of knowing – to the point of acting upon it, is a major component in the Aeolian Mode.

Hobson (1974) writing on loneliness says, 'In loneliness we are inarticulate.' He then develops the theme of the part that poetry can play in enhancing empathy. And empathy counteracts loneliness. As far as it can.

> 'The poetry is no literary adornment. I can find no better form of words to intimate what happens in therapeutic meetings . . . interpretation of resistance, analysis of the transference, and the saga of the cosmic battle between good and bad breasts – all these, when they do not obstruct, are useful in so far as they provide opportunities for apprehending, sharing, and (of the utmost importance) letting go, moments of insight in which (to use Blake's expression) we see not only "with" but "through" the eye – a "seeing into" which is inhibited by those formulated explanatory phrases which often go by the name of "insight".
>
> Men *interact* – as do billiard balls. Men *communicate* – as do bees. But only men use language in which words, looks, gestures and actions are symbols which, as they expand in new and complex combinations, intimate more than is immediately present and known.'

Empathy is not only a technical professional activity for therapists, it is also inextricably woven into 'the infinite web of things'. Nevertheless, the mesh of the web needs constant adjustment. If it is too coarse, or too fine, it fails to contain a fragile relationship with a precarious young man, who left his left arm in Italy.

WAITING AND WITNESSING

We cannot proceed further without mentioning 'waiting' and 'witnessing' because both form part of the ethos and atmosphere in which Aeolian activity takes place – though both are known to be key aspects in classical psychoanalysis. Thus Gedo (1979) writes of the function of the analyst in these terms: There is 'free association in the presence of the analyst as an *empathic witness* who responds from a position of freely hovering attention'. And Klauber (1980), writing on the formulation of psychoanalytic interpretations, refers to 'the slow building of interpretative bridges. . . . It puts a high value on the analyst's capacity to *wait* until he finds himself interpreting spontaneously, though only in the context of much formal thinking' [our italics].

In one way or another, every patient calls for the therapist to wait with him, to wait for him, and, often, to wait upon him. He also needs the therapist as a witness. Not in the legal sense of being a witness who can 'give evidence' about him to a third party. On the contrary, the witnessing which the therapist provides is that of endorsing the patient's sense of being present. This facet of psychotherapy is particularly important at two dynamic junctures: first, during transference interpretation when the patient's sense of integration may be threatened because he has to cope with disturbing feelings in which past and present experience intermingle – at such times the patient needs 'presence intensification' in relation to the here-and-now relationship with his therapist; secondly, during regression in the severely borderline patient whose hold on reality is tenuous. Unlike Smike (see p. 113), it is not possible for him to be 'recalled . . . to the world outside himself' because of defective boundaries and an inadequate sense of self.

Discussing the role of the general practitioner, Berger and Mohr (1967) write 'when we call for a doctor, we are asking him to cure us and relieve our suffering, but, if he cannot cure us, we are also asking him to witness our dying. The value of the witness is that he has seen so many others die.' In a similar way, the psychotherapist is often called upon to wait with the patient and to witness his presence. This is because he has been present with 'so many others' in the turbulence and chaos of their decompensation and breakdown. The greater the degree of non-psychotic disturbance, the more does the patient fear that the therapist has no prior experience of 'someone as mad as I am!'. The lack of insight of the genuinely psychotic protects him from such preoccupations. He 'knows' that how he sees the world, is how it *is*.

The Aeolian Mode allows the therapist to wait and to witness without encroaching upon the patient's personal space until, paradoxically, the patient 'invites' such infringement of his carefully guarded boundaries. Responding to the patient's presence in the Aeolian Mode means that the therapist is aware of a hovering, encircling yet non-restricting attentiveness. It enables him to be active but not invasive, and to be attentive but not impatient. Having quoted Heidegger, 'we are to do nothing but wait', Scott (1985) continues: 'it is a great part of his distinctive office to teach us how to wait, to teach us how to approach the environing reality of the world in a spirit of meditative openness (in the spirit of *Gelassenheit*, of surrender, of abandonment) to the manifold influxions of Being'. Scott is here discussing the 'distinctive office' of the poet. And though it is not the 'greatest' part of the distinctive office of the therapist, waiting is an essential component – especially when it comes to his attentive witnessing of those endopsychic changes which the patient may need, but which he also fears. Vanstone (1982), though writing primarily about theology, says much that is of direct relevance to the role of the therapist who waits and witnesses. In *The Stature of Waiting* he writes: 'man must see his dignity not only in being a point of activity in the world but also in being a point of receptivity: not only in his manifold capacity for action but also in the many facets of his passibility; not only in his potential for ''doing'' but also in his exposure to ''being done to'' '.

Sometimes the patient has a deep-seated fear that disclosure will take from him that which he wants to retain. He is afraid of 'working through' because it may mean 'letting go' of that which is of value.

> 'It's a parasitic relationship. You don't *add* anything. You just take it away. You might not know the value of it. . . . If I tell you a story, I transfer it when I share it with you. It's then partly yours and there's nothing I can do to get it back.'

Such a patient calls for presence intensification and non-encroaching attentiveness. And associative reverberations allow the therapist to wait and to witness until the moment comes when a mutative metaphor can touch the depths before it stirs the surface. If the timing is right, such a patient will then find that she has told her story, but that it has not been taken away or devalued.

The therapist needs to be on his guard lest he presumes that psychotherapy is the only influence for integration active in the patient's life. And it is to Kubie (1971) that we owe the cautionary reminder the the patient who 'fell ill may fall well again!' This means that the patient may have achieved greater psychic integration or 'clinical improvement' for reasons other than the therapeutic relationship. Increased maturity, more satisfying relationships, greater outlet for creative expression, enhanced awareness of the benevolence of life, or a shift in *Weltanschauung* – all these may significantly influence the patient's inner and outer adaptation. After all, why should a professional relationship be the only dynamic in the direction of coherence? Kubie's comment is not cynical, it is crucial. There may be many years of hidden decompensation before the patient overtly 'fell ill' and it is important to remember that, for equally complex reasons, a patient may 'fall well again'. Discussing the play *Troilus and Cressida*, Joyce Carol Oates (1976) points out that certain sequences of events are only 'weakly explained' by preceding dynamics. B follows A but it is only weakly explained in terms of A. She refers to a vertical dimension which is at least as important as the horizontal one of causality. There are implications here for working within the Aeolian Mode.

Replying to a question about the degree to which he was still puzzled by the offences he had committed, an offender-patient spoke of 'the chain of events'. And, in this apt phrase with a double meaning, he has captured two essential aspects of assessment and therapy.

The chain of events may imply the way in which a man is 'chained' to his past by the restrictive hold of life-events. And assessment calls for appraisal of the 'hold' of the past on the present. On the other hand, it is usually taken to refer to the causal connection – the chain – between one event and another. Assessment also calls for dynamic formulation of the 'developmental line'. Here again we refer to Oates' notion of one event being 'weakly explained' by another. But, either way, therapy attempts to free man from the restrictive chain of past events, through the incursion of new freedoms experienced when primitive defences are relinquished and transference resolved.

The Aeolian Mode allows the therapist's attention to hover lightly over 'the chain of events', so that either 'the restrictive hold' or 'the causal connection' can be brought into focus as psychic circumstances dictate.

The therapist can wait without boredom, because *poiesis* inevitably maintains arousal. We have looked at this in greater detail in connection with the neuropsychological foundation of the Aeolian Mode. This section could perhaps be ironically summarized by saying that associative reverberations which are non-invasive enable the therapist to be actively present, so that he can 'wait' and 'witness' until a patient who 'fell ill, may fall well again'! In this eventuality, the therapist is acting in the capacity of a containing and holding environment in which psychological growth is facilitated. And there is a small group of patients for whom this facet of psychotherapy is predominant. Nevertheless, we need scarcely add that the vast majority of psychotherapy is undertaken for conventional interpretive or supportive indications. And it is for this reason that chapter 8 on

applications of the Aeolian Mode deals primarily with interpretive and supportive aspects of psychotherapy.

Heidegger described the way in which a 'clearing' made in a dense forest
allows whatever is present to become evident. It may be light, dark, dawn,
dusk, mist, or smoke. The forester does not create the mist, but his
creation of a clearing allows the mist to be seen for what it is. And a similar
phenomenon occurs in psychotherapy. The therapist's hovering attentiveness enables a clearing to be made within therapeutic space. He then must
wait and witness what appears. Like the forester, the therapist merely
created space, so that what was already present could become evident.

There is such an ominous precision about a psychotic's urge to kill in
order that he could create a 'clearing' in an overcrowded flat, that the
neurotic's histrionic acting-out of 'clearing' room to breathe in the
parental home, by burning a teddy-bear, seems 'safely' transitional.

The therapist working within the confines of a secure hospital is acutely
aware of the importance of Heidegger's 'clearing' image. For example, it
can never be presumed that a therapeutic group is necessarily the agent of
change, though it may very well be the setting, the 'clearing', in which
change becomes evident. Thus an increased capacity for empathy may be
clamantly clear within the confines of a small group, whereas it might pass
unnoticed within the daily bustle of ward life.

· Kuhns (1983) draws our attention to the importance of witnessing
enactments as 'the meeting ground for the interaction of primary and
secondary process thought'. He says that this is the property of style – in
his discussion of a psychoanalytic theory of culture. And in the Aeolian
Mode the therapist's attention is upon the present enactments and that
which is 'thrown alongside'. This being the etymological source of the
'parable' (see pp. 1 and 242).

Sue Jennings (1986a) has spoken of the collaboration between therapist
and patient in the creation of an empty stage. Waiting and witnessing –
sooner or later – allow meaning to emerge. This is contrary to the impetus
to intervene and 'do something' which 'will bring Act I to a close'.
Whereas discerning observation, in the presence of partial mystery, may
lead to clarification of what was previously obscure. The picture of a
forester, waiting at the periphery of a clearing in the forest, is a healthy corrective to that of restless 'therapeutic' overactivity. The Aeolian Mode
augments the therapist's capacity to wait and witness.

Witnessing: presence and transfiguration: vignette 6.1
'give me my robe'

The intense pathos of the unfolding sequence of events has such a hold on
the observer that he feels more of a participant than a witness. The sense of

irresistible engagement in that which is present is more reminiscent of Dostoevsky than Dickens. Although the setting, now to be described, is incontrovertibly Dickensian.

A man has reached the end of the road. Isolated from the outside world in his cheap, dirty bed-sitter in dockland, and beginning to sense the approaching isolation from the stream of his own existence, Tom lies propped up in bed. He scarcely notices that the blood he has coughed up is dripping on to the floor. He is dying from carcinoma of the lung and insists on chain-smoking till the bitter end. Emaciated and lonely, he speaks to Maureen, his social worker, who is now sitting at his bedside. Pointing to an old chest of drawers standing in the corner, Tom says:

'Bring that drawer here.'

Obeying the instruction, Maureen finds that the drawer has a lid, so that she is unaware of the contents. She turns towards Tom. He indicates that he wants her to place it on his bed so that he can 'open' it. His hands shake as he lifts the lid and his gaze sharpens.

'He was looking at me while I was looking at the drawer. . . . What
I saw were some old cosmetics and a faded dress.'

There was a death-bed 'statement' of a transvestite life-style hidden until he felt it was safe to make what was likely to prove the last disclosure of his life. Maureen continues:

'He looked at the drawer . . . then he looked at me.'
        'What were his eyes asking you?'
'Is it all right?'

It became clear that this disclosure of hitherto secret material was in the nature of a confession. Tom had been ashamed of wearing 'drag'. None of his friends had ever known. As he came to the margin of life, and while he still had the chance, he wanted to make an unequivocal statement about himself. While Maureen was describing this fragment of history involving furtive, anxious glances at garments of which the owner was ashamed, an almost clamant phrase from *Antony and Cleopatra* elbowed its way into my (M.C.) mind. It initially appeared to be a contrasting extreme . . . a contaminant to my concentration. But it would not go.

'Give me my robe, put on my crown'
(V. 2, 287)

There had been a transformation. In this transvaluation there was a terminal ego-enhancing sense of completion. Tom was finally able to say who he was and what he did. Tolstoy would have said he was talking now,

184

knowing that he was talking for the last time. So great was the impression of the linking between the discovery of 'old cosmetics and a faded dress' and the *royal robes and crown*, which decked the dying Cleopatra, that I asked Maureen to repeat *exactly* what Tom had said, and to tell me once again what was in the drawer. And to tell me *slowly*. Although I was interested in this fragment of history from its inception, I was astonished to hear the contents of the drawer being described for the second time.

'What I saw were some old cosmetics and a faded dress.'

This time, (*though not before*) she added:

'. . . *and a WIG.*'

This confirmed an intuitive reception that the hidden significance of this incident had indeed been climactic robing and crowning. A statement of undisguised completion and readiness for 'the great change'.

'What I saw were some old cosmetics and a faded dress. And a wig.'
'Give me my robe [dress], put on my crown [wig].'

Transfiguration had taken place at the death-bedside. Tom's facial expression said:

'Is it all right?'

Tom had needed her to wait and witness. And Maureen's silent nod implied that it was.

When she next visited dockland, Maureen was told that Tom had died.

THE RORSCHACH APPROACH

'HAMLET: Do you see yonder cloud that's almost in shape of a camel?
POLONIUS: By the mass, and 'tis like a camel, indeed.
HAMLET: Methinks it is like a weasel.
POLONIUS: It is backed like a weasel.
HAMLET: Or like a whale?
POLONIUS: Very like a whale.'

(*Hamlet* III. 2, 381)

The essence of creativity lies in the capacity for rapidly changing frames of reference. This is illustrated in Hamlet's discussion with Polonius. He swiftly transforms the perception of a cloud to a sequence of visual images. The poet uses similar dynamic shifts as he explores the edge of language. And we have already referred (p. 25) to Kaufmann's description of the play *Troilus and Cressida* as 'a collossal Rorschach inkblot test' and to metaphor's projective quality (p. 16). The key reference which confirms 'the pattern which connects' is Empson's *Seven Types of Ambiguity* (1930), because ambiguity lies at the heart of the Rorschach.

The Rorschach test with its 'accidental inkblots' (Rorschach 1921) provides a unique vehicle for observing genetic aspects of both perceptual and verbal processes. On Rorschach's card two the lower middle red region is often interpreted as a flower, and sometimes as female genitals. A schizophrenic patient described it as a 'Virginity-flower'. This was an expansion of the frame of reference, and was something new. But in the evaluation of neologisms and contaminations, the formalistic aspects tend to dominate, and there is no appreciation of the creative and positive impact of the unknown. There is a danger that neologisms may be filed away as 'signs of primary process', without due consideration being given to the possibility of inherent meaning. And the centrality of attunement in the Aeolian Mode implies that such meaning can never be disregarded. It is for this reason that we have devoted many pages to anti-reductive phenomenology (see p. 208), and have cited, at the outset, a schizophrenic's response to a Rorschach card.

The semi-structured quality of the inkblots, and the process calling for a synchronization of perceptual and verbal phenomena, help us to understand the patient's experiential world. The Rorschach test has numerous possibilities for gestalt-making. In everyday perception the surroundings are structured as clearly delineated, real objects. The observer's perception is constantly oscillating from one object to another. Yet such alternation is part of a 'perceptual hold', to use Schachtel's term (1967). The units the observer isolates are usually limited to certain real objects. Although the structure, spatial arrangements, colours, and shade-effects of the inkblot make it more likely that some parts tend to be processed as gestalts, there is a wider range of choice and emphasis than in perceptual structuring of the 'real world'. The quality of these structuring, interpreting processes varies significantly from one person to another. It can be tentative, hesitating, confused, anxious, vague, impulsive, patient, circumstantial, intuitive, playful, indolent, scrutinizing, absorbed, bored, injured, spontaneous, dreaming, critical, etc. Rorschach perception is thus a far more active process than is the case in routine observation.

Individual differences in perception, which are usually camouflaged by reductive labelling, become more pronounced in the active perception called for by the ink-blots. Everyday perception is often stereotyped and cliché-ridden. And even the metaphors to which we resort tend to be faded and shrivelled.

We meet the unknown in 'accidental forms'. And how we do so tells us about our capacity to experience the world in an open way. The instruction: 'What does it look like?' invites the subject to explore and throw himself into the unknown. Some welcome this challenge and find it fascinating. Others are anxious. Joan Rees (1978) describes how the dramatist may find himself facing terror and excitement in regions which he himself has opened up. Shakespeare might be afraid of what King Lear had to face. She writes: '*King Lear*, especially, produces the terror and excitement of pushing into unknown and fearful regions and the dramatist himself may well have held his breath as they opened out before him.' The miniature Rorschach-world, consisting of ambiguous ink-blots, does not deal with questions to which there are unequivocal answers. The Rorschach encounter may be maintained at the level of colours and patterns, but it may confront the observer with the chaotic inner and outer world confronting King Lear. 'This tempest will not give me leave to ponder / On things would hurt me more' (*King Lear* III. 4, 24).

Granville-Barker (1927) expresses a view which, if not opposed to that of Rees, is at least an effective counterbalance. While it may be true that Shakespeare is pulled towards that experience which King Lear has to endure, at the same time, as the creative artist, he needs to provide domestic detail which allows us adequate foothold and grounding to offset inner disintegration. Granville-Barker writes: 'Shakespeare has, besides, to carry us into strange regions of thought and passion, so he must, at the same time, hold us by familiar things.' In this he is mirroring life. Domestic crisis, no matter whether it is that of birth or death, by natural causes or by homicide, is usually described against a backcloth of details about familiar things. For example, 'He was sitting in his usual chair, and had just called out for a cup of tea, when . . .'. Likewise, the Rorschach ink-blots may also provide material for mirroring the realities of everyday life, such as butterflies and flowers.

The richer, the more versatile and open towards the world the subject is, the more variegated will his outer world be. On the other hand, he who represses much of his inner reality by selective inattention, or other avoidance mechanisms, cuts himself off from essential aspects of life. The way in which the world is perceived is reflected in the subject's style of processing the Rorschach cards.

In our discussion of neuropsychology (pp. 200ff) we refer to an active organizing principle which operates below the threshold of consciousness. This is associated with emotions, and creates the basis for the mediation of the two modes linked to the duality of the brain. The Rorschach cards' 'opacity' reflects both darkness and light. It also provokes both undifferentiated and differentiated experience. An encounter with the Rorschach cards calls for a temporary shift from a factual, logical, analytical attitude, to one of attunement which is creative and playful and evokes the capacity to synthesize. The Rorschach test provides 'potential space' for creative processes. Its strength lies in its ability to tap the complexity of the psychological operations in perception, association, thinking, and communication. This is especially true of experiences pertaining to the 'background' of our thoughts. It keeps the mind's door open to the unconscious. For example, the understanding afforded by the Rorschach test would elaborate and 'fill out' attunement to the patient whose enigmatic statement carried such existential weight as: 'I'm standing on the edge of all my days' (see p. 91).

In such words the patient offers us his experience. He tells us in oblique metaphor-laden language that he is 'standing on the edge' of his days. And when he is confronted by the Rorschach cards he describes not only what he saw, but how he saw it. The words in which an interpretation is clothed are relevant, as indicators not only of his way of thinking and communication, but also of his personality. 'Every Rorschach statement contains an impulsive, a defensive and an adaptive element' (Schafer 1954). Man's greatest invention – language – has helped to articulate his experience and to communicate it. And by augmenting the awareness of experience the experiential world is 'authenticized'. But words may also be used as substitutes, so that they prevent, obscure, and edit experience.

In a Rorschach interpretation this limited use of language is counteracted by the percept, so that words can no longer camouflage what is subsequently revealed. Attitudes, feelings, and strivings are most clearly disclosed in kinaesthetic and physiognomic responses (see pp. 130, 173). These categories of experience do not necessarily reflect a 'lower' stage of development.

Physiognomic perception itself is capable of considerable development which is synchronous with the degree of differentiation and refinement of the hemispheres. The physiognomic perception which underlies art and poetry shows 'a tremendous advancement over that of the young child' (Schachtel 1967). When applied to the Rorschach test, this means that the 'physiognomic perception' of an 'inkblot and its sensory qualities' may imply that a person 'is more fully in touch with reality than is a person whose record is completely lacking in physiognomic responses'. Nevertheless, it should be mentioned that a particular kind of physiognomic response occurs in pathological contexts (Theilgaard 1987).

In the visual perception of movement, which leads to kinaesthetic empathy, one ceases to be an outside observer merely registering what takes place. One participates in the experience. While man is usually aware of his feelings or attitudes – unless he is emotionally crippled by severe repression or denial – kinaesthetic experience is characterized not only by its physical quality, but also by the content of the perception, namely movement. And this reflects the inner experience of the intimate relation to the self and the capacity for empathic understanding of others. Rorschach felt that the capacity of inner creativity – represented in the test by movement-responses – is, in its highest development, identical with artistic inspiration and religious feeling. But, first and foremost, he saw it as a creative factor in experience, a way of relating which is potentially present in everyone.

When assessing a patient for dynamic therapy, it is essential to evaluate his capacity for being receptive and sensitive to both inner and outer experiences. The Rorschach test represents an excellent medium for evaluating the patient's potentialities for empathy and creativity. The encounter with the unfamiliar and the unknown is of crucial significance for man's life and development. The Rorschach cards may mirror the uneasiness in the face of the unknown, 'the as-yet pathless' (Schachtel). They may also inspire a creative urge to engage with material in a physiognomic and empathic manner. And the processing of the multifaceted symbolic material, so specific for the individual, always gives evidence of his degree of attunement to the world.

Ecclestone (1977) aptly brings this chapter to a close by reminding us that we can lose our capacity for attunement. A loss T. S. Eliot echoes on the next page.

'Becoming absorbed in the one-dimensional current of instant speech we are in danger of losing both will and ability to attend to echoes. Still less are we ready to wait on what lies beyond them.'

7

The three foundations

'Where is the Life we have lost in living?
Where is the wisdom we have lost in knowledge?
Where is the knowledge we have lost in information?'
(*Choruses from 'The Rock'*, T. S. Eliot 1934)

Of the three theoretical foundations we have chosen, none – considered in isolation – is sufficiently comprehensive. Taken together, however, they make a substantial contribution towards illuminating our understanding of the way we experience the inner and the outer world. And, as such, they throw light upon the Aeolian Mode.

Models and theories are vehicles for thought and should, at best, be regarded as tentative. And related hypotheses are instrumental, to be adapted to the special demands of the subject matter. One theory does not make another redundant and, for this reason, we feel justified in adopting an eclectic approach. Man is both a biological and a social being. Because of this, no solitary perspective has a monopoly of truth. This means that the reduction of an either–or logic is insufficient and must yield to the integrated coherence of interdisciplinary synergism. Nevertheless, this does not imply a dualistic viewpoint. On the contrary, we want to dismantle the Cartesian cage which still exerts a peculiarly rigid and tenacious hold in some clinical circles. We choose to view the human being as a bio-psycho-social unity. But psychological and biological disciplines differ in regard to their applied systems and attendant variables. At a microscopic level, dealing with receptor-cells, synapses, and transmitter substances – which are all molecular phenomena – there are no corresponding phenomenological data. The latter are macroscopic.

It is well known that the qualities of the whole are not merely a simple sum of the qualities of its subsystems. In the formulations of the gestalt-psychologists: The whole is more than the sum of its parts. This is illustrated by the relation between water and ice. An understanding of the altered characteristics of water, when frozen, cannot be derived from an understanding of its chemical components.

The two descriptive systems – the biological and the psychological – have a complementary relationship. 'Complementary' is used in the same sense as in atomic physics. The word characterizes the relationship between different empirical data, which can only be illustrated by heterogeneous experimental procedures. Sets of explanations appropriate to the two descriptive systems belong to different categories.

Compared to biochemistry, psychology works with 'large' units. It can therefore accommodate deterministic and causal explanatory concepts, similar to those used in classical physics. It can hardly be expected that a habitual conceptual frame referring to global phenomena will be equally valid when microscopic phenomena are under discussion. This parallels the fact that quantum mechanics necessitates principles of a new kind, which deny the use of deterministic descriptions. Consider Bernoulli's 'law of large numbers' (Watson 1986): 'Random events, provided there are enough of them, produce patterns with reason and meaning.'

In order to forward our understanding of the complex totality of the human being, it is necessary to counteract the reductionism and fragmentation which is introduced by increasing specialization. The categorization principles we adopt codetermine our observation. This makes us acutely aware of Bateson's warning (1979): 'The map is not the territory' and 'Quantity does not determine pattern.' And, whereas Bateson also said, 'Two descriptions are better than one', we invoke the aid of Lewis Carroll and suggest that three foundations are better than one. 'What I tell you three times is true!' ('The Hunting of the Snark').

We have now reached the point, promised on p. xxvii, where we launch into a detailed consideration of the 'tripartite foundation' upon which the Aeolian Mode rests. We hope to illustrate the dynamics which undergird Bachelard's axiomatic observation that 'The image has touched the depths before it stirs the surface.'

DEVELOPMENTAL PSYCHOLOGY

I felt a Cleaving in my Mind –
As if my Brain had split –
I tried to match it – Seam by Seam –
But could not make them fit.

> The thought behind, I strove to join
> Unto the thought before –
> But Sequence ravelled out of Sound
> Like Balls – upon a Floor.
>
> (Emily Dickinson)

Developmental psychologists do not have a monopoly of relevant commentary about human growth. Shakespeare saw seven ages of man from the 'mewling and puking' infant to the old person 'sans teeth, sans eyes, sans taste, sans everything' (*As You Like It* II. 7, 166). There would have been little progress in the field of psychological theory if Polonius' advice had been followed: 'Neither a borrower nor a lender be' (*Hamlet* I. 3, 75). Fruitful ideas are hard to trace to a single origin, and theoretical viewpoints overlap. All developmentalists are concerned with the nature and source of divergent directions of psychological growth, though the specificity of their interest varies.

The two giants in this field, Freud representing psychoanalysis and Werner representing organismic theory, are not to be construed as opponents. Indeed, we hope to demonstrate how they complement each other in the Aeolian Mode. Both have made major and original contributions towards an understanding of those psychological phenomena associated with genetic development and process. Yet they each have a different emphasis. Psychoanalytic theory, being firmly grounded in clinical practice, is largely concerned with defences, ego strength, and personality characteristics, whereas organismic theory deals with qualitative distinctions between different stages of development. It is sometimes erroneously postulated that psychoanalytic theory is mainly concerned with affect, whereas other developmental theories stress cognition. (This stricture applies to Piaget's viewpoint, but not to Werner's.) Those theories which provide our frame of reference are in fact concerned with both affect and cognition. This duality was stressed by Freud, on the one hand, and by Werner on the other. Their respective viewpoints are neither as polarized nor as irreconcilable as is sometimes suggested.

Mainstream psychoanalytic psychology

Without doubt, psychoanalytic psychology is the most widely influential psychological theory. Freud was endowed with formidable intellectual autonomy. His ideas continue to challenge us, and they form the backbone of our therapeutic work. His use of literary and mythological allusions served as a starting point for the subsequent development of analytically orientated literary criticism. In these pages we have provided copious evidence of the close relationship between dynamic psychology and the part *poiesis* plays in poetry, narrative, and therapy. Nevertheless, from the broad sweep of Freud's extensive theoretical contributions, we have chosen five which are axiomatic for the Aeolian Mode.

First, *the dynamic holistic view of man:*

'a full-bodied individual living partly in a world of make-believe, beset by conflicts and inner contradictions, capable of rational thought and action, moved by forces of which he has little knowledge and by aspirations which are beyond his reach, by turn confused and clearheaded, frustrated and satisfied, hopeful and despairing, selfish and altruistic, in short, a complex human being.'

(as summarized by Hall and Lindzey 1957)

Secondly, *the unconscious as a powerful developmental resource*. There are developmental changes in the relative significance of the unconscious, preconscious, and conscious. With increasing age the preconscious and the conscious occupy more and more of the mental territory, but the unconscious remains the largest area. In his topographical approach Freud (1917a) used a metaphor to describe the relationship of these regions:

'Let us therefore compare the system of the unconscious to a large entrance hall, in which the mental impulses jostle one another like separate individuals. Adjoining this entrance hall there is a second, narrower, room – a kind of drawing-room – in which consciousness, too, resides. But on the threshold between these two rooms a watch-man performs his function: he examines the different mental impulses, acts as a censor, and will not admit them into the drawing-room if they displease him.'

(p. 295)

Thirdly, *the significance of early experience*. One of Freud's bold statements about human development was that the first years of life are the most important ones for the formation of personality. Its development involves his well-known psychosexual stages. These sequential phases are only loosely integrated. Each builds upon and is dominant over the antecedent stage, which is never obliterated. Regression is an ever present possibility. It provides clinical evidence of sequential maturation. The final organization of personality contains components derived from each stage.

Fourthly, *the continuum between the normal and the abnormal personality*. According to Freud (1933), abnormal and normal personality obey the same principles; they merely occupy different positions in a continuum:

'Pathology, by making things larger and coarser, can draw our attention to normal conditions which would otherwise have escaped us.

Where it points to a breach or a rent, there may normally be an articulation present. If we throw a crystal to the floor, it breaks; but not into haphazard pieces. It comes apart along its lines of cleavage into fragments whose boundaries, though they were invisible, were predetermined by the crystal's structure. Mental patients are split and broken structures of this same kind. . . . They have turned away from external reality, but for that very reason they know more about internal, psychical reality and can reveal a number of things to us that would otherwise be inaccessible to us.'

(p. 58)

Fifthly, *the perception of meaning in primary process material*. Thought and feeling do not occur at random. Every psychological event has a meaning; so has primary process thinking. It is not difficult to see why the creative aspect of primary processes finds echoes in the Aeolian Mode. Freud spoke of a preconscious thought 'entrusted for a moment to unconscious elaboration' and its connection to a variety of creative or other inventive processes. Under certain conditions, the ego regulates regression. This results in a relatively brief, oscillating reduction of certain adaptive, integrative, and synthetic ego functions. In therapy, as in artistically creative processes, the temporarily diminished boundaries permit fusion of new wholes and new *Gestalten* emerge. This regressive process is a temporary return to previous levels, characteristic of childhood years, when the secondary process was still weakly developed. But it is also a topographical regression, so that primarily conscious functioning returns to the province of the preconscious and the unconscious. Perhaps Freud's most fundamental achievement was his description of the features of the primary process.

Analytic literature sometimes gives the impression that primary process thinking remains static and primitive from a developmental point of view. We do not see it in this way. Primary process thinking is not synonymous with chaos or random error, it mediates experience – as Holt (1967) expresses it: 'In the service of synthetic necessity'. Neither is it a living anachronism, in constant conflict with the ego. Indeed, creative people – including artists and scientists – often show a high degree of development and refinement in their primary process thinking. Synthesis, a function our culture has underestimated for a long time, is the characteristic of this mode of thinking.

In his investigation of the creative process in art and science Rothenberg (1979) found that, compared with 'controls', Nobel laureates showed significantly more Janusian and homospatial thinking. The former consists of the active simultaneous conception of two or more opposite or antithetical ideas, images, or concepts. The latter consists of actively conceiving two or more discrete entities occupying the same space, a conception which

194

leads to the articulation of new identities. However, Rothenberg regards both Janusian and homospatial thinking as secondary process phenomena. But we take the view that the paradoxical, spatial, and ikonic nature of these modes is more in keeping with the primary process, albeit on a mature level. Noy (1979) stresses that primary and secondary process modes develop in parallel and, under normal circumstances, operate in a balanced fashion (see Maslow 1965, p. xxviii).

Characteristics of primary process material which are of special significance for the Aeolian Mode are the presence of mutual contradiction, displacement, condensation, timelessness, *'pars-pro-toto* thinking', and replacement of external by internal reality. It is the road to understanding not only dreams and symptoms, but also the vicissitudes of emotional relationships. In particular, it enables us to appreciate the power and persistence of feelings intensified and encapsulated in the transference relationship. While the secondary process is concerned with discrimination of differences and heterogeneity, the primary process deals with registration of sameness, identity, and homogeneity.

The Aeolian Mode utilizes the primary process to aid the 'unfolding' of the patient's fantasies, and to render accessible those verbalizations of 'deep down things that keep on coming up'. But this 'translation' does not violate defences (Bachelard) to the same extent as a logical, discursive analysis of the thought content; and for this reason it is less likely to encounter resistance. On the contrary, the patient often feels enriched and finds the experience enhancing.

Group phenomena: Thus far our discussion of psychoanalytic psychology has dwelt upon classical individual developmental psychology, whereas many of the vignettes cited come from group psychotherapy. We have already referred to Foulkes and Bion in connection with vignette 3.5 ('It's cold enough for snow outside as well', p. 81).

For our present purposes it is sufficient to state that we are aware of this apparent inconsistency. But the literature on group psychology and group psychotherapy is so voluminous that two primary references must suffice. During a therapeutic group the therapist attempts to tune in to affect-laden disclosure sequences which are both part of an individual life and yet also have generic relevance for the group-as-a-whole. This skill partly depends upon his ability to perceive and facilitate the inductive significance of metaphor. And, within the context of a therapeutic group, this means that the 'containing' and 'holding' function of the group are understood as being integral facets of the 'group matrix' (James 1984).

We suggest that the Aeolian Mode is operative within the group matrix because 'the image touches the depths – not only of the individual psyche, but also the depths of the group-as-a-whole – before it stirs the surface' – to adapt Bachelard's words. Bloch and Crouch (1985) have provided an overview of the *Therapeutic Factors in Group Psychotherapy*, and, in various ways, the Aeolian Mode can play a part in facilitating each one.

Object relations: Increasing knowledge of the earliest periods of life, and the importance of these for the structuring of personality, have led to a growing interest in clinical conditions graver than the neuroses, and in their treatment. Klein, Kris, Hartmann, and Loewenstein, Spitz, Jacobsen, Mahler, Winnicott, Kohut, and Kernberg are among those analysts who have contributed to the development of object relations theory. They have modified classical technique when working with borderline and psychotic patients.

Wright (1984) has succinctly referred to object relations as 'the structurings "projected" outwards and "introjected" inwards which form the pattern of a self's dealings with the world, including other people'.

It will be recalled that the Aeolian Mode (p. xxvi) was described as a psychotherapeutic emphasis which depended upon the therapist's attunement and his capacity to use metaphor, the most useful metaphors being primordial and linked to the patient's self-esteem and the patterning of his relationships. It is on the basis of early object relations that subsequent patterning of intimate relationships depends. It is for this reason that a disturbed capacity for, or even an avoidance of, intimacy (see page 166) is so frequently the primary motivation for seeking therapy.

Dynamic psychotherapy therefore attempts to restore or re-align distorted early object relations through transference interpretation, and thus exert a beneficial effect on subsequent encounters.

Object relations also influence the way in which the wider world is perceived. Affective freedom and unbound perception allow 'things' – be they people, animals, or landscapes – to be 'seen' in an unblinkered way. The capacity to appreciate the phenomenology of things (p. 208) – in an unbiased way – is evidence of that inner freedom which stems from unfettered object relations.

The Aeolian Mode helps the ego to 'get rid of existing categorizations through a process of "dedifferentiation", whereby it "scatters and represses surface imagery"; that is to say, it will dispose of the mundane sortings of experience' (Ehrenzweig, in Wright 1984).

There is a clear Aeolian association to Bachelard in the reference to 'surface imagery'. And the paradoxical movement of 'depth before surface' is one of the reasons why the Aeolian Mode is suited to working with psychotic patients; particularly those whose disturbance of early object relations is greatest. It affords safety, in that gratification experience does not slide towards engulfment. Neither does 'affectionate distancing' become malignant abandonment. In borderline patients the Aeolian Mode gives an opportunity to integrate primary and secondary process phenomena. This improves ego-autonomy by the building up of intrapsychic structure, resting on internalization and identification.

Organismic psychology

Organismic psychology supplements the developmental aspects emphasized by psychoanalysis, and it does so by deepening our understanding of the qualitative changes determined by the sequential steps in the ontogenetic ladder. The approach advocated by Werner (1948) and Witkin *et al.* (1962) underlines two essential principles:

1. Each developmental stage is characterized by a unique patterning of experience.
2. A connection exists between specific developmental stages and specific psychopathological phenomena. These processes are analogical but not identical. It is possible to understand both the phenomenology and the underlying psycho-dynamics of a patient's symptoms by drawing a parallel between current psychopathology and phenomena which occur naturally in earlier stages of development. Thereby their *de novo* stamp is diminished, because they are explicable in terms of earlier experience.

All developmental changes take place systematically, and the regulating principle underlying these changes has been named 'orthogenetic' by Werner (1948). This principle implies that developmental progression moves from a relatively global state, characterized by lack of differentiation, to a state of increased differentiation, articulation, and hierarchical integration. This is in keeping with the psychoanalytic viewpoint which underlines the fact that in early developmental stages there is a limited differentiation between object and subject, between perception and thinking, and between feeling and action.

It is important to note that such a developmental viewpoint does not imply that antecedent levels are lost *en route*. They remain as integral parts of the more complex organization where more advanced processes dominate. This interweaving of different levels of experiencing takes place both in daily life and within therapeutic space. However, when treating the psychotic patient, the psychotherapist is constantly aware of the unification of experience which is universal in early childhood.

In the very early years a primordial functional unity exists in the fields of sensation and imagination, resulting in a merging of experience. The physiognomic, syncretic style of response is characteristic for the small child, whose percepts are deeply conditioned by emotional and motor behaviour (see p. 129). His psychological functions are more intimately

197

fused. With the adult they are evident in oceanic, pantheistic, or mystical experiences, where a melting together with universal rhythms is experienced (see p. 29 and Paffard (1976)).

The qualitative distinction between undifferentiated and differentiated, unorganized and hierarchically organized experience can be further clarified by the application of other descriptive words. We have already (p. 129) referred to the fact that the undifferentiated structure or process is syncretic, diffuse, labile, and rigid; whereas that which is differentiated and organized is discrete, articulated, stable, and flexible (Werner 1948).

Dynamization of experience lends the world a physiognomic stamp. Things which are in reality lifeless are imbued with life. This manner of perception indicates proximity, and it is radically different from conventional organization in which things are categorized according to their technical qualities such as number, size, and weight.

One of the merits of Werner's view was that he combined a developmental orientation with an organismic point of view. His approach threw the holistic aspects into relief. 'Holistic' covers both intraorganism relations and organism–environment relations. Every behavioural phenomenon depends upon its role in the overall function of the organism. Moreover, to secure a true understanding of behaviour it is necessary to take environmental factors into account. The orthogenetic principle provides a framework for viewing, ordering, and interpreting behaviour. Werner drew on a remarkably wide range of material from the fields of ethnology, ethology, developmental psychology, and psychopathology.

The Aeolian Mode invites associative freedom. It is augmented by the simultaneity of multiple meanings expressed in poetic, metaphoric form loaded with affective content. It enables us to extend our grasp of the patient's phenomenological world so that we stand a chance of obtaining deeper, more coherent understanding. This can lead to a creative synthesis.

Matte Blanco (1975)[18] has described two principles involved in the process of classification and in the general functioning of the mind. One is defined by asymmetry, and is concerned with the discrimination of difference and therefore of discerning relationships; whereas the other is defined by symmetry, and is concerned with registering sameness, identity, and homogeneity. Symmetrical logic is of the essence in metaphor, symbolism, and poetry.

Matte Blanco introduced these new terms because he was dissatisfied with the ambiguity of Freud's concept of the unconscious. Freud originally described 'the unconscious' as not just a quality, but a mode of being characterized by various other features essential to it in addition to the primary quality of being unconscious. This is in contrast to his later view expressed in *The Ego and the Id* (1923), where he employs the term 'unconscious' as a quality. According to Matte Blanco 'the quality of being unconscious is not inherent in or essentially inevitable to symmetrical being. It is, instead, a consequence of the nature of consciousness, which cannot contain within itself the symmetrical being.'

Consciousness, or the asymmetrical mode of being, cannot focus on more than one thing at a time. It must separate one thing from the next, whereas the symmetrical mode of being, by its own nature, is encompassing. It identifies the part with the whole: *pars pro toto*. The equivalence between the part and the whole constitutes an important characteristic of the unconscious mode of being.

Other characteristics of the 'system unconscious' as seen in this way are: condensation, displacement, replacement of external by psychical reality, timelessness, spacelessness, and presence of mutual contradiction. Matte Blanco emphasized that, when this principle is applied, all members of a set or class are treated as identical to one another and to the whole set or class. He gives the following simple example:

'If John is the brother of Peter, the converse is: Peter is the brother of John. The relation which exists between them is symmetrical, because the converse is identical with the direct relation. But if John is the father of Peter, the converse is: Peter is the son of John. In this case the relation and its converse are not identical. This type of relation is called asymmetrical. What the second principle affirms is that the system Ucs. tends to treat any relation as if it were symmetrical. In the example given: if John is the father of Peter, then Peter is the father of John. In Aristotelian logic this is absurd; in the logic of the system Ucs. it is normal.'

We have referred to Matte Blanco at this point because several of his ideas are relevant in the development of our theme.

'It soon becomes evident that we are always, in a given mental product confronted by a mixture of the logic of the unconscious with that of the preconscious and conscious.

In every one of its direct manifestations we can, if we look for it, detect the activity of its various levels, from the asymmetry seen in conscious thinking to the great proportion of symmetry at the deepest levels.'

Rayner (1981) comments on the therapeutic aspects, which are reconsidered in the light of Matte Blanco's viewpoints. In addition to the well known lifting of repression and the undoing of defences, Matte Blanco suggests

'an activity which can be described as "unfolding" or as a translating function . . . the new meanings are associated with the older conscious ideas because they have an identical root, based on symmetry, in the unrepressed unconscious. It is, as it were, that symmetrical experience is always "contained" by asymmetrical ideas and enrichment is gained by dipping into, or approximating to, infinite symmetrical experience from new asymmetrical points of view. The two sorts of therapeutic process can be distinguished in that the first, the undoing of defense, always encounters resistance. In unfolding, however, resistance does not occur, rather the patient quietly enjoys the process of enhancing.'

And this echoes the Bachelard quotation.

NEUROPSYCHOLOGY

The reader is likely to find that neuropsychology is the least familiar of the three foundations, but attempts to understand the Aeolian Mode cannot proceed without it, and if it was omitted our presentation would lack coherence. There are inherent difficulties in presenting it briefly. Although such a complex subject as the functioning of the brain and its relation to the Aeolian Mode cannot be dealt with comprehensively, we decided to supplement this condensed account with appropriate references, in case it is felt that we are guilty of oversimplification.

The link between neuropsychology and the Aeolian Mode

Paradoxically, the Aeolian Mode is inextricably linked with associative freedom, although it remains in keeping with dynamic determinism. It also encourages an appreciation of the simultaneous perception of multiple meanings. The image-producing potentiality of the Aeolian Mode depends upon the right hemisphere rather than the left, which is primarily concerned with linear informative communication. In the 'dominant' half of the brain, sensory data are subject to complicated analytical–conceptual processing. This depends upon language. But in the 'non-dominant' half of the brain they are processed in a more holistic way, so that they retain their immediate and rich affective value.

The novelty of input increases the general arousal state. When the right hemisphere is alerted an augmentation of awareness ensues. This means that ikonic, non-verbal experience, and deep-rooted feelings characteristic of early childhood, which words can only represent as 'faded poor souvenirs', can be brought into focus. Freud (1923; already quoted on p. 125) says:

'We must not . . . forget the importance of optical mnemic residues, when they are of *things*, or . . . deny that it is possible for thought-processes to become conscious through a reversion to visual residues. . . . Thinking in pictures . . . stands nearer to unconscious

200

processes than does thinking in words, and it is unquestionably older than the latter both ontogenetically and phylogenetically.'

(p. 21)

Freud's statement indirectly reflects the underlying coherence existing between the foundations we have chosen. Hammer (1978) describes the way in which 'imaged communication' can make 'contact through the defensive layer of repression'. He thus establishes close links with the Aeolian foundations under discussion.

> 'Through imaged communication, we move closer to where the patient's affect resides . . . the feeling below the surface can be reevoked on the surface by an accurate, focused image. Reevoked, it is now accompanied by an echo or tone of familiarity. At this point, surface and subsurface feelings, when congruent, move to join; in uniting, *they make an avenue of contact through the defensive layer of repression.*' [our italics]

The human being is unique in that he has the possibility of a reciprocal mediation between the worlds of imagery and experience, emotion and reason, and synthesis and analysis. These complex functions call for a balanced development of each hemisphere. Thus, under ideal conditions, the two modes work in harmony; whereas, in pathological conditions, they are discordant.

It is for this reason that dynamic psychotherapy underlines the importance of the concurrent interweaving of the two modes, although it is rarely described in these terms. We (Theilgaard 1973) drew attention to the relevance of the recent work on neuropsychology – and especially the functional asymmetry of the brain – for the understanding of primary and secondary process phenomena.

The Aeolian Mode enlarges the therapist's and the patient's armamentarium for reconciling dualities by the use of metaphor (see chapter 4). Furthermore, metaphorical language plays a very important role in creating bridges between sensory modalities. As Levin and Vuckovich (1983) point out, the bridging effect of the metaphor results from the fact that it constitutes an ambiguous stimulus that can arouse activity in each hemisphere. We suggest that it does so by appealing to the left brain linguistically and to the right brain ikonically. The novelty of the non-faded metaphor giving rise to an arousal of attention (see p. 207) also serves the purpose of catalysing synthetic activity. Thereby it allows the therapist to reach a more coherent understanding of the patient's phenomenological world.

By looking at the phenomena from different perspectives, for example from developmental psychology and neuropsychology, we are not attempting to make a theoretical fusion of the two fields by trying to reduce psychology to physiology. The two areas are descriptively different, as are the systems of variables they utilize (Theilgaard 1984). Provided no attempt is made to identify one with the other, it is permissible to examine the relationship between two sets of data. As Kety (1960) points out: 'One can acknowledge the existence of consciousness and of matter and energy without insisting that the one must be reduced to the other.' Hebb (1958) states: 'Even a physiologically based or neuropsychological theory of behaviour remains a psychological theory.' Freud himself explored the possibility of a neuropsychological basis to his pioneer analytic discoveries (Pribram 1962).

Developmental psychology and neuropsychology are mutually complementary. And though they come from different scientific fields, the humanities and the natural sciences, they share important theoretical ideas such as 'organizing principles' and 'holistic concepts'. Each discipline maintains that increasing differentiation is an essential feature in development, and that this is followed by hierarchical integration.

Both neuropsychology and organismic psychology look for analogical processes at different steps on the developmental ladder, assuming that there are no abrupt transitions in passing from one step to another. For example, the potential for *physiognomic* thinking (see p. 130) remains as an integral part of a more complex organization, in which more advanced processes predominate.

In recent decades endeavours to achieve an understanding of the working brain have paid increasing attention to the issue of functional asymmetry. This theory of the duality of the brain is supported by many findings. These are drawn from psychological experiments with normal subjects, as well as from investigations of patients with focal brain-damage. The older brain model, in which the right hemisphere was seen to be subordinate and without independent importance for cognitive functions, has been superseded by the double-dominance model. It is for these reasons that both clinicians and research workers now pay greater attention to the right hemisphere than hitherto, which has consequently achieved a higher 'status'. Each hemisphere possesses the potential for executing all mental and physical functions. During normal maturation the regulation of certain functions is assigned to one or other hemisphere. Thus as the child grows, the brain becomes more differentiated and the two hemispheres more specialized. The left is dominant in some functions, and the right in others. Such observations come from four different sources:

First, there are many accounts of the specific neurological symptomatology of patients suffering from focal and acute insults to the right hemisphere (Hécaen and Assal 1970; Dimond and Beaumont 1974; Suvorova 1975).

Secondly, the 'split-brain' syndrome furnishes evidence of those functions characteristic of the right hemisphere (Sperry, Gassaniga, and Bogen 1969; Milner, Taylor, and Sperry 1968).

Thirdly, patients in whom the left hemisphere has been temporarily inactivated, either by dominant unilateral electroshock or by pharmacological means, illustrate the importance of the right hemisphere (Cohen *et al.* 1968; Wada 1969; Heshe, Röder, and Theilgaard 1978).

Fourthly – and most important in the present connection – experimental procedures such as dichotic listening (simultaneous presentation of different auditory stimuli to each ear), studies of conjugate lateral eye-movement (CLEM), and experiments of interhemispheric transfer of information applied to normal subjects confirm the right hemisphere's specific responsibility for many cognitive and emotional phenomena (Bryden 1970; Bakan 1971; Kimura 1973).

Semmes (1968) maintains that cognitive functions are represented in different ways in the two hemispheres, 'tending to be focally represented in the left hemisphere, but diffusely represented in the right. Focal representation of elementary functions favors integration of similar units; conversely, diffuse representation permits an integration of dissimilar units.' Thus the right hemisphere may allow polysensory integration to take place across the modalities facilitating synaesthesia and metaphor.

We are following the convention of presenting neuropsychological material under the headings of cognition, emotion, and attention. This is solely for the purpose of description. In reality, they are part of a dynamic whole.

Cognition

The functions of the left hemisphere may be described by such adjectives as: verbal, analytical, abstract, rational, and temporal; whereas the functions of the right hemisphere may be characterized as: preverbal, synthetic, concrete, intuitive, and spatial. Inevitably, however, this listing of functions is an oversimplification. A short resumé cannot do justice to the many experiments reflecting the intricate and complicated working of the brain, with its wide variety of integrative potentialities. Nevertheless, there is one finding which is incontestable and of central significance. The brain has two *different strategies* at its disposal. One is synthetic, analogical, ikonic, and intuitive; whereas the other is univocal, digital, conceptual, and abstract.

The way in which organismic psychologists have described cognitive development is congruent with the idea of increasing differentiation, lateralization, and corticalization. The advantage of this lateral differentiation of the brain is in the effective integration between gnosis and praxis and between cognition, action, and speech. The disadvantage is that intuitive, colourful imagination represented in the right hemisphere has given way to the bleakened, more rigid ideas mediated by the left hemisphere. We (Theilgaard 1973) have pointed out that the left hemisphere is primarily concerned with the 'foreground', while the right hemisphere is responsible for the 'background'; for the sphere surrounding our thoughts.

Conrad has expressed this more poetically in *Heart of Darkness*. He refers to Marlow's stories, which 'contain their meaning . . . not inside like a kernel, but outside, enveloping the tale which brought it out only as a glow brings out a haze'.

If the right hemisphere is insufficiently differentiated and inadequately integrated with the left, there is a risk that the relationship between foreground and background may become tenuous. This precarious hold on the essential would bind imaginative ideas to words and concepts. The result would be reduced sensitivity to inner life and the world around, which is clinically evident as perceptual defence. This in turn would alienate the ikonic from the conceptual.

That the image may include fragments of spoken language is of no psychological consequence, because the bond between them is not that of grammatical logic. On the contrary, it is ideographic logic, which culminates in an order of spatial disposition totally opposed to discursive juxtaposition. It is the opposite of narration. The former is a right brain function, the latter is organized by the left hemisphere.

From a neuropsychological point of view, Pribram and Luria (1973) maintain that the role of imagery in cognition can be conceptualized as cognitive action. It is active in terms of simultaneous spatial systems and successive temporal systems.

The right hemisphere is the more primordial and it 'matures' physiologically earlier than the left (Giannitrapani 1967). During early development the right hemisphere is more involved in the learning process. It is without words, but not without images. These phenomena are more vivid, colourful, and ikonic than those represented by the conceptual, abstract, word- and letter-bound left hemisphere.

Usually, extensive communication occurs between the two hemispheres, which permits a variation of integrative potentialities in the brain. The many-faceted experience is multicoded in several sensory modalities, and in both modes of processing. The balanced functioning of both hemispheres seems to be a requisite of normal cognitive development. However, as Hadley (1983) points out: 'there appears to be a period early in development when both modes are operative and developing, but not communicating or co-ordinated. This would explain the frequent inaccessibility of early memories to evocation in the verbal mode.'

The fact that individuals differ with regard to the availability of their early – often preverbal – memories could be considered in relation to the pattern of myelinization of the interhemispheric connections. Split-brain studies have shown that information stored in the non-verbal mode is inaccessible to consciousness, unless it becomes integrated with the verbal store.

The myelinization process is far from complete at birth. As Meyersburg and Post (1979) state, the development of the striatum and limbic systems, as measured by the degree of myelinization, continues well beyond the first year of life. The cerebral commissures and non-specific thalamic radiations take longer to mature, and the development of the reticular formation continues beyond the first decade. Most interesting (and most encouraging!) myelinization continues to increase in intracortical association areas well beyond the fifth decade.

The view that the mind–brain relationship rests on a reciprocal interaction paves the way for an understanding of how the Aeolian Mode works in individuals with sub-optimally connected hemispheres. If during the early years the hemispheres are functionally hypo-connected, the probability of a separation of affects from age-appropriate meaning or ideas increases. This disconnection itself may be seen as a defensive or adaptive neurological mechanism during development. Levin and Vuckovich (1985) write:

> 'For each individual the question as to what is optimal might therefore depend upon the balance of two parallel developmental trends: the growing need and capacity for co-ordination and integration of hemispheric activity, and the need and capacity to develop coping mechanisms to avoid the danger of being chronically overstimulated. It would seem safe to conclude that the more rapidly and reliably the individual hemispheres develop tension-regulating capacity, the sooner their connection would form a more optimal system.'

Since the middle sixties it has been increasingly accepted in neuro-science that conscious experience may influence the way in which the brain actually functions. Thus Sperry (1976) views conscious phenomena as dynamically emerging characteristics of cerebral processes of a high order which are specifically designed to produce operational subjective effects. The causal potency of the hierarchy of control is seen mainly as the universal power which the whole exerts over it parts. Conscious cerebral processes contain systemic qualities which have a controlling effect over the physio-chemical elements. This means that words can influence biochemical processes. It exemplifies another facet of the neglected coherence.

> 'I understand a fury in your words
> But not the words.'
>
> (*Othello* IV. 2, 32)

Emotion

It has long been recognized that the limbic system and other basal parts of the brain are involved with emotions. Unconscious processes are also represented in the basal parts of the brain. There are more anatomical pathways from the right hemisphere to this area than there are from the left.

Hughlings Jackson (cited by Taylor 1932) postulated that certain functions could be mediated at several levels in the nervous system (hierarchical representation). More recent attention has been paid to the anatomical localization of the anterior–posterior parts of the brain, and it is now recognized that lateralization also plays a part in the mediation of emotions.

Several experiments have demonstrated that schizophrenic patients show disturbances of interhemispheric integration/communication (Beaumont and Dimond 1973). (For a comprehensive review see *The Psychology of Schizophrenia*, Cutting 1986.)

There is substantial evidence (Tucker 1981; Sackheim *et al.* 1982) that negative affective states are represented in the right brain rather than in the left; whereas the converse applies for positive affective states. As psychotherapy is often concerned with depression and anxiety, the role of the right hemisphere in the regulation of negative affects is of particular interest. Most research in this area has been undertaken with depressed patients (d'Elia and Perris 1973; Heshe, Röder, and Theilgaard 1978), and available evidence seems to favour the view that there is a predominance of right brain activation in patients suffering from depression. Greater relative right hemispheric involvement is also found in conditions of stress, where a larger proportion of left CLEM has been observed (Sackheim and Weber 1982).

Traumatic emotional experience during early childhood may create memories which have disruptive effects. They do so not only by facilitating anxious or depressive reactions to repetition of the catathymic stimulus, but perhaps also by exerting a delaying or inhibiting influence on the subsequent development of the neural structure. The Aeolian Mode provides possibilities for facilitating the activity of alternative neuronal circuits.

Basch (1983) describes what he calls 'episodic' and 'semantic' memory processes related to the right and left brain, respectively:

'The consciousness of self that we call "I" requires that the right brain self-experience, the episodic memory, be translated into verbal or other forms of discursive language. The self-experience can no longer be articulated and, therefore, cannot be either thought about or made conscious. That is, what is apprehended on the semantic, left-brain level in terms of language and logical categories cannot be translated into right-brain, episodic, self-experience. As Freud postulated, in both repression and disavowal affect is "eliminated".'

Attention

Recent studies have suggested that the two hemispheres differ in their connection to the subcortical parts of the brain which are concerned with arousal. As far as the Aeolian Mode is concerned, it is interesting to note that the right hemisphere is dominant in the field of attention (Heilman and Van der Abell 1980). They postulate that the cells in the right hemisphere are more likely to have bilateral receptive fields than cells in the left. This implies that neurones within the right hemisphere would be activated by novel or significant stimuli in either visual field on each side of hemispace – and such findings are supported by our (A.T.) experience of working with brain-damaged patients. But we do not want to create the impression that the duality of the brain is the only way to relate neurophysiological and psychological phenomena. Additional dimensions, such as the deeper structures of the brain, play a crucial part not only in emotional processes, but also in attentional ones. And the knowledge of the underlying neurophysiological development may serve to validate, elaborate, and modify the psychological theories.

Penfield (1958) interpreted the observation that 'electrical stimulation could evoke complex "memories" as evidence of a "tapping" of some segment of a distributed totality of a neural representation, which, interacting with deeper structure, could re-evoke the entire experience'.

It is probably legitimate to speculate once more that the Aeolian Mode with its application of multi-modal images, metaphors, and paradox, all emphasizing novelty, has a special capacity to reach the deeper structures.

Ever since Moruzzi and Magoun (1949) demonstrated that stimulation of the ascending reticular activating system (RAS) diffusely energized the cortex and produced concomitant desynchronization of EEG alpha-activity, there has been an increased interest in arousal. The idea of arousal as a general state or as an unequivocal concept has been criticized, as has the idea of isomorphism between arousal and reticular activity.

Novelty of input is of great importance in maintaining the state of arousal, and it is homologous with the psychological concept of *poiesis* (see p. 23). While the perception of something expected, or of something already familiar, is quickly labelled and 'filed away' in an established category, the unfamiliar or novel stimulus cannot be disposed of in this way. The novel, the unknown, and that which cannot easily be anticipated maintain the state of arousal. The subject therefore remains alert.

Work on attentional disturbance in schizophrenic patients (McGhie *et al.* 1965a and 1965b; Venables 1969, 1980) underlines the importance of providing adequate stimulation in the treatment of the withdrawn schizophrenic. Responding to such patients within the Aeolian Mode, the therapist utilizes the impact of novel associative stimuli which tend to augment the state of arousal. When this occurs, 'hovering attentiveness' serves as an evocative presence, rather than being a threatening stimulus which might intensify the patient's need to withdraw.

Sokolov (1963) describes the orienting reflex (OR) as an unspecific response, initiated by any qualitative or quantitative change of stimulus. When a stimulus is neither novel nor significant, habituation occurs by selectively influencing thalamic relay. As an explanation of the selective aspect in this process, Sokolov has introduced the hypothesis of a neuronal cortical model. Signals from the receptors are projected to the cortex as well as to the reticular activating system. Any stimulus incompatible with this model will produce an OR by activating the RAS. This function thus acts as a selective filter – another example of perceptual defence.

Sokolov's hypotheses are concordant with a range of physiological data. Furthermore, it is shown that an incoming stimulus is received at a cortical level before it reaches the RAS. This means that cortical 'evaluation' of a stimulus can take place before the same stimulus initiates reticular activity. The model serves as an explanation of such psychodynamic phenomena as subliminal perception, repression, and sensitization. For example, repression may be brought about by inhibitory impulses from the cortex to the RAS, which will then block further processing of the stimulus in question. It does so by raising the threshold of stimulation, so that its conscious perception is impeded.

In accordance with this hypothesis it seems also plausible that the novelty of input may increase the likelihood of 'bypassing' the repression barrier, so that 'depth is touched before the surface is stirred' (Bachelard op. cit.). This is yet another example of the complementarity between dynamic psychology and neuropsychology. To discover that a psychodynamic concept, such as repression, is congruous with recent research in the field of neuropsychology supports those who advocate theoretical coherence between fields so often regarded as antagonistic.

PHENOMENOLOGICAL EXISTENTIAL PSYCHOLOGY

'If we look long enough at anything it overwhelms us with its possibilities. The lump of coal in my hand becomes the diamond a little greater pressure might have made. I stare hard at a leaf until petiole snaps free from branch and the leaf is autumn circling in a turning wind. I see your sleeping hand and I become the touch of all familiar places I have never known.'

(Weston 1977)

'Everything seemed to be asking me to notice it.'
(*An Autobiography*, Edwin Muir 1940)

'Subjects sprang up at every step. . . . It would seem that there is no profession, no class, no corner of . . . life into which Chekhov has not peered.'
(Eichenbaum 1944, see Jackson 1967)

'Seems, madam! Nay, it is; I know not "seems".'
(*Hamlet* I. 2, 76)

'It was only the loss of that cloistral self-concern which hangs like a dark curtain before all our pre-conceptions, to dim the full light of experience.'
(Church 1957)

'This shaking keeps me steady. I should know.
What falls away is always. And is near.
I wake to sleep, and take my waking slow.
I learn by going where I have to go.'
(Theodore Roethke, 'The Waking')

On the contrary the mere fact of dealing with matters outside the general run of everyday experience laid me under the obligation of a more scrupulous fidelity to the truth of my own sensations. The problem was to make unfamiliar things credible. To do that I had to create for them, to reproduce for them, to envelop them in their proper atmosphere of actuality. This was the hardest task of all and the most important, in view of that conscientious rendering of truth in thought and fact which has been always my aim.'
(*Within the Tides*, Conrad 1915)

Hamlet's affirmation stands as a generic representative of the phenomenological significance of experience. To the observer, even someone as close as the subject's mother, the experience may have *seemed* to be particular. But to the experiential subject, who is the only one entitled or indeed able to know the experience at first hand, it does *not* merely *seem* to be particular, it *is*.

The link between phenomenology and the Aeolian Mode is best discussed in relation to a clinical vignette (see p. 211). Phenomenological existential psychology is one of the theoretical foundations because of the central emphasis it places upon the validity of experience. And the constant search for possibly greater fidelity to experience is a characteristic of the Aeolian Mode.

Søren Kierkegaard: the cry of alarm

The central motif in dynamic psychotherapy is that of an individual daring to enter and claim his experience in all its fullness, however much suffering this may involve. It is also a central theme in existential thinking, particularly that propounded by Kierkegaard. He distinguishes between two individuals and their knowledge of suffering. 'One is to suffer; the other is to become a professor of the fact that another has suffered.' It has been said of Kierkegaard that: 'His mission to men was thus formed in the matrix of his own need and suffering. He believed that his was the task of "introducing the unconditional . . . to utter the cry of alarm". It was a cry which was first sounded in and to his own soul. As Heim has said of Kierkegaard's type of thought, "a proposition or truth is said to be *existential* when I cannot apprehend or assent to it from the standpoint of a mere spectator but only on the ground of my total existence"' (Chaning-Pearce 1948). Dunne (1967) says:

> 'Kierkegaard underwent both dread and despair and attained at length to an assurance and transparency by facing, though not abolishing, the ambiguity that was the cause of his dread and despair. . . . Faith for him consisted of facing this dreadful thing, his own individuality, and accepting it, like Saint Francis of Assisi kissing the leper. Each man had a leper to kiss, we might say, but the leper was not another person as it was for Francis; it was himself in his own individuality. . . . As victory over dread Kierkegaard defined faith as "the inward certainty which anticipates infinity," an inner assurance in the face of the infinity of possibilities concerning himself that makes a man uncertain of himself.'

We hope that these condensed quotations from Kierkegaard himself, and from Kierkegaard scholars, which bring out the paradoxical, 'the passion of inwardness', and the cry of alarm which accompanies the unconditional, show how firmly Kierkegaard stands upon the ground where existentialism and psychotherapy meet. His stress upon the unconditional led Tillich (1965) to write upon that for which man shows 'ultimate concern'. And he points constantly to intellectualization as a defence, and to any other protective mechanism by which an individual is distanced and alienated from his own experience. Hamlet's mother spoke of Ophelia as being 'incapable of her own distress' (*Hamlet* IV. 7, 177). And Kierkegaard would strongly support the aim of therapy which was to put man in touch with his distress, as far as he was able to bear it. Such therapy diminishes disengagement from experience. Man then ceases to be 'a professor of the fact that another [part of himself] has suffered' and is progressively enabled to acknowledge his distress. At the end of his summary of Kierkegaard's psychology, Kresten Nordentoft (1972) writes:

> 'Kierkegaard operates (though not very explicitly) with the notion of a benign circle, a ''consistency of the good'', in contradistinction to the vicious circle of sin. In the vicious circle the individual cuts himself off from an adequate relation to himself (the obscured self-perception etc.), to God (despair being, essentially, offence at the religious), and to his fellow beings (encapsulation). In the benign circle he simultaneously loves God, his neighbour, and himself. . . . God is love and love is the ''ground'' of human life, behind the superficial layers of despair.'

There is a note of urgency in Kierkegaard's writing, and, as was said of John Donne, it is that of 'a dying man to dying men'. Therapeutic space is characterized by a sense of urgency which is ultimate. And it does not need to wait for suicidal threats to make it so. The engagement of man with man in a therapeutic group is metaphorically, and sometimes literally, that of dying men to dying men. The group has a built-in dynamic which centres down upon that which is essential, so that the relatively trivial becomes more so. Immediacy gives an italicized quality to that speech and that silence which betoken ultimate concern.

During an experiential workshop in which we were exploring *poiesis*, aesthetic imperatives, and points of urgency, an American psychologist brought Kierkegaard up to date in this imperative appeal:

> 'Cut out the minuets and the flim-flam,
> AND GET IN THERE.'

We have no doubt that Kierkegaard would have added his weight to this dynamic injunction, although his phrasing would have been slightly different. It recalls a comment on the text 'It is a fearful thing to fall into the hands of the living God' (*Hebrews* 10, 31): 'but it's much more fearful not to!' Another Kierkegaardian paradox.

VIGNETTE 7.1 LOCATION AND DISLOCATION
'The river Mersey'

Let us take a deceptively simple example which arose during the apparently inconsequential unfolding of a group psychotherapy session.

Mary is describing how she reached such a degree of desperate hopelessness that the only way forward was a determined suicidal attempt. She has never been able to swim. She waits until it is dark, goes to an unfrequented bridge which crosses a fast-flowing river with very strong currents. There is no towpath and everything on a dark night is black because there is no

211

artificial lighting. She tells the group how she climbed on to the stone parapet, thought for a few minutes, and then jumped.

The current was so strong that it pulled her to the side. She tried to walk back in, but the river was too strong for her. Eventually, wet, cold, and covered in slime and grit, she 'squelched home'.

With appropriate affect she described her sense of depression and way-outlessness. She told the incident neither histrionically nor with that muting of feeling which sometimes comes from distance.

The group remained silent, unsure how to respond to Mary's pain, and it was clear that many members were on the brink of describing their own echoing experiences. They, too, had tried to put a stop to the little that life seemed to hold in store for them.

The silence continued. It might be said that it was a reflection of Mary's 'fidelity to experience'. But, somehow, even though we had heard of her feelings which led up to what was certainly intended to be her last jump, there was something missing. It could be legitimately argued that if a woman is intent on drowning, then it matters little whether it is in a river or the sea, and whether the water is deep or shallow, warm or cold. And still the silence continued. Then, gratuitously, yet conveying that she was about to say something of such importance that she had previously been unable to tell the group, she added words which were apparently trivial, yet carried existential and phenomenological significance:

'IT WAS THE RIVER MERSEY . . . IT WAS DARK . . . IT WAS COLD.'

What difference did this geographical precision make? How could the location of a particular river, in which she had decided to end it all, make such a difference to the impact of the incident she was describing? The phenomenologist will say that it is the filling out of detail, the enhanced fidelity to experience. It *was* the river Mersey; and not the Thames or the Tyne. It meant that Mary was telling us exactly how things were for her. She was endorsing the fact that it was the local river . . . it was the one that was there! It was in the nature of greater confession and intimacy that we were told 'It was the river Mersey.' Previously she had 'hidden' behind 'a river' – even a dark, cold river. But now that the precision of location in the outer world had been increased, so had her feeling of disclosing deeper details of her inner world.

In this vignette phenomenology 'lingered with experience and allowed understanding to emerge' – to quote Romanyshyn again (1982). The Aeolian Mode encourages the patient to take an image and make it particular. 'A river' becomes 'the river Mersey'. A jump becomes *the* jump. This is reminiscent of Ibsen's account of those in *Rosmersholm* (1886) who,

212

watching a man approach a bridge, comment that they would not expect him to cross it . . . 'Not after *that* happened'. Again, detail advances intensity. That it was the here-and-now river, the river Mersey, recalls Ursula Fanthorpe's poem (1982, op. cit.) where even deeper and older rivers are described:

> 'It is the other rivers that lie
> Lower, that touch us only in dreams
> That never surface.'

Scarcely *Topophilia* (Tuan 1974) in the orthodox sense of 'love of place', but certainly a way of ensuring the importance of her own living–dying activity at the last chosen place on earth. But it is detail viewed against the background of the total situation of the experiencing human being. *Dasein* in Heidegger's terminology refers to man's being-in-the-world in an intentional way. In other words, man's placing in the world is not casual. Although he may be 'thrown', his location is affirmative.

Affirmative location

Patients, philosophers, and poets are unanimous in their emphasis upon the importance of knowing where they stand. In one way or another they are saying the same thing.

> 'It's where I stand . . . that's what I want to know.'

Is this a question about geographical location . . . in the orchard . . . under the clock? Or is this a deeper demand for knowing 'how things are with me'?

> 'I had nowhere to stand in court.'

Is this a statement about the facilities in a crowded courtroom? Could it be saying 'there was no "platform" on which I could stand to state my case'? Or is it an existential statement of being groundless and having no ground on which to stand?

> 'Here stand I, I can do no other.'
>
> (Martin Luther)

It is on this affirmative declaration that I take my stand.

> 'I am standing on time/thyme.'

This was the double answer given by a Greek guide at Delphi when she was asked about the name of the copious flowers which formed a carpet on which she was standing. She was standing on thyme. And, in that archaic setting, she was also standing on time.

These statements and the ensuing reflections underline a way of looking at phenomena which was constantly emphasized by Heidegger. There is both the metaphorical and the concrete linking of meanings. Each being incomplete without the other. When a catatonic schizophrenic patient wants to know where he 'stands', he is simultaneously asking how things are with him, in the sense of what his being in the world implies, and he also needs to know his precise location in the world. Both meanings converge upon the importance of affirmative location. Man only knows where he stands (geographically) when he also knows where he stands in terms of his relationships with others. And this matrix of relationships is not only those who stand around him in the prevailing present. There is the internalized standing of other generations which influence his perspectival world. They are a great cloud of witnesses and they influence his experience. Working within the Aeolian Mode there is always a reminder that the patient standing in front of the therapist needs to know where he stands.

Displacement

Displacement is usually regarded as an intrapsychic defence. It is not uncommon to hear 'displacement' discussed during case conferences when the psychopathology of an offender-patient is under consideration. For example, an attack on a solitary old lady in the corner shop may be taken as evidence of the displacement of aggression originally directed towards the assailant's mother.

However, there are wider frames of reference in which a man may be perceived as a 'displaced person', a constant fugitive who has no place of his own. In this instance, displacement is a societal defence.

And this has links with a man's appreciation of his place in 'the larger story' (see p. 241), for until he is at home in himself man has many of the characteristics of the displaced person. He is then seen as primarily dislocated and dis-placed until he becomes rooted in the ground of his being. In chapter 10 we touch upon the relationship between the ground of our being and the Ground of our Being, which influences our degree of awareness of displacement.

Many authors have described the displaced person, but, as an associative link, it is not surprising that Dickens comes to mind. In *Bleak House* he describes Jo whose life consisted of sweeping 'crossings' and keeping them free of mud, faeces, and filth so that others could walk without dirtying their shoes. Jo was often harrassed by the police who told him to 'keep moving on'. And when an officer was challenged as to exactly where it was that Jo had to go, he replied, 'I don't know. My instructions didn't go that far.' The prime fact was that Jo had to 'keep moving on'. His message from life was that he was not wanted where he was, except when clearing filth from the crossing.

Jo can stand as a paradigm of the displaced person, whose message from society is to 'keep moving on'. Many such rootless, ungrounded people find their way into various kinds of asylum. They often feel that a therapeutic group or the ward in a hospital is the first place where they have been attended to. And the usual stigmatic comment 'he is attention-seeking' is an exact, relevant, and non-cynical statement of his human need.

Literature and drama are rich in associative passages on this theme. But none more so than these words attributed to Jo:

'Never done nothink to get myself into no trouble, 'sept in not moving on. . . . But I'm moving on now. I'm a-moving on to the buryin ground – that's the move as I'm up to.'

'You move on,' he says.

'when I was moved on as far as ever I could go and couldn't be moved no furder . . .'

It is interesting to note Jo's increasing passivity just before his death. In the first quotation he says 'I'm moving on', whereas in the second, he says 'when I was moved on'.

'The group, absorbed in their own memories, started to sob as Mrs Kor spoke to the ground: "I have not forgotten you all this time."'
(Auschwitz survivor revisits the ground, as reported in *The Times* 28 January 1985)

This brief section on the phenomenology of displacement has been written as a reminder that there are connotations of displacement other than that of being an intrapsychic defence. But when defences *are* relinquished, the patient himself wants 'to take it further enough . . . and further still' – a reminder from the beginning of the story (see p. 3).

A faithfully perceived current of life: psychotherapy as rehearsal

'The fable develops . . . in the midst of a simple, faithfully perceived current of life. The nameday, Shrovetide, the fire, the departure, the stove, the lamp, the pianoforte, pies, drunkenness, twilight, night, the living room, the dining room, the girls' bedroom, winter, autumn, spring, etc., etc., etc.'

This quotation comes from a discussion about rehearsing a production of *The Three Sisters* (Jackson 1967). It takes us straight into that amalgam of dynamic activity (the current of life) and the phenomenology of things ('the fire . . . pies . . . winter . . . etc.') which characterizes the patient's concern to fully tell his story. If he only conveys 'the current of life', he is ungrounded and dislocated. If he only conveys a 'faithful perception' of the fire–pies–winter, he is too circumstantial and concrete. He needs to convey both. It may have been Chekhov's clinical training that made him so attentively observant and faithfully descriptive of both inner and outer phenomena. In any event, he is ideally suited to introduce this section.

There is considerable overlapping between drama, psychodrama, and dramatherapy on the one hand (Jennings 1973; 1975; 1986b; 1987), and space, location, and psychotherapy on the other (Pedder 1977), though creative expression permeates them all. Throughout this book there have been numerous references and quotations from dramatic material. It is now our intention to dwell on psychotherapy as 'rehearsal' – which conveys the notion of repetition and preparation, as well as recounting. There are obvious inferences from group psychotherapy whose spontaneous evolution depends upon no predetermined script, and whose interchangeable 'actors' and audience are contained within a homospatial setting (see p. 194). There are echoes here of Pirandello's *Six Characters in Search of an Author* (1921).

One of our hospital groups contained not only one of the actors in the hospital play but also two prompters! Aeolian activity was greatly facilitated by this discovery. It requires little effort to see the comparison between the task of the prompters during rehearsal and performances of the play, when there was a script, and their activity during a therapeutic group when there was not. Indeed, a paradoxical headline would be: *Eight prompters: no script*.

It is as we move from the stage towards the inner world of the participant – here exemplified by one of Shakespeare's most opaque lines – that we appreciate the prompting function of Aeolian attunement. Just before her death, Ophelia was said to be: 'As one incapable of her own distress' (*Hamlet* IV. 7, 178). Distress is what Ophelia experiences – yet it is so extreme that she is 'incapable' of it. And we have shown how dynamic psychotherapy operates across exactly that threshold: a boundary at which the unconscious becomes conscious. Through being put in touch with her feelings Ophelia might have gradually found that she became capable of experiencing her distress. Indeed, psychotherapy can be considered as a process in which the patient gradually becomes 'capable' of his own distress. Rehearsal has just been described and, though it is etymologically linked with 'hearse' (coffin-carrying; death-bearing), the connection is rarely made. It was almost as a neologism that Shylock said of Jessica:

> 'I would my daughter were dead at my foot, and the
> jewels in her ear! Would she were *hearsed* at my foot,
> and the ducats in her coffin.'
> (*The Merchant of Venice* III. 1, 91)

In psychotherapy, however, constant re-hearsing takes place, so that death-wishes, murderous thoughts, and aggressive affects can be 'de-hearsed' – taken out of the coffin – and their restrictive legacy and the binding of past experience be abolished. In this way the current of life is not only faithfully perceived; the response to it is also changed. And this comes about within that space and location which is both within the patient and around him. It is facilitated by the many facets of drama and its link with therapy – not least in drama therapy – and the various aspects of poetry and its association with the *poiesis* of therapy. Each is enriched by the Aeolian Mode's assistance in enhancing the therapist's capacity for 'fine tuning'.

Hitherto our consideration of 'story' has underlined the importance of that particular story which constitutes the patient's 'history'. And psycho-analytic psychology helps us to understand the significance of the telling of the story and of those parts of the story that cannot yet be told. In the words of Erikson (1959), 'we cannot lift a case history out of history'. It is often claimed that interpretation of events is one of the essential tasks of the historian, a claim which carries additional relevance for the analytically orientated psycho-historian. And Dance (1960) draws our attention to the 'bias' of history in *History the Betrayer*:

> It is commonly supposed that history is over and done with, and therefore unalterable. The basis of this idea is that history is the past. But history is not the past – it is the record of the past. If there is no record, there is no history; if there is a record, it has a recorder, whose views and prejudices enter into his record, and colour it.'

Dance's comment blends well with Spence's concern (1982) about the relationship between narrative truth and historical truth. And the 'bias' of history is peculiarly apt when the history under scrutiny is the autobiographical clinical history.

Nevertheless, there is a counterbalancing way of thinking about the patient's story when it is considered under the heading of phenomenological existential psychology, although, as we have repeatedly stated, this is not an either/or perspectival stance. It is both/and.

In addition to wanting his story understood, analysed, and reflected, the patient so often needs to have it clearly heard, registered, and recorded. He wants his statement of 'how it is' to stand. He needs his story to count in the wider significance of things. It is here that he asks the therapist to revive the ancient task of acting as a 'chronicler'. The phenomenological approach can register these specific characteristics of a story-teller as much as it registers the details of the story told. It is called for when man has a precarious sense of his own identity, and feels that he has lost touch with those inner and outer landmarks which can give a sense of trustworthy bearings in his inner world and points of reference in that which surrounds him. We recall the deictic emphasis when a borderline patient, after telling us that 'some kid died in a fire and God came then', added 'I prayed for certain things.' But the stress was upon *'certain* things'. She was not praying for 'some things' or 'several things'. She needed certainty and it was *'certain things'* for which she prayed. When external boundaries become shrouded or fragile the Aeolian Mode can help to confirm that the patient's story 'stands'. It *has* been registered. Presence has prevailed. In the Shakespearean sense, the patient's existence and his experience has become 'remarkable'.

As Macquarrie (1972) points out, phenomenology 'offers a description in depth . . . causing us to notice features that we ordinarily fail to notice, removing hindrances that stand in the way of our seeing, exhibiting the essential rather than the accidental, showing interrelations that may lead to a quite different view from the one that we get when a phenomenon is considered in isolation'. A 'description in depth' comes close to witnessing – and both are linked to empathy (see p. 170). The phenomenologist – be he psychologist, psychiatrist, or philosopher – regards all data experienced as falling within his field. The Greek word *phainomenon* is usually translated as 'appearance'. But translation from one language to another is often burdened by the fact that it may lack precision, or be loaded with ambiguity. For example, a word used with enthusiasm by German phenomenologists, *Anschauung*, has no equivalent in English and is generally translated as 'intuition'. It is the immediacy of the experienced which is essential. Brentano (1924) referred to that 'clear knowledge and full certainty' which is derived from the immediacy of our consciousness of existence. His viewpoints inspired Edmund Husserl, who developed the science of phenomenology.

In his influential book *Cartesian Meditations* (1931) Husserl recommended the placing of traditional prejudices in 'brackets' in order to derive the essential indisputable aspects of experience. He saw all experience as self-validating; like Descartes he held the view that consciousness assumes only itself. He was opposed to 'naive realism', in which *the world is as it is*, regardless of who experiences it.

When the phenomenologist places his implicit assumptions in brackets, he invites the criticism that there is no observation without 'prejudice'. But it is possible to try to identify one's biases and temporarily suspend them, or – at least – to change systematically from one assumptive position to another.

Descriptive phenomenology was introduced to psychiatry by Karl Jaspers, and he saw this approach as an important tool in the exploration of psychopathology. In *General Psychopathology* (1963) he stressed that the purpose of a phenomenological approach was to gain as lucid and vivid a representation as possible of that which the patient experiences. The more spontaneous and detailed such accounts are, the more useful they become.

The gestalt school also took up phenomenology. And Koffka's *Principles of Gestalt Psychology*, published in 1935, contains the following passage:

> A good description of a phenomenon may by itself rule out a number of theories and indicate definite features which a true theory must possess . . . For us phenomenology means as naive and full description of direct experience as possible.

Merleau-Ponty also emphasizes the importance of the descriptive aspect. In *Phenomenology of Perception* (1962) he stresses that the description of experience is more than its explanation or analysis. To return to things in themselves is to return to the world which antecedes knowledge, a world about which knowledge always speaks, and in relation to which scientific schematizing is an abstract and derived sign-language, as geography is in relation to the landscape. However, faithful description does not exclude the indication of causal relationships, although its prime aim is to understand phenomena: to seek to understand the 'what' before the 'how' and the 'why'. Such an approach is not primarily explanatory; understanding is its goal. To grasp a phenomenon – an experience – is to get close to what is being explored on its own terms. It is to discover and participate in the experience until it shows its meaning. It is to grasp that which appears, rather than a predetermined search for theoretical confirmation. It is in the nature of an epiphany being understood for what it is. Premature closure, and the isolation and naming of a condition, can give a spurious impression of insight. They do so by forming boundaries and thus run the risk of introducing estrangement and relegating further consideration to oblivion. As soon as we start observing the individual we are part of his world (*Umwelt*), and thereby we become part of the relationship between him and his environment. Long before academic psychology entered the field, myth, tradition, and culture housed that encounter with self which today forms the basis of psychological enquiry. We need only mention Homer, Shakespeare, and Tolstoy to underline this point. Such awareness exists in different ways and in varying degrees of transparency. 'All people know the same things' as Kierkegaard says – 'only some know that they know'. Man achieves the awareness that he is 'standing out' (*existare*) from his biological and social nature. He transcends this predisposition by means of a time-dependent symbol function.

The reconstruction of the world of another person involves an opening of the self to the other self. Endeavouring to gain objectivity through the automatized collection of data does not necessarily lead to a truer picture of the world. Indeed, it may induce a sterile, estranged world.

It is the dwelling and being-in-the-world that matters. It is to be concerned with the world, to be engaged in ceaseless interaction with the things in the world that counts. Bonifazi (1967) has elaborated this theme in *A Theology of Things*. Existence is not static and fixed, but always something which is coming into being. It is therefore not the experience as such which we try to explore, but always the whole human being at the centre of his experiencing. And it is this 'coming into being' which directly links this theoretical section with the process of *poiesis* – one of the Aeolian Mode's dynamic components – in which 'that is called into being which was not there before'. In the example cited, we discover that a river had become 'the river Mersey'. And this particular river, the river Mersey, had – in Mary's retelling – not been there before.

One of the most important contributions the existentialists made was in the exploration and development of themes related to the conative and affective processes. As Cohn (1984) points out: 'There is a sense of movement, of "being" as a process, not a fact.' The only world we can know is an intentional world, i.e. the world to which we have attributed meaning.

Existentialism and psychotherapy

Existentialism and Psychotherapy calls for a heading of its own, not least so that we can introduce some of the major references which approach this topic from various angles. We find that *Existential Foundations of Medicine and Psychology* (Boss 1979), *Existence – A New Dimension in Psychiatry and Psychology* (May, Angel, and Ellenberger 1958), and *Estrangement and Relationship: Experience with Schizophrenics* (Macnab 1965) are three useful starting points, to which Laing's numerous writings should be added. Siirala (1969) refers to 'one of the chief obstacles to therapy' as being 'the delusion that we have reduced diseases to mere object-things, entities that can be studied in isolation'. He speaks of this delusion as 'the delusion of reductive reification'. Elsewhere, he refers to the process of 'primary objectification'. This is relevant in all clinical work, but never more so than in offender-therapy when, for a plethora of reasons, an offence may be committed; after which 'reductive reification' may lead to the fact that a particular human being is regarded as nothing other than a rapist or an arsonist. This has obvious and close connections to Matza's concept (1969) of the 'controlling identity'.

Macnab's book, which has a foreword written by R. D. Laing, has a central chapter on existentialism and psychotherapy. He refers to the encounter which is a 'decisive meeting between two persons, and in this meeting the whole of one's outlook may undergo profound changes.

Although the concepts of transference and counter-transference are involved in this encounter, the concept itself is more comprehensive.' He describes the critical moment of *kairos*, which we (Cox 1978) have also explored in relationship to the sequential chronology of primary experience and its link with the sequential discontinuity of psychotherapy.

Minkowski's attempt 'to find the central unifying experience or event in the person's life-history and to orientate the person around this' is also discussed. 'Thus there developed the idea of meaning-structures in the person's life.' The 'central unifying experience' can easily be remembered through the mnemonic 'CUE'. And it is interesting to note that the dictionary entry under the word 'cue' is 'last words of a speech in a play serving as signal to another actor to enter or speak'. Serendipity comes to our aid by discovering that the central unifying experience is captured and epitomized in the fact that such experience serves as 'a signal to another . . . to enter or speak'. There could be few more precise pointers to the centrality of experience in relationship with others. And the cue is the CUE.

Siirala (1961) raises an interesting dynamic question about schizophrenia. He suggests that many symptoms of schizophrenia may be precipitated by an inherited predisposition not of the patient himself, but of the people around him, as an attempt to overcome tendencies in him which disturb their view of reality. This, as with many of Siirala's writings, is disturbing and provocative. But it is a viewpoint which can never be healthily ignored. It has strong links with the theme of invisible loyalties and Ibsen's statement about internalized ghosts of previous generations.

'He was very disturbed. But I had the history, so I was in hospital.'

In a paper written while he was still a registrar at the Tavistock Clinic, Laing (1957) studies Tillich's theory of anxiety and neurosis. In a provocative introductory sentence, he says: 'many psychiatrists may wonder if it is really possible for a theologian, however distinguished, but without direct clinical experience, to say anything that could be relevant and valuable for the clinician, and others may even be deeply suspicious of any utterances made by a theologian'. This becomes the more remarkable considering the theme is 'ontological presuppositions about man' who 'is subject to annihilation, that is, he is subject to non-being'. Nevertheless, Laing has condensed much of Tillich's thought which is central in any consideration of existentialism, in relation to both clinical work itself and the therapist's reflection upon the larger story that both he and his patient are 'in'. Laing writes: 'At any rate, Tillich regards non-being as the basic threat, in whatever way it presents, and that neurosis is the way of avoiding non-being by avoiding being.' It is not difficult to think of an intensely phobic neurotic who is so concerned with his symptoms and preoccupied with himself that, paradoxically, he has avoided being. He has succeeded in bypassing that appreciation of the larger life which, once tasted, would be hard to relinquish. As it is, obsessed with his own inner world, the abrupt ending of life, by accident or design, could be devoutly to be wished.

A recent book of poems has the title *Melting into the Foreground* (McGough 1986). This is of course a reversal of the usual phrase 'melting into the background'. But it is a relevant, though tangential, comment about the aim of psychotherapy. It could be legitimately argued that psychotherapy endeavours to enable the patient to 'melt into the foreground' of his own life; so that he is not preoccupied by constantly being 'centre stage' and dominating those around him; neither is he retreating into the wings, and merely living out the role of a voyeur, obtaining vicarious life through watching the lives of others. If a patient is enabled to 'melt into the foreground' of his own life so that he can be there, without constantly studying the impact he makes in his effective personal world, it would be congruous with the point Tillich was making. One of the ways in which some patients with narcissistic disturbances present is that they do everything possible not to melt into the background. On the contrary, they often present because, in one way or another, they are dominating and disturbing the foreground.

The existential approach maintains that processes, events, phenomena, all exist to the extent to which they are invested with meaning. Heidegger chose to call it *Sorge*: that consciousness at all times is referring beyond itself to a world in which a man is constantly defining himself. And we have discussed the capacity of psychotherapy to correct pathological self-definition (Cox 1973). The Aeolian Mode assists the patient in redefining himself by calling more of himself into being. Poetry, in Heidegger's view, is the topology of Being. And this is marked by presence and particularity: 'the river Mersey' again.

Existential literature (Sartre, Kafka, Camus, *et al.*) explores human possibilities. Previous events and experiences constitute the past. But the past which is decisive in psychoanalytically inspired literature is not a chain of once and for all completed events. On the contrary, man recreates the past every time he realizes that meaning with which the past endows the present. The past meets us in the future, and such realization comes not only from the depths of therapeutic work, it is known also to the poet.

> 'Time present and time past
> Are both perhaps present in time future
> And time future contained in time past.
> If all time is eternally present
> All time is unredeemable.'
> (*Burnt Norton I*, T. S. Eliot 1935)

Existentialism has often been accused of being atheoretical, and phenomenology has been seen as propædeutic to a science of psychology. Phenomenological existential psychology constitutes a framework which is different from, but no less theoretical than, the empirical sciences. This divergence becomes most pronounced in the difference between their respective modes of knowing. The phenomenologist stresses knowledge by participation, whereas the empiricist depends upon knowledge by observation (Macquarrie 1972). The main thrust of existentialism is not in the direction of abandoning thought, but of recognizing that it has many forms. Science is not a passive registration of the world, it is an active, selective, and adaptive response. It is therefore legitimate to contemplate different models and various ways of relating to the world. And it is this original investment in the world which is the essence of science, philosophy, and literature.

These three disciplines converged within therapeutic space, as demonstrated in vignette 3.1! (p. 66):

'I've gone blank . . . of course I've always known I've been frozen.'

We return to Eliot's question: 'Where is the wisdom we have lost in knowledge?' Our intention has been to explore the dynamics underlying 'the life lost in living', and the 'going blank' through which Martha was reminded that she had 'always been frozen'.

8
Clinical applications of the Aeolian Mode

'One cannot flee from oneself; flight is no help against internal dangers.'

(Freud 1937, p. 237)

This is the shortest chapter in the book. Its brevity is due to the fact that the applications[19] of the Aeolian Mode are stated rather than 'justified', though numerous examples have been provided.

The indications for the Aeolian Mode can be discussed under three headings: psychotherapy; assessment; supervision.

In skeletal outline, *dynamic psychotherapy* can be classified in this way:

1. Supportive	(a) Individual
	(b) Group
2. Analytic (also called exploratory, or interpretive, or uncovering)	(a) Individual
	(b) Group

Although it is equally reasonable to view it as follows:

1. Individual	(a) Supportive
	(b) Analytic
2. Group	(a) Supportive
	(b) Analytic

Counselling

The Aeolian Mode also has a part to play in the large spectrum of therapeutic energies which fall under the heading of counselling. For example, one of the many facets of the probation service is to provide a counselling service for clients who may be poorly motivated and hostile towards authority. Such counselling involves working with those whose offences range from trivial legal infringements to major offences against the person.

224

In this context, the probation officer stands as a representative for counsellors from other disciplines. The Aeolian Mode is equally 'at home' in a custodial or a non-custodial setting, and it can further the possible scope of the holding function of therapy and counselling in a 'holding environment' (see Cox 1986).

The Aeolian Mode can play an integral part in any of these options, and we have already furnished clinical vignettes which exemplify its flexibility in both individual and group psychotherapy (see chapter 3). However, its scope is not limited to the precise operational field of psychotherapy *per se*. It can also feature in initial or reappraisal *dynamic assessment sessions*. This is because of its ambiguous qualities which enable it to function like a semi-structured projective test. For example, the cognitive style with which a subject handles a metaphor serves as a guide to his psychological minded-ness and flexibility.

Its third field of relevance is in *psychotherapy supervision*. Here again, it is its adaptive capaciousness which provides the supervisor with a useful instrument. The Aeolian Mode can be confidently used at both ends of the spectrum of the 'teaching–therapy' debate: a debate which still continues to permeate discussions on the nature of supervision; although each 'school' admits that 'absolute' positions are usually out of court.

The three dynamic components (*poiesis*, the aesthetic imperative, and the point of urgency) are always interrelated, although their predominance varies in significance in each of the three areas of application under discussion. Thus psychotherapy, dynamic assessment, and supervision each call for different ranking of priorities in relation to the dynamic components. For example, the point of urgency may be most important in psycho-therapy; whereas the novelty of *poiesis* may have pride of place in assessing a psychologically bored, 'test-sophisticated' patient with a personality disorder. Such a patient's whole demeanour and attitude is that he has 'seen it all before'. But, by definition, the novel must be novel. The previously cited instance (Cox 1983), in which a narcissistic killer is confronted, not by the clinical–forensic fact of 'death', but by the illusive–allusive 'unclassifi-able' novelty of 'death's pale flag' makes the point.

The creative use of the mutative metaphor links the verbal and the non-verbal aspects of analytic work, which inevitably include both assessment and therapy. Writing on this theme, Khan (1972) comments:

'It is my belief that in all psychotherapeutic work with patients, psychotherapists and analysts have to provide two distinct types of relating from their side. One type of relating is covered by interpret-ative work, which helps the patient to gain insight into his internal conflicts and thus resolve them. The other sort of relating, which is harder to define, is more in the nature of providing coverage for the patient's self-experience in the clinical situation. The knack of any psychotherapeutic work is to strike the right balance within these two types of functions in the therapist.'

The choice of the word 'coverage' is an interesting one. We speak of junior hospital staff having clinical 'cover' or protection from a consultant. We also refer to the 'coverage' of a newspaper, meaning the breadth of its scope or the extent of its interest. Khan's connotation embraces both meanings.

Analytic and supportive psychotherapy

It is our contention that metaphor, as it is used in the Aeolian Mode, can satisfy both these criteria. In other words, although the Aeolian Mode can play an integral part in analytic work, it also enables the patient to experience coverage for his 'self-experience'. Pushed still farther, it could be said that the Aeolian Mode can enable the therapist to meet the patient whether he experiences malignant 'regression aimed at gratification' or benign 'regression aimed at recognition' (Balint 1968). Pedder's paper on 'Attachment and New Beginning' (1976) is of relevance here.

Its freshness allows the Aeolian Mode to be an appropriate instrument whenever analytically orientated or supportive psychotherapy is called for. It is presumptuous to list the clinical criteria for each modality, and we have nothing new to add to the list. Nothing, that is, unless the extreme narcissistic personality manifested clinically as a psychopath, or the fragmented psychotic, is not regarded as being within the therapeutic range. If this is the case, then the perennial novelty, on which the Aeolian Mode rests, stands a good chance of engaging with the psychopath and 'taking him by benign surprise' (see Cox 1982b). Moreover, the psychotic often welcomes the 'bespoke' quality of 'tailor-made' metaphor – see, for example, 'the swelling of Jordan' (p. 13). The young woman who said 'How will I be tonight?' was suspicious, afraid, and profoundly distrustful of 'professional' initiatives. But the metaphor induced calm in deep waters, without stirring the surface. Eva Basch-Kahre (1985), referring to a state of borderline psychotic functioning writes: 'When there is chaotic functioning, I have found that the analyst has to put himself into a state of empathic reverie, as a nursing mother would with her baby.' Such a state of nurturing empathic reverie can be catalysed by the Aeolian Mode.

Recognition

The significance of 'recognition' for the severely regressed patient who needs 'a new beginning' is often a major concern in psychotherapy undertaken with the disturbed, the difficult, and the dangerous patient. This applies with even more validity to the psychopathic or psychotic offender-patient. In one way or another, such a patient seeks attention and meta-phorically (or literally) cries out to be recognized. The *Oxford English Dictionary* entry under the word 'recognize' is as follows:

1. Acknowledge validity or genuineness or character of claims or exist-ence of, accord notice or consideration to, discover or realize nature of, treat *as*, acknowledge *for*, realize or admit *that*.
2. Know again, identify as known before.

It is evident that each of these meanings is relevant to the disturbed patient whose sense of identity, validity, and self-esteem is at best precarious, and at worst almost non-existent. Indeed, such words taken from a dictionary cover a wide range of psychopathology underlying disturbed experience and behaviour. The patient is frequently desperate to be 'known again and identified as known before'. And dynamic psychotherapy is concerned with 'new beginnings' in many ways. The patient is given a chance to re-experience that which he did not genuinely experience 'first time round'.

The dynamic processes which energize, and are energized by, interpret-ive psychotherapy usually involve slow, repetitive movement in which the fixed flux of hitherto fossilized feelings is slowly mobilized and worked through. Essentially, change occurs through transference interpretation. But these processes can only take place when there is a sufficiently firm framework of mutual recognition by which the therapist and patient acknowledge each other's presence. When supportive psychotherapy is undertaken with a precariously poised neurotic, or an openly fragmented psychotic, or a suspiciously hesitant psychopath, the prime healing force may in fact be that of recognition. The Aeolian Mode offers a rich variety of avenues of access to the patient's inner world. It is through these that he may be acknowledged as the unique individual he is. King Lear asked: 'Who is it that can tell me who I am?' (I. 4, 230). And a psychotic was asking a deeper question than 'What diagnostic category am I?' when she asked 'What am I?' But the answer which satisfied her most, was that to another, as yet unspoken, question, namely

'Who am I?'
'You are Mary.'

This was of a more enduring and settling nature than the logically correct answer might have been. We know that the depths of the disturbed patient may be reached before the surface is stirred (Bachelard op. cit.). And the depth of the disturbed patient is sometimes reached most rapidly and most completely through the use of an apposite image or metaphor. It is then that *recognition* occurs through *poiesis*. Hamburger (1969) has described the poet's 'flashes of recognition within a particular context' which cannot be codified as though they were 'the articles of a creed'. And he underlines that existential immediacy of recognition in which a patient realizes that he is seen as 'himself' ('You are Mary'); and not as an 'article of a creed' or an inhabitant of a particular diagnostic category.

This function of the Aeolian Mode as an endorsement of presence is closer to the existential and phenomenological end of its spectrum of dynamic activity than to its facility as a mobilizer of mutative capacities in the course of transference interpretation. We have discussed this emphasis on page 208 under the heading of phenomenology.

It is encouraging to note that Frosch, who wrote *The Psychotic Process* (1983), referred to supportive psychotherapy 'as a challenging and complex endeavour' (1986), when reviewing *The Practice of Supportive Psychotherapy* by Werman (1984). 'It is David Werman's contention that supportive therapy is widely practised but not systematically taught.' We suggest that the pleomorphic character of mutative metaphor enables the Aeolian Mode to be an appropriate style of psychotherapy for the patient who needs support. Yet, at the same time, it has the potential for facilitating insight-orientated, expressive, or exploratory psychotherapy. However much analytic purists may claim that supportive psychotherapy is fundamentally different from analytic therapy, we are among those who consider that there is always a measure of support in the deepest and most rigorous analysis. At the other end of the spectrum, there is often an almost haunting introspective urge towards exploration of the inner world in the patient who is a 'classical case' for support. The Aeolian Mode possesses the advantage of flexibility, so that it can be facilitative, irrespective of the dynamic demands.

The borderline personality

We have given the borderline personality a separate heading for two reasons: first, because of its topicality. It has been the subject of a recent plethora of books and articles, and publishers' promotional lists carry yet further titles; secondly, because of the peculiar aptness of the Aeolian Mode as a therapeutic *modus laborandi* for engaging with the borderline personality (see also p. 58).

In essence it is the capricious and unstable nature of such a patient's personality structure which can make conventional analytic or supportive approaches hazardous. This is because the patient may present as an *apparently* florid psychotic, whereas within minutes an entirely different clinical picture emerges. What is constant is the poverty of stable introjects at the beginning of therapy, and the stormy trajectory of transference phenomena.

The course of such therapy is punctuated by doubt, tenacious clinging, fear of abandonment, difficulty in trusting, copious testing-out, and acting-out. In spite of such an ominous list of potential risks, stable introjects can take root through transference interpretation. Without doubt, the work will prove to be prolonged, arduous, and demanding. Nevertheless, personality change can ensue and the capacity for stable relationships result.

The Aeolian Mode offers the therapist a flexible approach in which he may be able to 'follow' the patient's unpredictable and explosive affective lability. Paradoxically, as we have tried to show, it can both loosen the structures of engagement and tighten them up as the occasion demands. Thus it can enable the therapist to tune in to the patient's multiple needs at the same time. For example, a borderline patient may be 'behaving' like a regressed child – explosively showing 'a temper' and throwing objects across the room – while he is also aware that the anger towards the therapist has a 'here-and-now' component which is superimposed upon earlier deprivations and frustrations. A capacious metaphor allows empathic support, interpretive reflection, and an existential encounter to take place concurrently.

We have already given several vignettes wherein the Aeolian Mode and the psychotic are discussed in detail. Oversimplistic it may be, but for our present purposes we can consider the borderline patient as a transient, intermittent, and particularly unpredictable psychotic. Although such patients posit the most difficult of all personality structures to work with, yet *pari passu* this is where the Aeolian Mode seems to have most to offer. And even if a full-blown episode of psychotic aggression ensues, this therapeutic approach does not cease to operate (Cox. In press).

Assessment and supervision

The ambit of the Aeolian Mode is wider than therapy. It is also useful in the course of clinical assessments. And it also has a part to play in the rapidly burgeoning field of psychotherapy supervision. Much has been written about the different models of therapy supervision (see Ekstein and Wallerstein 1958; Nadelson and Notman 1977).

In *The Quiet Profession* Anne Alonso (1985) has not only described various aspects of the process of psychotherapy supervision, she has also written about the supervisor himself/herself. Indeed the subtitle of the book is *Supervisors of Psychotherapy*. Under the heading 'What do supervisors do?' she explores the following issues: didactic teaching; imparting an appropriate attitude toward patients; expanding the affective capacity of the therapist; developing the capacity to work in the metaphor of the transference; supporting the therapist.

We suggest that there is much scope for Aeolian initiative in this field, and our experience as supervisors is in tune with Anne Alonso's approach. In a discussion of the presence of the supervisor at certain phases of supervision, Pines (1986) commented 'at their best, they are almost invisible'; and 'at times they experience creative curiosity that tests new horizons'. There is certainly an aspect of *poiesis* in the process of supervision.

Discussion ranges over the similarities and differences between the 'teaching' and 'therapeutic' aspects of professional training in psychotherapy. But it is in our joint experience of working in various settings, with various disciplines, that the flexibility of the Aeolian Mode comes into its own. It seems to be relevant to both the 'teaching' and the 'therapeutic' aspects of training supervisors in psychotherapy supervision. In other words, even in the supervision of potential supervisors the adaptability of the mutative metaphor can be both supportive and tolerably incisive as the occasion demands.

Joan Fleming and Thérèse Benedek (1964) illustrate the way in which a supervisor can demonstrate the ability to use – and isolate – his own associations. He does so in the course of trying to find an appropriate response to the therapist's associations. And the Aeolian Mode leads to the creative isolation/incorporation of the therapist's association as 'screened' through the presence – or absence – of an aesthetic imperative.

Existential re-cognition

Finally, we return to Balint's discussion of *The Basic Fault* (1968), and we wish to extend his reference of those intrapsychic needs which call for recognition. At the deepest level, man, who knows he is going to die, calls for recognition in his existential state of 'thrownness' into life. He did not choose to be where he is. He was 'thrown' there.

> 'The world is entire, and I am outside of it, crying, "Oh save me, from being blown for ever outside the loop of time!"'
>
> (*The Waves*, Virginia Woolf)

The language of religion often calls for protection and cover:

> 'Cover my defenceless head with the shadow of thy wings.'
>
> (Charles Wesley)

But the need for cover is not confined to a 'religious' quest. It is ubiquitous and transgenerational. It falls within the scope of recognition, because man's sense of being at home in a potentially alien cosmos depends upon recognition of the familiar. More precisely, *it depends upon being known and 'known again' (re-cognized) by that which has not yet been encountered, but which is still 'trusted' as though it were familiar*. Man needs to find the familiar in the unknown. And re-cognition, as an intrapsychic activity, can illuminate his exploration of the unknown which originally surrounded him, and which internalization has seated within him.

Prickett (1986) writes: 'The original participatory poetic vision is only rediscovered, with a shock of "recognition" as something both new and unconsciously familiar, through the now conscious artifice of poetry.' In this passage he reminds us that recognition and the aesthetic imperative are interwoven.

This chapter on the clinical applications of the Aeolian Mode closes with a section on existential re-cognition. We have briefly indicated its scope in psychotherapy, dynamic assessment, and supervision. Each is concerned with discerning that which is particular within an established framework. And the specific is always re-cognized with the 'shock of "recognition" '.

> 'I know that voice. . . . Is't not the King?'
>   *(King Lear* IV. 6, 95, 107)

9

Narrator, narration, and narrative

'I'm going to have to use the manner of a story because I can't fit it in to today.'

'I've been so many shorter lives than one long life. . . . There's no period of time that feels like "those days", because everything was shifting all the time.'

'If only one long story could begin which held all the others in it.'

We return now to 'the story' and 'the telling' with which the book opened, to look at the link between the written word of 'literature' and the spoken word of therapeutic dialogue. Such an exercise is inevitably highly selective in content and must reflect the authors' bias. Nevertheless, the ebb and flow of the tidal movement between both worlds is of interest, irrespective of perspectival allegiance. Spence (1982) looks in depth at the degree of congruity between the story the patient 'tells' and the story the therapist actually 'hears'. Barbara Hardy, in *Tellers and Listeners: the Narrative Imagination* (1975), states that: 'story-telling may be dramatic, imagistic, lyrical, and mythopoeic, but it always narrates, retails a sequence of events.' This author adds that narrative 'will almost always yield *other significances*. Narrative is hardly ever, if at all, simply and solely narrative' [our italics]. When the narrator is a patient, whose narrative is disclosed during psychotherapy, the 'other significances' often assume major proportions. Sometimes such other significances are detailed and 'domestic', but they may be catastrophic with extensive social ramifications if the 'teller' is an 'offender-patient'.

Again, Barbara Hardy's evocative comment upon her namesake, Thomas Hardy, finds many echoes in the life which unfolds in therapeutic space: 'Hardy takes us to the very verge of human telling and listening.' And:

'Hardy makes his plots out of the narrative forms we all use. His crises and climaxes turn on confidence, confession, warning, encouragement, revelation, history, and on reticence, lies, secrets and silence. What is told, and what is withheld make up the comic or tragic pattern of his people, whose destinies are woven by a story-teller particularly alert to the dangerous power of memory and fantasy and to the difficulty of telling our friends and lovers enough, but not too much or too little, of our own story.'

No therapeutic session is without that verge of human telling and listening at which 'not too much or too little' is the decisive issue.

This chapter could equally well be entitled: 'Teller, telling, and what is told'. But, close though it is, 'Writer, writing, and what is written' takes us into another country with other significances; not least, the many connotations of distancing (see Slatoff 1985, on *The Look of Distance*). In a passage in which he discusses 'professional literary study' Slatoff writes:

> 'Not only its power to move, excite, and trouble its readers but its offering of certain kinds of truth – those imparted by the mysterious and irreducible innards of metaphor and by the moment-to-moment experience of reading – above all, those truths that come into being only when armor and distance are removed or when the reader permits himself to read as nearly as possible with what Coleridge has called the whole of one's soul.'

In an earlier book, *With Respect to Readers: Dimensions of Literary Response* (1970), Slatoff grapples with a topic which is so deceptively self-evident that it is often overlooked. He draws our attention to the fact that books are written with the intention that they will be read, and looks at the various ways in which the reader may respond to a work of literature. His study throws light upon the variety of ways in which the therapist may respond to a patient's silent presence or flow of disclosure. There are indeed wide areas of congruence between cognitive–affective qualities expressed in literature, or drama, and those expressed in therapeutic space. Such expression evokes a response in the reader, or the audience, in the first instance and in the therapist or his patients in the second. The point of divergence is implicit in Slatoff's chapter entitled 'The Presence of Narrators'. He refers to 'this human presence' in 'almost any literary work'. There 'is the sense that we are being talked to by someone'. However, it is unnecessary to amplify the nature of this 'divergence' because the presence of a narrator is a *sine qua non* of the therapeutic process. A large part of psychotherapy consists of a narrator slowly giving as much of his 'narration' as he can. Lambert (1981) describes the phenomenon of 'literary microscopy': 'the fascination of seeing more and more things swarming and changing *where there had seemed to be nothing at all* [our italics]' (see p. 116 on deictic stress). This is crucial in that particular genre of narration which takes place in therapeutic space.

There are many reasons why a narrator may be unable to narrate what needs to be narrated. He will be unaware of repressed material. He may be diffident about disclosing fragile facets of his inner life. Slatoff quotes Aiken's reference to 'progressive and partial and delayed disclosure' when the narrator used 'rapid and unsequential temporal shifts – such as the idiot narrator in *The Sound and the Fury*'. When a patient is eventually fully able to be his own narrator it is evidence that he is at greater ease with himself. This affirms that the prolonged inner struggle which is an inevitable part of the psychotherapeutic process is over, and that the confrontation with self has led to self-acceptance. Such a confrontation is often almost unimaginable at the outset of psychotherapy, as is the possibility of achieving a stable resolution in the 'history-laden present'.

'The desperate act of coming in here to face unbearable things has gone. The last vestige of wanting to hide from the truth has been stripped.'

We have dealt at length with the nature of disclosure elsewhere (Cox 1978) and do not intend to dwell upon it further. We wish to look at the narrator–narration relationship from a different angle. A few quotations may set the scene:

'Where the story-teller is loyal, eternally and unswervingly loyal to the story, there, in the end, silence will speak.'

(Isak Dinesen 1957)

'what is concealed in what is proclaimed. The poem is . . . a pronouncement of which the meaning . . . can be determined only much later, and by illumination from a context unpredicted and remote from the original utterance.' [For our purposes, we could read 'disclosure' for 'poem'. Kermode's thesis is on *The Genesis of Secrecy: On the Interpretation of Narrative*. It is thus pertinent to our theme at many points.]

(Frank Kermode 1979)

'*there is danger that cryptic messages are not listened to*. It is essential that the therapist be familiar with the psychotic utterances of his patients because they may contain important information and valuable clues.' [our italics]

(Hilde Bruch 1974)

'Whether I shall turn out to be the hero of my own life, or whether that station will be held by anybody else these pages must show.'
(Opening sentence of *David Copperfield*, Charles Dickens 1849)

234

'Conrad seems ''to have done admirably in cutting short his story just on the *threshold of the horrible*''.' [our italics]

(*The Conditioned Imagination*, Echeruo 1978)

There is one cardinal distinction between the reader's response to the written word and the therapist's response to the spoken word. It is an unassailable fact that the therapist's response influences what follows, whereas the reader's response does not! Although the reader's cognitive–affective style of responding to the written word may influence his future perception of what is presented to him because of the effects of a self-fulfilling prophecy, it does not, *per se*, influence the intrinsic nature of the material.

The reader may develop an attitude to a character in a novel which influences his feeling about subsequent encounters. But he cannot influence what appears on the printed page. (Nevertheless, recent work (Hutcheon 1980) points to *poiesis* as an aspect of reading – as well as writing.) For better or worse, the therapist's cognitive–affective presence inevitably influences the content, the pace, and even the very existence of subsequent disclosures, though in each instance responding to disclosure is a sequential phenomenon. It is for this reason that the therapist must be on his guard lest self-fulfilling prophecies based on previous disclosure tend to preclude the entertainment of new possibilities.

The psychotic patient in particular challenges the therapist to re-appraise his own frames of reference. It is so easy to dismiss categories of experience which the therapist does not share, especially if they do not fit neatly into theoretical formulations based on developmental psychology.

We suggest that certain events occur which are not explicable solely in terms of their antecedent history. At least, it appears this way to us because of our restricted vision and our limitations in understanding '*ex nihilo*' phenomena.

This takes us into a rich interdisciplinary realm of discourse. Words doing things. Words changing things. The narrator becoming the narration. Again and again the therapist notices that, when a patient is disclosing the deepest, hitherto repressed material, he says directly or in an implicit paraphrase:

'My talk is becoming me.'
'What I say *is* me.'

There is a point wherein the history or narrative which the auto-historian originally 'gave' becomes an embodiment of the patient himself. There are familiar echoes here. 'The Word became flesh' (*John* 1, 14). The narration is the narrator. T. S. Eliot's words are relevant: 'but you are the music / While the music lasts' (see p. 125).

We soon discover the limitations of words in trying to describe an experience which sometimes defies and goes beyond the possibility of expression. But sometimes there is a quality of experience within therapeutic space which Maslow might describe as a 'peak experience'. Then the individual patient or the group-as-a-whole is the music, and 'while the music lasts' may be for a brief or an extended duration measured in terms of *chronos*. But in terms of *kairos* such an experience is an unforgettable, unanalysable epiphany of 'the thing itself'.

On these occasions there is an existential sense that what appears to be is, in fact, 'the thing itself'. Camouflage and cosmetic deception have gone. And so has all pseudo-disclosure or 'seeming', which Buber (1957) has cautioned so strongly against. How often the therapist hears such words in accents of relief:

'This is it . . . At last I've said it . . . it's been bottled up for years . . . I never even knew I had such feelings in me.'

Such words not only apply to cathartic release of unexpressed emotion. They also apply to the fresh encounter with self which eventually comes about through psychological work undertaken in the Aeolian Mode.

In our view, the risks of overanalysing what is irreducible and unanalysable, are greater than those of not analysing what should be analysed. When primitive defences have been relinquished and the patient can say 'My words *are* me' the narration has become the narrator.

There is a moment of reconciliation at the end of *The Tempest* (V. 1, 198) when Prospero says, 'Let us not burthen our remembrance with / A heaviness that's gone.' This could sum up an appropriate termination of psychotherapy. Previous 'heaviness' has gone. Much that was inexplicable is now understood. It would indeed be pathological to 'burthen our remembrance' with what has gone. Tears are often tokens of catharsis and it is not surprising that Prospero's words are immediately followed by those of Gonzalo: 'I have *inly* wept' (our italics). Insight, recently gained, often causes catharsis. There can be few deeper satisfactions than understanding what had been bewildering, frightening, and, as such, often at 'the threshold of the horrible'.

There is every reason for Gonzalo to say 'O, rejoice / Beyond a common joy', because many of his fellow travellers had made worthwhile discoveries. But, most of all, because the companions on the voyage found 'all of us ourselves / When no man was his own'. Perhaps the best paraphrase in 'basic English' of the task, and occasionally achievement, of psychotherapy is expressed in these words. The patient found himself whereas, previously, he had not been 'his own'.

We have already affirmed that there is usually a 'narrator' in therapeutic space. Sometimes the narrator may be an individual patient who gradually narrates his own narrative. Sometimes the narrator is in fact the group-as-a-whole. Such 'narration' is only rarely an evenly flowing recital of events and experiences. Indeed, if it is presented too calmly it makes the therapist wonder whether it might not be a pseudo-narrative, because the thing itself is too tempestuous and overwhelming to describe. Once the narrator has engaged in the unpredictable, potentially frightening task of anamnestic free association, the pace and flow begin to fluctuate. There will be phases of deceleration due to repression or total blocks due to resistance. There will be phases of acceleration due, for example, to the need to 'rush into the secret house of death' in whatever form this particular death takes. Offender-patients who have withheld deep personal narrative for a variety of reasons often experience the need to rush the crucial aspects of disclosure, once the process has started. This has something of the characteristics of acceleration found in leading up to a 'high jump' or, using another analogy, there is a point before orgasm when it is impossible to hold back. The patient may experience the need to hurry across 'the threshold of the horrible' – as though he wants to take by storm what he cannot yet easily tolerate. Therapeutic space should allow the patient appropriate flexibility as he approaches these various thresholds. Blocks to free association are interpreted 'at the point of urgency', so that a mutative interpretation facilitates the acquisition of insight, at the same time as reducing the accompanying inner tension.

There is a sense in which the audience response to a dramatic production is half-way between that of the reader to the narrative contained in a book and that of the therapist to the existential, inevitably 'here-and-now' narrative which takes place in his presence. The text of *Macbeth* is known, but every performance is a fresh engagement between actors and audience. The presence of a responsive, living audience exerts a profound impact upon the ambience of a particular performance. So does the presence of an unresponsive, half-dead audience. We cannot get away from the *in vivo* reality of the human encounter which takes place between those who temporarily, though regularly, engage in the life of therapeutic space.

The threshold of the horrible

Both the reader and the therapist respond to disclosed material 'on the threshold of the horrible'. But that which is 'horrible' may be idiosyncratically construed as such in the mind of the author/patient or the mind of the reader/therapist. Sometimes the selection of new members for a therapeutic group involves choosing patients who each need to explore their own 'threshold of the horrible'. What makes such a group homogeneous is not that they each have identical psychopathology or matching clinical presentations, but that each is disturbingly aware of his existence at 'the threshold of the horrible'. Thus there may be a wide variety of disturbed object relations which lead to the patient's intense awareness of sado-masochistic fantasies. But whether he will act on them, or keep them in a 'secure' intrapsychic enclave, depends upon many factors. There are therefore many threshold phenomena, and other aspects of liminality, which activate the patient's defences as he approaches his 'threshold of the horrible'. This has been looked at from an anthropological point of view by Mary Douglas (1969). 'Matter issuing from them [the orifices of the body] is marginal stuff of the most obvious kind. . . . The mistake is to treat bodily margins in isolation from all other margins.'

In *Powers of Horror: an Essay on Abjection* (1982) Julia Kristeva says many things that are relevant to our theme but, unfortunately, they can only be mentioned *en passant*. One particular sentence which is pertinent to therapy at the threshold of the horrible – which in one way, applies to all psycho-therapy in which man confronts himself; and, in another, is of magnified significance in offender-therapy – is as follows: 'As counterpoise to a purity that found its bearings in disillusioned sadness, it is the "poetic" unsettlement of analytic utterance that testifies to its closeness to, cohabi-tation with, and "knowledge" of abjection.' The phrase 'the "poetic" unsettlement of analytic utterance' is one that almost automatically writes itself in italics in a chapter about narration, and it links with *poiesis* and the aesthetic imperative. But this, in itself, takes us back to an imponderable facet of psychotherapy training and experience. Namely, that *which the patient may need to describe sometimes crosses 'the threshold of the horrible' and leads to a quality of narration which is too horrible for the therapist to endure*. We have discussed this point elsewhere (Cox 1979; 1983) because it is a core issue when a narrative fragment includes the committing of 'basic crimes' which may be over the 'threshold of the horrible'. The therapist endeav-ours to avoid a defensive retreat due to undue emotional distancing from the predicament of his patient or, at the other extreme, the voyeuristic pathological overinquisitiveness in the spurious interest of obtaining 'vital clinical information'.

Many authors including Dickens, Tolstoy, Ibsen, and of course Shake-speare, exercise a useful endurance test in this respect. Dostoevsky in par-ticular always challenges the therapist's *Weltanschauung* – and it would be worrying if it were not so. When the therapist is confronted by almost overwhelming primitive fantasies, of which the patient needs to unburden himself, there can be the counterproductive limitations of an interpretive approach which Greenson (1975) describes in these words: 'I . . . suspect

that the giving of deep interpretations is a counter phobic act on the therapist's part, his way of overcoming his fear of the patient's primitive
fantasies.'

The horrible may not necessarily imply torture, mutilation, or sado-
masochistic activity. It has been said that the most frightening line in the
whole of Shakespeare may be that spoken by Iras as she tries to usher
Cleopatra into 'the secret house of death':

> 'Finish, good lady; the bright day is done,
> And we are for the dark.'
>
> (*Antony and Cleopatra* V. 2, 191)

Paradoxically, this may be received as more 'horrible' than an overt
'horror' passage such as that in *Macbeth* (II. 3, 63):

> 'Oh horror! horror! horror! Tongue nor heart
> Cannot conceive nor name thee!'

Some would regard the phrase 'we are for the dark' as menacing and
horrible, others would not. The impossible demand made upon the therapist, who has chosen to work in what Freud (1937) called 'an impossible
profession' is that he is required to be sufficiently at ease in the presence of
whatever the patient construes as horrible!

One of the undercurrents flowing through these pages is that the wide
cosmology of literature, drama, and poetry provides a powerful route of
'direct access' to the deepest human experience; this may be of love and
hate, the beautiful and the horrible. When integrated with clinical training, this exposure to experience of such a high intensity soon shows the
therapist how far he can tolerate engagement with these basic feelings. He
will learn about the precise location of his own 'threshold of the horrible'.
If he tries to work beyond this personal threshold, he himself will experience disturbance and he will cause an exacerbation of disturbance in his
patient. The patient must be allowed to make the necessary crossing of his
'threshold of the horrible' in the safety of therapeutic space. This should be
a 'listening landscape' where the patient safely, and at the right time,
confronts that area of experience which has hitherto been too horrible to
face, endure, and negotiate. Analytic training does not guarantee immunity from knowing the proximity of 'the threshold of the horrible', but
it should at least enable the therapist to know where he has sufficient available energy to provide 'a listening landscape'.

These recent pages may have given the impression that narration in
therapy is only of 'the horrible'. This is far from the truth. Indeed, if the

therapist's life has been devoid of adequate loving he may find that his patient's narration of satisfying love is another painful threshold.

Sometimes a patient narrates life-events in a detached manner:

'It was just a sort of narration, not a litany, not a reliving of the hurt.'

Sometimes there is a sense of an imminent, unavoidable encounter with self which might prove to be devastating:

'There's something I must talk through. It's getting nearer. Absolute truth is essential.'

'I've lived through this before and its coming again.'

Sometimes in 'mid-transference' there are evocations in the past–present of re-engagement with the introjected past. The patient has the experience of being 'thrown back on an old memory'. It should be noted that he is *thrown* back. It is as though he is a passive recipient of his own experience. It is not the active seeking of an old memory. Unconscious material cannot be reached by introspection. When this occurs the patient may meet areas of his own experience which startle him; they appear novel because they were repressed beyond accessibility. But once they are encountered, they have a new, yet archaic quality; they were lost, forgotten, and have been subsequently found. They are therefore recognized as an 'old memory'. There is always this buried-yet-familiar quality in such re-engagement with the past.

The analogy of personal archaeology is often used to describe this aspect of the psychotherapeutic task. Recent excavations at Ephesus offer other archaeological insights. The plans of the old city, much of which is still buried, have now been unearthed. This means that, although in general terms the excavators know the location and broad outline of what has not yet been uncovered, they do not know the details of what remains hidden. But at least they know where to dig. The wide world of personal and corporate, spoken and written narrative is also a pointer towards that which still needs to be told.

It is fitting that this chapter should be closed by further reflections from Barbara Hardy (1975) and Romanyshyn (1982):

'The stories of our days and the stories in our days are joined in that autobiography we are all engaged in making and remaking, as long as we live, which we never complete, though we all know how it is going to end.'

'The childhood home from which each of us journeys is as much a matter of one's destiny as it is of one's heritage.'

10

The larger story

'Story is the raw material of theology, not theology itself. . . . The narratives do not change, but their readers do.'

(S. W. Sykes 1987)

'He knew intuitively that without a story one had no clan or family; without a story of one's own, no individual life; without a story of stories, no life-giving continuity with the beginning, and therefore no future.'

(Laurens Van der Post 1961)

'In great poetry there is a confluence of all kinds of life into a single flame of consciousness.'

(Lascelles Abercrombie in Bodkin 1934)

'The original story-tellers of Greek mythology justified their variations simply with the act of narration, each in his own fashion, of the story. In mythology, to *tell* is to justify. The words: "It was told", which the reader of this book will so often encounter, are not intended to compensate for the fact that the tones of the original story-teller, and often, alas, the original narrative itself, are now extinct. They are intended to concentrate the reader's attention on the only thing that matters – namely, *what* was told. This, however it was shaped, was essentially and in all its forms, developments and variations the same permanent and unmistakable basic story. The *words* of the basic story have disappeared, and all that we have are the variations. But behind the variations can be recognised something that is common to them all: a story that was told in many fashions, yet remained the same.'

(Kerényi 1951)

'In the enchanted universe all things were signs and signatures of each other.'

(de Santillana and von Dechend 1977)

A chapter with this title can, at best, be nothing other than inferential. Detailed, dogmatic assertions about the answers to 'unanswerable' questions are completely out of court. Nevertheless, the question posed by Dunne (1973), 'What kind of a story are we in?', and his reference to 'the greater story that encompasses the story of [our] life', cannot be avoided. We have already made the link (p. 1) between the story and the parable, which is the greater story 'thrown alongside'. Dunne's phrasing recalls the wording used to describe three crucial concepts in Jaspers' thinking (1953): 'the Encompassing'; 'man's experience of limits and transcendence'; and 'the will to communicate'. Dunne's question and Jaspers' concepts are pertinent because psychotherapy inevitably operates within 'the Encompassing' of the greater story.

Dynamic psychotherapy has many of the characteristics of tragedy, described by Una Ellis-Fermor (1945) as an 'interim reading of life'. Discussing the equilibrium of tragedy, she writes: 'Precisely because it is an interim reading of life, it speaks to the condition of all but a few at some period of their lives; for it reveals that balance, that uncertainty, which sees two worlds of being and cannot wholly accept either.' Indeed, attempting to come to terms with distress due to 'that uncertainty' is an important therapeutic objective. It is not surprising that 'guilty man' features largely in psychoanalytic deliberations, which Kohut (1977) has linked with 'tragic man'. In his introduction to *Tragedy is Not Enough* (Jaspers 1953), Deutsch says of Jaspers: 'His is the great refusal of the idolatry of excessive commitment and of the premature closure of the search.' There is a point of delicate balance between commitment to the search for the neglected coherence and the inherent danger in premature closure of the search. We are kept on our toes by phenomena we encounter in clinical work which are broadly congruous with established knowledge, though they may be novel in the sense that there is no precise fit with pre-existing categories. This underlines the fact that, whereas it is easy to point to neglected coherences, it is a very different matter trying to bring neighbouring frames of reference together. Although we each approach 'the greater story' with different antecedents, and from different starting points, we find ourselves in agreement with the paradoxical words of dialogue described by Paul Claudel (see p. 128).

'ENDEVERCORS: Did you mean this world? Or is there another?
VIOLAINE: There are two of them and I tell you there is only one of them and it is enough.'

One world is enough

Art, science, and religion pose challenges and, at the same time, point towards coherent patterning. Art unites inner and outer world phenomena. As the Aeolian harp picks up the music of the wind, so art transforms the perception of the phenomenological world to that of the deeper meaning of life. Regardless of the specific character of the medium, there are hidden rules through which art relates to the structure of the mind and gives it coherence.

Although the *Zeitgeist* encircles the artist's consciousness and stamps his work, it is bound to deeper-layered primordial structures. Thus the poem is not merely an echo of the prevailing present. It voices the timeless within time. Timelessness and patterning are both exemplified in the quotations which follow.

Rilke (1957) thought of a perfect state of osmosis between inner experience and the world:

'Durch alle Wesen reicht der *eine* Raum: Weltinnenraum. Die Vögel fliegen still durch uns hindurch. O, der ich wachsen will, ich sehe hinaus, und *in* mir wachst der Baum. (Through all beings stretches the *one* space: World-inner-space. The birds silently fly right through us. O, I who wish to grow, I look outside, and the tree grows *inside* me.)'

And Éluard (1968) wrote:

'Sans soucis sans soupçons
Tes yeux sont livrés à ce qu'ils voient
Vus par ce qu'ils regardent

'(Without cares without suspicion
Your eyes are exposed to what they see
And are seen by what they look upon)'
(I, 394)

It was as long ago as 1798 that Novalis expressed the holistic view:

'Unser Denken was bisher bloss mechanisch – diskursiv atomistich oder bloss intuitiv – dynamisch – ist jetz etwa die Zeit der Vereinigung gekommen? (Hitherto our thinking has only been mechanical, discursive, atomistic, or intuitive – dynamic: – has the time not come for unification?')

Writing of poetic transcendence, Cardinal (1981) suggests that 'poetry allows us access to modes of perception which disclose aspects of the world upon which we would not normally focus, and in so doing, affords us a heightened sense of the meaningful presence of things'. There are such moments – as Baudelaire points out – 'of existence when time and space take on extra depth, and the feeling of existence is immensely amplified'.

When the world is experienced as an integrated whole, there is no discontinuity between intention and expectation.

Alain Jouffroy (1970), in words strikingly reminiscent of Claudel's on the previous page, writes: 'There isn't any poetic universe, there is just the universe, and that's enough.'

It is increasingly accepted that the sciences and the humanities are interrelated, though the degree and depth of their relationship is still a matter of debate. We have attempted to link these different perspectival emphases under the heading of 'the three foundations' (chapter 7). It is self-evident that no unitary approach can possibly have exclusive access to reality. Each model enables the world to be known in different ways. Nevertheless, there is an underlying coherence and, although this can never be fully described, it continues to invite exploration. Indeed, the exploration of coherence was described in a theological inaugural lecture, 'Frontiers of Theology', by Chadwick (1981): 'If the Theological Tripos can help undergraduates to glimpse the pattern of coherence underlying their apparently disparate studies, it will have done the most important thing.'

Science has been called 'organized curiosity'. And invitation and curiosity are akin to wonder.

> 'We hurried here for some such thing and now
> Wander the countless roads to seek our prize,
> That far within the maze serenely lies,
> While all around each trivial shape exclaims:
> "Here is your jewel; this is your longed for day",
> And we forget, lost in the countless names.'
>
> ('The Prize', Edwin Muir 1960)

A sense of wonder overcomes the epistemological obstacles separating art, science, and religion. In the search for his place in the world, man is energized by wonder and motivated by the call for coherence and continuity. This is stressed by Polkinghorne (1986) – a mathematician and a priest – in *One World: the Interaction of Science and Theology*: 'the two disciplines have in common the fact that they both involve corrigible attempts to understand experience. They are both concerned with exploring, and submitting to, the way things are.'

Religion looks at the larger story *sub specie aeternitatis*, 'in the light of eternity'. In other words, it asks 'what, in the long run, is this all about?' It also asks eschatological questions about the 'final things':

> 'What will you do when the end comes?'
>
> (*Jeremiah* 5, 31)

This brings us to the limit of human questioning. Such ultimate considerations are 'lurking beneath the surface of our everyday lives, exploding into explicitness in the limit-situation inevitable in any life' (Tracy 1981). The practice of psychotherapy brings us face to face with 'limit-situations'. For example, killing and the fear of killing cannot be other than 'limit-situations'. In the starkly lucid words of one of our patients:

'Killing is not an analogy.'

Edwin Muir refers to the victor who cannot win:

'And now, while the trees stand watching, still
The unequal battle rages there.
The killing beast that cannot kill.'

('The Combat', 1960)

And in his autobiography he says:

'What I was so afraid of I did not know; it was not Freddie, but something else; yet I could no more have turned and faced him than I could have stopped the sun revolving. As I ran I was conscious only of a few huge things, monstrously simplified and enlarged.'

(Muir 1940)

It is the 'few huge things' which call us to remember the larger story and to repeatedly ask 'what kind of story are we in?'. The few huge things mobilize our reflective capacities upon the *mysterium tremendum* which no man can healthily ignore.

In his strangely neglected book with the unforgettable title *A Theology of Things* Bonifazi (1967) refers to the need for creative attention and the nourishment of 'enthusiastic association'. On the final page the phrase 'compassionate attention' makes its appearance. Bonifazi points towards the depth within the phenomenology of things. This lies at the centre of therapy conducted within the Aeolian Mode. There is an enthusiasm for association which takes everything seriously.

Referring to the importance of things in themselves and the poetic imagination, Scott (1985) writes: 'But, in pressing its relentless quest for intimacy of relationship with all the rich singularity that belongs to "things" in their intractable specificity, the poetic imagination, as Heidegger says "deconceals" that wherewith they are inwardly sustained, that by which they are so assembled as to enable them to stand out before the gaze of the mind.'

'Intractable specificity' recalls our previous reference to Hamlet's assertion (I. 2, 76) that his experience did not seem particular, it was.

'Seems, madam! Nay, it is; I know not "seems".'

His experience had the intractable specificity which his mother could neither trivialize nor diminish. And so it is with every patient in psychotherapy who fears that his distress will be categorized. His experience is always his alone. Paradoxical though it at first appears, the associative intensification of experience upon which the Aeolian Mode depends does not reduce its singular particularity.

We maintain that the central dynamic of trusting the heart of fire of the primordial activates and sustains all those encounters at depth which are at the heart of therapy. Here we invoke the words of Wilshire (1982) again, where he refers to that presence which 'is the boundless horizon of all our experiences [and in which] the primordial constancy of everything else is sustained'. Such primordial constancy brings us – with constancy – to an unavoidable mystery. Ramsey (1964) writes: 'The only distinctive function theology can or need claim is that of being the guardian and spokesman of insight and mystery.' Ten years ago we (M.C.) wrote the following passage which seems, if anything, even more necessary now: 'Psychotherapy is frequently held to be the guardian of insight, but it is impoverished if it cannot co-exist with mystery. The ability to tolerate mystery, ambiguity and uncertainty alongside psychic determinism is linked to the therapist's *Weltanschauung* and how he construes the nature of his task' (Cox 1978).

Rowell (1983)[20] quotes Pusey's *Lectures on Types and Prophecies*: '"It is not", he tells us, "in proportion to the clearness of our perception, that mysteries have their force"; rather "greatness and indistinctness commence together", so that it is "not the things which we know clearly, but the things which we know unclearly" which "are our highest birthright".'

At that point where theological study, philosophical reflection, and clinical concerns become coherent, we are called back to the centrality of the importance of our place in the larger story. Scott (1971) in *The Wild Prayer of Longing* writes:

'To affirm God's "existence", in other words, is not to assert that a particular being – the Supreme Being – dwells in some invisible realm behind or beyond the phenomenal world. It is, rather, to declare, as a matter of radical faith, that Being is steadfast, reliable, gracious, and deserves our trust. To say that God "exists" is, in short, to say that the Wholly Other, the uncreated Rock of reality, is *for* us, not against us.'

Shortly before this chapter was completed a patient was 'thinking aloud' about her story. This is what she said:

'There's an undercurrent of something very good and effortless and very. . . . It's a "being carried" sort of feeling by . . . I almost want to say benevolence. A feeling that something that was not on my side certainly is. I have a greater capacity to allow it to be. It makes more demands on me at the moment. And that's what I want. I don't feel left out.'

It is never easy to explain congruities which are as exact as this. A theologian writes: 'the uncreated Rock of reality is *for* us, not against us'. And a patient says: 'something that was not on my side certainly is'. In 'Reflections on Mirroring' Pines (1982) has studied aspects of mirroring in group psychotherapy. And Mary Caws (1981) writes 'About Thresholds', referring to 'the setting of settings one inside the other' and 'infinitely receding thresholds'. It seems to us that both authors, through the interlinking of mirroring and liminality, engage with vital aspects of individual-within-corporate experience. We are brought to the 'threshold of thresholds' when man, after much struggling with himself, can say that something that had not been on his side had certainly become so. This part of the story within the larger story could only be told because the story of stories is always set among the stories of others. And also because the inner world is where the decisive action takes place.

Towards the end of the last therapeutic group in Advent, with its wide ranging reflections upon the meaning of life, the word becoming flesh, the words spoken by 'the voices', and the pros and cons of various religious beliefs, one patient turned to the therapist and said:

'It'll soon be Christmas in Broadmoor.'

'Just in Broadmoor?'

'Yes . . . Bethlehem is still a place . . . isn't it?'

Whatever a formal psychodynamic appraisal would make of the patient's 'mental state', there was no doubt in the therapist's mind that 'concrete thinking . . . psychotic evasion' would be a cynical reduction. The concreteness of precise location 'Bethlehem is still a place' could also be seen as a 'disturbed' patient's way of cutting through layers of irrelevant philosophical abstraction, which distracted her attention from the one fact of which she needed to be certain. She knew that Broadmoor was still a place. That Bethlehem was also still a geographical location (interpret this how we will) was what mattered. Historically and theologically, the first Christmas was indeed remarkably localized.[21] She exemplified the forceful words by Robert Graves (see p. 5) which press towards an overall coherence:

> 'There is one story and one story only
> That will prove worth your telling.'

Graves ends this stanza with the following lines: 'That startle with their shining / Such common stories as they stray into.' Hopefully, for this patient, the Aeolian Mode had enabled her to recognize and tell part of the one story which, for her, was worth the telling. Though from a technical point of view it should be noted that the Aeolian Mode helped to tune the therapist's listening, rather than to influence what he said. In this instance, it was important to recognize that 'Bethlehem is still a place' was existentially significant for a patient who wandered, in mind and body, and needed a fixed point of reference. 'Bethlehem in Broadmoor' could be regarded as a clang-association or as evidence of psychotic confusion and dislocation. But it can also sustain prolonged reflection on the location of epiphany and apocalypse.

The story which the patient tells differs from the story which the therapist might tell. Indeed, it would be a travesty of the whole process if this were not so. But both will find that their story falls within the range of *parable*; the story-containing-story of how things are.

The therapist's perception of the larger story may involve the christian's *skandalon* of particularity ('Once, only once, and once for all', William Bright 1824–1901), when the Word behind the larger story became flesh. Or, as a patient said: 'There is one word, where *all* the words come from.' On the other hand, it may encompass the broader conviction that global reality 'deserves our trust', as Scott (1971) reminds us. Either way, we cannot see how a therapist can work without the awareness of some kind of personal affirmative depth. Just what it is that enables the therapist to be sufficiently at home with the possibility of experiencing the depths of others, sometimes even before their 'surface' is stirred, takes us beyond the confines of this book. It is to be hoped that the therapist's personal *Weltanschauung*, his professional training, and his cumulative clinical experience enable him to have that necessary degree of hospitable equanimity in the face of the unknown, and possibly unknowable depths of another. The therapeutic process is inevitably blocked if the therapist is unable to receive those cognitive–affective disclosures which form the substance of transference interpretation and other authentic exchanges.

Affirmative depth allows the freedom for 'new things to be called into being' (*poiesis*); an appreciation of the possibility that there could be 'a pattern which connects' (aesthetic imperative), however fragmented its initial appearance; and an awareness that associative linkings may bring together integrative resources at clinical 'points of urgency'.

The therapist also needs to work within the assurance that a sense of affirmative depth implies more than naive optimism. And this is never more important than at those phases in psychotherapy when the patient reflects upon the limit-situations of dying and/or killing. At his proximity to 'the great void' man so often questions himself about that which 'reasonably' enables him to say:

'Call me when my life shall fail me.'
(Anima Christi)

Leaving aside the 'sterile' and sometimes spurious safety offered by technical jargon, we might say that the patient usually seeks therapy at the point at which he becomes aware that his life is failing him. And the therapist himself is not immune from this ubiquitous human experience. Indeed, should the patient's demand for vicarious life exceed that available energy which the therapist has to offer, the therapeutic process itself can sometimes lead to the therapist's awareness that his life is almost failing him. Such a constellation is, fortunately, rare. It is likely to occur if the therapist's personal life involves 'limit-situations' and, at the same time, the patient is poised at the brink of 'the great void', a void which may lead to the psychic abyss of dying or killing. But such encounters are inevitable if authenticity prevails. It would be a travesty of human experience if 'adequate professional training and awareness of countertransference phenomena' could obviate the possibility of such eventualities. When this occurs the therapist is acutely aware of the significance of the larger story. Upon what, and to whom, does the therapist call when his life begins to fail? And if this experience is intensified by the patient's failing life, the therapist will find himself repeatedly drawing upon affirmative depths.

Such encounters are bound to raise the question of the nature of the curious amalgam of the translation of such human predicament into the language of 'clinical data'. The early experience which wounded the patient may be re-opened during psychotherapy so that, ultimately, he may be healed. Once again, this may only 'make sense' against the background of a larger story. A book title and a sentence from the first page are strangely apposite here. In *The Wound of Knowledge*, Williams (1979) writes: 'The questioning involved here is not our interrogation of the data, but its interrogation of us.'

But this questioning does not necessarily wait until life 'fails'. The shadows are swarming with intimations that beckon and evoke response.

> 'I tell you that, if these should hold their
> peace, the stones would immediately cry out'.
> > (*Luke* 19, 40)

> 'Stones have been known to move and trees to speak.'
> > (*Macbeth* III. 4, 122)

Without at least an attempted engagement in this struggle, man re-enacts that anxious, floating, groundless response to life described by Heidegger (1936). Man is then part of 'The age for whom the ground fails to come'.

Tillich (1957) refers to 'The Ground of our Being'. But intrapsychic defensive forces may so overprotect a man that he runs the risk of keeping this Ground at too great a distance from the ground on which he must tread.

Gilkey (1969) points to the fundamental question which stands upon the ground of our being. The question is not 'How can I become whole?' It is similar. Yet it differs profoundly:

'How can I become whole *again?*'

In that single word 'again' is contained the implication that one world is enough. In a later work (1979) he takes up Kierkegaard's suggestion that there are two sets of polar categories which characterize our passage through time:

'(i) *Destiny* – what we and our world have been given and so what they are – and *freedom* – the capacity to shape both ourselves and our world into the future; and (ii) *actuality* – what is now arising out of what has been – and the *possibility* – what might be or become in the still undecided future.'

In a subsequent passage he extends this last category with a sweeping sentence with obvious and direct application to Aeolian therapeutic initiatives: 'Our present is saturated with possibilities.' When this phrase is set alongside another of Gilkey's injunctions, in which we are 'to speak seriously, and yet without despair', we are brought face to face with the clinical appraisal of 'how things are'. Yet, at the same time, we are to appreciate the degree to which our life can be saturated with possibility.

That man is accepted unconditionally is a central tenet in the thinking of Luther, Buber, and others. And, in our view, the meeting of patient and therapist must bear the stamp of an encounter between equals, *sub specie aeternitatis*.

'The rose is without why; it blooms because it blooms,
It cares not for itself, asks not if it is seen.'

(Angelus Silesius)

'This saying very greatly fascinated Heidegger. For a rose that does not fret about the enabling conditions of its existence, that is not constantly attacking the world and seeking to contain it within its own scheme of concepts and categories, that simply blooms because it blooms, being quite content to be ''without why'' – such a rose, in its undemanding openness to the Mystery, to the Ground of Being, became for Heidegger a kind of sign, an emblem of what man himself is like when he is most truly human.'

(Scott 1985)

The rose described by Silesius conveys an inferential echo of a more familiar passage about another species, which blooms because it blooms. 'Consider the lilies of the field, how they grow; they toil not, neither do they spin; And yet I say unto you, That even Solomon in all his glory was not arrayed like one of these' (*Matthew* 6, 28). Such a proclamation of acceptance, and the possibility of new beginnings, invests therapeutic endeavours with hope. It recalls the words of Levi (1975) which are so angular and luminous that they seem to fit into no prior category. Yet no *poiesis* could be more original, no aesthetic imperative more commanding, and no point of urgency more insistent:

'The vision of [his] compassion belongs to innocent eyes and it belongs also to us because our *innocence can be renewed*. The man who does not know this has not understood anything.' [our italics]

The nature of the encompassing larger story exerts its pervasive and un-avoidable influence on man's inner world. And therapeutic space will always carry the imprint of the therapist's perception of the larger story, albeit silently. One way or another.

> When it comes, the Landscape listens –
> Shadows – hold their breath –
> (Emily Dickinson)

Notes

1 The theme of the 'perspectival world' occurs as a regular outcropping throughout the book, though it is of particular relevance in chapter 6 on 'Attunement'. Its significance is self-explanatory. It refers to the phenomenon of seeing the world through the eyes of 'the other', from the same 'perspective'. Pool (1972) writes, 'Husserl takes as his guiding idea, his major instrument of investigation, the notion of *perspectives*, of a *perspectival world*. The objects in the world are seen from different perspectives. We move round them, seeing them and experiencing them in different modalities, while other people in the world do the same. We are all conscious that there is only one world, but we are also quite sure that we all see it differently, we all interpret it differently, and we all attribute different meanings to it at various times.'

2 We are aware that the words '*feeling like* a river' are, strictly speaking, the language of simile and not metaphor. Nevertheless, for our present purposes this is an academic distinction and irrelevant. There are, however, other instances where this is of diagnostic importance. Indeed, the differentiation of concrete and metaphorical thinking sometimes serves as a hallmark of psychotic thought disorder.

3 We are grateful to Theodore Nadelson, M.D., Boston, for comments about the therapist's changing threshold of risk-taking and 'venturing with the patient'.

4 Whereas textual criticism may not strongly support this 'castrating' interpretation, an experienced professional actress felt that this was confirmed by kinaesthetic empathy. It was 'beyond doubt when playing the part, *in vivo*'.

5 A footnote is an inappropriate location for four references which are cognate with central Aeolian issues, particularly when they each approach the field from different starting points. Nevertheless, our dilemma is that they were all encountered after our text was complete. Yet, having read them, it became incomplete without their inclusion! We mention them so that the reader can follow those ideas which beckon him.

   Kelman (1987) has described the process of resonant cognition 'whereby understanding of another [the patient] is obtained by observation of his impact on one's [the analyst's] psychology'. There are clearly Aeolian echoes here which become even more evident when he refers to the three types of resonant cognition. These are 'distinguished on metapsychological grounds: transference, empathy and induction'. It is interesting to note that Kelman's paper was 'received' in August 1985 which was shortly after we had been writing on poetic induction (see p. 48). In this way we exemplify some features of Jung's (p. 14) synchronicity to which Capra (1982) refers! Prickett (1986) in a chapter on 'Metaphor and reality' has much to say that links with the theme of primordiality and the larger story. 'Having lost the old primal participation with the natural world, humanity is now liminal: at once precariously marginal, and at the same time potentially on the threshold of a much more significant relationship with nature. Religious language, in this sense, can be seen as the language of liminality.' And Spengemann (1980) develops the thesis that there are three distinct kinds of autobiography: the historical, the philosophical, and the poetic. These are concerned with self-explanation, self-portrait, and enactment. This brings the reader to 'that autobiography we are all engaged in making and remaking, as long as we live, which we never complete, though we all know how it is going to end' (Hardy, see p. 240).

6 We are grateful to Adrian Grounds, M.R.C.Psych., The Institute of Criminology, Cambridge, for pointing out that the patient was making a direct statement about the transference. It was as though, in selecting his response, the therapist was asking himself 'do I deal with this head-on?'

7 If the therapist is over-analytic, it may have a subversive effect on his empathic capacity. Thus an ironic remark can become isolated from its context and be taken too literally.

8 On re-reading these vignettes we were struck by the frequency with which the cold, ice, and 'frozen introjects' appear. This is a reminder that much of the book was written in the winter. Some winters in London are cold, all winters in Copenhagen are.

9 This linking of the literal and the metaphorical aspects of 'washing' is reminiscent of Arieti's comment (1976): 'we sense that we are getting closer to touching a special truth that only metaphor can offer us'. And, strangely enough, he says this in a commentary on *Macbeth*.

10 See *Perfume* by Suskind (1986).

11 It is not the first time that the metaphor of 'being led up the garden path' has appeared (see p. 4). Nor is it the last.

12 Bedell Stanford, then Regis Professor of Greek in the University of Dublin amplified this in a personal discussion in 1981.

13 This is congruous with the views of Levin (1980) which we unfortunately came across too late to deal with in the text: 'Metaphors serve as bridges in a number of ways. At first they allow for the linking up of the two hemispheres. This results from the fact that metaphors constitute an ambiguous stimulus object that can arouse activity in each hemisphere, by appealing to the left hemisphere linguistically and to the right hemisphere by non-linguistic means.'

14 Our spontaneous choice of the word 'embark' shows how much metaphor

invades our thinking and our language. We did not try to 'think of a metaphor' which might be appropriate to this discussion. On the contrary, 'to embark' was exactly what we intended to do, although it was in its metaphorical connotation.

15 See note 3.

16 Geoffrey Rowell, Fellow and Chaplain of Keble College, Oxford, kindly introduced us to Newman's words (p. 135) which Elgar did not set to music. We have been greatly helped by his inter-disciplinary versatility and his concern for quotational precision.

17 That society 'will have no place for me' is an understandably frequent theme in psychotherapy undertaken in a custodial setting. The patient is sometimes unable to make realistic plans for life when he has been discharged from hospital, or released from prison. The poetic and archaic description by Oscar Wilde describes a frequent fantasy. Namely, that somehow or other 'Nature' will prove sufficiently hospitable, to the extent that 'other arrangements' do not need to be made. This may all be part of the essential aspect of reality-testing which all patients need to consider, before they are ready to face the increased societal demands 'on the other side of the wall'.

There is also a primordial ethos to this passage from *De Profundis* in which Oscar Wilde hopes to be cleansed and made whole by the sweet rains of Nature. This is in marked contrast to King Lear's confrontation with the elements. It is reminiscent of a psychotic patient who stood in the middle of a field during a cloud-burst and said 'I let the rain finish on me'. He was a human 'rain-conductor' which, he felt, protected his family from being washed away in the deluge. It will be recalled that there was a paranoid aspect to Lear's sense of being at the focal point of the storm. He did not say that he went out *when* it was raining. On the contrary, 'the rain came to wet me once and the wind to make me chatter' (*King Lear* IV 6, 100).

This takes us back to a recurrent theme. The more elemental and primordial the metaphor, the more powerfully does it convey the turbulence of the inner world.

18 Gerald Wooster, F.R.C.Psych., St George's Hospital, London, has drawn our attention to the link between the work of J. Matte Blanco and the Aeolian Mode. We are grateful for this and for his more general encouragement.

19 During a discussion at the Shakespeare Institute in 1983, we were asked about the 'literary implications' of the Aeolian Mode. We replied that whereas we were professionally qualified to suggest its clinical implications, this did not apply to its literary significance. Specialists in that field will decide whether there is any relevance – direct or oblique.

20 See note 16.

21 Sir Andrew Huxley, P.R.S., upon hearing of the question 'Bethlehem is still a place, isn't it?' in relation to a localized Christmas, commented, 'perhaps it is localized everywhere' (personal communication 1985).

Bibliography

Abrams, M. H. (1953) *The Mirror and the Lamp: Romantic Theory and the Critical Tradition*. Oxford: Oxford University Press.

Abse, D. W. (1971) *Speech and Reason: Language Disorder in Mental Disease*. Bristol: John Wright.

Ach, N. (1905) *Über die Willenstätigkeit und das Denken*. Göttingen: Vandenhöck & Ruprecht.

Alonso, A. (1985) *The Quiet Profession: Supervisors of Psychotherapy*. New York: Macmillan Publishing Company.

Altieri, C. (1971) Jean-Paul Sartre: the Engaged Imagination in the Quest for Imagination. In O. B. Hardison (ed.) *The Quest for Imagination: Essays in Twentieth-Century Aesthetic Criticism*. Cleveland: Case Western Reserve University Press.

Andersen, Hans (1979) *Fairy Tales*. Translated by Vera Gissing. London: Octopus Books.

Anne, Countess of Winchilsea (1945) In P. Pool *Poems of Death*. London: F. Muller Ltd.

Appelbaum, S. (1966) Speaking with the Second Voice. *Journal of the American Psychoanalytic Association* 14, 462–77.

Apter, N. S. (1975) Breaking the Rules. In J. H. Gunderson and L. Mosher (eds) *Psychotherapy of Schizophrenia*. New York: Jason Aronson.

Arieti, S. (1976) *Creativity: the Magic Synthesis*. New York: Basic Books.

Arlow, J. A. (1969) Unconscious Fantasy and Disturbances of Conscious Experience. *Psychoanalytic Quarterly* 38: 1–27.

Armstrong, E. A. (1946) *Shakespeare's Imagination: a Study of the Psychology of Association and Inspiration*. London: Lindsay Drummond.

Auerhahn, N. C. (1979) Interpretation in the Psychoanalytic Narrative: a Literary Framework for the Analytic Process. *International Review of Psycho-Analysis* 6: 423–36.

Bachelard, G. (1969) *The Poetics of Space*. Boston: Beacon Press.

Bakan, P. (1971) The Eyes Have It. *Psychology Today* 4: 64–7.

Bakan, P. (1979) Imagery, Raw and Cooked: a Hemispheric Recipe. Paper presented at First Annual Conference on Imagery of the American Association for the Study of Mental Imagery. June 22–4, Los Angeles, California.

Bakhtin, M. (1973) Problems of Dostoevsky's Poetics. Translated by R. W. Rotsel. Ardis Publications 1973. In T. Todorov *Introduction to Poetics*. Translated by R. Howard. Brighton: Harvester Press, 1981.

Balint, M. (1968) *The Basic Fault: Therapeutic Aspects of Regression*. London: Tavistock Publications.

Barfield, O. (1928) *Poetic Diction: a Study in Meaning*. London: Faber & Gwyer.

Barker, A. (1985) *Using Metaphors in Psychotherapy*. New York: Brunner/ Matzel.

Barry, S. (ed.) (1986) *The Inherited Boundaries: Younger Poets of the Republic of Ireland*. Portlaoise, Ireland: The Dolmen Press.

Barth, J. R. (1977) *The Symbolic Imagination*. Princeton, New Jersey: Princeton University Press.

Basch, M. F. (1983) The Perception of Reality and the Disavowal of Meaning. *The Annual of Psychoanalysis* Vol. II. New York: International Universities Press.

Basch-Kahre, E. (1985) Patterns of Thinking. *International Journal of Psycho-Analysis* 66: 455–70.

Bateson, G. (1979) *Mind and Nature: a Necessary Unity*. London: Wildwood House.

Beardsley, M. C. (1967) Metaphors. In P. Edwards (ed.) *The Encyclopaedia of Philosophy* Vol. 5. London: Collier Macmillan.

Beaumont, J. G. and Dimond, S. J. (1973) Brain Disconnection and Schizophrenia. *British Journal of Psychiatry* 123: 661–2.

Benedetti, G. (1976) Crucial Problems in Psychotherapy of Schizophrenia. *American Journal of Psychoanalysis* 36: 67–77.

Berger, H. and Mohr, F. (1967) *A Fortunate Man: the Story of a Country Doctor*. London: Penguin Press.

Bettelheim, B. (1976) *The Uses of Enchantment: the Meaning and Importance of Fairy Tales*. London: Thames & Hudson.

Bille, E. (1975) *Digte og Vignetter*. Copenhagen: Brøndum.

Blake, W. (1972) In G. Keynes (ed.) *Complete Writings*. Oxford: Oxford University Press.

Bloch, S. and Crouch, E. (1985) *Therapeutic Factors in Group Psychotherapy*. Oxford: Oxford University Press.

Blædel, N. (1985) *Harmoni og Enhed. Niels Bohr en Biografi*. Copenhagen: Rhodos.

Bodkin, M. (1934) *Archetypal Patterns in Poetry: Psychological Studies of Imagination*. London: Oxford University Press.

Bohr, N. (1982) Personal communication by Vilhem Bohr.

Bollas, C. (1980) Review of Rogers (1978). *International Review of Psycho-Analysis* 7: 117–19.

Bonifazi, C. (1967) *A Theology of Things: a Study of Man in His Physical Environment*. New York: J. P. Lippincott.

Boss, M. (1979) *Existential Foundations of Medicine and Psychology*. New York: Aronson.

Boszormenyi-Nagy, I. and Spark, G. M. (1973) *Invisible Loyalties: Reciprocity in Intergenerational Family Therapy*. New York: Harper & Row.

Bowra, C. M. (1951) *The Heritage of Symbolism*. London: Macmillan.

Brentano, F. (1924) *Psychologie vom empirischen Standpunkt*. Leipzig: Bunker & Humbolt.

Brockbank, J. P. (1971) 'Pericles' and the Dream of Immortality. In K. Muir (ed.) *Shakespeare Survey* Vol. 24. Cambridge: The University Press.

—— (1976) *Upon Such Sacrifices*. Sixty-sixth Shakespeare Lecture. London: British Academy.

—— (1982) Personal communication.

Brooke, R. (1928) *Collected Poems* (2nd ed.). Edinburgh: Turnbull & Spears.

Brooks, C. (1947) *The Well Wrought Urn*. London: Dennis Dobson Ltd.

Bruch, H. (1974) *Learning Psychotherapy: Rationale and Ground Rules*. Cambridge, Mass.: Harvard University Press.

Bruner, J. S. (1980) *Possible Castles*. Paper delivered at the Gordon Mills Lecture. Austin: University of Texas.

—— and Postman, L. (1949) On the Perception of Incongruity: A Paradigm. *Journal of Personality* 18: 206–23.

Bryden, M. P. (1970) Laterality Effects in Dichotic Listening. *Neuropsychologia* 8: 443–50.

Buber, M. (1957) Elements of the Interhuman. *Psychiatry* 20: 105–13.

Bugentan, J. (1965) *The Search for Authenticity*. New York: Reinhardt & Winston.

Burkart, E. (1963) 'Das Zeichen' in *Deutsche Lyrik: Gedichte seit 1945*. (Translated by Rosemary Combridge as 'The Sign'.) Munich: Deutsche Taschenbuch Verlag.

Cain, A. C. and Maupin, B. M. (1961) Interpretation Within the Metaphor. *Bulletin of the Menninger Clinic* 25: 307–11.

Capra, F. (1982) *The Turning Point: Science, Society and the Rising Culture*. London: Wildwood House.

Cardinal, R. (1981) *Figures of Reality: a Perspective on the Poetic Imagination*. London: Croom Helm.

Casement, P. (1985) *On Learning From the Patient*. London: Tavistock Publications.

Caws, M. A. (1981) *The Eye in the Text: Essays on Perception, Mannerist to Modern*. Princeton, New Jersey: Princeton University Press.

Cecil, D. (1949) *Poets and Story-Tellers*. London: Constable.

Chadwick, H. (1981) *Frontiers of Theology*. An inaugural lecture. Cambridge: Cambridge University Press.

Chaliff, C. (1973) Emily Dickinson and Poetry Therapy: the Art of Peace. In J. Leedy (ed.) *Poetry of Peace*. Philadelphia: Lippincott.

Chaning-Pearce, W. (1948) Søren Kierkegaard: a Study. London: James Clarke & Co. Ltd.

Chessick, R. D. (1977) *Intensive Psychotherapy of the Borderline Patient*. New York: Aronson.

Church, R. (1957) *Small Moments*. London: Hutchinson.

Cirlot, J. (1962) *A Dictionary of Symbols*. New York: Philosophical Library.

Claudel, P. (1978) The Tidings Brought to Mary. In R. J. O'Connell (ed.) *Art and the Christian Intelligence in St Augustine*. Oxford: Blackwell.

Clemen, W. (1951) *The Development of Shakespeare's Imagery*. London: Methuen.

Cohen, B. D., Noblin, C. D., Silverman, A. J., and Penick, S. B. (1968) Functional Asymmetry of the Human Brain. *Science* 162: 475–7.

Cohn, H. W. (1984) An Existential Approach to Psychotherapy. *British Journal of Medical Psychology* 57: 311–18.

Coleridge, S. T. In J. Shawcross (ed.) (1907) *Biographia Literaria*. Oxford: Oxford University Press.

—— Statesman's Manual. In K. Coburn (ed.) (1972) *The Collected Works*. Princeton, New Jersey: Princeton University Press.

Coulson, J. (1981) *Religion and Imagination: 'In Aid of a Grammar of Assent'*. Oxford: Clarendon Press.

Cox, M. (1973) Group Psychotherapy as a Redefining Process. *International Journal of Group Psychotherapy* 23: 465–73.

—— (1978) *Structuring the Therapeutic Process: Compromise with Chaos*. Oxford: Pergamon Press.

—— (1979) Dynamic Psychotherapy with Sex Offenders. In I. Rosen (ed.) *Sexual Division* (2nd edn). Oxford: Oxford University Press.

—— (1982a) 'I Took a Life Because I Needed One': Psychotherapeutic Possibilities with the Schizophrenic Offender-Patient. *Psychotherapy and Psychosomatics* 37: 96–105.

—— (1982b) The Psychotic Patient as 'Co-therapist'. In M. Pines and L. Rafaelsen (eds) *The Individual and the Group*. New York: Plenum.

—— (1983) The Contribution of Dynamic Psychotherapy to Forensic Psychiatry and *Vice Versa*. *International Journal of Law and Psychiatry* 6: 89–99.

Cox, M. (1986) The 'Holding Function' of Dynamic Psychotherapy in a Custodial Setting; a Review. *Journal of the Royal Society of Medicine* 79: 162–4.

—— (In press) The Psychopathology and Treatment of Psychotic Aggression. In R. Bluglass and P. Bowden (eds) *Principles and Practice of Forensic Psychiatry*. Edinburgh: Churchill Livingstone.

Cunningham, J. S. (1979) *'Where are They?': the After-Life of a Figure of Speech*. Warton Lecture. London: The British Academy.

Cutting, J. (1986) *The Psychology of Schizophrenia*. Edinburgh: Churchill Livingstone.

Dance, E. H. (1960) *History the Betrayer: a Study in Bias*. London: Hutchinson.

Davie, D. (1964) Yeats, the Master of a Trade. In D. Donoghue (ed.) *The Integrity of Yeats*. Cork: The Mercier Press.

Davis, D. R. (1981) Exchanges with the Humanities. *Bulletin of the Royal College of Psychiatrists* 5: 82–5.

Day, D. (1963) *Swifter than Reason: the Poetry and Criticism of Robert Graves*. Chapel Hill: University of North Carolina Press.

Day Lewis, C. (1947) *The Poetic Image*. The Clark Lectures, Cambridge (1946). London: Jonathan Cape.

D'Elia G. and Perris, C. (1973) Cerebral Functional Dominance and Depression. *Acta Psychiatrica Scandinavica* 9: 191–7.

Dickens, C. adapted by Edgar, D. (1982) *The Life and Adventures of Nicholas Nickleby*. New York: Dramatists Play Service Inc.

Dickinson, Emily (1970) *The Complete Poems*. London: Faber & Faber.

Dimond, S. J. and Beaumont, J. G. (1974) *Hemisphere Function in the Human Brain*. London: Elek Science.

Dinesen, I. (1957) The Blank Page. In *Last Tales*. Chicago: University of Chicago Press.

Donoghue, D. (ed.) (1964) *The Integrity of Yeats*. Cork: The Mercier Press.

Douglas, M. (1969) *Purity and Danger*. London: Routledge & Kegan Paul.

Dunne, J. S. (1967) *A Search for God in Time and Memory*. New York: The Macmillan Company.

—— (1973) *Time and Myth: a Meditation on Storytelling as an Exploration of Life and Death*. London: SCM Press Ltd.

Dymond, R. (1949) A Scale for the Measurement of Empathic Ability. *Journal of Counselling Psychology* 13: 127–33.

Ecclestone, A. (1977) *A Staircase for Silence*. London: Darton, Longman, and Todd.

Echeruo, M. J. C. (1978) *The Conditioned Imagination from Shakespeare to Conrad: Studies in the Exo-cultural Stereotype*. London: Macmillan Press Ltd.

Egan, R. (1972) *Drama within Drama: Shakespeare's Sense of his Art*. New York: Columbia University Press.

Eichenbaum, B. (1944) Chekhov at Large. In R. L. Jackson (ed.) (1955) *Chekhov: a Collection of Critical Essays*. Englewood Cliffs: Prentice-Hall Inc.

Ekstein, R. and Wallerstein, R. S. (1958) *The Teaching and Learning of Psychotherapy*. New York: Basic Books Inc.

Eliot, T. S. (1934) *Choruses from 'The Rock'*. London: Faber & Faber.

—— (1935) *Murder in the Cathedral*. London: Faber & Faber.

—— (1935) *Burnt Norton*. London: Faber & Faber.

—— (1940) *East Coker*. London: Faber & Faber.

—— (1941) *The Dry Salvages*. London: Faber & Faber.

—— (1957) *On Poetry and Poets. The Music of Poetry*. London: Faber & Faber.

—— (1969) *The Complete Poems and Plays*. London: Faber & Faber.

Ellis-Fermor, U. (1945) *The Frontiers of Drama*. London: Methuen.

Éluard, P. (1968) *Oeuvres Complètes*. Paris: Gallimard.

Empson, W. (1930) *Seven Types of Ambiguity*. London: Chatto & Windus.

Erikson, E. H. (1950) *Childhood and Society*. New York: W. W. Norton.

—— (1959) *Young Man Luther*. London: Faber & Faber.

Fanthorpe, U. (1982) *Standing To*. Poems. Plymouth: Harry Chambers/ Peterloo Poets, Latimer Trend & Co.

Faulkner, W. (1935) *As I Lay Dying*. London: Chatto & Windus.

Fell, J. P. (1979) *Heidegger and Sartre: an Essay on Being and Place*. New York: Columbia University Press.

Fenichel, O. (1953) On Identification. In O. Fenichel (ed.) *Collected Papers*. New York: Norton.

—— (1955) *The Psychoanalytic Theory of Neuroses*. London: Routledge & Kegan Paul.

Fet, A. (1982) *'I Have Come to Greet You': Selected Poems*. Translated by J. Greene. London: Angel Books.

Fleming, J. and Benedek, T. (1964) Supervision: a Method of Teaching Psychoanalysis. *The Psychoanalytic Quarterly* 33: 71–96.

Foreman, R. (1979) *New York Times* 14 January.

Forrest, D. V. (1965) Poiesis and the Language of Schizophrenia. *Psychiatry* 28: 1–18.

Forster, E. M. (1910) *Howard's End*. London: Edward Arnold.

Forsyth, N. (1971) Gaston Bachelard's Theory of the Poetic Imagination. Psychoanalysis to Phenomenology. In O. B. Hardison (ed.) *The Quest for Imagination: Essays in Twentieth-Century Aesthetic Criticism*. Cleveland: Case Western Reserve University Press.

Fossi, G. (1985) Psychoanalytic Theory and the Problems of Creativity. *International Journal of Psycho-Analysis* 66: 215–30.

Foulkes, S. H. (1964) *Therapeutic Group Analysis*. London: George Allen & Unwin Ltd.

Freud, S. (1900) *The Interpretation of Dreams*. Standard Edition Vols 4 and 5. London: Hogarth Press and the Institute of Psycho-Analysis.

—— (1905) *Fragment of an Analysis of a Case of Hysteria*. Standard Edition Vol. 7. London: Hogarth Press and the Institute of Psycho-Analysis.

—— (1914a) *On the History of the Psycho-Analytic Movement*. Standard Edition Vol. 14. London: Hogarth Press and the Institute of Psycho-Analysis.

—— (1914b) *On Narcissism: An Introduction*. Standard Edition Vol. 14. London: Hogarth Press and the Institute of Psycho-Analysis.

—— (1917a) *Introductory Lectures on Psycho-Analysis*. Standard Edition Vols 15 and 16. London: Hogarth Press and the Institute of Psycho-Analysis.

—— (1917b) *Transference*. Standard Edition Vols 15 and 16. London: Hogarth Press and the Institute of Psycho-Analysis.

—— (1923) *The Ego and the Id*. Standard Edition Vol. 19. London: Hogarth Press and the Institute of Psycho-Analysis.

—— (1933) *New Introductory Lectures on Psycho-Analysis*. Standard Edition Vol. 22. London: Hogarth Press and the Institute of Psycho-Analysis.

—— (1937) *Analysis Terminable and Interminable*. Standard Edition Vol. 23. London: Hogarth Press and the Institute of Psycho-Analysis.

Frick, M. (1972) *All the Days of his Dying*. London: Alison & Busby.

Friedman, N. (1953) Imagery: From Sensation to Symbol. *Journal of Aesthetics and Art Criticism* 12: 25–37.

Frosch, J. P. (1983) *The Psychotic Process*. New York: International Universities Press.

—— (1986) Review of D. Werman *The Practice of Supportive Psychotherapy*. *International Review of Psycho-Analysis* 1: 121–4.

Frost, R. F. (1955) *Selected Poems*. Introduction by C. Day Lewis. Harmondsworth: Penguin.

Garland, C. (1981) *The State of Play*. London: Unpublished dissertation. The Institute of Group Analysis.

Gedo, L. (1979) *Beyond Interpretation: Toward a Revised Theory for Psychoanalysis*. New York: International Universities Press.

Giannitrapani, D. (1967) Developing Concepts of Lateralization of Cerebral Functions. *Cortex* 3: 353–70.

Gilkey, L. (1969) *Naming the Whirlwind. The Renewal of God-Language*. New York: The Bobbs-Merrill Company.

—— (1976) *Reaping the Whirlwind: a Christian Interpretation of History*. New York: Seabury Press.

—— (1979) *Message and Existence: an Introduction to Christian Theology*. Minneapolis: Seabury Press.

Giovacchini, P. L. (1967) The Frozen Introject. *International Journal of Psycho-Analysis* 48: 61–7.

Gordon, W. J. J. (1961) *Synectics: the Development of Creative Capacity*. New York: Harper & Row.

Granville-Barker, H. (1927) *Prefaces to Shakespeare: King Lear*. London: Sidgwick & Jackson.

Graves, R. (1961) *Collected Poems*. London: Cassell & Co. Ltd.

Graves, R. P. (1979) *A. E. Housman: the Scholar-Poet*. London: Routledge & Kegan Paul.

Green, A. (1979) *The Tragic Effect*. Cambridge: Cambridge University Press.

Green, H. (1964) *I Never Promised You a Rose Garden*. New York: Holt, Rinehart & Winston Inc.

Greenson, R. R. (1967) *The Technique and Practice of Psychoanalysis Vol. I*. New York: International Universities Press.

—— (1975) The Limits of an Interpretive Approach. In J. G. Gunderson and L. R. Mosher (eds) *Psychotherapy of Schizophrenia*. New York: Jason Aronson 205–7.

Gunderson, J. G. and Mosher, L. R. (1975) *Psychotherapy of Schizophrenia*. New York: Jason Aronson.

Hadley, J. L. (1983) The Representational System: a Bridging Concept for Psychoanalysis and Neurophysiology. *International Review of Psycho-Analysis* 10: 13–30.

Haefele, J. W. (1962) *Creativity and Innovation*. New York: Reinhold Publishing Corporation.

Hall, C. and Lindzey, G. (1957) *Theories of Personality*. New York: John Wiley & Sons.

Halliburton, D. (1981) *Poetic Thinking: an Approach to Heidegger*. Chicago: University of Chicago Press.

Hamburger, M. (1969) *The Truth of Poetry: Tensions in Modern Poetry from Baudelaire to the 1960s*. London: Weidenfeld & Nicolson.

Hammer, E. F. (1968) *Use of Interpretation in Treatment*. New York: Grune & Stratton.

—— (1978) Interpretations Couched in the Poetic Style. *International Journal of Psychoanalysis & Psychotherapy* 7: 240–53.

Hardy, B. (1975) *Tellers and Listeners: the Narrative Imagination*. London: The Athlone Press.

Havens, L. L. (1976) *Participant Observation*. New York: Jason Aronson.

—— (1986) *Making Contact: Uses of Language in Psychotherapy*. Cambridge, Mass.: Harvard University Press.

Hebb, D. O. (1958) Alice in Wonderland or Psychology Among the Biological Sciences. In H. F. Harlow and C. N. Woolsey (eds) *Biological and Biochemical Bases of Behavior*. Wisconsin: University of Wisconsin Press.

Hécaen, H. and Assal, G. (1970) A Comparison of Constructive Deficits Following Right and Left Hemispheric Lesions. *Neuropsychologia* 8: 289–305.

Heidegger, M. (1927) *Sein und Zeit*. Halle: Max Niemeyer. Translated as *Being and Time* by J. Macquarrie and E. Robinson (1962). Oxford: Basil Blackwell.

—— (1936) What are Poets For? In *Poetry, Language, Thought*. Translated by A. Hofstadter (1971). New York: Harper & Row.

Heilman, K. M. and Van der Abell, T. (1980) Right Hemisphere Dominance for Attention. *Neurology* 30: 327–30.

Heilman, R. B. (1963) *This Great Stage: Image and Structure in King Lear*. Seattle: University of Washington Press.

Held, R. (1961) Exposure History as a Factor in Maintaining Stability of Perception and Coordination. *Journal of Nervous and Mental Disease* 132: 26–32.

Hendry, J. F. (1983) *The Sacred Threshold: a Life of Rilke*. Manchester: Carcanet New Press.

Henn, T. R. (1956) *The Harvest of Tragedy*. London: Methuen & Co. Ltd.

Heshe, J., Röder, E., and Theilgaard, A. (1978) Unilateral and Bilateral ECT. *Acta Psychiatrica Scandinavica. Suppl. 275*. Copenhagen: Munksgaard.

Hillyer, R. (1966) *Country Boy*. London: Hodder & Stoughton.

Hingley, R. (1982) *Nightingale Fever: Russian Poets in Revolution*. London: Weidenfeld & Nicolson.

Hobson, R. F. (1974) Loneliness. *The Journal of Analytical Psychology* 19: 1, 71–89.

—— (1985) *Forms of Feeling: the Heart of Psychotherapy*. London: Tavistock Publications.

Hoffman, D. (1967) *Barbarous Knowledge: Myth in the Poetry of Yeats, Graves and Muir*. Oxford: Oxford University Press.

Hogg, J. (ed.) (1969) *Psychology and the Visual Arts*. Harmondsworth: Penguin.

Holland, N. N. (1985) *The I*. New Haven: Yale University Press.

Holloway, J. (1961) *The Story of the Night: Studies in Shakespeare's Major Tragedies*. London: Routledge & Kegan Paul.

Holmes, J. (1985) The Language of Psychotherapy: Metaphor, Ambiguity, Wholeness. *British Journal of Psychotherapy* 4: 240–54.

Holt, R. (1967) The Development of the Primary Process: a Structural View. In R. Holt (ed.) *Motives and Thoughts: Psychoanalytic Essays in*

Memory of David Rapaport. Psychological Issues. Monographs 18/19. New York: University Press, 345–83.

Holt, R. (1972) On the Nature and Generality of Mental Imagery. In P. Sheehan (ed.) *The Function and Nature of Imagery*. London and New York: Academic Press.

Homan, S. (1980) *Shakespeare's 'More than Words can Witness': Essays on Visual and Nonverbal Enactment in the Plays*. London: Associated University Presses Ltd.

—— (1981) *When the Theater Turns to Itself: The Aesthetic Metaphor in Shakespeare*. London: Associated University Presses Ltd.

Hopkins, G. M. (1967) *The Poems of Gerard Manley Hopkins*. 4th edn (eds) W. H. Gardner and N. H. MacKenzie. London: Oxford University Press.

Housman, A. E. (1933) See Graves, R. P. (1979).

—— (1939) *Collected Poems*. London: Jonathan Cape.

Husserl, E. (1931) *Cartesian Meditations*. The Hague: M. Nijhoff.

—— (1970) *Logical Investigations*. Translated by J. N. Findlay. New York: Humanities Press.

Hutcheon, L. (1980) *Narcissistic Narrative: the Metafictional Paradox*. Ontario: Wilfred Laurier University Press.

Hölderlin, F. (1953) *Sämtliche Werke*. Stuttgart: Kohlhamer.

Ignatieff, M. (1984) *The Needs of Strangers*. London: Chatto & Windus: The Hogarth Press.

Irvine, E. (1974) *Literature and the Study of Human Experience*. Lydia Rapoport Lectures. Northampton, Mass.: Smith College School for Social Work.

Jackson, J. Hughlings (1932) On the Nature of the Duality of the Brain. In J. Taylor (ed.) *Selected Writings of John Hughlings Jackson*. London: Hodder & Stoughton.

Jackson, R. L. (ed.) (1967) *Chekhov: a Collection of Critical Essays*. Englewood Cliffs: Prentice-Hall Inc.

Jacobsen, E. (1965) *The Self and the Object World*. London: Hogarth Press.

James, D. C. (1984) Bion's 'Containing' and Winnicott's 'Holding' in the Context of the Group Matrix. *International Journal of Group Psychotherapy* 34: 201–13.

James, W. (1890) *Principles of Psychology*. United States: Henry Holt & Co.

Jaspers, K. (1953) *Tragedy is Not Enough*. Introduction by K. W. Deutsch. London: Victor Gollancz.

—— (1963) *General Psychopathology*. Translated by J. Hoenig and M. H. Hamilton. Manchester: Manchester University Press.

Jennings, S. (1973) *Remedial Drama*. London: Pitman Publishing.

—— (ed.) (1975) *Creative Therapy*. London: Pitman Publishing.

—— (1986a) Personal communication.

—— (1986b) *Creative Drama: In Groupwork*. London: Winslow Press.

—— (ed.) (1987) Dramatherapy: Theory and Practice for Teachers and Clinicians. London: Croom Helm.

—— (in press) The Loneliness of the Long Distance Therapist. *British Journal of Psychotherapy*.

Johnson (1751) *The Rambler* 168. 26 October.

Jouffroy, A. (1970) *La Fin des Alternances*. Quoted in R. Cardinal *Figures of Reality* (1981) New Jersey: Barnes & Noble Books.

Jung, C. G. (1964) *Man and his Symbols*. New York: Doubleday & Co. Inc.

—— (1972) *Synchronicity*. London: Routledge & Kegan Paul.

—— and Kerenyi, C. (1951) *Introduction to a Science of Mythology*. Translated by R. F. C. Hull. London: Routledge & Kegan Paul.

Kandinsky, W. (1913) *1901–1913*. Berlin: Der Sturm.

Kane, L. (1984) *The Language of Silence: On the Unspoken and the Unspeakable in Modern Drama*. London: Associated University Presses Ltd.

Katz, G. A. (1983) The Noninterpretation of the Metaphors in Psychiatric Hospital Groups. *International Journal of Group Psychotherapy* 33: 53–67.

Kaufmann, R. J. (1965) Ceremonies for Chaos: the Status of *Troilus and Cressida*. *English Literary History* 32: 139–59.

Kelman, H. (1987) On Resonant Cognition. *International Review of Psycho-Analysis* 14: 111–23.

Kenner, H. (1948) *Paradox in Chesterton*. London: Sheed & Ward.

—— (1983) *A Colder Eye: the Modern Irish Writers*. London: Allen Lane.

Kerényi, C. (1951) *The Gods of the Greeks*. London: Thames & Hudson.

Kermode, F. (1979) *The Genesis of Secrecy: On the Interpretation of Narrative*. Cambridge, Mass.: Harvard University Press.

Kernberg, O. F. (1975) *Borderline Conditions and Pathological Narcissism*. New York: Jason Aronson.

Kety, S. (1960) A Biologist Examines Mind and Behavior. *Science* 132: 1861–70.

Khan, M. M. R. (1972) The Finding and Becoming of Self. In Khan (1974) *The Privacy of the Self*. London: Hogarth Press.

Kierkegaard, S. (1962). In A. B. Drachmann, J. C. Heiberg, and H. O. Lange (eds) *Samlede Værker* VI. Copenhagen: Gyldendal.

Kimura, D. (1973) The Asymmetry of the Human Brain. Readings from *Scientific American* (San Francisco) 228: 70–8.

Klauber, J. (1980) Formulating Interpretations in Clinical Psychoanalysis. *International Journal of Psycho-Analysis* 61: 195–201.

Klein, M. (1977) *Love, Guilt and Reparation. And other works 1921–1945*. London: Hogarth Press.

Knights, L. C. (1980) Poetry and 'Things Hard for Thought'. *International Review of Psycho-Analysis* 7: 125–36.

Koffka, K. (1935) *Principles of Gestalt Psychology*. New York: Harcourt Brace Jovanovich.

Kohut, H. (1959) Introspection, Empathy and Psychoanalysis: an Examination of the Relationship between Mode of Observation and Theory. *Journal of the American Psychoanalytic Association* 7: 459–83.

Kohut, H. (1977) *The Restoration of the Self*. New York: International Universities Press.

—— (1982) Introspection, Empathy, and the Semi-circle of Mental Health. *International Journal of Psycho-Analysis* 63: 395–407.

Kragh, U. and Smith J. (1970) *Percept-Genetic Analysis*. Copenhagen: Gleerup.

Kris, E., Hartmann, H., and Loewenstein, R. M. (1964) *Papers on Psychoanalytic Psychology*. New York: International Universities Press.

Kristeva, J. (1980) *Desire in Language: a Semiotic Approach to Literature and Art*. Translated by T. Gora, A. Jardine, and L. S. Roudiez. New York: Columbia University Press.

—— (1982) *Powers of Horror: an Essay on Abjection*. Translated by L. S. Roudiez. New York: Columbia University Press.

—— (1984) *Revolution in Poetic Language*. Translated by M. Waller. New York: Columbia University Press.

Kubie, L. (1971) The Retreat from Patients. *Archives of General Psychiatry* 24: 98–106.

Kuhns, R. (1983) *Psychoanalytic Theory of Art: a Philosophy of Art on Developmental Principles*. New York: Columbia University Press.

Lacan, J. (1977) *Écrits*. Translated by A. Sheridan. London: Tavistock Publications.

Laing, R. D. (1957) An Examination of Tillich's Theory of Anxiety and Neurosis. *British Journal of Medical Psychology* 30: 88–91.

Lakoff, G. and Johnson, M. (1980) *Metaphors We Live By*. Chicago: University of Chicago Press.

Lambert, M. (1981) *Dickens and the Suspended Quotation*. New Haven: Yale University Press.

Langer, S. K. (1942) *Philosophy in a New Key: a Study in the Symbolism of Reason, Rite and Art*. Cambridge, Mass.: Harvard University Press.

Lankton, S. and Lankton, C. (1983) *The Answer Within*. New York: Brunner/Mazel.

Lascelles, M. (1980) *The Story-teller Retrieves the Past: Historical Fiction and Fictitious History*. Oxford: Clarendon Press.

Latham-Koenig, A. L. (1984) Letter to *The Times* 19 November.

Leedy, J. J. (ed.) (1969) *Poetry Therapy: the Use of Poetry in the Treatment of Emotional Disorder*. Philadelphia: J. B. Lippincott & Co.

Lehmann, A. (1913) Om Stemninger i Naturen. In *Oversigt over Det*

Kongelige Danske Videnskabernes Selskabs Forhandlinger 5: 367–88. Copenhagen.

Leighton, A. H. (1959) *My Name is Legion: Foundations for a Theory of Man in Relation to Culture.* New York: Basic Books.

Leishman, J. B. (1964) Introduction to *Rilke: Selected Poems.* Harmondsworth: Penguin Books Ltd.

Leishman, J. B. and Spender, S. (1939) Introduction to *Rilke: Duino Elegies.* London: The Hogarth Press.

Lerner, A. (ed.) (1978) *Poetry in the Therapeutic Experience.* New York: Pergamon Press Inc.

Levi, P. (1975) *In Memory of David Jones.* London: The Tablet.

Levin, F. M. (1980) Metaphor, Affect and Arousal: How Interpretations Might Work. *The Annual of Psychoanalysis* 8: 231–45. New York: International Universities Press.

—— and Vuckovich, D. M. (1983) Psychoanalysis and the Two Cerebral Hemispheres. *The Annual of Psychoanalysis* 11: 171–97. New York: International Universities Press.

Levinson, S. C. (1983) *Pragmatics.* Cambridge: Cambridge University Press.

Lewin, K. (1926) Vorsatz, Wille und Bedürfnis. *Psychologische Forschung* 7: 330–85.

McDougall, J. (1974) The Psychosoma and the Psychoanalytic Process. *International Review of Psycho-Analysis* 1: 437–59.

—— (1978) Primitive Communication and the Use of Countertransference. *Contemporary Psychoanalysis* 14: 173–209.

—— (1985) *Theaters of the Mind: Illusion and Truth on the Psychoanalytic Stage.* New York: Basic Books.

McGhie, A., Chapman, J., and Lawson, J. S. (1965a) The Effect of Distraction on Schizophrenic Performance – (1) Perception and Immediate Memory. *British Journal of Psychiatry* 111: 383–90.

——, ——, and —— (1965b) The Effect of Distraction on Schizophrenic Performance – (2) Psychomotor Ability. *British Journal of Psychiatry* III: 391–8.

McGough, R. (1986) *Melting into the Foreground.* Harmondsworth: Penguin Books Ltd.

McGuire, P. C. (1985) *Speechless Dialect: Shakespeare's Open Silences.* Berkeley: University of California Press.

Macnab, F. A. (1965) *Estrangement and Relationship: Experience with Schizophrenics.* London: Tavistock Publications.

MacNeice, L. (1935) in G. E. Grigson (ed.) *The Arts Today.* London: John Lane.

Macquarrie, J. (1972) *Existentialism.* New York: World Publishing Co.

Mahler, M. S. (1958) Autism and Symbiosis. *International Journal of Psycho-Analysis* 39: 77–83.

Malan, D. (1979) *Individual Psychotherapy and the Science of Psychodynamics.* London: Butterworths.

Marcus, S. (1984) *Freud and the Culture of Psychoanalysis: Studies in the Transition from Victorian Humanism to Modernity.* Boston: George Allen & Unwin.

Maslow, A. H. (1965) Isomorphic Interrelationship between Knower and Known. In Kepes, G. (ed.) *Sign, Image and Symbol.* New York: Brasiller.

Masterson, J. F. (1976) *Psychotherapy of the Borderline Adult: a Developmental Approach.* New York: Brunner/Mazel.

Matte Blanco, I. (1975) *The Unconscious as Infinite Sets: an Essay in Bi-logic.* London: Duckworth.

Matza, D. (1969) *Becoming Deviant.* Englewood Cliffs, New Jersey: Prentice-Hall.

May, R., Angel, E., and Ellenberger, H. F. (1958) *Existence – a New Dimension in Psychiatry and Psychology.* New York: Basic Books.

Maycock, A. L. (1963) *The Man who was Unorthodox: a Selection from the Uncollected Writings of G. K. Chesterton.* London: Dennis Dobson.

Mellers, W. (1980) *Bach and the Dance of God.* London: Faber & Faber.

Meltzer, D. (1984) *Dream-Life: a Re-Examination of the Psycho-Analytical Theory and Technique.* Clunie Press: Roland Harris Trust Library.

Merleau-Ponty, M. (1962) *Phenomenology of Perception.* Translated by C. Smith. London: Routledge & Kegan Paul.

Meyersburg, H. A. and Post, R. M. (1979) A Holistic Developmental View of Neural and Psychological Processes: a Neurobiologic–Psychoanalytic Integration. *British Journal of Psychiatry* 135: 139–55.

Milner, B., Taylor, L., and Sperry, R. (1968) Lateralized Suppression of Dichotically Presented Digits After Commisural Section in Man. *Science* 161: 186–8.

Milroy, J. (1977) *The Language of Gerard Manley Hopkins.* London: André Deutsch.

Modell, A. H. (1976) 'The Holding Environment' and the Therapeutic Action of Psychoanalysis. *Journal of the American Psychoanalytic Association* 24: 285–307.

Moi, T. (ed.) (1986) *The Kristeva Reader.* Oxford: Basil Blackwell.

Moltmann, J. (1980) *Experiences of God.* London: SCM Press Ltd.

Moore, M. (1968) *The Complete Poems of Marianne Moore.* London: Faber & Faber.

Mortensen, V. K., Møller, L., Theilgaard, A., and Ziegler, H. (1987) *Rorschach-testning: En Grundbog.* Copenhagen: Dansk Psykologisk Forlag.

Moruzzi, G. and Magoun, H. W. (1949) Brain Stem Reticular Formation and Activation on the E.E.G. *Electroencephalography and Clinical Neurophysiology* 455–73.

Muir, E. (1940) *An Autobiography*. London: The Hogarth Press.

——— (1960) *Collected Poems*. London: Faber & Faber.

Murphy, J. L. (1984) *Darkness and Devils: Exorcism and King Lear*. Ohio: Ohio University Press.

Murray, G. (1927) *The Classical Tradition in Poetry*. Oxford: Oxford University Press.

Myers, F. W. H. (1904) *Fragments of Prose and Poetry*. London: Longman, Green & Co.

Nadelson, C. and Notman, M. (1977) Psychotherapy Supervision: the Problem of Conflicting Values. *American Journal of Psychotherapy* 31: 275–83.

Nisbet, R. A. (1969) *Social Change and History: Aspects of the Western Theory of Developments*. Oxford: Oxford University Press.

Nordentoft, K. (1972) *Kierkegaard's Psychology*. Copenhagen: G.E.C. Gad.

Norman, C. (1958) *The Magic-Maker: e. e. cummings*. New York: The Macmillan Co.

Novalis (1798). Quoted by K. D. Hoppe (1975) Die Trennung der Gehirnhalften. *Psyche* 10: 919–70.

Nowottny, W. (1962) *The Language Poets Use*. London: The Athlone Press.

Noy, P. (1979) Form Creation in Art: an Egopsychological Approach to Creativity. *Psychoanalysis Quarterly* 48: 229–56.

Oates, J. C. (1976) *The Edge of Impossibility: Tragic Forms in Literature*. London: Victor Gollancz.

Ogden, T. H. (1982) *Projective Identification and Psychotherapeutic Technique*. New York: Jason Aronson.

——— (1985) On Potential Space. *International Journal of Psycho-Analysis* 66: 129–71.

Olinick, S. L. (1982) Meanings Beyond Words: Psychoanalytic Perceptions of Silence and Communication, Happiness, Sexual Love and Death. *International Review of Psycho-Analysis* 9: 461–72.

Paffard, M. (1976) *The Unattended Moment: Excerpts from Autobiographies with Hints and Guesses*. London: SCM Press Ltd.

Patterson, G. (1971) *T. S. Eliot: Poems in the Making*. Manchester: Manchester University Press.

Pedder, J. R. (1976) Attachment and New Beginning: Some Links Between the Work of Michael Balint and John Bowlby. *International Review of Psycho-Analysis* 3: 491–7.

——— (1977) The Role of Space and Location in Psychotherapy, Play and Theatre. *International Review of Psycho-Analysis* 4: 215–23.

——— (1979) Transitional Space in Psychotherapy and Theatre. *British Journal of Medical Psychology* 52: 377–84.

Penfield, W. (1958) *The Excitable Cortex in Conscious Man*. Liverpool: Liverpool University Press.

Pines, M. (1982) Reflections on Mirroring. Sixth S. H. Foulkes Annual Lecture of the Group-Analytic Society. *Group Analysis* 15: Supp. 1–26.

—— (1986) Psychoanalysis, Psychodrama and Group Psychotherapy: Step-children of Vienna. *Group Analysis* 19: 101–12.

—— (1986) Personal communication.

Pirandello, W. (1921) *Six Characters in Search of an Author*. London: Eyre Methuen, 1979.

Polkinghorne, J. (1986) *One World: the Interaction of Science and Theology*. London: SPCK.

Poole, R. (1972) *Towards Deep Subjectivity*. London: Allen Lane.

Porter, P. (1978) *The Cost of Seriousness*. Oxford: Oxford University Press.

Pound, E. (1934) *A.B.C. of Reading*. London: Routledge & Kegan Paul.

Powell, A. (1982) Metaphor in Group Analysis. *Group Analysis* 15: 127–35.

Press, J. (1958) *The Chequer'd Shade: Reflections on Obscurity in Poetry*. Oxford: Oxford University Press.

Pribram, K. (1962) The Neuropsychology of Sigmund Freud. In A. Bachrach (ed.) *Experimental Foundations of Clinical Psychology*. New York: Basic Books.

—— (1973) *Psychophysiology of the Frontal Lobes*. New York: Academic Press.

—— and Luria A. R. (1973). In A. R. Luria (ed.) *The Working Brain*. Harmondsworth: Penguin.

—— and McGuinness, D. (1975) Arousal, Activation and Effort in the Control of Attention. *Psychological Review* 182: 116–49.

Prickett, S. (1986) *Words and 'The Word': Language, Poetics and Biblical Interpretation*. Cambridge: Cambridge University Press.

Raine, K. (1967) *Defending Ancient Springs*. Oxford: Oxford University Press.

—— (1981) *Collected Poems 1935–1980*. London: George Allen & Unwin.

Ramsey, I. T. (1964) *Models and Mystery*. Oxford: Oxford University Press.

Rapaport, D. (1951) *Organization and Pathology of Thought*. New York: Columbia University Press.

Rayner, E. (1981) Infinite Experiences, Affects and the Characteristics of the Unconscious. *International Review of Psycho-Analysis* 62: 403–12.

Rees, J. (1978) *Shakespeare and the Story: Aspects of Creation*. London: The Athlone Press.

Reik, T. (1936) *Surprise and the Psycho-Analyst: On the Conjecture and Comprehension of Unconscious Processes*. London: Kegan Paul, Trench & Trubner & Co.

—— (1948) *Listening with the Third Ear*. New York: Strauss & Co.

Rich, A. (1978) *The Dream of a Common Language*. New York: W. W. Norton & Co. Inc.

Ricks, C. (1984) *The Force of Poetry*. Oxford: Clarendon Press.

Ricoeur, P. (1977) *The Rule of Metaphor*. Toronto: University of Toronto Press.

Rilke, R. M. (1957) Sämtliche Werke, vols I and II. Frankfurt: Insel.

—— (1964) *Selected Poems*. Translated and Introduced by J. B. Leishman. Harmondsworth: Penguin.

Robinson, M. (ed.) (1981) *Is There Anyone Out There?* An Anthology of Poems by Sufferers from Schizophrenia. Eastbourne: Downlander Publishing.

Rochester, S. and Martin, J. R. (1979) *Crazy Talk: a Study of the Discourse of Schizophrenia Speakers*. New York: Plenum.

Rodgers, A. T. (1979) *The Universal Drum: Dance Imagery in the Poetry of Eliot, Crane, Roethke, and Williams*. Pennsylvania: The Pennsylvania State University Press.

Roethke, T. (1968) *The Collected Poems*. London: Faber & Faber.

Rogers, R. (1978) *Metaphor: a Psychoanalytic View*. Berkeley: University of California Press.

Romanyshyn, R. D. (1982) *Psychological Life: From Science to Metaphor*. Milton Keynes: The Open University Press.

Rommetveit, R. (1968) *Words, Meanings, and Messages*. New York: Academic Press.

Rorschach, H. (1921) *Psychodiagnostik*. Bern: Verlag Hans Huber. *Psychodiagnostics*. New York: Grune & Stratton, 1944.

Rose, G. J. (1980) *The Power of Form: a Psychoanalytic Approach to Aesthetic Form*. New York: International Universities Press.

Rosenbaum, B. and Sonne, H. (1986) *The Language of Psychosis*. New York: University Press.

Rothenberg, A. (1972) Poetic Process and Psychotherapy. *Psychiatry* 35: 238–54.

—— (1979) *The Emerging Goddess*. Chicago: University of Chicago Press.

—— (1983) Creativity, Articulation, and Psychotherapy. *Journal of the American Academy of Psychoanalysis* II: 1, 65–85.

Rowell, G. (1983) *The Vision Glorious: Themes and Personalities of the Catholic Revival in Anglicanism*. Oxford: Oxford University Press.

Rubin, E. (1915) *Synsoplevede Figurer*. Copenhagen: Gyldendal.

Rupp, G. (1969) *Patterns of Reformation*. London: Epworth Press.

Sackheim, H. A. and Weber, S. (1982) Functional Brain Asymmetry in the Regulation of Emotion: Implications for Bodily Manifestations of Stress. In Goldberger, L. and Breznitz, S. (eds) *Handbook of Stress – Theoretical and Clinical Aspects*. New York: Macmillan Publishing Inc.

—— Weinman, A. L., Gunz, R. C., Greenberg, M., and Hungenbuhler, J. P. (1982) Pathological Laughing and Crying: Functional Brain Asymmetry in the Expression of Positive and Negative Emotions. *The Archives of Neurology* 39: 210–18.

Sackville-West, V. (1926) *The Land*. London: William Heinemann Ltd.

Samuels, A. (1985) Symbolic Dimensions of Eros in Transference–Countertransference: Some Clinical Uses of Jung's Alchemical Metaphor. *International Review of Psycho-Analysis* 12: 199–214.

Santillana de G. and von Dechend, H. (1977) *Hamlet's Hill: an Essay on Myth and the Frame of Time*. Boston: David Godine.

Sartre, J. P. (1950) *What is Literature?* London: Methuen & Co.

Schachtel, E. G. (1950) Projection and its Relation to Character Attitudes and Creativity in the Kinesthetic Responses. *Psychiatry* 13: 69–100.

—— (1967) *Experiential Foundations of Rorschach's Test*. London: Tavistock Publications.

Schafer, R. (1954) *Psychoanalytic Interpretation in Rorschach Testing*. New York: Grune & Stratton.

—— (1959) Generative Empathy in the Treatment Situation. *Psychoanalytic Quarterly* 28: 347–73.

Schilder, P. (1914) Zur Kenntnis Symbolähnlicher Bildungen in Rahmen der Schizophrenie. *The Journal of Neurology and Psychiatry* 26: 201–44.

Schlack, B. A. (1979) *Continuing Presences: Virginia Woolf's Use of Literary Allusion*. Pennsylvania University Park: The Pennsylvania State University Press.

Scott, N. A. (1971) *The Wild Prayer of Longing: Poetry and the Sacred*. New Haven: Yale University Press.

—— (1985) *The Poetics of Belief: Studies in Coleridge, Arnold, Pater, Santayana, Stevens and Heidegger*. Chapel Hill: University North Carolina Press.

Sechehaye, M. A. (1951) *Symbolic Realization: a New Method of Psychotherapy Applied to a Case of Schizophrenia*. New York: International Universities Press.

Sedgwick, W. E. (1944) *Herman Melville*. Cambridge, Mass.: Harvard University Press.

Semmes, J. (1968) Hemispheric Specialization: a Possible Clue to Mechanism. *Neuropsychologia* 6: 11–26.

Shakespeare, W. The Arden edition (London: Methuen) has been used throughout.

Sharpe, E. F. (1930) The Analyst: Essential Qualifications for the Acquisition of Technique. *International Journal of Psycho-Analysis* XI: 251. In *Collected Papers on Psychoanalysis* (1950). London: Hogarth Press.

—— (1937) *Dream Analysis*. London: Hogarth Press.

Siirala, M. (1961) *Die Schizophrenie des Einzelnen und der Allgemeinheit*. Göttingen: Vandenhoek & Ruprecht.

—— (1969) *Medicine in Metamorphosis: Speech, Presence, and Integration*. London: Tavistock Publications.

—— (1983) Schizophrenia: a Human Situation. In *From Transfer to Transference*. Therapeia Foundation, Helsinki, and in *American Journal of Psychoanalysis* 28: 39–66.

—— (1985) Personal communication.

Sitwell, E. (1948) *A Notebook on William Shakespeare*. London: Macmillan & Co.

Slatoff, W. J. (1960) *Quest for Failure: a Study of William Faulkner*. Ithaca: Cornell University Press.

—— (1970) *With Respect to Readers: Dimensions of Literary Response*. Ithaca: Cornell University Press.

—— (1985) *The Look of Distance: Reflections on Suffering and Sympathy in Modern Literature – Auden to Agee, Whitman to Woolf*. Columbus: Ohio State University Press.

Slochower, H. (1970) *Mythopoesis: Mythic Patterns in the Literary Classics*. Detroit: Wayne State University Press.

Smith, B. H. (1968) *Poetic Closure: a Study of How Poems End*. Chicago: The University of Chicago Press.

Sokolov, E. (1963) *Perception and the Conditioned Reflex*. Oxford: Pergamon Press.

Sontag, S. (1978) *Illness as Metaphor*. New York: Farrar, Strauss & Giroux.

Soskice, J. (1985) *Metaphor and Religious Language*. Oxford: Clarendon Press.

Spence, D. P. (1982) *Narrative Truth and Historical Truth: Meaning and Interpretation in Psychoanalysis*. New York: W. W. Norton & Co.

Spengemann, W. C. (1980) The Forms of Autobiography: Episodes in the History of a Literary Genre. New Haven, Conn.: Yale University Press.

Sperry, R. W. (1976) A Unifying Approach to Mind and Brain. In M. A. Corner and D. Swaab (eds) *Perspectives in Brain Research*. Amsterdam: Elsevier.

—— Gassaniga, M., and Bogen, J. (1969) Interhemispheric Relationships: the Neocortical Commissures and Syndromes of Hemispheric Disconnection. In P. Vinken and E. Bruyn (eds) *Handbook of Clinical Neurology*. Amsterdam: North Holland Publishing Co.

Spiegelberg, H. (1972) *Phenomenology in Psychology and Psychiatry: a Historical Introduction*. Evanston: Northwestern University Press.

Spitz, R. A. (1953) Aggression: Its Role in the Development of Object Relations. In R. M. Loewenstein (ed.) *Drives, Affects, Behavior*. New

York: International Universities Press.

Stanford, W. B. (1936) *Greek Metaphor: Studies in Theory and Practice*. Oxford: Oxford University Press.

States, B. O. (1978) *The Shape of Paradox: an Essay on Waiting for Godot*. Berkeley: University of California Press.

Steiner, G. (1978) *Heidegger*. London: Fontana Paperback.

Stern, A. (1986) Psychoanalytic Investigation of and Therapy in the Border Line Group of Neuroses. In M. Stone (ed.) *Essential Papers on Borderline Disorders: One Hundred Years at the Border*. New York and London: New York University Press, 54–73.

Stevens, W. (1954) *Collected Poems*. New York: Knopf.

Stone, A. A. and Stone, S. S. (eds) (1966) *The Abnormal Personality Through Literature*. New Jersey: Prentice Hall.

Stone, M. H. (ed.) (1986) *Essential Papers on Borderline Disorders: One Hundred Years at the Border*. New York: New York University Press.

Storr, A. (1972) *The Dynamics of Creation*. London: Martin Secker & Warburg.

Strachey, J. (1934) The Nature of the Therapeutic Action of Psycho-Analysis. *International Journal of Psycho-Analysis* 15: 127–59.

Suskind, P. (1986) *Perfume: the Story of a Murderer*. London: Hamish Hamilton.

Suvorova, V. V. (1975) Functional Asymmetry as a Problem of Differential Psychophysiology. *Voprosy Psikhologii* 5: 26–33.

Sykes, S. W. (1987) The Role of Story in the Christian Religion: an Hypothesis. *Literature and Theology* 1 (1): 19–26.

Taylor, J. (ed.) (1932) *Selected Writings of John Hughlings Jackson*. London: Hodder & Stoughton.

Theilgaard, A. (1968) Oversigt over nogle psykologiske perceptionsteorier. In A. Theilgaard and R. Willanger (eds) *Klinisk – Psykologiske Tekster. Neuro-og perceptionspsykologiske emner*. Copenhagen: Akademisk Forlag.

—— (1973) Psykologiske Funktioners Repræsentation i Hjernen. *Nordisk Psykiatrisk Tidsskrift* 7, 484–94.

—— (1980) Klinisk Psykologi. In J. Welner (ed.) *Psykiatri, en Tekstbog*. Copenhagen: F.A.D.L.'s Forlag.

—— (1984) *A Psychological Study of the Personalities of XYY and XXY Men*. Acta Psychiatrica Scandinavica Sup. 315. Copenhagen: Munksgaard.

—— (1987) in Mortensen *et al.*

Thelwell, N. (1967) *Up the Garden Path: Thelwell's Guide to Gardening*. London: Methuen & Co.

Thomas, D. (1952) *Collected Poems 1934–1952*. London: J. M. Dent & Sons.

Thompson, S. and Kahn, J. H. (1970) *The Group Process as a Helping Technique*. Oxford: Pergamon Press.

Tillich, P. (1957) *Systematic Theology* Part III. Chicago: University of Chicago Press.

—— (1965) *Ultimate Concern*. London: SCM Press Ltd.

—— (1966) *On the Boundary*. New York: Charles Scribner's Sons.

Tillyard, E. M. W. (1934) *Poetry Direct and Oblique*. London: Chatto & Windus.

Titchener, E. B. (1908) *Lectures on the Elementary Psychology of Feeling and Attention*. New York: Macmillan.

Tracy, D. (1981) *The Analogical Imagination: Christian Theology and the Culture of Pluralism*. London: SCM Press Ltd.

Tuan, Y. (1974) *Topophilia: a Study of Environmental Perception, Attitudes and Values*. Englewood Cliffs, New Jersey: Prentice-Hall.

Tucker, D. M. (1981) Lateral Brain Function, Emotion, and Conceptualization. *Psychology Bulletin* 89: 19–46.

Turbayne, C. (1962) *The Myth of Metaphor*. New Haven: Yale University Press.

Turner, V. (1974) *Dramas, Fields and Metaphors: Symbolic Action in Human Society*. London: Cornell University Press.

Usandivaras, R. J. (1986) Foulkes' Primordial Level in Clinical Practice. *Group Analysis* 19: 113–24.

Van der Post, L. (1961) *The Heart of the Hunter*. London: Hogarth Press.

Vanstone, W. H. (1982) *The Stature of Waiting*. London: Darton, Longman & Todd.

Venables, P. H. (1969) Sensory Aspects of Psychopathology. In J. Zubin and C. Shagass (eds) *Neurobiological Aspects of Psychopathology*. New York: Grune & Stratton.

—— (1980) *Primary Dysfunction and Cortical Lateralization in Schizophrenia*. In M. Kloc and A. Lehmann (eds) *Functional States of the Brain: Their Development*. Amsterdam: North Holland Biomedical Press.

Victor, G. (1978) Interpretations Couched in Mythical Imagery. *International Journal of Psychoanalysis and Psychotherapy* 7: 225–39.

Voth, H. M. (1970) The Analysis of Metaphor. *Journal of the American Psychoanalytic Association* 18: 359–61.

Wada, J. A. (1969) Interhemispheric Sharing and Shift of Cerebral Speech Function. *Excerpta Medica International* Congress Series 193: 296–7.

Watson, L. (1986) *Beyond Supernature*. London: Hodder & Stoughton.

Weatherhead, A. K. (1967) *The Edge of the Image*. Seattle: University of Washington Press.

Wells, H. W. (1924) *Poetic Imagery Illustrated from Elizabethan Literature*. New York: Columbia University Press.

Werman, D. (1984) *The Practice of Supportive Psychotherapy*. New York: Brunner/Mazel.

Werner, H. (1948) *Comparative Psychology of Mental Development*. New York: International Universities Press.

Weston, S. (1977) *Wallace Stevens: an Introduction to the Poetry*. New York: Columbia University Press.

Whalley, G. (1953) *Poetic Process*. London: Routledge & Kegan Paul.

White, F. (1964) *West of the Rhone: Languedoc, Roussillon, the Massif Central*. London: Faber & Faber.

Whitman, W. (1968) *A Choice of Whitman's Verse*. Introduction by D. Hall. London: Faber & Faber.

Wicker, B. (1975) *The Story-Shaped World: Fiction and Metaphysics: Some Variations on a Theme*. London: Athlone Press.

Wilde, O. (1898) The Ballad of Reading Gaol; (1949) De Profundis. *Selected Essays and Poems*. Harmondsworth: Penguin Books, 1954.

Williams, R. (1979) *The Wound of Knowledge: Christian Spirituality from the New Testament to St. John of the Cross*. London: Darton, Longman & Todd.

Wilshire, B. (1982) *Role-playing and Identity: the Limits of Theatre as Metaphor*. Bloomington: Indiana University Press.

Winnicott, D. (1963) The Development of the Capacity for Concern. *Bulletin of the Menninger Clinic* 27: 167–76.

—— (1967) The Location of Cultural Experience. In Winnicott 1971, 112–21.

—— (1971) *Playing and Reality*. London: Tavistock Publications.

Witkin, H. A., Dyk, R. B., Faterson, H. F., Goodenough, D. R., and Karp, S. A. (1962) *Psychological Differentiation*. New York: John Wiley.

Wolfe, H. (1928) *This Blind Rose*. London: Victor Gollancz.

Woodworth, R. S. (1938) *Experimental Psychology*. New York: Henry Holt & Co.

Woolf, V. (1927) *To the Lighthouse*. London: Hogarth Press.

—— (1929) *A Room of One's Own*. London: Hogarth Press.

—— (1931) *The Waves*. London: Hogarth Press.

Wright, E. (1984) *Psychoanalytic Criticism: Theory in Practice*. London: Methuen.

Wright, K. J. T. (1976) Metaphor and Symptom: a Study of Integration and Its Failure. *International Review of Psycho-Analysis* 3: 97–109.

Wundt, W. (1904) *Principles of Physiological Psychology*. New York: Macmillan.

Yalom, I. D. (1975) *Theory and Practice of Group Psychotherapy*. New York: Basic Books.

Yeats, W. B. (1950) *The Collected Poems of W. B. Yeats* (2nd edn). London: Macmillan.

Name index

Subject index

Literary index

15482990R00177

Printed in Great Britain
by Amazon